TRUE
STORIES
OF
GREAT
ESCAPES

Reader's Digest

TRUE
STORIES
OF
GREAT
ESCAPES

VOLUME ONE

The Reader's Digest Association Limited
London, Sydney, Cape Town

True Stories of Great Escapes

Editor: Charles S. Verral
Art Director: Robert Grant
Research Editors: Monica Borrowman, Susan Brackett,
        Rita Christopher
Copy Editors: Rosemarie Conefrey, Natalie Moreda,
        Susan Parker
Art Researcher: Erika Pozsonyi

FIRST EDITION 1977
Reprinted 1995
The Reader's Digest Association Limited
Berkeley Square House, Berkeley Square, London W1X 6AB

The credits and acknowledgments that appear on pages 351–352,
Volume Two, are hereby made a part of this copyright page.

ISBN 0-276-42202-3 (Volume One)
ISBN 0-276-42204-X (2 volume pack)

Printed and bound in Hong Kong

CONTENTS

Many authors of fiction have written stories in which their characters make breathtaking escapes. Yet no matter how fertile a writer's imagination, a fictional escape rarely surpasses those that happen in real life.

History abounds with such thrilling episodes: the flight of Moses and the Israelites from the Egyptians; Napoleon's getaway from the prison island of Elba; Harriet Tubman gaining her liberty after years of slavery; General MacArthur slipping away from the Japanese during World War II. The list goes on and on.

When Reader's Digest decided to publish an anthology of escape stories, the editors began a search of past issues of the magazine, going back to its beginning year of 1922. They found many accounts of true escapes—some well known, others now almost forgotten. But all these stories contained one common ingredient: courage—the courage of men, women, and sometimes children who risked life itself to be free.

From these true stories, 40 were selected to appear in this two-volume set. They range from the miraculous mass escape of almost an entire British army in World War II to the feat of one young man who crossed the Atlantic Ocean hidden in the wheel well of an airliner.

To these Reader's Digest stories have been added six other escape dramas. Two are booklength condensations: "The Long Walk," the saga of a breakout of seven men from a Soviet labor camp in Siberia and their trek toward India, 4,000 miles away; and "The Colditz Story," an account of a prison in Germany that the Nazis believed escapeproof and of the Allied POW's who proved them wrong. —THE EDITORS

From the day the wall went up in Berlin, groups
of East Germans tried every means of escape. On January 24,
1962, a band of refugees crawled into West Berlin
through a tunnel they had laboriously dug. Here is the story of
that tunnel. It is a drama of breath-catching suspense,
eloquent proof of man's passion for freedom.

The January Tunnel

By William A. H. Birnie

T HE BECKER HOUSE was like hundreds of other homes throughout
East and West Germany. Its two-story stucco walls squatted
sturdily beneath a massive peaked roof covered with red tiles. With
its tiny vegetable and flower garden and five or six dwarf fruit trees,
the house bespoke reliability, frugality, and strong family ties. To be
sure, a startling conical dovecote towered above the roof, but what
really distinguished the Becker house was its location.

In the quiet East Berlin suburb of Glienicke, it stood directly on
the border that separates East from West, tyranny from freedom.
Only 30 yards from the rear of the house lay the suburb of Frohnau,
in the French sector of West Berlin.

In between lay the Berlin Wall—at that point composed of four
rows of barbed wire and a picket fence—which was constantly patrolled by details of heavily armed Volkspolizei ("People's Police"),
commonly called Vopos.

Late on Monday afternoon, December 18, 1961, two of the Becker
boys, Erwin and Guenther, arrived home from work together. The
instant they opened the front door, they heard a dull pounding coming from the cellar. Dashing down the steps to investigate—anything
out of the ordinary put nerves on edge in tense East Berlin—the boys
found their handsome, blond brother Bruno energetically chipping
away at the cellar wall with hammer and chisel. There was no need to
ask what he was doing.

Bruno looked up and wiped the stone dust from his damp forehead. "I know you think I'm crazy," he said. "But I've had it! That
damned wall gets longer and higher every day. Tunneling through
here is our only hope."

"Sure," said Guenther, his voice edged with sarcasm. "How long have you been working?"

"About three hours."

Guenther pointed to the wall. "And take a look at what you've accomplished!"

The surface of the stone-hard glazed bricks that lined the cellar wall had scarcely been scratched.

"Come on, Bruno," said Erwin. "There's some beer upstairs. Let's talk this over quietly."

So the three went upstairs to the kitchen, where Bruno continued to argue for his tunnel.

"You remember what happened when we planned to cut through the barbed wire," he said bitterly.

They remembered all right. It had been only a month since they had tried, vainly, to escape overland. That night at 9:30 they had turned off all the lights, so that the patrols would think they had gone to bed. Then they sat in the darkness, waiting. They didn't know that the patrols had been reinforced because a few people down the road had escaped several days before. All they knew was that the Vopos, with police dogs that growled at the slightest suspicious sound, came by with dismaying frequency. They were still waiting for the right moment when dawn broke.

After that failure Bruno had wanted to start digging a tunnel. But his brother Erwin disagreed, and now in the Becker kitchen he reviewed his reasons.

"Look at it this way, Bruno. If we cut our way through the wire, most of us will probably make it, even if one or two get caught or shot. But with a tunnel what chance have we got? The Vopos would be sure to hear us digging. Then we'd be sent to prison—or worse—with all our friends who knew about the tunnel and probably a lot of others who didn't."

Reluctantly, Bruno again agreed to his brother's suggestion that they make one more effort to cut their way through the wire. They would now time the attempted breakthrough for as soon as possible after the New Year.

The Beckers had never been politically minded. All they asked of politicians was to be left alone. But after the wall had gone up, imprisoning them, along with more than a million other East Berliners on August 13, 1961, their nerves were drawn to such a point of desperation that they preferred risking their lives to living under a suffocating Communist regime.

Frau Clara Becker, 53, slim and gracious, with a quiet smile, had been left a widow with six children when her husband died in a Russian prisoner-of-war camp in 1945. Released herself from a refugee camp in 1947, she and the youngsters had eventually settled down in suburban Glienicke.

Life was far from easy, but they managed to get by. An uncle who lived in the United States periodically sent money and food parcels until he died in 1955.

In 1950 the Becker family moved into the house on the border. The three younger sons completed their schooling and found jobs. (Arnold, the eldest, had gone to live with Frau Becker's brother in Dortmund, West Germany.) By 1961 Erwin, 27, was earning an above-average salary as chauffeur for the president of East Berlin's Art Academy. Bruno, 21, brought home fairly good pay each week from his job as an electrician, and his twin Guenther also did pretty well as a steamfitter.

The oldest daughter, Gerda, 22, crossed over into West Berlin every working day. There she had a job as a hairdresser and earned a good salary. Her sister, exuberant 18-year-old Christel, was training to become a salesgirl.

They were an industrious, optimistic family, and their home became a sort of informal community center for a number of the young people in the neighborhood.

"It certainly wasn't paradise," Frau Becker later recalled. "But it wasn't too bad either. We could go over to the bright lights of West Berlin any time we wished."

Then came the wall, and the Beckers' world closed in.

On Monday morning, August 14, 1961, Gerda started off for her job in West Berlin as usual. Half an hour later, much to her mother's astonishment, she was back home.

"The Vopos stopped me," Gerda reported. "They said I was no longer permitted to cross over."

"But what about your job?"

"They told me to forget about it, about *ever* going across again. They said we were now all standard-bearers in the People's Democracy. They said—"

Her voice broke, and her mother put an arm around her shoulders. "Now don't get upset, Gerda. In two or three days everything will be all right again."

But the next day the Vopos and "volunteers" from the factories came pounding along Oranienburger Chaussee, the border highway

13

that adjoins the Becker home, and with them came trucks carrying huge rolls of barbed wire.

The Vopos unreeled mile after mile of the ugly wire strands, continuing the prison wall from the Brandenburg Gate to quiet little Glienicke and far beyond.

Life behind the wall became a series of small crises. Gerda got a job as a hairdresser in an East Berlin establishment, but her new salary enabled her to buy less than half what she could with her West Berlin pay. In addition, the management, following the party line, encouraged her fellow workers to distrust her because she had been a *Grenzgänger* ("border crosser"). The Communists were spreading the word that anyone who had worked in West Berlin was probably infected with "capitalistic decadence."

The men in Bruno's electrical shop were told to volunteer for duty in the People's Army—which might be ordered any day to fire on fleeing fellow Germans. Bruno got out of it, thanks to a doctor's certificate attesting to deafness in one ear, but the threat still hung over him. Guenther was urged by a fellow worker, who identified himself as a member of the Security Police, to report anyone making subversive, antiregime remarks.

Every third or fourth evening a pair of Vopos would knock on the Beckers' front door and check the identification papers of all the inhabitants. Each time one of them would be sure to flick on the living-room radio—to see whether it had been left tuned to a West Berlin station. If it had, the Beckers were liable to prison terms as "ideological defectors."

FOOD SHORTAGES grew acute. Meat, potatoes, butter, milk, and vegetables were scarce everywhere. Actually, the Beckers were better off than most of their neighbors, because they had a well-tended garden and those few fruit trees. But, like most Germans, they were fond of liver and bacon, and it seemed there was no liver to be had anywhere in East Berlin.

"You know," Christel said, smiling, one night, "Herr Ulbricht, our dictator, has accomplished at least one miracle: he has raised a generation of animals without livers."

But the jokes grew fewer as the shadow of the wall grew longer. Petitions were circulated through the factories and the schools urging all workers and students to agree that neither they nor anybody in their families would accept any mail or food or clothing parcels sent in from the West.

Worse than the facts were the rumors. (East Berliners have learned through bitter experience that the worst rumors tend to come true.) Two in particular troubled the Beckers. First, a universal conscription law (later enacted) would make all able-bodied young men liable for service in the East German armed forces; that would likely take the Becker boys. Second, it was rumored that all border residents were to be resettled somewhere deep within East Germany far away from the West and all border houses destroyed; that would mean the destruction of the Becker home.

Having agreed to make one more try at escaping through the wire, the Becker brothers finally decided to stage the hazardous attempt on January 13, 1962. It was a Saturday night, and this time the Beckers were not to be alone.

First to show up that afternoon were the Schwartzes—Franz, 50, a sober-minded mechanic, and his wife, Ilse. (Fictitious names have been used except for members of the Becker family.) Recently the Schwartzes had thought of nothing else but crossing over from East Berlin. When the wall went up, Herr Schwartz had been cut off from his good West Berlin job. But, more important, two of the Schwartzes' four daughters were married and now living in West Berlin; and the two youngest, 16 and 18, had been crossing over each day to attend school there.

The wall abruptly separated the younger daughters from school and schoolmates. Then they found that they couldn't even gain admittance to an East German school. Invariably they were told, "As former border crossers you should *prove* your loyalty to the People's Democratic Republic by getting jobs in factories."

The two girls had no desire to wait for the inevitable: assignment to a factory of the regime's choice. They begged their parents to escape, but their father had been adamant. Like Frau Becker, he felt that the wall was only a passing horror.

"There's no need for anybody to risk his life," he repeated firmly. "Just be patient, that's all."

But 16 and 18 are no ages for patience. Knowing that they could not persuade their parents to change their minds, the girls made secret plans. After lunch on Saturday, September 16, 1961, they slipped across the border on their own. (This was scarcely a month after the wall had been erected, and there were still some loopholes in the security system.)

Three days later the Schwartzes received a letter: the girls were living with their married sisters in West Berlin. Thereafter, every few days all four girls stood on a hilltop in Frohnau and waved to their mother. Frau Schwartz watched them through binoculars, her eyes blurred with tears.

At first, Franz Schwartz was infuriated that the girls had tricked him and his wife. But as the days and weeks ticked off and life behind the wall turned increasingly sour, the Schwartzes, too, became determined to escape.

One afternoon Herr Schwartz went to the Becker house to ask Bruno if he could fix a television set. While they were talking, Franz kept looking through the windows facing Frohnau.

"You're *really* on the border, aren't you? Have you ever thought of cutting through?"

"Maybe," said Guenther. "Why?"

Schwartz told them what was on his mind. Frau Becker sensed the sincerity in his voice and instinctively trusted him.

"We're going to make a try for it Saturday night," she told him. "If you want to join us, you and your wife come over for dinner. Then after it gets dark . . ."

Shortly after dinner that Saturday evening another couple appeared—the Alfred Muellers. They were in their middle thirties, and with them was their blond, roly-poly, eight-year-old daughter, Gisela. Unlike the Schwartzes, the Muellers had decided to move to the West even before the wall. All through July 1961 they had smuggled shoes, clothing, and other essential articles across the border and stored them in the West Berlin office where Herr Mueller worked as a heating engineer.

After the wall trapped them, they determined to make the break as soon as possible. On the bus he took to work each day, Herr Mueller had struck up an acquaintance with Christel Becker. When he learned that her family's house was directly on the border in Glienicke, he dropped by one night. Within an hour Frau Becker and her sons had invited him and his family to come along on the Saturday night escape expedition.

That night the three families—Beckers, Schwartzes, and Muellers—drank coffee and talked about everything except what was on their minds until it was pitch-black outside. Then they concentrated on the tramp-tramp-tramp of the Vopos, who seemed to come by all too regularly. Occasionally the Vopos would flash their lights on the windows, instantly silencing all conversation inside the house until reassuring darkness returned.

At 11:45 Frau Becker's nerves were at the breaking point. "I

haven't heard the Vopos for a long time," she said, "Maybe now's the time. I'm going out to see."

"I'll come with you," said Herr Schwartz.

"I think it's too early," said Erwin. "Take a look if you want, but be very careful."

Frau Becker and Franz Schwartz walked out into the garden. All was quiet. Then, suddenly, from off to the left, came the sound of voices and the tread of boots. There wasn't time to dash back into the house, and they had no reasonable explanation for being out in the darkness right there on the border.

"Quick, lie down," whispered Schwartz.

They lay on the icy ground behind a pine tree and, as fortune would have it, the two Vopos stopped not 10 feet away. For half an hour at least—Frau Becker thinks it was two hours—the Vopos discussed the weather and when they would get off duty, and how much better life was back in Dresden.

(Most of the border police were brought in from other sections of East Germany so they wouldn't have personal ties with East Berliners and be tempted to assist would-be escapees.)

Scarcely breathing, Frau Becker and Herr Schwartz lay in the garden until the Vopos finally moved on. When they got back inside the house, Frau Becker was near hysteria.

"We'll *never* make it!" she cried.

It had been a frightening, frustrating night. It produced one positive result, however: The men were now convinced that they could never escape overland.

The Becker boys invited Herr Schwartz and Herr Mueller to come down into the cellar. There Erwin pointed to the dents that Bruno had made in the glazed-brick wall.

Instantly, Herr Schwartz said, "Of course—a tunnel! That's the only way to do it!"

Now the Becker boys were all enthusiasm, and Schwartz agreed to pitch in on the project immediately. Mueller, engineering-minded, was skeptical. For an hour they talked over possibilities, techniques, and the obvious dangers.

Finally, Mueller said quietly, "All right. I agree. Shall we start the first thing Monday morning?"

"Perfect," said Erwin. "We'll report sick at our jobs. Let's make it 7 o'clock Monday, then?"

"*Jawohl.*"

ON MONDAY MORNING Herr Mueller arrived at the Becker house before the sun was up, carrying an electric drill he had "borrowed" from the shop where he worked. Bruno's eyes sparkled when he saw it; he knew it could save hours of exhausting work. In the cellar he connected it, listened to it hum, and then shoved it against the spot on the brick wall where he had chiseled. Instantly, all hell broke loose. He cut the switch hastily.

"We can't use it!" he said. "A banging like that could bring the Vopos on the run."

So the drill was put aside, and for the rest of that day the men took turns with Bruno's hammer and chisel.

Herr Schwartz joined the group on Wednesday and worked during the mornings. (To avoid suspicion he did not yet want to report sick at his regular job, which required him to work only in the afternoon.) By then the others had equipped themselves with the necessary hammers, shovels, and pickaxes—smuggled into the Becker house under cover of their overcoats.

They soon discovered that the cellar wall, built in the late 19th century, was two feet thick and all glazed brick. Working in shifts of two at a time, their eyes and lungs filling with stone dust, they took three days to cut a hole four feet high and two feet wide. They wanted it large at the beginning because they suspected that, regardless of their ambitions, the tunnel would inevitably tend to grow smaller and smaller as freedom came closer.

By Wednesday, about 5 P.M., they had conquered the cellar wall and were up against the sand and clay outside. From then on the job progressed with exhilarating rapidity.

But now new difficulties had to be solved. First, there was the problem of dirt disposal. Guenther suggested an easy solution: dump the dirt down an abandoned well in the garden at the rear of the house. The others vetoed the idea; the Vopos might notice and, besides, they would have to spend most of their time and energy carrying the debris upstairs and outside. Instead, the men put up crude partitions like old-fashioned coal bins and piled the dirt right there in the cellar. (Eventually there was just a single churchlike aisle left leading to the tunnel opening.)

The second problem was the need for light. Already the tunnel was getting black inside, and the two who worked at the front could barely see. Electrician Bruno solved that by stringing an overhead extension cord into the tunnel and, as they dug on, lights were added every nine feet or so.

Their third difficulty was that the farther they dug, the more dirt they had to handle, and the harder it became to remove. Even at 10 feet out from the cellar, it was time-consuming and enervating to throw the dirt back by hand.

The twins, Guenther and Bruno, solved this problem. They found a wooden box two feet square and one foot deep. They cut holes on opposite sides and attached long ropes. The diggers in the tunnel would fill the box and then call softly, "Full up." Those waiting in the cellar then would haul the box back and dump the earth into the bins. Hour after hour the operation continued in virtual silence, broken only by the men's panting and the soft swish of the shovels digging into the sand.

By Friday, January 19, they were beyond the first barbed-wire fence and, more dangerous, directly under the highway that constitutes the border. Just three feet beneath the pavement, the diggers could hear the tread and even the voices of the Vopos as they tramped by directly overhead.

"If we can hear them," said Guenther, "why can't they hear us?"

"It's a risk we have to take," Mueller said grimly. "We'll just have to try to work quietly."

Bruno put down his beer. "*Nein,* we can do better than that. We'll use the lights in the tunnel as a signal. I'll connect a switch upstairs, and Gerda can stand by the window and keep watch. Every time she sees the Vopos coming, she can switch the lights off, and we can stop working until they're gone."

Thus began Gerda's vigil at the window. Henceforth, from dawn to dusk, she scanned the border, switching the lights off and on as the Vopos came and went. Usually the delays were only a minute or two in length, but once she had to leave the diggers in darkness a while longer when a pair of young Vopos stopped and called up to her, "Hey, what are you doing at that window?"

Gerda's heart pounded. "Thinking over my homework," she answered quickly.

One of the Vopos chuckled. "When I get off duty, I'll come up and do some homework with you." He nudged his companion. "My pal, too. How about it?"

"You do," said Gerda evenly, "and I'll just have to inform your commanding officer."

"Oh, that sort," said the first Vopo. The two men swaggered on down the border highway, and with a sigh of relief Gerda switched the lights back on.

Inside the tunnel it was hot, dirty, sweaty work. Thus far, fortunately, there had been no cave-ins. At the entrance they had shored up the tunnel with boards, but under the foundations of the highway they found it unnecessary. Even so, droplets of melting snow kept coming through, making them wonder uneasily if the tunnel would continue to stand firm.

Then, on Saturday, January 20, while Bruno was digging, an avalanche of sand suddenly deluged him and a stick of wood hit him on the head. The lights flashed frantically.

In a moment Gerda's voice reached Bruno from the cellar. "For God's sake, do something quick! One of the fence posts has slipped down, and the barbed wire is sagging. The Vopos will see it the second they come by."

Bruno thought quickly. "Go back upstairs and flash twice when the fence looks all right."

He grasped the post and pushed it up through the ground slowly, until two flashes came from Gerda.

Then he called to Guenther, "Here, make a brace for this post. We'll tunnel around it."

On Monday, January 22, the end of the job seemed imminent.

Herr Schwartz announced that he had also reported sick at his job and would now be able to work full time. That made five diggers, and the pace quickened. On the same day, the men estimated that they already had reached the West.

They decided to push up a rod from the end of the tunnel. From the window Gerda was to flash once if it came up in the West, twice if it was still in the East.

Bruno and Guenther shoved up the rod and watched the lights. For a moment, the lights stayed on. Then they flashed off and on, off and on. The boys pulled the rod down hastily and crawled back through the tunnel to confer with Gerda.

She was breathless. "You're still at least 10 feet inside the border," she said, "and two Vopos were coming. You got that rod down just in the nick of time."

Swiftly the men returned to attack the last 10 feet. When they quit work that night, they announced jubilantly that they were sure they would be able to break into the West the next day.

To FRAU BECKER, that last Tuesday remains a kaleidoscope of nightmarish impressions. The mere thought that the tunnel was there, and the dread of what would happen to them all if it was discovered, chilled her. Then, to her astonishment, the house began to fill with unexpected guests.

First to arrive were a courtly white-haired gentleman, his 71-year-old wife, and another woman only a few years younger. Frau Becker had never laid eyes on any of them.

"Herr Mueller was kind enough to invite my wife and myself," the man explained, "and we took the liberty of bringing Frau Zeller here. You see, she is a widow; her two daughters married our two sons, and they live in West Berlin. We just couldn't go without her. I do hope you understand?"

"Of course," said Frau Becker, forcing calm into her voice. "Won't you please come in?"

In the next few hours Frau Becker found herself hostess to a bewildering succession of friends and strangers. Among them was Hilda, 19, a plump, quiet-spoken girl who had been in and out of the house for months. During the tunneling she had often helped brush off the men's clothes and given them a nod of approval before they left the house. Frau Becker regarded her as Bruno's sweetheart, but that night Bruno announced that she was his fiancee.

Even more surprising was the arrival of a tall, blue-eyed teenager whom Guenther introduced as his girl friend. (He had never before mentioned her to the family.)

Christel had left the house after lunch. Her brothers would have been furious if they had known she was inviting several of her friends to join in the night's adventure. But Christel's instinct proved to be correct; nobody informed on the Beckers—not even the few who declined to go along.

For Frau Becker the most agonizing moment came when the doorbell rang around 8 P.M.

Frau Schwartz answered, then reported, "There's a lady to see you—a very stout lady."

"Dear God," Frau Becker whispered to herself.

She knew who it was—Frau Krauss, a friend and close neighbor. Frau Becker had desperately wanted to invite her to come through the tunnel, but Frau Krauss was an unusually large woman, and her husband was asthmatic.

"He might have an attack," the diggers had insisted, "and she could never fit through at the far end."

So Frau Krauss had not been told about the tunnel, and now, with the house filled with strangers, Frau Becker knew she could not even ask her friend to come in.

She went slowly to the door. *"Liebe* Frau Krauss—"

"I was passing by and thought I'd drop in for a minute."

"How nice! But I'm so sorry, I—my head aches and I was just about to go to bed."

But Frau Becker couldn't leave it like that. "Please wait a second," she said. "I have something for you."

Frau Becker went back into the living room and picked up her mother's Bible. Then she returned to the door.

"I've been meaning to give this to you for some time," she said. "You mentioned once that your family Bible was lost when your home was bombed. . . ."

Afraid that she couldn't control her voice any longer, she leaned forward and kissed Frau Krauss on both cheeks. "Sleep well."

Frau Krauss thanked her and slipped off into the darkness. (Less than four months later Frau Krauss, her husband, and 10 others escaped through a tunnel dug from the cellar of the Krauss border home, only a few hundred feet from the Becker house.)

By 10:30 there were 28 people scattered through the rooms of the Becker house. All the lights had been turned off, and they waited in darkness, each one absorbed in thoughts of the past and future.

In the cellar all attention was focused on a new crisis. Tunneling upward to break out into the open, the diggers had run into a concrete conduit four feet in circumference. Mueller, the engineer, studied it from below and decided that it contained telephone lines. The problem was whether to tunnel farther under or to cut up beside it and risk coming out in the East Zone.

"How long will it take to tunnel under?" asked Erwin.

"Another 24 hours."

"I vote that we take our chances and dig straight up," said Erwin.

"Agreed," said Mueller.

Now, as Bruno and Guenther dug upward, they began to encounter roots of trees and bushes.

"Get me the shears," whispered Bruno.

Forty-five minutes later—just before 1 A.M. on Wednesday, January 24—Bruno broke through.

Bruno and Guenther scrambled back to the cellar. "Let's get going," Bruno said quietly.

Thoughtfully Herr Mueller said, "Wait a minute. When we come out, we should have some protection. The Vopos might hear us and start shooting. I suggest that somebody go through first and get the West Berlin police to stand guard by the opening."

"Good idea," Bruno said. "Who?"

Guenther pointed to Mueller. "You."

Mueller nodded and crawled into the entrance.

Bruno went upstairs and whispered the news to his mother.

"All right," she said, "tell the others, and ask Gerda and Christel to go through with me."

She went down into the cellar, her two daughters close beside her. The others followed silently. Bruno crawled in first.

"I'll show the way," he said.

Ten people lay silent in the tunnel, and 17 waited in the cellar—all the women in their Sunday best—while Herr Mueller clawed and fought his way up and out of the opening. He discovered with horror that they had come out directly under the picket fence. They were still three feet short of the small posts that mark the actual beginning of the West. Technically they were still within the East Zone, and technically the Vopos had the right to shoot.

Then from down the road came the tread of approaching Vopos.

"Quiet!" he whispered back to Bruno. "They're coming."

"Quiet," Bruno whispered back to his mother.

Scarcely breathing, Herr Mueller lay in the bushes as the two

Vopos passed. In the tunnel Frau Becker and the others lay listening to the ominous footsteps just three feet over their heads.

During those last, unbearable moments of tension, the thoughts of many of the refugees turned strangely to the everyday world. Christel thought of her pet tomcat, Peter. Unable to find him that night, she had left behind a note with some money, asking that someone take care of him. Now she wondered: "Who will get Peter?"

Erwin thought: "I'm glad the last thing I did was to go upstairs and hack down our rubber plant. Why should *they* get it?"

Frau Becker thought of Frau Krauss: "May God forgive me, and may Frau Krauss forgive me in the morning."

Then the Vopos were gone, and Herr Mueller whispered to Bruno, "All clear. I'm off."

They waited in stifling blackness while he clambered up the Frohnau hill, stumbled half a mile along the path, and knocked at the first house he came to. It was now 1:15 in the morning. A light came on, and an infuriated man opened the door. "What in the name—"

Herr Mueller blurted out his story. "Have you a telephone?"

"Yes, the only one within a mile. You're lucky. Come in."

A half hour later Mueller was back at the tunnel entrance with

three armed West Berlin policemen. Each of the policemen had a flashlight ready to turn on to reveal himself and his gun if any Vopos started trouble.

Up and out, the refugees emerged, dirty, gasping, trembling. First came Bruno, then Gerda.

"Mother's next," she whispered to Bruno.

Daughter and son reached down into the hole, took hold of their mother's arms, and pulled her out gently.

Disdaining help, Christel pulled herself up.

"This is nothing." she whispered.

But the wait in the tunnel had taken its toll of everybody's nerves, and a moment later she was lying beside her mother on the frozen grass, looking up at the stars and murmuring over and over, "Thank you, God. Thank you."

In the Beckers' cellar, those who were waiting crawled singly into the tunnel as it emptied from the other end. Frau Mueller strapped a doll around the waist of her eight-year-old daughter, Gisela.

"Courage, little one," she whispered.

Gisela was delighted that she could stand and walk at the beginning of the tunnel, but soon she, like all the others, had to crawl.

They came through quickly now, with military precision. Frau Schwartz caught sight of a uniform in the dim moonlight, thought the man was a Vopo, and ducked back into the tunnel. But her husband, with the confidence of desperation, reassured her, and the West Berlin policeman helped her out.

Last person into the cramped, 87-foot passage was the 71-year-old grandmother who insisted that her husband precede her: "You have always led, *Geliebter.*"

On the way through she lost a shoe, and as she tried to crawl out of the hole at the end, she fainted. Tenderly, her husband and one of the policemen pulled her out. A moment later she was lying on the ground beside Frau Becker.

"You know," she said, "I do believe that policeman thought I fainted. Isn't that ridiculous?"

The Becker tunnel, dug through desperation and hope, was empty at last. It had enabled 28 men, women, and children to crawl from tyranny to freedom.

The escapees spent the next few days at the Marienfelde Refugee Camp in West Berlin recovering from their ordeal before they left for their new homes in West Berlin, Dortmund, Hamburg, Munich, and other cities of free Germany.

A week to the day after they had crawled through, Gerda and Christel returned to the snow-covered Frohnau hillside across from their home. They descended the hill and looked at the tunnel opening, already caved in and surely blocked on the other side.

"It's so little," Christel said in a suddenly awestruck voice. "I don't see how we ever got through."

Just then the inevitable pair of Vopos came by, and the irrepressible teenager in Christel broke out. "Why don't you come over here?" she cried. "You know you'd like it much better."

Eyes straight ahead, the Vopos marched on, and the girls were left alone. Across the border and the barbed wire, their home stood empty and abandoned.

"Peter," Christel called to her tomcat. "Come, Peter. Come."

But Peter didn't come, and Gerda put her hand on Christel's shoulder and said, "Let's go, Christel. That life is over."

The girls then climbed back up the hill toward their new lives.

*For the captured Danish Resistance fighters
there seemed no hope of escape from the
tightly guarded Nazi prison—until the day the
planes came and the bombs fell.*

Breakout

By Christen Lyst Hansen

THE FIRST OF THAT day's series of improbable events occurred when a key grated in the lock of my tiny attic cell. The solid wooden door creaked open and there stood the chief of the Nazi prison guards, Trappart himself.

"Get your things together," he said. "You're leaving."

Leaving? I couldn't believe it. For four long months I had been a prisoner on the sixth floor of this sprawling, U-shaped building, once the Copenhagen offices of the Shell Petroleum Company but now Danish headquarters of the German Gestapo. I shared the prison with 35 other Danish Resistance leaders, and I had feared that I'd never leave the place alive.

"We are sending you to Froeslev concentration camp," Trappart said. "The car will be leaving in 15 minutes."

The door clicked shut and he was gone.

Incredulously, I glanced at my watch. It was 8:10 A.M. on March 21, 1945. For just a moment my future seemed immeasurably brighter. I knew Froeslev to be an easy camp; my chances of survival there would be much better than where I was.

Though I had once organized a Danish underground police force, the Gestapo had apparently come to consider me too unimportant to remain in Shell House attic, where they kept only those leaders suspected of being most dangerous to them. They were much more interested now in "interrogating" Danes who had masterminded the sabotage of German-run war factories and railways.

Naturally, I was glad to be getting out of that infamous building, but I felt a sharp pang of regret at leaving so many of my friends behind to die. From the interrogation room on the fifth floor just

27

below, I could hear the cries of fellow Danes undergoing "questioning." More and more of our group were being arrested every day, and many of them were being forced to talk. Consequently, the Gestapo's massive intelligence files, kept on the first three floors, were fast nearing completion.

Soon the Nazis would finish piecing together their complex jigsaw puzzle of information. Then most of my friends in the attic would be shot, or put to slower deaths. Worse, when the Gestapo's files were completed, scores of other Danish Resistance leaders would be arrested and executed. Our whole regional underground movement would be defeated.

8:30 A.M. The surly German guard named Wiesmer marched me across the corridor to the washroom for the last time. As we went in, Prof. Poul Brandt Rehberg came limping out, and I was shocked to see how badly crippled he was from Gestapo beatings. This eminent Danish physiologist, who had helped most of Denmark's 7,000 Jews to safety, was now paying a heartbreaking price for his valor.

On the way back to my cell, I caught a glimpse of young Poul Bruun, who had planned many acts of sabotage. We had all heard whispers of his impending fate.

"We've found out you have been lying to us," an SS officer had informed him the evening before. "Tomorrow you will tell us the whole story—if we have to tear it from you."

For the slightly built, gentle Bruun it was now "tomorrow."

Again conscience stabbed me. What right did *I* have to escape, when men who had done so much more for our cause and country would stay here and perish?

8:40 A.M. Back in my cell I listened to the rising moan of the wind. It would be gray and raw outside. No weather for flying. *They won't come today,* I thought—and was forced to smile grimly at the wild fantasies that desperation can bring to the mind. There was no sensible reason to believe "they" would ever come.

"As long as we've got you up here under the roof," our jailers had always reminded us, "your RAF friends will never attack. They know you'd be the first ones killed by their bombs. Besides, your Allied friends are too busy in Europe to be interested in a cause as trivial as yours. They've forgotten you."

Discouragingly logical arguments. Yet drowning men clutch at straws, and we prisoners in the attic had long clung to a last forlorn hope. If, we reasoned, our Resistance leaders outside should determine that Shell House must be destroyed at any cost, if they could prevail on the Royal Air Force to attempt the job, and if the pilots could single out our building in a crowded district where all the steep-tiled rooftops looked alike, then the damning records in Shell House *might* be destroyed and our underground movement saved. And the terrible ordeal might be quickly over for us "expendable" prisoners locked up in the attic.

8:55 A.M. The poker-faced Wiesmer and two other soldiers came to escort me out of the building. As we passed the second and first floors, I glimpsed the vast rows of filing cabinets filled with the incriminating records that threatened to doom my comrades. How I longed for a hand grenade!

We reached the door leading outside, but there Wiesmer stopped and swore furiously.

"The morning car has already gone. Now we'll have to wait until 1 o'clock for the next one."

So it was back to the attic—at 9:02.

I attached no significance to the delay, nor to the fact that I was now placed not in my old cell, Number 10, but in Number 6. What did a few more hours matter when, without even a word of farewell, I'd soon be leaving my friends forever? I kept glancing at the hands of my watch, slowly edging toward my departure time.

Ten o'clock came . . . 11:00 . . . 11:15 . . . little did I know that the long-hoped-for "impossible" air attack was almost upon us, that, using the bad weather as an element of surprise, 46 Allied planes—18 Mosquito bombers and 28 Mustang fighters—were streaking for their target—Shell House.

11:18 A.M. At the whine of diving planes, I jumped up. As the bombs hit Shell House, the attic floor heaved violently beneath my feet. Dust filled the air, making it difficult to see or breathe. The bed danced out across the floor, and everything loose in the cell whirled around me. This, I realized, was only the salvo from the first wave of bombers. Could they destroy the records just 30 feet below without destroying us, too?

I picked up my wooden stool and hurled it against the cell door. To my amazement, the panel shattered. Rushing into the corridor, I saw Wiesmer blocking my path. I grabbed him by the shoulders and shook him violently.

"The keys!" I roared at him. I was frantic. "Give me the keys to the cells! Hurry up!"

Wiesmer, however, was paralyzed with terror, and for a second we both stared in awe at the gaping hole that a bomb had torn in the roof.

29

Planes roared unbelievably overhead; machine guns stuttered and flicked red tongues. Bombs crashed all around us. I could hear the other prisoners beating away at their doors.

"The *keys*!" I screamed at Wiesmer again.

Slowly he began to pull a chain from his pocket. I snatched it from him and began unlocking the cell doors.

Here was my big chance—the one I'd thought would never come. But would there be time?

In seconds, I unlocked Cells 7, 8, and 9. Number 10, my old cell, was open and empty. As I rushed toward Number 11, the whole building reeled and shook with a new series of explosions, but I managed to reach and open 11 and 12, and, as a sheet of flame from the ruined west wing swept toward me, 13, 14, and 15.

Rushing out of their cells into the dust-choked corridor came leading figures of the Danish Resistance. Some, like Professor Brandt Rehberg, were limping so badly from "interrogations" that they could barely walk. But we were out—every one of us from the attic's south wing was free.

Some of us ran to help prisoners in the west wing, but found them impossible to reach; a bomb had ripped a gigantic hole in the floor, and we couldn't get across.

"Come on," I yelled. "Time to get out of here."

With the others behind me, I raced for the northeast stairs. A lucky choice: They proved to be one of the only two stairways in the building still left standing!

The few prisoners still alive in the blazing west wing were making even more spectacular exits. Poul Bruun, experiencing an even rougher day than had been promised him by the Gestapo, had fallen straight through to the fifth floor. His skull was fractured, but he was vaguely aware of fire surging toward him. It was either jump—from a fifth-story window—or burn to death. Bruun jumped. Spinning down, he landed in a tangle of barbed wire.

Meanwhile, our group raced down the stairs and burst into the open. There had been no time to think of the guards and guns that might await us there, but a glance revealed only corpses; the lucky guards had fled.

The gate of the barbed-wire fence was standing open. We ran through it, wildly, headlong.

By another freak of chance, the barbed-wire entanglement, our last obstruction, had been blown to bits, and a path was cleared for us precisely where—and when—we needed it.

31

The streets were mercifully deserted and filled with smoke. By now practically everyone else had dived into the air-raid shelters (among them, I learned later, my wife and 15-year-old son, who had watched the bombing from a shop not 700 yards away).

For a moment we seemed to have the entire city to ourselves. Only when the last ground-shaking explosions ended did we turn to look back. Shell House attic—about 90 seconds after we left it—had collapsed in a torrent of flames.

We quickly scattered in various directions, and in seven minutes I had reached a friend's house.

That evening I learned more about the air raid, one of the most daring and perilous of the war. Launched in cooperation with the Danish Resistance, the mission had been led by Britain's Air Vice-Marshal Sir Basil Embry himself. The bombing attack on Shell House had cost four RAF bombers, two fighter planes, and the lives of nine of the airmen.

But the assault had accomplished its mission. Though eight of the attic prisoners had died, the incriminating Gestapo records lay in ashes. Scores, perhaps even hundreds, of Copenhagen Resistance fighters had thus been placed beyond the reach of terror.

For us and for our families and friends it was a night for exuberant, if incredulous, celebration.

Christen Lyst Hansen, who died in 1974, was honored by King Frederik of Denmark with a decoration for his heroism during the bombing raid on Shell House.

*The weather-beaten Soviet trawler sailed across the
Black Sea under orders to proceed to a repair yard.
But its captain had a different plan—to defect to a Western
country with his ship and crew.*

Desperate Voyage

By George Feifer

EVENING WAS APPROACHING when distant thunder rumbled
through the air of Kerch, a Russian port on the northern shores
of the Black Sea. The weather would have seemed threatening to
most sailors, but to Pavel Ivanovich Dudnikov, captain of the elderly
Soviet fishing trawler *Vishera*, the prospect of a storm was pure balm.
From the wheelhouse he gave the order to cast off and rang down
"slow ahead." It was 7 P.M. on August 10, 1972. The *Vishera* had
begun her desperate voyage to freedom.

Nothing seemed unusual about the 160-ton trawler. Her gray and
white anonymity was enlivened only by the canary-colored hammer
and sickle painted on a red band around her narrow funnel. Her
orders were to proceed to a repair yard in Odessa, 485 miles to the
west. In fact, however, Captain Dudnikov and his first mate, Vladimir Dyusov, shared a daring plan: to strike south across the Black Sea
to the Bosporus, thence through the strait and on to Greece, the
nearest Western country where they considered it safe to ask for
political asylum. Though slow, the ship was newly refitted and fully
provisioned: 11 tons of fuel (enough for 10 days' sailing), plenty of
food and water for the crew of eight.

The notion of defecting with an entire ship was audacious indeed.
All craft movements throughout the Black Sea were closely watched
by Soviet patrols. Capture of a defector, with a likely charge of
"crimes against the state," could mean up to 10 years in a labor
camp—even, in rare cases, death.

Dudnikov and Dyusov could not tell the crew of their plan for fear
of risking denunciation to the Soviet police. At least one member of
every Soviet fishing crew is an informer. Fortunately, the identity of

the *Vishera's* informer was obvious: Engineer David Tskhadaya, 57, a dogmatic, slogan-spouting Communist Party member. Even knowing this, the captain could not always contain his feelings about Soviet rule. A few days earlier he and Tskhadaya had stood on deck, gazing at the hills above Kerch.

Tskhadaya had said: "If I were a local party secretary, I'd build a large statue of Lenin up there, dominating the city."

"This country has a million statues of Lenin," Dudnikov blurted

out. "I'd build a restaurant where people could go and *enjoy* themselves for a change!"

Aghast, Tskhadaya warned the crew of this "impertinence" and threatened: "When we get back, the KGB will look into this case."

Pavel Ivanovich Dudnikov had been born in 1929 of Russian peasant stock in a village bordering the Caucasus Mountains. In 1930 Communist Party officials forced farmers to give up their land and join collective farms. To acquire resources to start the collectives, the officials arrested some of the hardest-working farmers and their families as "exploiters," confiscated virtually everything they owned, and exiled them to the wilderness of the northern Ural Mountains. Among the victims was the Dudnikov family.

At 17, after an adolescence in near-famine conditions, Pavel became a seaman. Over the next decade he rose to the rank of mate, earning 150 rubles a month—enough to support a bachelor. But when he married and had to provide for a family, his pay did not suffice. He resorted to occasional smuggling and black-market transactions to make ends meet.

In 1962 the desperate Dudnikov bought some Western currency from an underground trader, intending to purchase and resell some

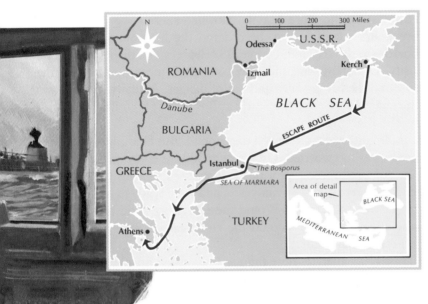

foreign clothing so that he could buy extra goods for his family. But he was caught and sentenced to eight years in a labor camp. In his first year there he learned that his wife had divorced him.

The harsh experience set his goal in life: to flee the Soviet Union. Shortly after his release from the labor camp in 1970, he met Vladimir Dyusov, whose ideas about the Soviet regime matched his own.

Three hours out of Kerch, a guard-ship signal light—"Identify yourself"—stabbed furiously at the *Vishera*. Dudnikov's first impulse was to ignore the challenge, even though the trawler was still on her assigned course. His slow response aroused suspicion, and the guard ship at once ordered the *Vishera* to come alongside.

Through a bullhorn, an officer asked, "Why didn't you answer? What are you trying to do?"

"Sorry," shouted Dudnikov.

He saw the officer pick up the radiotelephone to call the Command Point for Control of Ship Movements in Kerch. Five minutes seemed like hours. Then he was told he could proceed and was warned: "Watch yourself—or we'll watch you!"

Leaving the guard ship, the *Vishera* headed almost due south, instead of moving westward along the coast to Odessa. Luckily, Command Point had ordered all vessels to give a wide berth to the coast, where naval units would be engaging in night-firing exercises. This, of course, suited Dudnikov, since it would take him out into the Black Sea, away from the more heavily patrolled shore.

Five hours out of Kerch, he ordered the helmsman to come to starboard—to the freedom course, 232 degrees. To dispel the crew's curiosity, Dudnikov said this new course was necessary to take the ship around the firing zones and out of danger. Actually, the *Vishera* was heading directly for the Turkish Bosporus, 500 miles southwest across the Black Sea.

At midnight Dyusov relieved the captain. But Dudnikov could not sleep. He was too worried. On a recent 300-mile voyage the *Vishera* had encountered three patrol boats. These sea sentries knew the assigned location of every Soviet vessel and were ready to intercept any ships that were off course. Would these high seas and bad visibility provide effective cover? Would the electrical storms interfere with coastal radar surveillance?

August 11 dawned to more thundery squalls. The morning horizon was empty, and the *Vishera* seemed alone in the Black Sea's 170,000 square miles. Dudnikov was required to radio his ship's position twice daily, but he told his radio officer to contact no one. An industrious Lithuanian, the officer thought the order a curious one, but he did not question it.

However, the captain was soon suffering the disquieting presence of Tskhadaya, who climbed to the bridge to inspect the chart.

"Why are we so far from shore?" he asked.

"It's this rotten visibility," said Dudnikov. He gestured with his hand. "The coast is right over there."

In truth, they were more than 100 miles from land on a course slightly south of the major sea-lane.

Just after noon the next day a speck appeared ahead. Dudnikov and Dyusov were relieved when it turned out to be a Soviet freighter. Even so, merchant vessels had standing orders to report any Soviet ships considered off course. The two men watched the ship lumber past. No signal. Their luck was holding!

Several times in the tense hours that followed, the *Vishera* took evasive action to avoid Soviet merchantmen. These maneuvers did not go unnoticed by the crew. Some of them guessed correctly—but privately— what was afoot. Dudnikov and Dyusov became aware of a kind of tacit conspiracy as they saw some of the sailors exchange meaningful looks.

At 3 P.M. the magic moment arrived: the first view of Turkey to the south. Although five hours of steady steaming remained to reach the Bosporus, they would soon be in Turkish territorial waters. If a Soviet cutter appeared, Dudnikov could race for the shore, beach the ship if necessary or swim to land. Meanwhile, the crew had to be told what was up—everyone, that is, except Tskhadaya, who was down below in the engine room.

"I offer you my congratulations," Dudnikov said to each sailor in turn. "You are now in Turkish waters and a free man if you choose. I intend to sail to Greece. You can join me in requesting political asylum. If you want to return to the Soviet Union, you may do so when we reach Athens. The choice is yours."

The crew's reaction was not long in crystallizing. "Free!" they rejoiced. "We're going to be free!"

Tskhadaya obviously had to be told something. So he was informed that the ship had received radio orders to change course from Odessa to Izmail, a Soviet port located about 45 miles up the Danube delta from the Black Sea. Tskhadaya checked with the radio officer who, as instructed, confirmed the change.

There was still the serious business of getting safely through the Bosporus. At the rail Tskhadaya watched idly as the *Vishera* began negotiating "the Danube." The delicate passage took well over an hour. It was only at the south end of the Bosporus, opposite Istanbul itself, when the Sultan Ahmet Mosque, a famous Turkish landmark, came into view that Tskhadaya jerked back in disbelief.

"What does this mean?" he shouted. "This is Turkey!"

"Yes, I see," Dudnikov replied blandly. "Apparently I made a slight mistake."

"I will report to the Soviet Consulate in Istanbul immediately," spluttered Tskhadaya.

The captain proceeded through the Bosporus, then anchored and opened six bottles of Russian champagne to mark the occasion. Calmly he made Tskhadaya an offer: he would not lock him up if Tskhadaya stood watch until allowed to leave the vessel in Greece. Crestfallen, the informer agreed.

As it turned out, Tskhadaya never reached Greece. Shortly after, in the Sea of Marmara, a Turkish parol boat drew up to inspect the *Vishera*. As the vessels touched, Tskhadaya leaped onto the deck of the Turkish boat. Babbling in Russian and schoolboy German, both incomprehensible to the Turkish crew, he was whisked ashore with them. The Turks were convinced that he was seeking asylum from the Soviet vessel.

But this episode posed a new problem. The Soviet Navy kept an average of 50 ships in the Mediterranean. If Tskhadaya got word to Soviet officials before the *Vishera* could reach Greece, there was still danger of interception. Dudnikov ordered the trawler's identification markings painted out. (As it happened, Tskhadaya remained enmeshed in Turkish red tape too long to relay a timely warning to the Soviets.) In the early morning hours of August 14 the *Vishera* safely dropped anchor off Piraeus, the seaport of Athens.

When a Greek patrol boat came alongside, Captain Dudnikov told its skipper: "We want to ask for political asylum."

"You mean you yourself want asylum," the Greek corrected him.

"No, the whole crew!"

And so ended the voyage of the *Vishera*, the first Soviet craft to defect since World War II.

On January 8, 1973, Captain Dudnikov, First Mate Dyusov, and the rest of the Vishera's *crew boarded the Italian liner* Cristoforo Colombo *at Piraeus and sailed for the United States. Two eventually returned to the Soviet Union; the others took jobs in various parts of the United States. The fate of Engineer Tskhadaya remains unknown.*

Green Beret officer James "Nick" Rowe was captured by the Viet-cong in South Vietnam in 1963. Throughout his 62 months of imprisonment, during which he suffered extreme physical and mental torture, he managed to keep a diary. The following amazing account of how one man endured a lonely, uneven struggle against a totalitarian system is based on that diary.

Five Years to Freedom

By Maj. James N. Rowe, U.S. Army

THE STOCKY VIETCONG soldier shoved me violently forward. My arms were tied at the wrists and elbows, and this prevented me from balancing as I slipped and struggled in the muddy rice paddy. Another VC prodded me with his bayonet.

"*Mau di!*" he commanded ("Move fast!").

I stumbled into one of the deep irrigation trenches that bordered the paddy. Underwater, panic seized me as I kicked, trying to get to air. But the sides of the ditch were slick and offered no foothold. Then I felt something solid and pushed myself upward, breaking the surface and taking a deep breath before going under again. I heard a harsh chuckle from one of the VC as the water closed over me.

A hand grasped the cloth binding my elbows and raised me. I managed to roll onto dry land. Then I was pulled to my feet and once more pushed along the path atop the canal bank where a short time ago we had been shooting at one another.

I was exhausted, but through the whirling haze in front of my eyes, I saw crumpled bodies strewn across the mud. Many of the bodies were stripped, but on a few were the camouflage uniforms worn by the South Vietnamese Special Forces. Each had a gaping hole in the head, the face unrecognizable after the explosive exit of the bullet. The VC were taking no wounded Vietnamese prisoners.

This was Vietnam in October 1963—before the arrival of United States jets, artillery support, and combat units. I was an adviser, and now, on patrol in Vietcong territory with three companies of South Vietnamese, a fight had broken out and I had been captured.

I heard a commotion behind me, and Dan Pitzer, a medic, came shuffling past, two VC trotting behind him.

"I'm sorry, Nick," he said as he passed.

A third American had also accompanied the patrol, Capt. Humbert "Rocky" Versace, an intelligence adviser. He had been hit in the knee, and I had just put a compress on the wound when the VC took me. I prayed that they hadn't killed him.

At a shouted command, my guards halted. I stood with my head hanging, trying hard to get my breath, dimly seeing a pair of sandaled feet in front of me.

"My khong?" came a rasping voice ("Is it an American?").

"Da Phai!" snapped a guard, and a fist came straight at me. My head snapped back; pain shot across my face, then blackness.

I came to with a guard kicking me in the back. I could feel the wetness of blood on my face, and I couldn't breathe through my nose. Yanked to my feet, I was led down the canal and put in a long, narrow boat. Shortly the boat pulled away, and I passed out.

I awoke blindfolded with one of the guards wiping my face, using a rag dipped in canal water. He swabbed my mouth and nose almost gently, for which I was grateful. Later, I was led ashore into what was apparently a small village and, in the company of Dan Pitzer and several Vietnamese prisoners, given some rice to eat. The blindfold had been removed.

I had no idea where we were. I recalled a chapter in the pamphlet

Escape and Evasion that said: "One should attempt to escape as soon after capture as possible, before the enemy can move you to a secure area." I wished that the author had included at least one paragraph on how to do it.

Night fell, and we came to a hut. To my relief we found Rocky Versace inside, lying on the floor. He was in obvious pain from his wound, but the bleeding had stopped. Most important, he was alive.

Again by water we moved on, blindfolded, accompanied now by Rocky. I lost all sense of direction. When we finally stopped and the blindfolds were removed, I could see low, thick-leaved trees, ferns, and reeds. I followed a guard through knee-deep water into a grove where we came to a cagelike structure with a low thatched roof and a floor. The walls were made of poles spaced about six inches apart vertically and horizontally.

We entered, and our arms were untied. We were given sleeping mats and mosquito nets. I asked for a drink of water. In a short time, a boy brought me a cup, and I drank greedily. Too late, I felt the slimy moss in my mouth. The water had been scooped up from the stagnant swamp outside our enclosure.

I was too tired to think any more about it. We climbed under the mosquito nets, and the guards departed, leaving one man outside the cage with a submachine gun.

The patrol on which we were captured had been directed against the village of Le Coeur, located in Vietcong-dominated territory some 140 miles southwest of Saigon. It was a countryside of rice paddies, banana and coconut groves, and scattered hamlets, located on the edge of the U Minh Forest. We had never ventured into this area before, and the close proximity of the legendary "Forest of Darkness," a Vietcong sanctuary, had made it a cinch for a fire fight. But instead of encountering the irregular guerrilla units we had expected, we had run into a main force battalion. Our retreat had been cut off with heavy losses. As a matter of fact, Dan, Rocky, and I were very lucky to be alive.

The sun was above the trees the next morning when I awoke. I gingerly felt the bridge of my nose and was rewarded with a sharp pain. I also had a graze wound on the thigh and several small punctures in my chest and legs from mortar fragments. Dan, who had caught fragments in his shoulder, cleaned our wounds.

Rocky Versace was a more serious problem. A trimly built, 26-year-old West Point graduate, he had volunteered for a six-month extension in Vietnam after a year as an adviser. His outthrust jaw and penetrating eyes were indications of his personality; his steel-gray hair looked as if it belonged on someone much older.

He was in severe pain, and his knee had begun to swell. Dan loosened the compresses, which had stuck to the dried blood, giving Rocky a little relief; but medical care was a necessity. Apparently this was not available, for we received only boiled water, some soap, and a mild antiseptic. We washed the wound as thoroughly as we could, and Dan rebandaged it.

The guards also gave us a breakfast of rice. I wondered how long I could go without some sort of real food. I was still thinking in terms of American rations. Before I finished my meal, I experienced wrenching stomach cramps. The guard responded to my frantic gestures by pointing toward a shaky walkway that led away from the cage into the brush. I barely made it to a small platform nailed above the water between two trees. The guard stood about 15 feet away as I went through the spasms of oncoming dysentery. Soon I was spending most of my time running to the latrine.

After a couple of days, Rocky was moved out of the cage, supposedly to be taken to a hospital. Later, we were assured that his wounds were being treated. Dan and I wondered what was in store for us. Before Rocky's departure, he had talked about another American who had been captured earlier and released after six months. We set that as the outside limit of our own detention.

On November 14 Dan and I were taken on a four-day trip to another prison camp among the mangrove swamps of the southern Camau Peninsula. This camp was more elaborate than the setup we had left. There was a log dock over the entry canal and long, narrow huts built on poles to raise them above water level.

Rocky Versace was already there in a thatched hut next to a small kitchen and mess hall. Dan and I were put in a separate hut with barred walls and were not allowed to communicate with him. It was becoming clear that the reason for his separation was not "hospitalization," which he had never received. Rocky, who spoke fluent Vietnamese, had assailed the Vietcong movement from his first encounter with the guards and had been marked as a "reactionary." Dan and I, who spoke little Vietnamese, were unknown quantities.

On the evening of our fourth day in the new camp, we heard excited shouts near Rocky's hut. The guards scrambled for their weapons and then disappeared into the trees, wading in mud up to their thighs, rifles held overhead. Shouting continued as they spread into a line, sweeping through the palms and fern thickets.

A camp official appeared before our cage carrying leg irons, and we were forced into them. We asked why. Visibly incensed, the man snapped, "Versace was very bad."

With a wounded leg and surrounded by deep mud and a camp full of guards, Rocky had tried to escape. He had more guts than brains to try it at this point, and he was caught pulling himself through the slime toward a canal. I learned later that he was attempting to reach the canal, where he could swim and possibly make it northward to a friendly outpost. The VC had assumed from Rocky's opinions that they had a hard case on their hands. Now they knew it.

The camp was run by a major who wore a khaki uniform. The VC also had a political representative there, Mr. Muoi. He wore black trousers and shirt, as did a third man. He was Mr. Ba, whom we called Plato because of his tendency to philosophize.

Plato spent part of each afternoon at the cage with Dan and me, gently probing our ideas about the U.S. involvement in Vietnam. He made no effort to contradict anything we said. His central theme was the generosity and leniency of the National Liberation Front toward prisoners. Then he began to push for a letter to our families stating that we were well and thanking the NLF for its lenient treatment. I refused, and eventually a compromise was worked out. We wrote to the International Red Cross, giving our names, ranks, and serial numbers, and stating that we were in reasonably good health.

One day Plato brought a piece of paper to be filled out. It was titled: "Red Cross Index Data Card." Beneath this heading were: Name, Rank, Serial Number, Date of Birth—all as prescribed by the Geneva Convention. But these questions were followed by a great many others of a military and personal nature.

"Mr. Ba," I said, "this form contains questions we cannot answer."

He looked surprised that I would refuse. "All the Front wishes to do is to notify your family that you are not killed."

"We wrote letters to the Red Cross," I reminded him. "They will notify our families that we are alive."

"No!" His answer was emphatic. "The Red Cross is a tool of the imperialist aggressors, and the Front does not recognize it. Consider your decision carefully. I will come back."

I was still attempting to determine several things. First, what was their purpose in taking us prisoners rather than killing us? Second, what requirements would be placed upon us that we could not fulfill? Finally, to what lengths would they go to ensure fulfillment?

My dysentery, which had grown worse, was now accompanied by

43

fever and nausea, but the probing of our thoughts went on. Ba and Muoi came in periodically, and on one visit Muoi asked, "Do you know that your President Kennedy was killed?"

I thought he was trying to shake us up. We had been told earlier that Ngo Dinh Diem had been overthrown and killed and that the government in Saigon was toppling. The possibility that these reports might contain some truth made me wonder what was happening on the outside. I dismissed them as false, but it was my first taste of an uncertainty that would grow to monstrous proportions.

Early in 1964 Dan, Rocky, and I were separated and moved to another camp, about two hours away by boat. Plato came to visit me soon after my arrival and pulled out the index data card again.

"You must complete the form," he said.

"What if I refuse?" I asked.

"Do not fear torture," he reassured me. "We are not barbarians who rely on torture to gain information." Then he explained a theory that I was to learn well in the days to come. "If you take an individual and control his body, you do not necessarily control the man. But if you can control his mind, you control the whole. Soon you will attend a school that will show you the truth about Vietnam."

I asked what happened if an individual refused to cooperate.

"He may rest here for a long time," Plato said calmly. "If we are unsuccessful in our instruction the first time, we must recommence."

On February 18 a guard marched me to the school hut. The inside had been decorated with slogans, painstakingly printed in English: "Welcome the lenient policy of the Front toward POW's," "Do not die for the profit of Capitalist-Imperialist." Two khaki-uniformed Vietnamese sat behind the desk. As I slid onto a bench, one began to lecture in a precise voice. Plato translated:

"The National Liberation Front has dispatched us to present to you the just cause of the revolution and the certainty of final victory. Your release will depend upon your good attitude and repentance of your past misdeeds."

My mind was fixed on the phrase "good attitude," and I barely heard Plato begin translating the first lesson: *Vietnam la mot* ("Vietnam is one country").

The next day it was Rocky's turn. I had learned that he was being held in both leg and arm irons, and I watched as he hobbled along to the school. From the angry expressions on his guards' faces, I could tell he was not going willingly.

His first words as he entered the school were: "I'm an officer in the

United States Army. You can force me to come here, you can make me sit and listen, but I don't believe a damn word you say!" "Rocky," I thought, "bless you. You're a hard-core s.o.b.!"

The school continued through March 24 and covered a sketchy history of the war against the French, the Geneva Accords of 1954, Ngo Dinh Diem's accession to the presidency in South Vietnam, and the suffering that, they said, had occurred because of Diem and the intervention of the United States. Any facts that refuted their version of history were conveniently omitted from their recital of events.

On the evening of April 8, I heard Mr. Muoi's voice yelling in the direction of Rocky's cage. Rocky's voice was fainter, but clear, "All or just me?" They were moving Rocky out! In the commotion, I strained to see through the darkness, but the guards blocked my view.

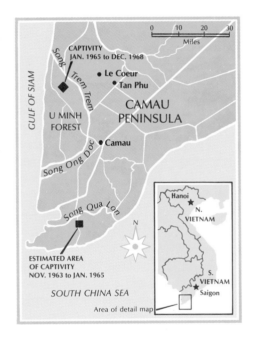

The next morning I was allowed for the first time to walk from my cage to the kitchen to get rice. Along the way a pile of bloody gray rags caught my eye. They were the pajamas given to Rocky, torn into shreds. I forced myself to look at Rocky's cage. Bars had been ripped from the side of the hut and either hung crazily from the tangle of poles or were strewn in the mud. The image of what had happened fixed itself slowly in my brain. Rocky must be dead.

Plato visited my cage later in the day, his mood unusually somber. He told me it was unfortunate that the Front had been forced to take drastic action, but they had no other choice. Rocky had shouted at him and questioned his instruction. Because Rocky had opposed the Front, he had paid. Plato said he hoped my attitude would improve.

I sat, trying to contain my boiling anger. My one thought was not to strike back until I could hurt them. It would have been useless to batter my head against a wall and only lose what slight freedom I had. My ultimate goal was clear: to gain my freedom without compromising my beliefs or harming my country.

45

Nearly six months had passed, and clearly our hope for an early release had been ill-founded. In fact, another year would pass in much the same way. It was a strenuous period of being moved from one camp to another, of deteriorating health, and of continual VC attempts to extract military information while instilling a proper attitude—acceptance of their version of the war.

I devised a cover story that allowed me to deny knowledge of the areas my questioners were interested in. I concealed the facts that I was a graduate of West Point and that I had trained in artillery and the Special Forces. Instead, I became an engineer with no knowledge of tactics. Bridges, roads, buildings I could discuss, but beyond these subjects I was useless.

I was trying to avoid any open opposition, since this would allow them to bring to bear on me whatever pressure they wished. I wasn't certain that I could hold out as Rocky had done, particularly when the pressure could be maintained for as long as they wanted.

The case of Rocky had a startling twist. One afternoon a guard was at my cage talking to me about the war and particularly about the good treatment given prisoners. I questioned this, saying that the POW's never knew when one of them might be executed. The guard, in defense of his statements, blurted out, *"Khong My chet!"* ("No American is dead!").

Later, I discovered that this was true. While bathing in a canal I overheard Rocky's voice coming from some huts in a clump of thick vegetation about 100 yards from ours. His "murder" had been staged; it was purely a deception meant to weaken our resistance. (Rocky's days, however, were numbered. In September 1965 we were to learn from a Radio Hanoi broadcast that he had been executed in retaliation for the execution of three VC terrorists in Danang.)

As the weeks passed, my health began to disintegrate. The diarrhea became so bad that the guards brought me a crock resembling a large flowerpot so that I wouldn't have to be released from the cage five or six times a night to go to the latrine. I also developed a fungus infection that began like ringworm, spreading rapidly until the raised red areas linked up in a patch extending from my knees to my arms. The constant itching became almost unbearable.

Curiously, after losing a lot of weight, I began to fill out again, although there had been no change in our diet: rice twice a day with *nuoc mam* (a kind of salty fish gruel) and an occasional piece of fish. I felt extremely tired, however, and noticed pains in my lower legs. Within a few months I had practically ceased to urinate, and the weight was an abnormal swelling in my legs and abdomen. I had beriberi and was bloated with stored fluid.

A VC medic, whom we called Ben Casey after the television doctor, treated me with injections of strychnine and vitamin B_1. Within three hours I was experiencing intense pain in my legs, and shortly after dark I began urinating, continuing through the night. The result was a thoroughly emaciated American. I stared at my skinny arms and legs in horror.

Dan was in bad shape, too. Once, for resisting being put in irons, he was strung up from trees outside his cage, spread-eagled, his wrists and ankles bound with wire that cut so deeply it left scars. Worse, however, was the slow starvation. He was little more than bone, and I was reminded of pictures I had seen of the Nazi concentration camp at Dachau. Any exertion left him exhausted.

In December our camp came under attack by American helicopters, and we had to flee into the jungle; then we were moved to a new camp. Dan passed out, going into a near coma for almost two weeks.

LATE IN JANUARY 1965 we moved back to the area where we had been captured, and in March our political indoctrination began again. Dan and I were taken to a hut and introduced to a man named Mr. Hai. He fixed us with a frigid stare.

"I can kill you. I can torture you," he said coldly. "But no, I choose to allow you to fulfill the requirements of the Front and display your knowledge on certain questions."

Back in my cage I was given paper, ball-point pen, and a questionnaire entitled "My Revelation," which asked for biographical and military data and essay-type answers dealing with religion, politics, and economics. I read and reread the form, fitting my cover story into the framework of the questionnaire. Then I began on the essay questions and merrily scribbled inane comments about home economics, mechanical drawing, and a number of other courses I had—and had not—taken in high school.

On April 9 I again met with Mr. Hai. Dan was already there, and I sat with him on the floor. Mr. Hai looked at me with a malefic stare. Suddenly he slammed the papers down hard on his desk. His eyes were flaming with rage.

"This is useless! You have not shown repentance! You continue to resist the Front!" His voice lashed out, carrying a physical impact with each word. "I can no longer allow you to live under the lenient policy. You will go where conditions will reflect your attitude."

I was sent to a separate camp, which I named the Salt Mines. It consisted of just four huts, one of them the familiar barred cage. Dan did not accompany me, but on May 15 another American was brought in, bedraggled but still defiant. This was Sgt. Dave Davila, who had first been captured in December 1964. (The names Dave Davila, Tim Barker, and Ben Wilkes have been fictionalized to protect the families of the actual prisoners.) Davila was a helicopter gunner from Hawaii. He had escaped from a nearby camp and had managed to evade capture for two days. His punishment was to be sent to the Salt Mines.

Two and a half months of utter hopelessness followed. The guards no longer talked about release. Our diet was reduced, and both Dave and I knew we were slowly starving. My fungus infection became much worse, threatening to cover my face and eyes. For days at a time there was no water to drink. I could feel the lining of my mouth drying and tightening as the weeks passed.

We both knew that we couldn't survive much longer. An attempt to escape, whatever the result, would be better than rotting away. I had been planning for months, and in our infrequent meetings Dave and I began to lay the groundwork for a getaway, sketching rough maps, hiding bits of dried fish.

By late August 1965 we were ready.

The night of the 28th was perfect. Rainstorms that rolled in at half-hour intervals would cover any noise we might make. The guards were all in their hut by the kitchen, leaving the path to the canal open. With my last bit of hoarded ink in an old piece of ball-point-pen filler, I drew out a false escape route. This I was going to drop near my cage as we left, hoping the guards would find it. It might keep them off our backs for a couple of extra hours.

About midnight Dave's voice came softly:

"Ready, Nicko?"

We checked our gear and slid into the dark. The paper with the false route was lying outside the cage as if I'd dropped it accidentally. Our guard was curled up, asleep.

The night was totally black. It took us about 10 minutes to cover the 60 feet to the reed-lined canal. Once there, we moved more rapidly, but found the canal less clearly defined the farther we got from camp. Dave suggested heading overland, going what we thought would be due east until we hit a larger north-south canal that we could follow. We decided to try it and found ourselves in a tangle of ferns and reeds. We sounded like a herd of elephants as we splashed

48

through them. The mosquitoes were like a second skin, driving their stingers into every inch of our bodies.

We tried to move faster, but we were both tiring rapidly.

"Don't let me stop," Dave gasped.

Exhausted, we pushed on through high grass, reeds, and clumps of trees, driven by the thought of freedom. After two hours we came upon a canal, but we could no longer tell if it ran north to south or east to west. We moved on through the reeds, hoping frantically that we were heading east.

At last the sky lightened, and I decided to climb a tree, checking for the sunrise that should be ahead of us.

As I reached a vantage point, I almost wept. The sun was breaking through the clouds *behind* us. We had been traveling west. Worse, I saw the path that we had left in the tall grass. It marked our trail as if we had left road signs.

Desperately, I tramped out several false trails from our main path, terminating each in an area where the grass stopped and where we could conceivably have continued without making a distinct trail. We then backtracked for about 100 yards and headed due south, making certain to close the grass over our path as we moved away.

I cursed at our slow pace. I could picture the guards, like a bunch of bloodhounds, rapidly sweeping the area.

We had traveled another hour when we heard voices from a boat along a nearby canal. They had got near us too damn fast.

I couldn't think of anything that would aid us in evading them now, aside from a tremendous amount of luck. Dave and I camouflaged the narrow trail we had made into a dense clump of ferns, then lay down in the water, covered to our necks, with our heads pressed in close to the ferns. All we could do was wait.

I could hear my heart thumping as the voices came closer. I thought of the movies I'd seen as a young boy about the war in the Pacific, and how the hero had always miraculously escaped. What happened in real life?

A guard we called Cheeta suddenly broke into the patch of grass, his Russian burp gun carried in a ready position. Behind him came two other guards. We heard more voices from the south. Another group was sweeping in to link up with the others. I was suddenly very tired, very sick.

Cheeta shouted in alarm and jumped back. He had almost stepped on Dave. The others rushed over, training their guns on Dave as he unwillingly got to his feet.

"Where's Rowe?" Cheeta demanded. *"Toi khung hieu"* ("I don't understand"), Dave replied in a lifeless voice.

The guards fixed bayonets and began to tramp through the ferns, jabbing at the water.

I was only six feet away, sliding backward through the undergrowth as quietly as possible, when one of them tripped over me. Instantly there were bayonets all around my face, and I was ordered to get to my feet.

Dave sank to his knees utterly exhausted, only half conscious. A

guard named Leo shouted for him to stand, pointing his burp gun at him. I knelt beside him and lifted an eyelid. I saw nothing but white; he was passing out.

I told Cheeta I would have to help him. Instead, they bound my arms at the elbows. Dave started to slump.

I bent my knee, giving him something to hang onto. Deep strain twisted his mouth. His hand found the bend in my arm. He clung, pulled, and with his face contorted almost beyond recognition, stood upright, leaning heavily.

For six days after that I was held in leg and arm irons. My arms were pulled back and upward while my feet and legs were stretched painfully in the opposite direction. It was like being on a rack. I was released only to eat twice a day—rice with salt and almost no water. I was not allowed to go to the latrine. So for that period, still suffering from dysentery, I lay encrusted in my own filth.

If I were to repent of my crime, I was told, and to promise that I would never try to escape again, the Front would be lenient with me. I replied that I'd rather die trying to regain my freedom than starve in a prison camp. Then, late one night, the guard who had been on duty when we escaped came into my cage and kicked me viciously twice in the ribs. I decided then that enough was enough and agreed to their terms if both Dave and I would be allowed to resume our normal prisoners' life.

A guard handed me a piece of soap and a towel and told me to bathe. I felt a sudden catch in my throat and turned away, ashamed at the urge to cry. The relief was so beautiful!

I looked toward Dave's cage and saw him sitting by the door. He was a skeleton. The escape had pushed him to the limit. In his eyes was the reflection of the last months in the punishment camp, the slow death there, the near death in front of Leo's submachine gun, and now this. It was a tightening vise that left a man no place to turn, no hope for maintaining the shreds of individuality, self-esteem, or belief without sacrificing his life for that privilege.

On September 7, 1965, we were taken back to a camp we called the No K Corral and rejoined Dan Pitzer and another American prisoner, a black master sergeant named Edward "John" Johnson. John was in leg irons because he was thought to have been an accessory in Dave's earlier escape attempt.

On the morning of January 8 all of us heard a deep voice speaking English in the guard area. The man was talking extremely slowly, almost as if he were drugged. One of the guards called Dan over, and a few minutes later he reappeared at the edge of the compound. I caught my breath in shock. There, clinging to Dan's shoulder, was a hulk of human wreckage, a huge bone structure covered with tightly stretched, fungus-infected skin. What must have been a grin of joy at seeing other Americans looked like a leering death's-head. The deep voice echoed from the cavernous chest. "God! Americans!"

This was our introduction to Capt. Tim Barker, U.S. Army, captured a year before. One look at him and a strong feeling of kinship and responsibility swept through us. He must have lost at least 80 pounds, and his festering fungus sores were alarming. The first thing we did was to get him a bath and some clean clothing.

I spoke to the cadre about medication for Tim, and on January 13 we were given vitamins, a horse-liver extract, and several bottles of a fungicidal liquid. Our days now became a constant struggle to some-how keep Tim alive. But a year of imprisonment and starvation had destroyed his will to live.

On the morning of February 4, I went to Tim's net to help him get out and eat. He was crouching at the rear of the net, his eyes enor-mous, his pupils dilated.

"I don't want any rice!" he gasped. "I won't eat it!" Then he curled up in a tight ball and began to have spasms from the waist down, his legs twitching and jerking.

Dan slipped in beside me and called for John to get Intern, a VC medic. He arrived with a syringe of respiratory stimulant, injected it, and left. Tim's chest began to heave for a moment, then slowed and stopped. We rolled him onto his stomach, and I began artificial respi-ration. "Don't . . . die! Don't . . . die!" The rhythm went through my mind as I applied pressure, then released.

Intern came back and told us to carry Tim to the canal, where he would be put in a boat and taken to a "hospital." But as we placed him in the boat and shaded his head with a sleeping mat, I knew it would be the last time we would see Tim.

A few weeks later Dave Davila began to have a problem with rice. He would eat and vomit, try again and vomit again, until he finally got the rice to stay down. Soon he began to remain all day in his net, except when he had to go to the latrine. Then he refused to eat, just as Tim Barker had done. I went to see Major Bay, the camp command-er, telling him another American would die unless he was given ade-quate food. His reply was an apologetic refusal.

I RETURNED DETERMINED not to let Dave die. We had been through the Salt Mines together, survived the escape attempt, and made it through the "correction" period. I knew he could lick the physical problem, but the psychological one was tougher—Tim Barker had shown Dave a new way to escape. I prayed for an idea that might help this Hawaiian boy get back to the islands he loved.

On the night of March 19 Dave's condition worsened and he be-came incoherent. It was agonizing to lie there in leg irons and listen to a man die, calling the names of old friends, his mind a thousand miles away. In the morning I tried to feed him, but it was impossible. He couldn't even get a cup of water down. Intern arrived and decided that Dave also had to be moved to the "hospital."

I gathered his belongings in a small bundle, and we carried him to the canal. As we lifted him into the boat, he clung to my forearm with a grip far beyond anything I imagined possible. I realized that it was the ancient warrior's arm clasp. Dave was bidding me farewell.

The impact of this second death drove our morale to abysmal depths. I felt bitterness and hatred building, feeding off the constant frustrations and anxiety. I knew that I could destroy myself if I allowed such negative emotions to dominate my thinking. So I turned to the one positive force our captors could never challenge: God.

I had never questioned religion, nor had I ever really accepted it. It was something I had lived with, because that's the way things were done. Now I was left with only the intangibles that form the core of our existence: faith, ethics, morals. I could only turn to the Power I believed to be so far greater than that which now imprisoned me. After Dave's death I really began to believe: "The Lord is my Shepherd; I shall not want."

The next months—indeed, the next year and a half—were a struggle as first one, then another of us succumbed to illness and sought desperately to find enough to eat to sustain the will to live.

Political indoctrination during 1966 and 1967 continued as before. The guards would bring the camp radio over for us to hear the English broadcast by Radio Hanoi. This was supposed to keep us abreast of the conflict so that we might evaluate the validity of the lessons taught us. For the first time we learned of the antiwar movement in the United States. Hanoi reported protests on campuses across the nation, which we took as normal exaggeration, but it stayed with us where the battle reports didn't.

Major Bay conducted several classes on "the just cause of the revolution and the injustice of the U.S. dirty war of aggression." He always claimed that no North Vietnamese troops were present in South Vietnam, and there were specific instructions to the cadre to deny any link with the Communist Party of Vietnam, headed by Ho Chi Minh. This link was the first thing an American prisoner looked for to justify his own beliefs. If the VC could convince him that a Communist-inspired insurgency didn't even exist, the rest of the POW's beliefs could be attacked.

Had I not understood some Vietnamese, I might have missed hearing the daily political classes attended by the guards in which the doctrine *Marx-it, Le-nin-it,* was taught to even the youngest. It was incongruous to hear the cadre teaching Marxist philosophy to the guards, yet denying any connection with communism when talking with Americans. The fact that the cadre felt the need to lie strengthened my conviction that I was right in my beliefs.

On September 14, 1967, the first indications of some big event began to unfold. A group of high-level interrogators and a VC journalist paid us a visit. Dan and John Johnson met with them together, and then, separately, so did I and Jim Jackson, a Special Forces medic who had joined us a month earlier. The journalist, who spoke English, informed me that these men were representatives of the Central Committee and had come to the camp to determine our condition and review our "progress." They asked me a few perfunctory questions and seemed to be bored by my answers. Then I was told that my attitude had been judged unsatisfactory.

Nonetheless, their visit sparked speculation about the possibility of release, and our hopes seemed justified, for soon our diet was improved. A second indicator came when John suddenly declared that he couldn't eat and began vomiting. This time medication came into the camp in amounts and types exceeding anything we had seen in all the other years combined.

On October 18 Mr. Hai reappeared to see if John was well enough to travel. That was the tip-off to what followed. Preparations were made by the guards for a trip, and the next day Dan, Jim, and John attended a special meeting with Mr. Hai and a cadre that had arrived with him. That afternoon my summons came, too.

I sat on a stool before the cadre, while Mr. Hai translated:

"You are POW Rowe, and you are here to learn the decision of the National Front for Liberation of South Vietnam. Your comrades are no longer prisoners. They are to be released under the lenient policy of the Front and allowed to return to their homes."

I knew what was coming, but it was still a shock. "You have shown a bad attitude," Mr. Hai continued. "You have foolishly tried to escape. You cannot recognize the just cause of the revolution. For these reasons you cannot be released."

He paused, then added, "Do not think that merely because the war ends you will go home. You can remain here after the war."

I felt like sliding through the floor poles. The thought of staying here alone until I died was terrifying.

That evening I ate my last meal with the other three. I gave Dan a message for my parents and wished them all a heartfelt Godspeed on their journey to freedom. Late that night they climbed into a boat and were gone. On November 3, I was told that they had reached Cambodia and would soon be home.

The loneliness after they left produced an overwhelming depression. At the same time, I was happy that they were free. I knew that none of them had bought the line that the cadre was throwing at us.

Christmas was approaching, and I planned to celebrate it no matter what the circumstances. The day before Christmas I spent the morning catching enough of the tiny *ca ro* fish for a substantial surplus. I was declaring the next day a holiday. I made a wreath out of tree branches and pieces of colored thread. Purple wild grapes took the place of holly berries.

As I prepared the evening meal, I sang Christmas carols, picturing the brightly lighted tree at my parents' home, the table spread with food, and, most important, the people. The fireplace in our living room was the window through which I saw Mom and Dad, seated on the couch, as the small dancing flames of my cooking fire became the roaring blaze on our hearth.

Mr. Hai had given me some cookies and tea to celebrate, "just like you do in America." I made the tea and offered a cup to my guard, Cheeta, with some cookies. He was surprised, but ate them with obvious enjoyment. Then he locked me in my leg irons for the night.

I now entered a terrible period of harassment and pressure to force a compromising statement from me. Adding to my torment, my fungus infection again developed into a serious problem. It covered most of my body except for my head.

The political lessons became almost more than I could take, as I had to sit and listen to the guards degrade my country and voice their confidence in our defeat. I was troubled by the increased use of American sources to substantiate the violence that seemed to be erupting across the United States. I began hearing more statements alleged to have been made by U.S. senators and congressmen, not only opposing our presence in Vietnam, but supporting the NLF.

DURING THE TET OFFENSIVE the news got worse. I heard that the NLF had hit major cities over the length of Vietnam (despite their own proposed seven-day cease-fire). City after city was being overrun, the South Vietnamese forces were disintegrating, and the American command was in turmoil.

Confused and anxious, unable to sleep, I developed a case of dysentery that soon became unbearable. I was denied medication unless I wrote an "appeal" to U.S. servicemen to go home. I resisted at first, but at last consented, signing the message just as my keepers wrote it, leaving in every grammatical error and inaccuracy. I felt lost when I gave them the paper.

News continued to pour in. The assassination of Robert Kennedy was carried on all broadcasts. I sat stupefied. First, President Kennedy, then Martin Luther King, now Bobby. My United States was being turned upside down. Escape was a remote dream, for I was told that the Tet offensive had broken Saigon's control of the countryside. Even if I did escape, there would be no place to go.

Finally, on August 18, Mr. Hai —who had once said, "I can kill you. I can torture you"—returned to camp, and I was called before him. I listened as he went through his main points: the hopeless struggle, the antiwar movement, President Johnson's decision not to run for reelection. I could feel the confusion building, the feeling of having to defend something that perhaps wasn't defensible.

"And now," Hai continued, "you must write for me your thoughts on the war and how it can be resolved. You must recognize the unjust cause of the U.S. imperialists, who sent you to die so that they might become enriched. You must believe that my recommendations are well received by the Central Committee and, if you show progress, you can be released."

The desire for release was strong, and writing what he wanted was the only way I could see to come out alive. The reasons I'd had for being willing to hang on, no matter what came, had been torn away from me. I couldn't condemn my country, yet I didn't want to die for supporting a lost cause. "Mr. Hai, I can't write those things." The words were out before I realized I'd said them. I panicked as I saw the coldness come into his eyes.

He retrieved his paper without speaking, then looked at me with a slight smile, confident in his control of the situation. "Go back to your house," he said. "We will talk again about this matter."

That night my clothes and mosquito net were taken from me. Mr. Hai, the s.o.b., had set this up. I cursed under my breath as the first group of mosquitoes bit into my exposed skin. I could actually feel the pulpy mass in my hand each time I slapped at a concentration of 50 or more. There was not a portion of my body that wasn't bitten. Blood and crushed mosquito bodies smeared my skin.

The hours wore on without relief. The rough metal of my irons made raw red stripes on my legs as I twisted and turned. My diarrhea broke loose, and I was unable to make the crock I used at night. The odor, the filth, the stings, the hopelessness made me want to cry out: "—you, Mr. Hai, and all your ancestors!" That was my final coherent thought before I was aroused by a guard.

My clothes were given back, and later I was ordered to Mr. Hai's hut. His countenance was a mask of innocence as he said, "I see your face is swollen. Why do you not use your mosquito net?" Then he launched into his spiel for several hours, ending by saying, "Now you can write for me what you have learned in our discussion."

"Mr. Hai, I'm tired," I said, "and can't really think straight."

His voice cut like a knife. "You must not try the patience of the Front! Consider carefully your path."

That night was a repeat of the previous one. My clothes and net were taken away again.

"Mr. Hai," I asked in the morning, "please tell me—am I being punished for something?"

"You are a criminal," he replied. "The U.S. aggressors have brought much suffering to our country, and they must pay their blood debts. If you do not repent your crimes, the Front can no longer allow you to enjoy the lenient policy."

No longer enjoy the *lenient* policy!

For a third night I suffered without my clothes or net. During periods of rationality, my one thought was: "I've got to stop this." I decided to make a trade, giving Mr. Hai something he wanted—in as ambiguous a form as possible—in exchange for relief and sleep.

The next morning I indicated my willingness to write for him, and the following day, after a satisfying rest, I listed the events of the war as Hai had related them. (A few days earlier, for example, he had told me: "In the dry-season counteroffensive launched by the imperialist aggressors in 1966 and 1967, 28 U.S. battalions were annihilated and 85,243 U.S. and satellite troops were wiped out.")

I had reached the point where the war in Vietnam was a mass of confusion in my mind. I had to buy time and try to get my physical condition under control. Mr. Hai left, and for two weeks I fed myself as well as I could and treated my ailments. He returned late in August with five lessons—"corrections" to my thoughts. The sessions ran through the days and into the nights. I knew I'd lie naked to the mosquitoes again unless he got what he wanted. There was too much to fight at one time. I wrote in my diary later: "Sessions a mental meat grinder—repeat, repeat, repeat, write. Enough truth to confuse the rest—certain points are unclear as compared with before—*have* to know *our* side!"

Mr. Hai left again, but returned a few days later and announced that I was to prepare for a "three-day excursion." The Central Committee had decided that I had progressed, but that my "writing" was still incomplete. So I was to be taken to my old post at Tan Phu, where the base had been overrun and the area "liberated," in order

for me to see the "reality of the situation in South Vietnam."
We left on September 14 by boat. Hai explained the ground rules:
no talking to civilians, keep my head lowered, look repentant in the
presence of civilians, and rely on the cadre to protect me from the
wrath of the people.

We spent the first night in a nearby village, then continued our
journey. I didn't recognize the terrain until we came to a point where
our canal intersected with a larger one and Hai pointed to a reed-
covered bank. "There is Tan Phu post," he declared. I stared in
disbelief. There wasn't anything there—no concrete bunkers, no
watchtower, no people, only the reeds swaying in the hot breeze. Tan
Phu had ceased to exist.

Hai took advantage of my surprise to emphasize the NLF's
strength as proved by their ability to wipe out the post. I had no
reply. It was obvious that nothing had been spared, and the confidence they had shown traveling through this zone seemed justified.

AT DUSK WE STOPPED at a village where the people were holding a
meeting to discuss the revolution. This would be dangerous for me,
Hai cautioned, since the villagers hated Americans. When he mentioned the name of the village, I was startled. We had run medical
patrols to it in 1963, bringing food and clothing, and had developed
quite some rapport with the people.

When we arrived, Hai spoke to the assembled crowd, pleading
with them to realize that I was a prisoner and was learning of the
crimes I had committed in order to repent and join the Vietnamese in
their struggle for freedom. There was silence from the people as rows
of curious eyes fastened on me. Then I felt a hand on my shoulder
and flinched. *"Manh khong, Trung-Uy?"* ("Are you all right, Lieutenant?") a voice behind my ear asked. I managed to nod. The hand
patted me and there was one word: *"Tot"* ("Good.").

Then I was roughly pushed out beside Hai by a guard and exhibit-
ed as a prize of war. A commotion broke out to my right, and a
scrawny man leaped from the crowd with his fist upraised, screaming, "Down with the American imperialists!"

I tensed, awaiting the blow. But nothing happened. I glanced up,
and the man was standing in front of me, his fist still clenched. This
unusual tableau continued until suddenly a member of the cadre
stepped belatedly forward and blurted out, "My compatriots, restrain
your anger. Do not strike the prisoner."

It was like a grade-school play during which someone had missed his cue. When the speech was finished, the man in front of me was even more uncertain what to do next. Finally, he managed a sheepish grin and shuffled back into the crowd. Someone laughed.

Hai had just begun a closing speech when an old grandmother, chewing betel nut, walked up to me and poked a bony finger into my ribs. She squeezed my forearm until she touched bone. "Do you mistreat him?" she asked. "I remember this boy when he came to our hamlet. He was strong, and now he looks weak and sick."

A chuckle went through the crowd at the idea of this little old lady putting a powerful leader in a tight situation.

Hai slipped into his standard line. "You must remember that the Americans are criminals. But the Front is lenient. . . ."

The old woman interrupted him. "I know what it is to be hungry and sick, and there is no leniency in inflicting that on another."

Hai looked desperately at me. "Tell her you are well treated," he ordered. I lowered my head and looked repentant.

Two days later I was back in my forest cage, not knowing what to expect next, but feeling better equipped to deal with my confusion about the war. I had seen the vast difference between what the cadre wished me to believe and what actually existed. These people had known nothing but war for two decades, and out of its destruction they had always rebuilt. I had seen, if only in this area, the spark of resistance still burning. If they, in a Communist-controlled zone, were willing to resist, I was willing to help.

One morning, a few weeks after my trip to Tan Phu, I was called to a meeting in the guards' mess hall. Entering the hut, I saw not only Hai and his cadre but also an older man in his late 50's sitting at the head of the table. All the guards from the immediate area were gathered, too. I had been thinking constantly of release, but I felt only animosity from the assembled group.

The man at the head of the table spoke: "I am a representative of the Central Committee and have come to say a few words to you. It is fortunate that the peace- and justice-loving friends of the South Vietnam Front for National Liberation in America have provided us with information that leads us to believe you have lied to us."

My throat constricted, and my stomach wrenched. The guards' eyes all seemed to be boring into mine.

"According to what we know, you are not an engineer. You were not assigned to the many universities that you have listed for us. You have much military training that you deny. The location of your family is known. You were an officer of the American Special Forces.

59

Your father's name is Lee, and your mother's name is Florence."

The words became a blur. He was picking me to pieces. Desperately, I tried to remember the points he attacked, so I could build some sort of answer, but there was no way to cover all of them.

After five years of captivity, my whole miserable world had collapsed. Who would give them information about me? An American wouldn't do that to one of his own. I could understand opposition to war and a strong desire for peace. Dissent was a part of American life, but to support the enemy at the expense of another American was inconceivable. Yet there was no other place the VC could have got their information. I felt sick.

Shortly thereafter I discovered a frightening new development. During mealtime the guards spent at least 40 minutes in their mess hut, leaving me alone. Periodically, I went to their sleeping hut during this interval and leafed through the papers they kept in a .30-caliber ammunition box. In this way I was able to determine roughly what action of major importance was pending.

One day in December I was quickly checking the new papers in the box when one caught my eye. My name was on it! I read the heading and saw that it had come from the political office of the headquarters zone. I tried to decipher the sentences relating to me. *"Sang chuyen"* ("to transfer"). *"Ban dan dich van."* I was to be transferred to the Enemy and Civilian Proselyting Section at headquarters. Transfer meant the VC felt that the resources to deal with me at this level had been exhausted. I knew that at headquarters there was no pretense of "leniency and humanitarianism." I could expect to give them what they wanted or face execution.

THE MORNING OF DECEMBER 31, 1968, was dark and cold as my guard, nicknamed Porky, unlocked my leg irons. We were camped atop a low bank formed by the mud dug from a canal and now covered with the same cattail and bamboo reeds that filled the fields on both sides of us. A faint glimmer of a fire brushed the reeds with an orange glow. I could hear the other guards talking in low voices.

For 10 days our area had been under intensive attack by B-52's, F-100's, and helicopter gunships. We had been forced to leave our camp, keeping on the move during the day, bivouacking where we could at night. Rice was running short; we were limited to one meal a day. As the food supply dwindled, so did my value to the VC.

I was just cleaning my eating cup when I heard the sound of helicopters. They were heading straight for us. My throat went dry, even though the sound had been a common one during the past days.

The piercing foghornlike sound of a minigun, the electronic multi-barreled machine gun, caused all heads to snap in its direction. The aircraft had found something.

An HUI-A (Huey) command ship orbited in wide circles above us, observing the action. Below it four smaller choppers flew in pairs, sweeping back and forth across a huge field near us, almost touching the reeds. The first ship was blowing the reeds apart with the violent downdraft from its rotor blades, and as the reeds parted, the trailing ship would gun down anything that showed.

It was obvious that I, wearing Vietnamese pajamas, would look like one of the VC to a pilot, and my deeply tanned face, even with a beard, would be just another VC face. On the other hand, the guards had a standing order to kill an American prisoner if they couldn't guarantee his security. My chance for survival looked slim.

A Light Observation Helicopter made a pass directly over us. I was flat on the ground, anticipating the rain of steel that would follow. Reeds were battered down all around us by the prop wash, exposing our bodies to the trailing gunship. They began firing, but apparently at targets in the next field. Cold sweat covered my face. I heard one of the younger guards, his voice soft, sobbing, *Ma, ma.* How lost he sounded. How strange that he turned back to the source of love and comfort he had known before joining this revolution.

Porky, who was monitoring a radio, announced, "Troops are being sent into the area!" Mr. Sau, head of the military cadre, ordered us to move, crossing to the field of reeds behind us. The idea was to get as much distance between us and our campsite as possible.

It was a confused exodus, and I noticed that discipline was disintegrating. The helicopters continued their hunt, causing us to crouch frequently in the thigh-deep water. Sau still maintained a weak grip on the reins of authority, but the muttering behind me from Porky and another guard indicated their dissatisfaction with his leadership.

Sau called a halt and had a guard climb a low tree to observe. I turned and spoke quietly to Porky. "It is dangerous to put him where the helicopters will see him."

Porky's face was stoic. "Sau is not a wise soldier." he said. A break in confidence between cadre and guard! If only I could exploit it.

We set off again, and I could hear Porky muttering to himself as we slogged through the murky water. I frequently pointed out maneuvers that I had noticed the choppers using, assuring Porky that Sau was going to get us killed. Porky told me to be quiet, but after a while we began to fall farther and farther behind the main group. I murmured a quick prayer, asking the good Lord please to do what He would—I was going to try my best.

I stopped and turned to Porky, whose face was upturned, watching the gunships. "I'm afraid to follow Sau any farther, because the helicopters will spot him soon. If we go by ourselves, making a small trail, you will be able to fight later, while the others will be dead." I paused, studying his face for reaction.

"Di!", Porky commanded (*"Go!"*). He was pointing to the left, perpendicular to our line of travel and away from the main group! I followed, first taking my mosquito net out of my pack. It would be wise to wave something white at the helicopters.

Porky was breaking the reeds ahead of me, opening the minimum path that would allow us to pass. His attention was divided between the trail and the helicopters, and I found myself ignored. He had slung his burp gun across his back and was bent forward, enabling him to use both hands as he tunneled through the grass. The weapon was temptingly exposed, and from the position of the bolt I could see that there was no round in the chamber. All I had to do was get rid of his magazine! I reached forward and tripped the release at the rear of the magazine. Porky straightened up seconds later, and as he stepped forward, the magazine dropped unnoticed into the water. I stepped on it as I passed, grinding it into the mud.

Now the choppers appeared to be making wider circles, skirting the fringes of this field as if preparing to transfer their operation to another area or to depart entirely. I couldn't allow that. I searched the clumps of reeds for one of the numerous fragments of dead tree branches, selecting a short limb almost two inches in diameter. I stepped quickly behind Porky. The sharp blow caught him at the base of the skull. He sagged and dropped without making a sound. I chopped him twice with the edge of my hand, delivering the blows to the side of his neck below the jawbone. I didn't intend to kill him, but as I laid him across the reeds, I noticed blood running from his mouth and nostrils. It was too late to worry about it now.

I moved quickly across a narrow ditch and leveled an area of reeds, which allowed me to see the helicopters. Then I began to wave my white mosquito net wildly. One of the gunships passed overhead and banked sharply, circling me. It was joined by a second sleek craft, and now my heart was beating so hard I thought my whole body would vibrate. "They've seen me! I'm okay! They've seen me!" I was exuberant and waved even more frantically.

Up in the helicopters (I learned later) the radio crackled. "There's a VC down there in the open."

From the other ship came the reply, "Gun him!"

Then from the command ship came the voice of Maj. Dave Thompson, group flight commander. "Wait. I want a VC prisoner. Cover me. I'm going down."

The helicopters swept the surrounding terrain, laying a devastating hail of bullets on the hidden VC, who were firing at the descending ship. I watched as the Huey circled wide around me, then lined up for a low pass. The door gunners kept their fingers against the triggers of their machine guns as they waited to foil any trap. All of a sudden one of them, looking down, spotted my beard.

" Wait, sir!" The shout went over the microphone with a unique urgency. "That's an *American!*" The response was immediate.

I saw the helicopter swing into a tight, low turn, braving the fire directed against it, and settle at the edge of the water not more than 15 yards from me. I ran, stumbling, seeing nothing but the interior of the chopper. I dived onto the cool metal flooring and heard myself shouting, "Go! Go!"

The chopper lifted off. I watched as the trees and reeds began to drop away beneath the speeding craft. After five years I was out of the "Forest of Darkness." How many times I had looked up at airplanes, wishing that I could be in them above the mud, mosquitoes, and filth, flying free over the confines of my green prison. Now I could see the horizon—and the world seemed beautiful.

Twenty minutes later Lieutenant Rowe reached the U.S. base at Camau, where he learned that during his imprisonment he had been promoted to major. His first real meals, his first sight of friendly faces, his exuberance at having escaped were almost indescribable experiences. That night, bedded down on a soft, "capitalist-imperialist" mattress, he was unable to sleep and finally arranged his blankets on the floor.

Major Row was awarded the Silver Star and the Bronze Star for his actions as a POW. He left the army in 1974 and, after a try at politics, turned to writing.

*General Giraud had been captured by the
Germans once before and had escaped. Now he was
determined to gain his freedom again.*

The Elusive
French General

By Frederick C. Painton

O N MAY 10, 1940, German infantry flowed out of the woods near
Le Catelet, France, and surrounded a French machine-gun
nest. After the emplacement had been pulverized by mortar fire, the
German officer called on the survivors to surrender. To his amazement, among them appeared a six-foot, gray-mustached man with the
five stars of a general on his kepi. For the second time in 25 years
Henri Honoré Giraud was a German prisoner of war.

It was a bitter humiliation for a man whose career had just reached
its peak. Giraud had been an outstanding officer since the turn of the
century. But ill luck followed him into battle. In the First World War
Giraud, then a captain, was wounded while leading a bayonet charge.
He was captured by the Germans and placed in a prison camp in
Belgium. But even before his wounds healed, he managed to escape
and, although permanently lamed by his wounds, finally rejoined his
regiment in France.

During the peace years he served with distinction in Africa and
commanded a military district at Metz. Then came the Second World
War, and he was made commander in chief of the Allied forces before Laon. When the Germans broke out of the Forest of Ardennes,
he rushed to the front to see how the tide might be stemmed, only to
be caught in a forward machine-gun nest.

Giraud had escaped before, yes. But now he was 61, and the rigors
of making an escape demanded youth. Nevertheless, he refused to
give his word not to make the attempt. He was taken to the fortress of
Königstein, perched on a sheer cliff 150 feet high, with all entrances
double guarded.

Immediately Giraud began to scheme for escape. He practiced his

65

German until he could speak it well. He obtained a map of the surrounding country and memorized every contour. With the twine from packages sent to him he patiently wove a rope that would support his 200 pounds. When it proved not strong enough, friends from France sent him 150 feet of copper wire in an adroitly prepared ham. He was allowed, of course, to write letters; his jailers did not know that an invalid prisoner, who had been repatriated, had conveyed a code to the general's wife. Using this, he sent out details of his plan bit by bit in the form of seemingly innocent letters.

He had only a French general's undress blue uniform to wear, but his raincoat could pass for a civilian garment. Presently, among the packages arriving for him was another luscious ham. If the Germans had looked inside it, they would have found a jaunty Tyrolean hat.

On the morning of April 17, 1942, Henri Giraud stood on the balcony, looking out over the sentry walk. Tied to his waist was a package containing chocolate, biscuits, the Tyrolean hat, and the raincoat. When the guard had passed, the general knotted his homemade rope to the balustrade and started his 150-foot descent. He wore gloves, but even so the skin was chafed from his hands. At last he reached the ground safely.

He limped to the cover of some trees, shaved off his mustache, and put on the Tyrolean hat and the raincoat. Two hours later he reached a bridge at Bad Schandau, five miles away. Calmly he leaned against the parapet and ate the lunch from his pack. There, at 1 o'clock, a lean young man carrying a suitcase and a hat in the same hand strolled toward Giraud. This was the prearranged signal. The young man had been sent by friends. Giraud and the young man went to the railroad station, boarded the first train that came along, and went into a lavatory. Giraud opened the suitcase and found his own Paris clothes. There were also identity papers bearing the name of an industrialist, a photograph that looked like him (without his mustache), and money. A few minutes later a grave, distinguished-looking businessman emerged from the lavatory.

Now Giraud put into operation part two of his escape plan. The alarm was out and the frontier guards would be extra alert. He could hope to avoid arrest only by traveling continuously on trains through Germany until the uproar died away.

Once, near Stuttgart, Gestapo agents began working through the train, verifying heights against the passengers' identity cards. Giraud's six feet could not be disguised. But he happened to be seated opposite a young *oberleutnant* of the Afrika Korps. He smiled at the lieutenant and remarked that he, too, had spent much time in Africa. The German dropped his magazine, delighted to find someone who knew the desert. They conversed animatedly.

By the time the Gestapo man arrived at his seat, Giraud was illustrating graphically with his hands his idea of how Rommel could beat the British. The German lieutenant watched, his eyes eager, his own hands poised.

The Gestapo man touched Giraud's shoulder. "Your papers,

please, gentlemen." The lieutenant, boiling to present his own point, looked up angrily. "Go away! How dare you interrupt us?" The man did as Giraud had guessed he would: apologized and backed off.

On another occasion, as the general was about to board a train, he saw Gestapo agents searching every passenger. He dallied outside until the train began to move. Then, with a supreme effort of the will, Giraud ran—without limping. His glasses jiggled. His cheeks puffed out. He had all the appearance of a flustered German businessman trying to make a train. His very boldness carried off the affair. One of the Gestapo agents actually helped the panting old gentleman aboard.

Finally he crossed the border into occupied France. He hoped to slip over the line into the unoccupied area, but found that German guards were stopping every man over 5 feet 11 inches tall. Back he went by train across southeastern Germany to the Swiss frontier. That, too, seemed tightly closed. But there were mountain trails that could not all be watched. One night he struck out over an unfrequented trail. Climbing and twisting among craggy peaks, he came suddenly upon three soldiers. Bayoneted rifles swung to cover him.

Then a soldier spoke—in a Swiss dialect. He was safe. The guards took Giraud into Basel, where he made his identity known. The Germans were furious, but the Swiss refused to surrender him.

Giraud finally made the dash for unoccupied France. He resorted to an old trick—that of changing cars several times on the lonely Swiss roads. The cars entered unoccupied France by different roads. The Gestapo stopped the wrong car.

In 1914, when he had first escaped from the Germans, Giraud had sent his wife a telegram when he reached Holland safely: "Business concluded excellent health affectionately Henri." Now he sent her another: "Business concluded excellent health affectionately Henri."

Yet Gen. Henri Giraud was not a free man. His escape had caught the imagination of a saddened French people, and he had become a public idol. The Germans had lost face. When Marshal Pétain refused the German demand to return Giraud under arrest, the Nazis tried to assassinate him. He was forced to go into hiding. Giraud found that he had merely escaped into a different kind of prison.

History, however, was to summon Henri Giraud from obscurity. On October 24, 1942, in an Arab farmhouse in Algeria, Lt. Gen. Mark W. Clark conferred secretly with pro-Ally French officers about the possible Allied occupation of French North Africa.

During the conference the French officers raised the point of choosing a leader around whom the many French factions could rally. General Mast said: "I can only suggest—General Giraud."

General Clark objected: "But that's impossible. He's practically a prisoner in France."

"He must be got out—by submarine."

Such a plan was put into effect a few nights later when a submarine reached the southern coast of France. The British secret service had informed Giraud, and he was ready. He arrived in North Africa in time to play an important part in the Anglo-American invasion.

Gen. Henri Honoré Giraud died in 1949 after being decorated with the Croix de Guerre and the Médaille Militaire. He was laid to rest at Les Invalides in Paris, where Napoleon and other great French military heroes are buried.

*The East German doctor had made careful
plans for his escape. But when he entered the
hostile waters of the Baltic Sea, he wondered if he could
endure the hours of struggle ahead.*

The Lone Swim

By Peter Döbler

IT WAS A WARM SUMMER afternoon in 1971. I was spooning down a
vanilla sundae and watching the throng of bathers at Kühlungsborn, one of East Germany's finest beaches on the Baltic Sea. From
time to time, armed patrols of border guards sauntered past. I was
wearing part of my scuba diver's wet suit, and my body glistened
with the kind of heavy grease used by Channel swimmers, but nobody seemed to be taking any special notice of me.

At about 5 o'clock I headed for the water, carrying a bundle with
the rest of my wet suit, together with diver's weights and a few
personal possessions. I paddled the bundle out to a sandbank and let
it sink, marking the spot mentally. Then I swam to and fro, to become part of the scene and also to watch the patrol activity. For,
unlike the other bathers, I was not there for recreation.

As the crowds began to leave for home about an hour or so later, I
dived for my gear and put on the rest of my suit in the water. The wet
suit and mask now covered my entire body, except for part of my
face. I had fins on my feet and homemade scoop-shaped swimming
aids fitted on my hands.

Tucked into the suit were a deflated plastic life belt for extra buoy-
ancy in an emergency and a roll of strong tape for mending defective
equipment. Next to them, wrapped in watertight plastic, I carried
two bars of chocolate, identification papers, and 50 East German
marks, plus a tube containing painkillers. On one wrist I wore a
compass, on the other a watch with a luminous dial. I was all set for a
28-mile swim—to freedom. If all went well, I reckoned I would be in
West Germany in another 26 hours.

It would not be my first trip to the West. A decade before, while still at school, I had visited "capitalist" Hamburg, where I defended our peasants' and workers' state against skeptical West Germans. Yet I took back to my hometown of Rostock memories of the way West Germans spoke out freely, of their better-quality and less-expensive shoes, of the shiny new cars that even ordinary people drove.

I kept these impressions to myself while at school, learning to give the outward assurances of loyalty that our state required. In the summer of 1959 I confidently applied to study medicine at the University of Rostock, listing forestry as a second choice. But although I had always done well at school, the university administration informed me that there was no room in either department.

This rejection painfully reminded me of something I had found it convenient to forget. In a country where almost everything is state-owned and state-run, my father, an accountant, worked hard to keep his own small accounting firm private. This was enough to place our family outside the peasant and worker category, whose children were given preference in education.

That summer, however, my father died. When I subsequently reapplied to the university, this time as the son of a state employee (my mother worked in a state enterprise), I was promptly admitted to study medicine.

For a full year after I had completed my basic medical studies, I was unable to get a hospital post in Rostock. When they offered me a job as a doctor on a large fishing vessel I took it—with the consent of my wife, also a doctor, whom I had married that year. Since there were no apartments available in Rostock, we decided the shipboard job would be a practical solution until the housing authority found living quarters for us. Yet after three voyages to North Atlantic fishing grounds, there was still no apartment. My wife continued to live with her parents, and I went back to my mother.

Finally, there was a job for me in Rostock, at one of the most modern and best-equipped hospitals in East Germany. But the work was demanding and the pay poor. Because my wife and I worked different hours, we spent only an occasional Sunday together. Sadly but inevitably in our fourth year of marriage she and I agreed that life together had been a fiction, and we decided to get a divorce. In court I spoke out, blaming our breakup on the inability of the state to find us accommodations. Needless to say, this didn't make me any friends, but it did make me feel better.

Escaping to the West then became my main preoccupation. I proceeded to explore the Baltic coast so thoroughly that even to this day

I can draw a detailed map of it from memory. To check on conditions after dark, I took up night fishing at all the likeliest escape points. I familiarized myself with the movements of the mobile searchlight batteries that nightly scan the waters up to nine miles out and the patrol routines of the police boats and naval craft.

I also started on a program of physical conditioning. I took lengthy swims, the longest lasting about 20 hours. When I emerged after that, I was elated to discover that I still had energy left. At night I swam in rivers or lakes, avoiding the sea because it might arouse suspicion. To strengthen my arm muscles, I began rowing and lifting weights. I changed to a protein-rich diet, and to harden my body, I took regular winter dips in the Baltic.

For my starting point, I chose Kühlungsborn because it was not in a maximum-surveillance zone, not being especially close to either Denmark or West Germany. I plotted my course carefully on a sea chart and memorized it. For the first nine miles I would swim straight out; then, following an estimated $8\frac{1}{2}$ hours of swimming, I would turn left toward the coast of Schleswig-Holstein. My next checkpoint would be Buoy Number One of Sea Lane Number Six, between Gedser in Denmark and Lübeck. From the buoy it would be another 14 hours' swim to shore.

On the evening of Friday, July 23, I dictated a tape stating my reasons for fleeing and stressing that I had informed no one of my plan. I put the tape in the desk of my room at the hospital. As I had the weekend off, I would be missed on Monday at the earliest; and if I had to call off my escape, there would be time to retrieve the tape.

At Kühlungsborn on Saturday morning the weather looked quite promising. The wind was strong enough to provide a gentle helping push and the surface chop I needed for concealment. Water temperature was ideal. Still, I delayed, afraid that something unforeseen might occur. But after finishing my vanilla sundae, I decided that it was now or never.

As I struck out from the sandbank, the lead weights held me low in the water. To make me even harder to spot, I swam the breaststroke, slower than the crawl but causing less splash. I had decided to stay with this stroke at least until darkness, then jettison my weights and switch to the crawl.

By nightfall I had passed the first buoy that marked the three-mile territorial-water limit. I stopped to check my compass and picked the star closest to my desired heading to guide me. Since I knew from long practice how fast I was swimming, I needed only to consult my watch to work out my progress and position. I glanced at my watch—and at first I didn't want to believe what I saw. It had stopped. One of my main navigating aids had failed. I would just have to rely on estimated time.

Meanwhile, searchlights from the coast were beginning to feel out the waters. One beam brushed directly over me, and I ducked until the darkness oozed back. I was past the three-mile limit—yet I knew very well that East German patrols pick you up, or shoot you, wherever they find you, except in another country's territorial waters.

For the rest of the night I concentrated mostly on my stroke. Occasionally, I rolled over on my back to relax, and once I munched a chocolate bar. In the misty half-light of predawn I calculated elapsed swimming time and made my left turn. Above the surface the only sound was my own rhythmic splashing; beneath the surface I was able to detect the continuous pulsations of faraway ships' propellers and the unsettling whoo-whoo-whoo of East German patrol boats.

About an hour after dawn I raised my head to look around. There, directly ahead, I saw a dark object in the mist. It seemed as high as a patrol boat, and I could make out a mast. Gingerly, I paddled ahead until the silhouette became sharper. Then I almost laughed out loud in relief. Before me lay Buoy Number One on Sea Lane Number Six. I had calculated correctly.

Now I could hear the thump of an approaching vessel. It was a large ferryboat bound for West Germany. I waved and shouted, but it slid past without stopping. More ships kept passing that day, but they were all too far away to spot me. Soon I gave up even attempting to hail them; it sapped too much strength.

Then I sensed that first warning twinge, and a cramp seared through my right calf. I went into the drill I had practiced many times. I wrenched off my hand fins, tucked them into my suit, bent the cramped leg, crammed the disabled toes behind the knee of the other leg, and gripped them between my good calf and thigh. I also swallowed a painkiller, washing it down with a gulp of seawater, and floated. Then I tested my leg; it seemed all right, and on I swam.

But now dark clouds loomed overhead, and a world of gray surrounded me—gray sea all around, gray sky above. Suddenly, in mid-afternoon, the skies opened, pouring forth sheets of rain. Lightning flashed, the wind whistled, and I found myself bobbing up over wave crests and down into troughs. I had been in the water more than 20 hours; my mouth felt crusted with salt, and I had to stop myself from swallowing water through my snorkel.

The thunderstorm lasted about an hour. When it finally lifted, there was land ahead. Before me lay the West German island of Fehmarn. Pleasure craft dotted the seascape, and one of them was coming in my

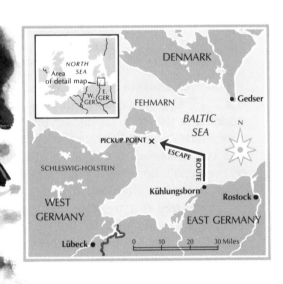

direction. "East Zone! East Zone!" I yelled. A man and two boys gaped down at me. Then they lowered a ladder, and I stumbled aboard. The next thing I knew, I'd downed a whole pot of steaming coffee. I was very cold now, my shoulders and legs ached, and the skin of my body was bluish-white and incredibly wrinkled. But I had made it!

Later on I was able to obtain work at a West German hospital and began to feel at home. People ask me if I would do it over again. If there were no other choice, I certainly would. As a doctor, I am accustomed to handling people's lives as a precious trust. But I also know that if a patient loses trust in his doctor, it's his privilege to switch to another. My new one is much better. His favorite remedy—freedom—is doing wonders for me.

73

The almost incredible story of a teenage boy
who escaped from his native Cuba by
flying the Atlantic Ocean stowed away in the
wheel well of a DC-8 airliner.

Stowaway

By Armando Socarras Ramírez
as told to Denis Fodor and
John Reddy

THE JET ENGINES of the Iberia Airlines DC-8 thundered in ear-splitting crescendo as the big plane taxied toward where we huddled in the tall grass just off the end of the runway at Havana's José Martí Airport. For months my friend Jorge Pérez Blanco and I had been planning to stow away in a wheel well on this flight, No. 904—Iberia's once-weekly nonstop run from Havana to Madrid. Now, in the late afternoon of June 3, 1969, our moment had come.

We realized that we were pretty young to be taking such a big gamble; I was 17, Jorge 16. But we were both determined to escape from Cuba, and our plans had been carefully made. We knew that departing airliners taxied to the end of the 11,500-foot runway, stopped momentarily after turning around, then roared at full-throttle down the runway to take off. We wore rubber-soled shoes to aid us in crawling up the wheels and carried ropes to secure ourselves inside the wheel well. We had also stuffed cotton in our ears as protection against the shriek of the four jet engines. Now we lay sweating with fear as the craft swung into its about-face, the jet blast flattening the grass all around us. "Let's run!" I shouted to Jorge.

We dashed onto the runway and sprinted toward the left-hand wheels of the momentarily stationary plane. As Jorge began to scramble up the 42-inch-high tires, I saw there was not room for us both in the single well. "I'll try the other side!" I shouted. Quickly I climbed onto the right wheels, grabbed a strut, and twisting and wriggling pulled myself into the semidark well. The plane began rolling immediately, and I grabbed some machinery to keep from falling out. The roar of the engines nearly deafened me.

As we became airborne, the huge double wheels, scorching hot

74

from takeoff, began folding into the compartment. I tried to flatten myself against the overhead as they came closer; then, in desperation, I pushed at them with my feet. But they pressed powerfully upward, squeezing me terrifyingly against the roof of the well. Just when I felt that I would be crushed, the wheels locked in place and the bay doors beneath them closed, plunging me into darkness. So there I was, my five-foot–four-inch, 140-pound frame wedged in a maze of conduits and machinery. I could not move enough to tie myself to anything, so I stuck my rope behind a pipe.

Then, before I had time to catch my breath, the bay doors suddenly dropped open again, and the wheels stretched out into their landing position. I held on for dear life, swinging over the abyss, wondering if I had been spotted, if even now the plane was turning back to hand me over to Castro's police.

By the time the wheels began retracting again, I had seen a bit of extra space among all the machinery where I could safely squeeze. Now I knew there *was* room for me, even though I could scarcely breathe. After a few minutes I touched one of the tires and found that it had cooled off. I swallowed some aspirin tablets against the head-splitting noise and began to wish that I had worn something warmer than my light sport shirt and green fatigues.

Up in the cockpit of Flight 904, Capt. Valentín Vara del Rey, 44, had settled into the routine of the overnight flight, which would last 8 hours and 20 minutes. Takeoff had been normal, with the aircraft and its 147 passengers, plus a crew of 10, lifting off at 170 miles per hour. But right after takeoff a red light on the instrument panel had remained lighted, indicating improper retraction of the landing gear.

"Are you having difficulty?" the control tower asked.

"Yes," replied Vara del Rey. "There is an indication that the right wheel hasn't closed properly. I'll repeat the procedure."

The captain relowered the landing gear, then raised it again. This time the red light blinked out.

Dismissing the incident as a minor malfunction, the captain turned his attention to climbing to assigned cruising altitude. On leveling out, he observed that the temperature outside was -41° F. Inside, the stewardesses began serving dinner to the passengers.

SHIVERING UNCONTROLLABLY from the bitter cold, I wondered if Jorge had made it into the other wheel well and began thinking about what had brought me to this desperate situation. I thought about my parents and my girl, María Esther, and wondered what they would think when they learned what I had done.

My father is a plumber, and I have four brothers and a sister. We are poor, like most Cubans. Our house in Havana has just one large room; 11 people live in it—or did. Food was scarce and strictly rationed. About the only fun I had was playing baseball and walking with María Esther along the seawall. When I turned 16, the government shipped me off to vocational school in Betancourt, a sugarcane village in Matanzas Province. There I was supposed to learn welding, but classes were often interrupted to send us off to plant cane.

Young as I was, I was tired of living in a state that controlled *everyone's* life. I dreamed of freedom. I wanted to become an artist and live in the United States, where I had an uncle. I knew that thousands of Cubans had got to America and had done well there. As the time approached when I would be drafted, I thought more and more of trying to get away. But how? I knew that two planeloads of people were allowed to leave Havana for Miami each day, but there was a waiting list of 800,000 for those flights. Also, if you signed up to leave, the government looked on you as a *gusano* ("worm") and life became even less bearable.

My hopes seemed futile. Then I met Jorge at a Havana baseball game. After the game we got to talking. I found out that Jorge, like myself, was disillusioned with Cuba. "The system takes away all your freedom—forever," Jorge complained.

Jorge told me about the weekly flight to Madrid. Twice we went to the airport to reconnoiter. Once a DC-8 took off and flew over us; the wheels were still down, and we could see into the well compartment. "There's enough room in there for me," I remember saying.

These were my thoughts as I lay in the freezing darkness more than five miles above the Atlantic Ocean. By now we had been in the air about an hour, and I was getting lightheaded from the lack of oxygen. Was it really only a few hours earlier that I had bicycled through the rain with Jorge and hidden in the grass? Was Jorge safe? My parents? María Esther? I drifted into unconsciousness.

The sun rose over the Atlantic like a great golden globe, its rays glinting off the silver-and-red fuselage of Iberia's DC-8 as it crossed the European coast high over Portugal. With the end of the 5,563-mile flight in sight, Captain Vara del Rey began his descent toward Madrid's Barajas Airport. Arrival would be at 8 A.M. local time, the captain told his passengers over the intercom, and the weather in Madrid was sunny and pleasant.

Shortly after passing over Toledo, Vara del Rey let down his landing gear. As always, the maneuver was accompanied by a buffeting as the wheels hit the slipstream and a 200-mile-per-hour turbulence swirled through the wheel wells. Now the plane went into its final approach; now a spurt of flame and smoke came from the tires as the DC-8 touched down at about 140 miles per hour.

It was a perfect landing—no bumps. After a brief postflight check Vara del Rey walked down the ramp steps and stood by the nose of the plane, waiting for a car to pick him up, along with his crew.

Nearby there was a sudden, soft plop as the nearly frozen body of Armando Socarras fell to the concrete apron beneath the plane. José Rocha Lorenzana, a security guard, was the first to reach the crumpled figure. "When I touched his clothes, they were frozen stiff as wood," Rocha said. "All he did was make a strange sound, a kind of moan."

"I couldn't believe it at first," Vara del Rey said when told of Armando. "He had ice over his nose and mouth. And his color—" As he watched the unconscious boy being bundled into a truck, the captain kept exclaiming to himself, "Impossible! Impossible!"

THE FIRST THING I remember after losing consciousness was hitting the ground at the Madrid airport. Then I blacked out again and woke up later at the Gran Hospital de la Beneficencia in downtown Madrid, more dead than alive. When they took my temperature, it was so low that it did not even register on the thermometer. "Am I in

Spain?" was my first question. And then, "Where's Jorge?" (Jorge is believed to have been knocked down by the jet blast while trying to climb into the other wheel well. He was arrested by Cuban police and served a short term in prison before being released.)

Doctors said later that my condition was comparable to that of a patient undergoing "deep freeze" surgery—a delicate process performed only under carefully controlled conditions. Dr. José María Pajares, who cared for me, called my survival a medical miracle.

A few days after my escape, I was up and around the hospital, playing cards with my police guard and reading stacks of letters from all over the world. I especially liked one from a girl in California. "You are a hero," she wrote, "but not very wise." My uncle, Elo Fernández, who lived in New Jersey, telephoned and invited me to come to the United States to live with him. The International Rescue Committee arranged my passage.

(Armando Socarras now lives in Florida. He is happily married and a college student.)

I want to be a good citizen and contribute something to this country, for I love it here. You can smell freedom in the air.

I often think of my friend Jorge. We both knew the risk we were taking and that we might be killed in our attempt to escape from Cuba. But it seemed worth the chance. Even knowing the risks, I would try to escape again if I had to.

AN EXECUTIVE OF THE Douglas Aircraft Co., makers of the DC-8, later said that there was "one chance in a million" that a man would not be crushed when the plane's huge double wheel retracts. "There is space for a man in there, but he would have to be a contortionist to fit himself in among the wheels, hydraulic pipes, and other apparatus."

Armando should also have died from both the lack of oxygen and the extreme cold. At the altitude of Flight 904 (29,000 feet), the oxygen content of the air was about half that at sea level, and the temperature was -41°F. An expert at Brooks Air Force Base School of Aerospace Medicine in San Antonio, Texas, said that at that altitude, in an unpressurized, unwarmed compartment, a man would normally retain consciousness for only two or three minutes and live only a short while longer.

Perhaps a Spanish doctor summed up Armando Socarras' experience most effectively: "He survived with luck, luck, luck."

Led by a brave girl and dedicated to a just cause,
the young heroes risked death at the hands of the Nazis
to win freedom for Allied servicemen.

The Lifeline Called Comet

By W. E. Armstrong

O N SUNDAY, OCTOBER 22, 1972, more than 200 men and women
met in Brussels for a great reunion. Ambassadors and aristo-
crats, French, Dutch, and Belgian peasants, and a party of 35 wartime
veterans of Britain's Royal Air Force—they gathered as they had
every October for 27 years, to commemorate one of the war's strang-
est and most inspiring ventures. All had played a part in Comet, the
escape line along which Allied airmen, shot down in northwestern
Europe, were funneled back to Britain.

Many such lines were organized by courageous men and women in
Holland, Belgium, and France. But whereas other chains were professional—under the guidance of trained agents and limited to getting escapees home—Comet was idealistic and passionate, dedicated
to making a real contribution to victory by helping to keep the Allied
air forces fully manned.

A conspiracy of youth, with few escorts or couriers older than 25, it
was braver, more imaginative—and the most successful. Of 2,900
airmen returned to Britain by all escape lines between the outbreak of
war in September 1939 and the Allied invasion of Normandy in June
1944, Comet was responsible for 770—nearly one in four.

The cost of this lifeline was grievous. Two hundred and sixteen of
Comet's members, both French and Belgian, were shot or died in
concentration camps. At least 700 were imprisoned for the duration
of the war. Many were tortured and risked their lives—but the line's
boost to aircrew morale was immense. RAF Sgt. George Duffee,
whose Halifax bomber was shot down in Holland, recalls: "The
knowledge that unknown friends were waiting below to pick you up
was an enormous comfort on a raid, like having extra armament."

The Comet Line began as the compassionate impulse of an ardent young Belgian girl, Andrée de Jongh. At her home near Brussels, she and her sister were taught by their schoolmaster father, Frédéric de Jongh, to revere the memory of Edith Cavell, the heroic English nurse executed by the Germans in 1915 for helping Allied soldiers to escape. Andrée vowed that if ever war came again to Belgium, she would follow Edith Cavell's example.

In May 1940, when the Germans invaded her country, 24-year-old

Andrée promptly acted on her vow. For some seven months she nursed Belgian and British wounded in a Bruges hospital, under such strict German surveillance that any scheme for rescue was impossible. Then she returned to Brussels and took stock of the situation. With the Channel coast and all the Low Countries in enemy hands, hundreds of Allied servicemen hidden in Brussels and other big towns were trapped. As the German police got to work, more were captured and their hosts condemned for harboring them. Some way of escape to Britain was urgently needed.

The only route, Andrée decided, was via Gibraltar. It meant nearly 600 miles through Nazi-occupied France and almost another 600 through pro-Nazi Spain. It meant crossing three national frontiers and several military zones. It meant recruiting hundreds of underground workers willing to risk death for strangers in a cause that much of the world thought lost. It meant outwitting the most efficient and cruelly repressive secret police in Europe.

Even for a well-subsidized, experienced Resistance group, this was a daunting project.

Andrée de Jongh set to work alone, without funds, and with only a young fellow Belgian named Arnold Deppé, her father, and her own dauntless spirit to help her.

Escapees, they decided, would travel by train to the Belgian frontier at Quievrain; then would come a Somme crossing near Amiens, to bypass German checkpoints at the entrance to France's Occupied Zone; a train to Paris; a night train to Bayonne, some 20 miles from the western end of the Spanish frontier; a bicycle ride to Anglet, near Bayonne, for a day's rest in a "safe" house; a hike to a farm in the mountains around Urrugne, the frontier village; an all-night forced march over the Pyrénées to San Sebastián in northern Spain, and finally, with the help of the nearest British consulate in Bilbao, a car journey to Gibraltar via Madrid.

To secure the receiving end of the chain, Arnold Deppé went south to Anglet, where he established contact with Elvire de Greef, mother of a family of Belgian refugees. A woman in her thirties, with iron health and ruthless energy, she was to become second only to Andrée in the organization. Tactician and quartermaster, she found bicycles for escapees, bought their black-market food, and recruited Basque smugglers as guides for the march over the mountains.

With the line's southern end assured, Arnold Deppé moved north, working out passwords, train timings, contacts with French and Belgian Resistance workers, and, in Paris, setting up a halfway house where escapees could rest and change their clothes. Upstream from Amiens, he arranged to have a rowboat hidden on the Somme's reedy bank. Returning to Brussels, he reported that all was ready.

At Andrée's end, too, all was ready: the false papers and identity cards, the cover stories. To raise the necessary cash, Andrée sold her few jewels and Arnold Deppé took a salary advance from his firm. Everyone now had a code name. Andrée was "Dédée," her father was "Paul," Elvire de Greef was "Tante Go." The escapees were known as "parcels," or "children."

The first batch of "parcels," 11 Belgians including an elderly woman, left Brussels in early June 1941, with Andrée and Arnold Deppé as escorts. All went well until the party reached the Somme, where they were appalled to see a tent pitched near the rowboat. With campers so close by, the boat was unusable, but the river had to be crossed, and only four of the fugitives could swim.

With typical resourcefulness Andrée obtained a long coil of wire and an inflated inner tube from a nearby farm. She waited until after nightfall, stripped, swam the 40 yards to the far bank, tied the wire to a tree, and returned.

Supported by Andrée or Arnold Deppé and clinging to the tube, which was threaded to the wire on a running noose, all the fugitives reached the other side. The operation took two hours; Andrée swam the dark river 11 times.

"She made me brave," said one fugitive that night, "braver than I ever thought I could be."

The party reached Anglet without further incident at the end of June. Here they were handed over to Elvire de Greef for the march across the Pyrénées, while Andrée and Arnold Deppé, elated by this apparent success, returned to Brussels.

In August they escorted eight Belgians and a Scottish soldier. Only Andrée, with two Belgians and the Scotsman, got through; Arnold Deppé and the others were arrested by German police while changing trains at Lille. Deppé was tortured by the Gestapo but, knowing that the line's future depended on his courage, he refused to reveal the name of his leader.

In Anglet Andrée received more bad news: the Spanish government had repatriated all 11 Belgians in her first batch. Bitterly disappointed that people brought out so dangerously had been sent back to the Germans, she resolved in the future to help mainly British fugitives, who stood the best chance of reaching Gibraltar, and, further, to give priority to those who could resume the battle against the Nazis—at that stage of the war, aircrew.

Andrée now had to enlist the help of the British Consulate in Bilbao, 100 miles away. With her three "parcels," led by a smuggler-guide, she took the hazardous 14-hour night march across the Pyrénées. After a day's rest in San Sebastián, she reached Bilbao and confronted Vice-Consul Vyvyan Pedrick. Although by profession Pedrick had to be skeptical, he was deeply impressed by the candid girl with her eager face and remarkably youthful appearance.

"I was particularly struck by Andrée de Jongh's single-mindedness," he recalls, "and the passionate determination that showed clearly in her blue eyes."

Andrée soon convinced Pedrick of her good faith, but the consulate was required to carry out routine security checks. She was asked to return in a few weeks.

When she reappeared on October 17, this time with two Scottish soldiers, she got all she wanted from the British: money for the expenses of every fugitive brought from Brussels and for the Basque guides. About one condition she was adamant: her organization must be an entirely Belgian enterprise, completely independent of London. She would have no professional agents, no radio contact, no interference whatsoever.

With finances assured, results followed quickly. By Christmas 1941 Andrée had made her fifth crossing of the Pyrénées, escorting four airmen. She had found a new guide, a rugged Spanish Basque called Florentino, who became one of Comet's bravest and most faithful workers. Apparently as lighthearted and confident as ever, Andrée was now under great pressure, for the Gestapo in Brussels had been questioning Frédéric de Jongh about her movements. A wanted woman, she could not return to Belgium. Her father got a message through to her by courier: he would take over her role in Brussels while she continued to direct operations in France.

This was a solution typical of the line's impressive resilience—a resilience that may have inspired MI-9, the department of British Intelligence concerned with escape routes, to name the line Comet, because it is the nature of comets in general to vanish and reappear again.

Detailed vigilance became more and more necessary. Freedom could hang on the faulty tilt of a beret or an awkward gait in clogs. Since so few fugitives knew the French language, to speak was often fatal; sometimes, surprised airmen would find themselves locked in a sultry embrace with Andrée as police or customs men approached.

It was a grim, nervous game, but there were hilarious moments. Flight Sgt. Brin Weare, hidden in a German-infested area for months, was finally borne to safety in a coffin by grieving Resistance members, as punctilious Germans presented arms.

At Austerlitz station in Paris, when "informers" warned the Nazis that an airman was disguised in the garb of a priest, the escapee and his aghast but giggling escort watched in amusement while dozens of indignant ecclesiastics, bound on a pilgrimage to Lourdes, were unceremoniously frisked.

In February 1942 the Gestapo paid another visit to the De Jongh home near Brussels. Andrée and her father were both away, so the Gestapo took her elder sister for questioning and put a watch on the house. On his return to Brussels six weeks later, Frédéric de Jongh only just escaped arrest and fled to France. Within a few days three leaders of his organization were in prison.

To MI-9, which had been following reports of the line's activities with admiration and anxiety, the disruption of its northern section seemed to be the end of Comet. But a new leader, 36-year-old Belgian aristocrat Jean Greindl, materialized to tie the broken ends. He quartered Belgium into regions with reporting centers at Ghent, Namur, Liège, and Hasselt, where patriots brought airmen they had been hiding. The system paid off at once. Between June and October 1942, 54 aircrew, brought south in 13 teams, crossed the Pyrénées.

Safely back in Britain, the airmen told of the cheerful efficiency of their escorts; the long night journeys in crowded trains; the chilling police checks; the isolated farmhouse in Urrugne, where they rested before the last hard march into Spain—and, finally, of San Sebastián's lights, the heady lights of freedom. Above all, the airmen talked of Andrée. Some broke down when they remembered her, fearful that so gallant a spirit should be at risk.

Andrée was at greater risk than they knew. In November 1942 two German agents slipped through weak security in Brussels. As a result, from Brussels to Bayonne, more than 100 men and women were arrested and deported or sent to prison; none broke under torture.

Then, on the misty afternoon of January 15, 1943, Andrée was arrested with three pilots at Urrugne as she was about to start on her 37th passage through the Pyrénées. Since August 1941 she had personally escorted 118 servicemen to freedom.

Elvire de Greef, with her usual energy, organized two daring attempts to rescue Andrée from prison in Bayonne. They failed. Soon Andrée was moved to other prisons and eventually to Germany. In no less than 21 severe interrogations in various prisons, and in Ravensbrück and Mauthausen concentration camps, she gave only one piece of information. To protect her father from Gestapo suspicions, she admitted that she herself was the mastermind behind Comet.

To MI-9 and British observers in Spain, the line seemed destroyed beyond all mending. But, amazingly, a batch of airmen reached Bilbao a fortnight after the roundup at Urrugne. Once again Comet's vitality had triumphed. A new leader emerged in the south: a 23-year-old Belgian, Jean-François Nothomb, code-named "Franco," who had worked for months with Andrée. Meanwhile, time was running out for Comet's top men in the north. Jean Greindl was arrested, tortured, and condemned to death. He was killed—a bitter irony—when an Allied plane bombed the barracks in which he was held.

By spring 1943 Allied air strikes were drumming over northern Europe, and the escape lines had never been busier. Comet, handling 60 airmen a month, needed more escorts. In May, Frédéric de Jongh, who had his daughter's courage but not her cunning, recruited as guide a plausible Belgian youth called Jean Masson—a pathological traitor. Within a month De Jongh and his principal assistants were under arrest.

Still the line endured. Throughout that summer Comet kept up the flow of airmen into Spain. By now all its members were very tired, but the ardor of Andrée's undefeated spirit, coming from the misery of Mauthausen, upheld them.

"We felt we couldn't let her down," recalls Elvire de Greef. "Dedée was not simply the founder of Comet, she *was* Comet."

Meanwhile, the Nazis hardened their campaign against the escape lines. On October 20, eight of Jean Greindl's lieutenants, arrested with him, were shot on the military rifle range at Brussels, against the grass bank where, 28 years before, Edith Cavell had died for the same cause. In his last letter one of them wrote what could be a motto for the Comet line: "I die for the ideal we all shared."

In January 1944 "Franco," who had helped 215 men to freedom, was arrested in Paris. By February nearly all Comet's operators in the north were in Gestapo hands.

On March 28, 1944, Frédéric de Jongh was shot by the Germans near Paris. The line had begun with this gentle, scholarly man, for it was he who had inspired his daughter to create it. And, fittingly, the line ended shortly after his death, for the massive bombings that followed the Normandy invasion made the operation of escape lines virtually impossible. Instead, under a plan code-named "Sherwood," the airmen were gathered into forests on the Belgian frontier and in central France and supplied by parachute drops until the Allies liberated them in September.

Andrée was eventually freed from prison. Along with two other Comet members, she received the George Medal for her contribution to the Resistance. Later on she continued working for others by nursing lepers in Ethiopia. What force sustained her? As one airman she guided to freedom put it: "Andrée de Jongh was one of those rare beings who felt the misery of the world and would not let it rest."

The young prisoner had all but given up hope of
breaking out of escapeproof Brandenburg
prison in East Germany. Then a solution came from
an unlikely source—his Communist guard.

The Only Way

By Claus Gaedemann
and Robert Littell

THE FILE ON ALFRED LAUTERBACH, prisoner No. 1880 in Brandenburg Penitentiary, East Germany, was meager. It showed only that he had been sentenced to 25 years for the crime of conspiracy against the German Soviet State. The file did not tell how, in the last days of the war, this young German artist had watched his brother die by torture at the hands of Soviet soldiers. In retaliation, he had thrown himself into underground resistance, had been arrested, "tried" by a Russian military court, and summarily sentenced.

When our story begins, in May 1952, Lauterbach had been in prison three years. His hair was cropped; his restless, burning eyes were sunk deep in his drawn face; and he had lost 57 pounds.

Worst of all for artist Lauterbach was the knowledge that his skill of hand and eye was rusting away. All day he sat alone with his thoughts in a cell where he could hear children playing and laughing in the free world beyond the walls, yet never see them.

But one day Lauterbach was shown some Communist propaganda posters and asked to paint others like them. Though he hated the East German regime, he jumped at the chance to hold a paintbrush in his hand once more.

A young police officer escorted him to a long, narrow room with a high window on the top floor of the prison. On a trestle table lay paper, pencils, cloth streamers, and pots of paint. Then, given a dozen slips of paper with the text of slogans typed on them, he was locked in. Lauterbach shoved the table under the window, set the chair on the table, and climbed up for his first glimpse of freedom in three years. Then he went to work. There was such sheer joy in watching color spread under his brush that time flashed by; before he knew it, his guard was standing at the door to take him to his cell.

Noticing that the guard seemed unusually young for the master sergeant's stars he wore, Lauterbach looked at him more closely. Smart blue uniform, straw-blond hair showing under the jaunty cap, unblinking eyes set like marbles in an almost baby-pink poker face. Here was a perfect specimen of the new Communist-trained People's Police: green as a cucumber but hard as nails.

The guard, Horst Bock, was indeed young. Born in 1930, he had known only the Germany of Hitler, the war, and the Soviet regime. At 17, urged by a People's Policeman who was the father of one of his friends, he enlisted in the Volkspolizei—the Vopo. But Bock's politics went no further than the naïve belief that the Soviet regime was responsible for East Germany's postwar recovery.

Even the massive doses of Marx and Lenin that he got at police school didn't seem to affect him. If you were a good recruit, you stood dutifully in the rain, whether the downpour consisted of words or water. He learned to take it—and also to dish it out; he became fluent in Communist doctrine.

At the proper time he was told to join the Communist Party. He hesitated—until his friend's father pointed out to him that if he didn't join, he couldn't hope for promotion. "I saw no harm in it," Bock said later. "I just went along."

He emerged from his schooling a specialist. At Brandenburg he was assigned to the prison's three-man political division, where he censored East German newspapers before they were given to the inmates, looked after the library for the prison staff of 300, and lectured to them regularly on Communist history and ideology.

Life was good. Bock's young wife, also a Vopo, worked in the prison's teletype department. They had two small children, lived practically rent-free in one of the comfortable staff houses near the prison, and by East German standards were well paid.

If Bock was not a convinced Communist, he was at any rate an obedient, industrious, and appreciated servant of the state. He had no idea of "choosing freedom" or indeed anything but the path ahead of him—which clearly led upward.

From time to time during the weeks that followed, Bock would march his shaky, gray-faced prisoner to the studio workroom, to the task of painting posters or of blowing up to several times life-size the paunchy figures of puppet President Pieck or Premier Ulbricht. Words between them were few. But each was sizing up the other.

Lauterbach saw in Bock a tool of the power he feared and loathed.

But how ruthless or how pliable a tool, he did not know. So he kept his mouth shut and watched and waited.

Lauterbach, on the other hand, impressed Bock more and more by his talent, his concentration, and the passion he put into making a good job of dreary slogans. Bock could not feel, he said later, that Lauterbach was a criminal; rather, he thought of him as an opponent of the regime whom it was logical to lock up.

Imperceptibly, as time went on, the ice melted. The tone of Bock's commands softened. Occasionally he would offer a word of praise, now and then a mild joke. Curious about the prisoner, Bock looked up his record. It was starkly brief: There had been a two-minute trial, followed by a five-word explanation of a 25-year sentence. Bock wanted to know more.

One day in September when he went to take Lauterbach down from the workshop, Bock asked: "Just what are you in prison for?"

Impulsively, Lauterbach burst out: "I was branded as a criminal because I fought against crime!"

It was as if the cork had been pulled from a bottle; everything came pouring out. Lauterbach told the tale of heartless injustices so many people had suffered—decent people whose crime had been indignation and protest—and of sentences of a third of a lifetime for offenses they hadn't committed.

Bock's duty, according to regulations, was to interrupt the prisoner, accuse him of telling lies, and report him. Instead, he listened, fascinated. "He may be lying," Bock remembers saying to himself. "I must find out if it checks."

At one point in Lauterbach's tirade, Bock went to the door and opened it to see if anyone was listening. By this gesture, though neither of them realized it at the time, Bock had crossed the line: He and Lauterbach were on the same side of the fence.

Later, in his cell, Lauterbach was horrified at what he had done. Bock would report him. It meant weeks in the punishment cell deep underground—no light, no bed, and only dry bread to eat.

For a week he sat alone in dread, waiting for the ax to fall. And then one morning Bock came for him, escorted him upstairs, and set him a task as if nothing had happened.

But in Bock's mind and heart a great deal had happened. At that time the first steps toward an amnesty of political prisoners were being taken in Soviet Germany. Many of the inmates of Brandenburg were being questioned in the hope that some would confess and beg the government for mercy.

It was part of Bock's job to help with the preliminary questioning. Under this cover he talked to almost 100 prisoners and unearthed a sickening succession of cases of doctors, lawyers, teachers, and civil servants who had been sentenced to 10, 15, or 25 years for political "crimes" that were trivial, trumped-up, or grotesquely vague. Lauterbach had not been lying.

Bock said nothing, but Lauterbach sensed the change and began to push a little. He showed Bock selected newspaper clippings: "Ten Thousand Cheer Party Leaders," a Communist headline would boast—and Bock, who had been to the meeting himself, knew that only a few hundred had turned out.

One day Lauterbach launched into a savage attack on puppet Premier Ulbricht. Bock let the prisoner fire away. He was moved by Lauterbach's eloquence, his unanswerable facts. At the end he remarked: "Be glad you said all this to me and not to someone else."

Bock had committed himself.

And now, he began to try to help many of the prisoners. There were the smuggled notes between inmates, for example. When a note was intercepted by a guard and taken to Bock, he would secretly consult Lauterbach. If Lauterbach said the prisoner was OK, nothing more would happen to him. Even more dangerous was Bock's identifying, to Alfred Lauterbach, the stool pigeons among the prisoners. Lauterbach would then discreetly pass the word around that so-and-so was not to be trusted.

Then Bock fell ill. For four weeks he was at home with plenty of time to think things over. It became clear to him that he had in effect joined the underground. Sooner or later he would betray himself. There was only one solution. When he went back to the prison, he fastened his cool, steady eyes on Lauterbach and said: "The only way out of all this is—*out.*"

"That should not be difficult for you," replied Lauterbach.

"It's going to be extremely difficult," said Bock, "because when I go I shall take you with me!"

Lauterbach was speechless. A policeman and an inmate escaping together from Brandenburg—it was mad!

Brandenburg Penitentiary was what penologists call an "institution of maximum security." The buildings were enclosed within a 20-foot wall, at each corner of which stood a watchtower manned by guards with machine guns. At night searchlights glared pitilessly down upon a strip of bright-yellow sand just within the wall. Any prisoner who stepped onto this blinding beach was instantly shot. Everyone and everything that passed through the prison's double gates were scrutinized. At unpredictable times there were spot checks when men and goods were meticulously searched. No one had ever escaped from Brandenburg Penitentiary.

But Bock's determination was unshakable. Carefully he went over all the possibilities: fake papers, a guard's uniform, throwing the switch on the searchlights and scaling the wall in the dark, even the wild idea of arming enough prisoners to stage a gigantic delivery of all of them. And once he and Lauterbach were out, how would they cross the Havel River between Potsdam and West Berlin?

They were working hard on their plans when suddenly Bock was transferred to a post in Kottbus Prison. He left Brandenburg Penitentiary on a few hours' notice.

A stouter heart even than Lauterbach's would have despaired. He was seldom asked to paint now, or to letter posters. Time stretched out and out; nearly a year went by. Then Horst Bock was in Brandenburg again, transferred back at his own request. Lauterbach's hopes blazed when he realized that his guard was as keen as ever to attempt the double escape. Bock had been to Berlin and could easily have crossed over to freedom alone. Instead, he had come back for his friend Lauterbach.

Again for weeks they watched, planned, and eliminated one escape scheme after another. And then, when the whole thing seemed utterly hopeless, Bock had a flash of inspiration. A shortage of some 100 marks had turned up in the accounts of his political section. A small matter, but it caused a flurry among Bock's superiors. Why not make up the deficit by selling the old newspapers piled high in the top-floor storeroom? The authorities, relieved, told him to go ahead.

At 8 A.M. on Thursday, July 8, 1954, a covered truck backed up to the doors of the prison office building. It waited there while a squad of inmates, with M. Sgt. Horst Bock in charge, climbed back and forth to the storeroom, where Lauterbach handed each man a heavy bundle of newspapers.

The last bundle was taken down by Lauterbach. Inside it was hidden a suit of civilian clothes. Under the windows of the office staff, he carried the bundle of papers into the truck. Bock climbed in after him and quickly stacked the bundles around and over him.

It was raining as the truck pulled out. At the first gate two guards stepped out of their room. Turning up their collars against the rain, they peered into the truck. They saw Bock, who outranked them, sitting on top of a load of old newspapers. They waved the driver on.

The guards at the second gate were also satisfied. "Pass!" they said.

When Lauterbach heard the truck start up again, he peeled off his prison uniform and changed into the civilian clothes. As the truck slowed for a stop sign, he hopped off. A moment later Bock followed him. The two men walked into the city of Brandenburg 100 yards apart, like strangers.

It was now after 9 o'clock. At noon there would be a roll call of the inmates. As soon as Lauterbach was found missing, a crash alarm with roadblocks, radio cars, and police launches would triple-seal the border between Potsdam and West Berlin.

The two men had 30 miles and a risky swim before them. By taxi and bus the fugitives rode taut as watch springs into Potsdam. Then they walked, not too quickly, through the lawns and hedges of Babelsberg, where many Russian officers had their villas, and down to a deserted spot on the Havel River. They waded into the water and struck out for the far shore.

The rain made visibility bad, and the wind raised waves. Lauterbach, weakened from his prison fare, could not make good time. Halfway across they heard the sound they had dreaded most: the put-put of a motorboat. A police launch was bearing down on them.

Or was it? Unbelievably, the Soviet police, whom the men could see huddled in the cabin, did not spot them. The launch came abreast, a few dozen yards away, and then put-putted on.

They swam on, stumbled ashore, saw the friendly uniforms of the West Berlin police, and surrendered at last to freedom.

The rest, like all happy endings, is quickly told. After the usual screening, both men were granted political asylum and flown to West Germany. Bock's wife was placed under house arrest for some weeks but, being pregnant, was finally allowed to consult a doctor. Taking her two young children with her, she slipped into West Berlin, and from there to a small Bavarian town where the Bock family finally settled. Horst took up the study of photography.

Alfred Lauterbach directed his art talent to carving. He produced beautiful wood figures in the tradition of his native Saxony: a tiny goose teasing a little girl, dappled deer no larger than a watch charm, fairy-tale figurines sturdily but delicately alive.

For the Bocks and for Lauterbach, bound together by an act of patient, selfless courage, life hasn't been easy. But it's been free.

*The Cuban truck driver had a daring scheme so risky
that it defied belief. If it worked, it would bring
freedom to many. But if it failed, imprisonment or death
before a firing squad would swiftly follow.*

The Truck That Fled

By *William Schulz*

EUFEMIO DELGADO WAS a man obsessed with a single dream: getting out of Cuba. The wiry, 28-year-old father of four had vowed to himself that somehow, someday, he would take his wife and children to freedom. During the day, as he drove a huge tractor trailer for Fidel Castro's Transportes Nacionales, and lying awake at night, he searched for a solution. Finally, by the summer of 1968, he had a plan—a scheme so daring that it defied belief.

Strong-willed and outspoken, Delgado was just one of countless Cubans who felt themselves trapped and stifled in Castro's police state. On three different occasions he had blurted out anti-Castro sentiments within earshot of a government informer. And each time he had been arrested by G-2, the secret police, on "suspicion of counterrevolutionary activity."

"Is it a crime to say that the people don't have enough food?" he had stubbornly insisted. But he also knew that he could remain no longer in Guanajay, a town 30 miles southwest of Havana. The local G-2 chieftain had threatened to have him sent to a forced-labor camp. Reluctantly but realistically, Delgado moved as far away as he possibly could—615 miles away—to the little town of Contramaestre in Oriente, Cuba's easternmost province.

Even there life became unbearable. The terror of the regime had been stepped up. Neighbors simply disappeared, victims of G-2. The 8 hours that Delgado worked each day became 12 and sometimes 14 as he and hundreds of thousands of other Cubans "volunteered" to work overtime.

"We are told by the commissar that we are volunteering," he said to his dark-haired wife, Olga. "If you protest, you go to jail."

He received no pay for the extra work, but it made little difference. The pesos that he brought home each month were all but useless. Literally everything that money could buy was stringently rationed or simply unavailable. In a land where food was once plentiful, each of the Delgados was limited to a pound of beans, a half pound of meat, and a pound of lard per month.

"If you have ever heard a child cry from hunger, it is something you never want to hear again," Olga said when her husband returned from three weeks of hauling sugarcane.

"That does it!" he shouted. "We've *got* to get out of this place."

But how? The twice-daily Freedom Flights that carried refugees to Miami were available only to those with relatives in the United States. The Delgados had none. (The Freedom Flights, begun in September 1965, were discontinued in April 1973.) Escape by sea seemed impossible. The heavily patrolled waters between Cuba and the American mainland were known as Machine Gun Alley.

Delgado knew that he was by no means alone in his desperate desire to flee Cuba. Long-distance hauls took him to Havana, where he found almost everyone he knew bitter and disillusioned by the Castro revolution.

Joaquín Martínez (names have been disguised when necessary) was a victim of the 1968 "revolutionary offensive," during which Castro shut down 55,000 of Cuba's privately owned shops and restaurants. Jobless waiter Martínez found himself drafted into an agricultural brigade, in which he worked from 6 in the morning until 6 at night, seven days a week. And there was Lucila Cardona, who rose every morning at 4 to join the long lines at the nearest food outlet. Often, after hours of waiting, she would find the shelves bare, which meant that her children would subsist again on sugar dissolved in water. Or Gloria Morales, who was married to a dedicated Communist naval officer and lived a privileged life in Castro's Cuba. But the young couple had an 18-month-old daughter, a beautiful, curly-haired little girl who would be taken from home when she reached school age and sent to a revolutionary boarding school—the Círculos Infantiles. "She will not grow up a Communist," vowed Gloria.

Delgado had no idea how he could help his friends and relatives reach freedom. "But somehow we'll make it," he promised an older brother. "You have my word."

Then, in the summer of 1968, Eufemio was dispatched to Caimanera, a small town near the U.S. naval base at Guantánamo Bay, to pick up salt for delivery to Havana. There he learned of still others anxious to flee Cuba: blacks who had found the revolution a cruel hoax; fugitives from forced labor; students hungry for a taste of freedom. He established contact with the group's leader, a mechanic named Francisco Alonso, and in a series of clandestine meetings gained his confidence.

"Escape to the American base is possible," Alonso reported, "but risky. The Cuban side is heavily patrolled, and escapees are shot or captured and sent to concentration camps for 30-year terms. But if we could get a truck, we might be able to crash through."

"I'll supply the truck," Delgado said, referring to his 1958 American-built White, a large green van whose cab was now powered by a Soviet diesel engine. "We'll work together."

Alonso pulled from his shirt a soiled, much-studied map of eastern Oriente. For hours the two analyzed government defenses, discussed strategy, made plans. As Delgado headed back toward Havana, he felt relieved for the first time in many months. "I don't know whether we'll make it," he thought. "But at least we're trying."

Coordination between Delgado, who was now required to spend most of his time at Transportes Nacionales headquarters in Havana, and Alonso in Guantánamo was difficult. Both were reluctant to use the telephone for fear it was tapped by G-2. Finally, plans were completed: Eufemio would send 22 relatives and friends by train from Havana to Santiago, on the southeastern coast of Cuba some 50 miles from Guantánamo. They would wait there until picked up by him in his truck; then all would proceed to the city of Guantánamo, 15 miles from the U.S. base, for the rendezvous with Alonso's group and the break for freedom.

The escape was set for December 17. At first all went according to plan. With his wife and children already aboard the truck, Eufemio picked up his 22 passengers in Santiago on the morning of the 17th and headed for Guantánamo. But when he braked the truck to a stop at the final pickup site, he knew immediately that something was wrong. Only Alonso was there, and he was obviously distraught.

"G-2 is wise to us," he stammered. "They've got an ambush waiting at the base. You've got to turn back."

Delgado, stunned, climbed into the trailer and broke the news to the others. An auto mechanic slammed his fist into his palm in bitter frustration; several women wept silently.

"This is only a temporary setback," Delgado declared, trying to keep his voice steady. "We will return to our homes and move again when the time is right. There is nothing to worry about."

But Delgado knew this was untrue. As he drove back toward Havana, questions ran through his mind. How had G-2 learned of the escape? Could there be an informer in the group? Would G-2 be waiting when he returned to Transportes Nacionales headquarters? Fortunately, nothing untoward occurred.

On December 31 a courier whom Delgado knew only as Pedro arrived. An escaped political prisoner and comrade of Alonso's, Pedro brought welcome news: "Everything is set for January 6." That would be the Feast of the Three Wise Men, the day on which Latin Americans traditionally exchange Christmas presents. "It is some gift we will give ourselves and Fidel," thought Delgado.

He checked his work schedule and found that he was supposed to drive west that week from Havana to Pinar del Rio Province and then back to Camagüey, less than 250 miles from Guantánamo. A perfect cover. He next communicated with the friends and relatives who had made the first trip. No one backed out; indeed, others who had learned of the plan begged to come along. By January 3, when they left by train for Santiago, the Havana group had swelled to 36.

Delgado left Havana that same morning for a youth camp in Pinar del Rio. There he picked up 80 men who were to be transported to a sugar mill in Camagüey.

The trip took 22 hours. Bone-weary, Delgado delivered his workers, grabbed a few hours' rest, then headed for Contramaestre. He arrived home at 3 A.M. on January 5, parked the truck, and waited through the "longest day of my life."

At 1 A.M. on January 6, Delgado and his family walked out of their home for the last time, leaving behind everything they treasured. In less than two hours they reached Santiago, where the Havana contingent was waiting, disguised as agricultural volunteers on their way to the cane fields. Eufemio gave no hint of recognition as he herded them into the truck. "Hurry up! Get moving!" he barked. "There's cane to be cut."

Within minutes the van was heading toward Guantánamo, where Delgado would pick up Alonso and 20 more passengers. But, again, a surprise greeted him. When he arrived at the rendezvous, he was horrified to discover nearly 100 people—middle-aged women, teenage boys, babies in their mothers' arms—instead of the expected 20.

"There are too many. They make the escape too difficult," Delgado protested to Pedro.

"What can we do?" Pedro replied. "We cannot deny them."

Delgado agreed, then asked for Alonso. "He has pulled out," Pedro said. "He couldn't get any machine guns, and he says that without them we have no chance of holding off the guards."

Eufemio cursed bitterly—but he had come too far to turn back. "We've got the truck and two pistols," he said. "We will make it now—or die trying."

It was still dark when Delgado pulled out of Guantánamo with his 130-odd passengers shoehorned into the truck. Knowing that the crack Cuban guards stationed outside the U.S. base relaxed somewhat during daylight, he pulled off the road to mark time. Half an

hour later, with the first signs of dawn, he continued toward Caimanera along the three-lane road that would take him past the base. Four miles outside Caimanera, he saw the base, a mile off to the right. Driving parallel to it, he was passing guard posts every quarter of a mile, and he studied them intently, looking for the weakest point. He made his selection, then proceeded into Caimanera. There he asked a passerby for directions to a fictitious address. Informed that there was no such place, Delgado headed back the way he had come.

The sun was shining brightly as he approached the spot he'd chosen for the breakout. Slowing down as little as possible, he suddenly swerved off the road and headed for the Cuban-built barbed-wire barrier. In his rearview mirror Eufemio glimpsed eight soldiers sprinting from the nearest guardhouses. He pressed the accelerator to the floor. Machine-gun bullets whizzed past the truck; a tire blew. Delgado struggled desperately to keep his vehicle under control as it lurched across the bumpy terrain at 60 miles an hour. A quarter mile from the wire, his luck ran out. The truck careened into a ditch. He jumped out and opened the trailer doors. "Head for the fence!" he shouted. "Keep low! Keep low!"

Delgado and Jorge Pérez, an old friend from Havana, ducked behind the truck and fired at the rapidly closing guards. They dropped two, but their pistols were hardly a match for Czech-built automatic weapons. A half-dozen refugees fell as they neared the fence.

"Down!" Delgado screamed to the others. "Keep down!"

He and Pérez abandoned the truck to go to the help of the stumbling women and children.

Those who reached the barrier—four feet high and four feet across—ripped themselves badly as they clambered over. But still they fought, screaming and bleeding, across the wire.

Delgado got Olga and his own four children over, then heard Gloria Morales cry despairingly for help: "I can't make it. Take the baby. Get her to freedom!"

Eufemio took the child just as he saw his own brother and sister-in-law captured 50 yards away. The guards were moving in quickly now, taking prisoner after prisoner.

"Cross over! Cross over!" Olga screamed from the other side of the fence. Delgado tossed the baby across the barbed wire; then, with nothing left that he could do, he crawled over himself.

Less than 20 minutes had passed since he had turned off the road. When U.S. Marines arrived on the scene minutes later, they found 88 courageous men, women, and children who had made it to freedom. Sadly, more than 40 others had not.

It was 8 A.M., January 6, the Feast of the Three Wise Men. Eufemio Delgado had engineered the largest single escape in the 10 years of Fidel Castro's Communist regime. A frail little woman, her arms and legs streaked with blood, grabbed Delgado and sobbed her thanks. "You have given us the greatest gift of our lives," she cried. "We can never forget."

*The young lawyer had carefully prepared an elaborate
hoax to hoodwink the Communist authorities
in East Germany. On its successful conclusion rested
the liberty of five political prisoners.*

Operation Liberty

*By Frederic Sondern, Jr.,
and Norbert Muhlen*

THE WEST BERLIN RADIO interrupted its regular program one day
in the summer of 1952 to make a startling announcement. Five
prominent political prisoners of the Communists had escaped from
the supposedly escape-proof East German prisons of Zwickau and
Waldheim and had made their way to the safety of Berlin's Western
sector. As details came in, it became clear that they had not broken
out. They had been released by the Communist prison authorities,
who had been hoaxed by forged release orders and telephone calls
from a spurious state's attorney.

While West Germany laughed, the enraged State Security Service
and People's Police dropped all other business to find the authors of
the plot. Sixty officials were discharged. The Communist press and
radio screamed that dastardly American agents had been at work.

Actually, the skulduggery had been devised by a young German
ex-Communist named Hasso Lindemann and two of his friends.

Lindemann, a bookish, 23-year-old law student, had been rocketed
to a position of Communist power by circumstances not unusual in
East Germany. In 1949 the Communist authorities of Leipzig had
discharged most of the experienced judges and prosecutors in the
district as "politically unreliable." A milkman, an organ-grinder, and
a 21-year-old girl became Leipzig's People's Prosecutors. They had
power of life and death over their fellow citizens, but they needed
someone to advise them about legal procedure. Lindemann, who had
worked as a clerk in the Ministry of Justice, seemed "politically ac-
tivistic" and obedient. He was made assistant to the state's attorney.

Comrade Lindemann was a shrewd investigator and wrote brilliant
briefs in impeccable Communist legal style. His record was soon

impressive. Several prominent industrialists whose cases he investigated had their properties expropriated and were sent to prison for long terms. A dozen young anti-Communist agitators went to jail after Lindemann had made the cases against them. Wisely modest and retiring, Lindemann let the People's Prosecutors take credit for these triumphs. As a result, he was very popular with his chiefs. He was well fed and housed, relatively well paid, and had a promising career ahead of him.

But Hasso Lindemann had a conscience. He had been a convinced and faithful Communist, but as the parade of Red injustice and cruelty—the trumped-up charges, faked evidence, and brutal sentences against innocent people—crossed his desk, he began to rebel.

"All the Communist philosophy in the world," he later said, "could not excuse for me the monstrous thing I was doing. Somehow I had to set these people free."

One afternoon, when most of the personnel of the state's attorney's staff were at their weekly Communist Party "indoctrination meeting," Lindemann took from his chief's desk a number of form letters used to order the release of prisoners, then fled to West Berlin.

"The forms, the clothes on my back, and a few marks were all I had," Lindemann recalls. "Everything else—job, future—I left behind. But I felt much, much better."

There were five cases that he was determined to rectify at once. Seventy-year-old Karl Mende had committed no crime, even under Communist law—the government had simply wanted his prosperous glass factories. He was convicted of "industrial sabotage" and sentenced to six years at hard labor; his factories were expropriated. Arthur Bergel, a prominent woolen manufacturer, was the victim of a similar conviction. His offense had been to pay his 1,700 workers a higher wage than the government allowed. Horst Schnabel, a high-school boy of 17, had been sentenced to two years in the penitentiary, to be followed by transportation to the uranium mines, for possessing a book banned by the Communists. Jürgen Poppitz and Ekkehard Schumann, 20-year-old students, had received four-year terms for firing rockets that showered Leipzig with anti-Communist leaflets.

The obstacles in Hasso Lindemann's way seemed insuperable. As a former Communist, he was suspect to the various refugee organizations in Berlin. Then, after he had finally convinced the principal anti-Communist committees that he was sincere, a new state's attorney, whose signature Lindemann did not know, was appointed for Leipzig. The new incumbent ruled that no release order was to be obeyed unless the prison director checked its validity by a personal phone call to the state's attorney or to his immediate subordinate.

It took Lindemann three months to obtain from a friend in Leipzig a document signed by Chief State's Attorney Adam, more time to practice a flawless forgery of the signature. Through a complicated system of couriers and deftly worded, seemingly innocent letters, he learned the exact technique and timing of the telephonic verification.

Finally, the months of preparation came to an end. One of Lindemann's aides, Hans Schmidt, was put in charge of the first operation. Lindemann had wanted to perform it himself, but his face was too well known to People's Police and State Security Service men.

With forged release orders for Mende and Bergel in his briefcase, Schmidt set out for Leipzig and for the particular postbox from which the state's attorney's communications were always mailed.

Twice Schmidt almost met disaster. Two police officers suddenly appeared in his train compartment and ordered him to open his briefcase for inspection. Such spot checks are routine in East Germany. Schmidt obeyed, his heart in his mouth. The policemen saw the envelopes stamped "Chief State's Attorney's Office."

"You are a courier of the Herr Oberstaatsanwalt? " one of them asked. "Of course," Schmidt replied.

"We are sorry to have disturbed you, sir."

Heels clicked, salutes were exchanged, and, without asking for his papers, the officers departed.

At the postbox in Leipzig, Schmidt had his other bad moment. Two People's Police were watching the box, on guard against the mailing of clandestine leaflets. But again the official envelope commanded immediate obeisance, and one of the Volkspolizei even politely held up the box flap as Schmidt dropped the letters in.

That night neither Schmidt in Leipzig nor Lindemann in Berlin slept a wink. The release orders should reach the warden of Zwickau Penitentiary in the morning. If the warden telephoned the state's attorney's office before the plotters could act, the game would be up.

At the earliest feasible moment, Hans Schmidt braced himself and telephoned Zwickau.

"This is Oberstaatsanwalt Adam," he bellowed into the machine. "Give me the director at once."

Since the German bureaucratic caste system under the Communists is as strict as it ever was, Schmidt calculated that the voice of an exalted chief state's attorney would not be too familiar to a warden. He was right. The director answered with great deference.

"Have you received the release orders for Mende and Bergel?" snapped Hans Schmidt.

"No, Herr Oberstaatsanwalt. But I will attend to them personally the moment they arrive."

"See that you do," Schmidt growled. "No return call to my office is necessary to verify these orders. Is that clear?"

"Of course, Herr Oberstaatsanwalt. I will not disturb you. I have been deeply honored by your personal call."

When Schmidt hung up, he was sweating. But the most dangerous part of the operation lay ahead. Mende and Bergel, thinking their release was legal, would doubtless go home, where they would soon be rearrested. They had to be warned to flee at once to West Berlin. Schmidt went to Zwickau to wait for them.

Watching Zwickau Penitentiary is a hazardous task. Anyone loitering nearby is immediately reported by the guards to the People's Police. But Schmidt found a café from which he could watch the institution's main gate. He sat and drank beer—and more beer. He explained at great length to the café keeper that he was trying to drown his domestic troubles. A People's Policeman examined his papers, fortunately rather carelessly.

Finally, Schmidt decided that the forgeries had been detected. Dejectedly he returned to Berlin.

Actually, the release orders had merely been slow in reaching the penitentiary. When they arrived, Mende and Bergel were brought before the warden and the prison's dreaded political commissar.

"The highest authorities in our state have decided to forgive your crimes," the commissar announced cordially, even offering them cigarettes to put them at ease. "We are releasing you."

Presently the two men, provided with civilian clothes, money, and a ration of food for the journey home, stumbled out through the prison gate in a daze.

Their freedom might not have lasted long except for Lindemann's thorough planning. Fearing that Schmidt might be picked up by the police, Lindemann had dispatched another friend—Kurt Braun—to guide Mende and Bergel to Berlin. Braun waited in the neighborhood of the prison for almost 48 hours—without sleep and with only three apples for food. He didn't dare go into a restaurant for fear there might be a police checkup.

Almost collapsing from fatigue and hunger, Braun also finally gave up and boarded a streetcar for the railroad station. As the trolley rumbled away, he took one more backward look at the prison. Two gaunt men whose clothes hung loosely from their shoulders were coming out the prison gate!

Risking his neck, he jumped from the car. For several blocks he walked behind the two men to make sure they were the right ones (prison changes people's appearances). Finally, he sidled up and pressed a slip of paper into Herr Mende's hand.

"Follow these directions," he said quietly. "Get to West Berlin. Your families are there."

Fear and suspicion were plain on the men's faces. They both knew

that this might very well be a cleverly arranged police trap.

"Please, *please*," Braun urged desperately, "do as I say." With that, he vanished around the corner.

The next morning Herr Mende and Herr Bergel were safely in West Berlin. Still hardly able to believe their luck, they had found their families and had come to thank Lindemann.

"It was a strange interview—the former convicts and their former prosecutor," Lindemann reminisces happily. "But it was a very satisfactory one, particularly for me."

There were still three more prisoners to free—one in Zwickau, the others in Waldheim.

Schmidt was ready to start again for Leipzig when catastrophe struck. News of the two men's "escape" had leaked somehow, and a

West German radio station blared it out. Lindemann was beside himself with disappointment, when suddenly he realized that the trick might still work if they acted immediately. All Communist police and judicial chiefs habitually leave the city on Saturday for their country retreats and cannot be reached until their return around 11 o'clock on Monday morning. Lindemann was sure that his plan had more than an even chance of succeeding.

And he was proven right. The release orders arrived at Zwickau and Waldheim without delay. Schmidt repeated his first memorable telephone call to the two wardens. On Monday three bewildered boys found themselves on their way to West Berlin in the care of Hans Schmidt and Kurt Braun.

But it had been a close shave. Five minutes after the Zwickau gates had closed, a big car roared up to the prison. Herr Oberstaatsanwalt Adam himself, flanked by high-ranking police officers, stormed angrily into the institution.

The escape of Mende and Bergel had been discovered late Saturday by agents monitoring West German radio broadcasts. Gerhart Eisler, then propaganda minister, happened to be at his desk early Monday morning and was informed first. Roaring with rage, he tried to contact his colleagues. But no responsible police official could be reached until Monday noon. Then the entire State Security Service and People's Police was unleashed in an unprecedented manhunt. Trains were searched, automobiles stopped, innocent pedestrians dragged off to police stations for questioning throughout East Germany. They were too late.

In a comfortable restaurant in West Berlin Lindemann, his helpers, and his ex-victims were celebrating. The spare, usually shy young man raised his glass.

"We shall have to use other methods in the future," he said. "But I think we can do it again."

*As the airplane swooped low over the Communist cruise
ship, a man leaped from the stern into the
stormy, shark-infested waters of the Caribbean Sea.
It was all part of a daredevil escape plan.*

Rendezvous at Sea

*By Ken Agnew
as told to Kenneth Schaefer*

IT WAS NOW OR NEVER for Karl Bley. I put my single-engine air-plane into a steep turn and raced directly at the East German ship. My low pass was the signal for the 24-year-old machinist from behind the Iron Curtain to jump overboard.

Misgivings filled my mind. The Atlantic Ocean seven miles off the Florida Keys is hostile water at best, and on this day-after-Thanksgiving 1970, choppy swells were waiting to welcome his desperate leap to freedom. If he escaped the powerful suction of the ship's propeller, he would have to take his chances with the sharks until the rescue boat reached him.

For that matter, was Karl Bley even on board the ship? If he was, would he jump, or would he lose his nerve at the sight of that 40-foot drop into the churning wake?

Escape had been Karl Bley's dream since the night two years earlier, when, aboard the same East German cruise ship-freighter, the M.S. *Völkerfreundschaft*, he had sailed past the glittering lights of Miami. A thousand miles to the northwest in Villa Park, Illinois, lived his older brother, Eric. Eric Bley had made it out of East Germany in 1955, followed a year later by his fiancée, Marlis. The two were now U.S. citizens and were grateful to their adopted land. Eric had founded a successful machine-building firm in a suburb of Chicago.

For 15 years the brothers had corresponded regularly. (They had worked out a code to get their messages past the ever-watchful East German censors.) Immediately after his 1968 trip to Havana, Karl wrote Eric that if he ever got that close to America again, "I'm going to jump and swim for it." It was no idle boast. Eric knew the hunger his brother felt. He had felt it himself.

He also knew that the chance was slim of swimming the seven miles from ship to shore. So there had been desperation on both sides of the Iron Curtain. It was at that point—two months before—that I had been pulled into the affair.

Eric had come to the Florida Keys, south of Miami, looking for help in the escape plan that he and his brother had plotted. On Duck Key he saw a sleek charter boat, the *Pequod*, belonging to my long-time friend, Capt. Bob Lowe. Fast, in prime condition, *Pequod* was the perfect boat to overtake the *Völkerfreundschaft* when she ran by the Florida coast at 18 knots. Eric found Bob Lowe, who listened in silence as he outlined his scheme.

"You want to lay a rescue vessel alongside that Commie ship just when your brother is ready to jump?" Lowe demanded. "Is that the idea?"

Eric nodded. "That's right."

"It's going to need air-ground co-ordinating. And a definite signal to your brother that all's set before he makes the leap. It won't be easy."

Needing a pilot, Lowe brought Bley to see me. It was Lowe who sold me; I could tell that he liked what he saw in Eric Bley. Before he'd finished, I was as hooked as Bob by the desperate determination of a man fighting for his brother's life.

Eric had just about everything we needed to know about the cruise ship *Völkerfreundschaft*, thanks to an advertising brochure that Karl had mailed to him. Passengers would board at the Baltic seaport of Rostock, enjoy a trip to Havana, then return. The cover carried a picture of the ship; an inside page even gave the frequencies monitored by the ship's radio.

We worked out a plan. I'd fly the route most Communist ships take in making the Havana run: From the Bahamas they go straight toward Palm Beach, then follow the Florida coastline until they've nearly cleared the Keys. Once I'd spotted the ship, I would radio Bob and Eric, who would put out in the *Pequod*. As they closed in on the East German ship, I'd make a low pass in my light plane. That would be the signal for Karl to jump.

The second week of November Eric told us that Karl was aboard the ship. He would be off the Keys sometime on Thanksgiving Day. He would wear a bright jacket for quick spotting by his rescuers and would have a life preserver on under the jacket. But, the younger brother wrote, whether the rescue craft showed up or not, he was going to jump before the *Völkerfreundschaft* veered away from the last bit of America.

To provide day and night surveillance, we had enlisted George Butler, a retired engineer and enthusiastic pilot. For two days he and I had been flying our planes up to Palm Beach and across the 60 miles to the Bahamas, directly over the path the ship should take. We had also worked south along the Keys to American Shoal, an unmanned lighthouse 16 miles off Key West—the usual turnaway point of Soviet vessels bound for Cuba. We could report nothing but frayed nerves for our almost nonstop efforts.

At 5:30 on the morning after Thanksgiving a dejected Eric Bley was leaving his hotel on Duck Key for the airport and a reconnaissance flight with me. Suddenly, as he stared out at the blackness across the ocean to the east, he saw lights—*the ship!* He jumped into his car and roared off to the Marathon airport on Key Vaca. I was waiting for him, and the minute we lifted off the runway, we could see the ship, her whole stern lighted up like New York. I killed our wingtip lights and the brilliant strobe atop the fuselage so we wouldn't tip off our quarry. Flying high over the ship, we took out the brochure with its identifying picture. The sky and water were still dark, but with the deck lighting we had it—picture and ship matched exactly, even to the bright-red line along her hull.

In minutes we were back at Marathon, where a waiting Bob Lowe told us that there wasn't time to go north to Duck Key, get the *Pequod,* and still catch the cruise ship, now moving past the village of Marathon at a full 18 knots.

"It'll take a 40-knot boat to catch it," he said. "Come on, Eric! We'll get a boat even if we have to steal it!" Seconds later their car was speeding toward Big Pine Key, 19 miles to the south.

Butler had arrived by this time and was ready to fly the high watch at 2,000 feet while I took the low run. Just before we both took off, I asked Butler's wife to call the Coast Guard: "Tell them you got a garbled message that there's a man in the water off American Shoal and to get help out there right now!"

We had to have some kind of backup. I was afraid Bob and Eric wouldn't get a boat and that Karl had meant it when he said he'd jump even if there was no signal.

I flew down to Big Pine Key just as a 22-foot fiberglass outboard skiff came planing out of the Sea Center Marina, charging for the daylight beginning to show in the east. It was taking a brutal pounding as it hit the heavy chop of the open water. I didn't think Lowe could see the ship, and I skimmed over him to set him on an intercept course that would put him ahead of his target.

At that point the skiff went dead in the water! I watched Bob fiddle with the engine until it restarted. Another half mile and it quit again. "Bob's not going to make it!" I reported to Butler over the radio.

As I was debating whether to signal the jump anyway, I saw white froth behind the little boat as Lowe brought the engine alive once more. We were still in business!

I headed for my assigned point low and far ahead of the *Völkerfreundschaft* to wait until Butler called that the skiff was closing in.

"Now!" came the word finally.

"Right. I'm going in!"

Soon I was hell-bent for the bow of the unsuspecting liner, barreling down her port side, whitecaps only a few feet below me. I caught sight of passengers at the rail—two dozen of the most stunned expressions I'd ever seen. At the fantail I made a tight turn to the left, so close that the flagpole at the stern almost caught my wingtip. If Bley was aboard, he had to have heard me! But for one awful second there was nothing—just people gawking from the rail as I roared up the starboard side of the ship.

"Nobody jumped!" I bellowed at the mike in my right hand.

Then it happened. A figure went over the rail and plummeted to the water. *"He jumped!"* I yelled.

There was an abrupt squawk from my radio, and Butler called from overhead: "There're two in the water!"

I gaped in disbelief at what was happening. From the side window I now saw not two, but *three.* No . . . *four!* Eric had previously warned us:

"If this boy jumps, look out—you're liable to get more." We had them.

Lord, I thought, what a gamble! None of the three knew of our plot. No one but Karl had a life jacket—only life rings they'd tossed to the turbulent sea just before jumping. I circled the floundering figures below, and as they struggled toward those orange-colored rings in the water, I knew I was looking at raw courage.

Lowe's pilotage of the rescue boat was magnificent. Almost before the last man hit the water, Bob was past the liner and Eric was pulling Karl into the skiff.

Then came the ship's response. We had known that the Reds were prepared for the possibility of a man overboard, and we'd talked at length about how long it would take the *Völkerfreundschaft* to make a 180-degree turn. We had guessed wrong.

Eric and Bob were still dragging the men from the water when the ship rolled into a tight turn at full speed. It was amazing to see a liner lean like that, and I had the fleeting suspicion that the captain wanted everybody overboard.

It was close! By the time the last man was picked from the sea, the ship was bearing down on the tiny rescue craft. Bob raced at top speed for shallow water close to shore, where the *Völkerfreundschaft* could not possibly follow. Finally, the East German ship broke off the chase, made a turn, and took the southerly heading for Havana. It was all over.

Afterward, I sat beside Karl in a room at the Key West Coast Guard station and looked at the earnest face of this slender, dark-haired youth from East Germany. His dream had come true out there in the ocean when he waved his arms in a sign of triumph and screamed at the man in the bow of the rescue boat, "Bruder! Bruder!"

The men who had leaped to freedom with him were Dr. Manfred Kupfer, a 37-year-old neuropathologist from Leipzig; his brother, Dr. Reinhold Kupfer, a 33-year-old pathologist from Zwickau; and Dr. Peter Rost, 37, a microbiologist, also from Zwickau. They had come on the cruise with unspoken hopes that just such a chance might be theirs. Karl's bold leap was the inspiration they'd hoped for so desperately.

Through Eric's interpreting, I learned that Karl had been on deck since early morning watching the lights along the Keys, studying the shoreline through binoculars for any sign of action. "I saw you when you took off from the airport," he told me. "I saw your bright light go out, and when I heard you in the dark high above the ship, I knew that Eric was coming."

Looking at this 24-year-old, who I knew now would have made that leap, signal or no, I suddenly realized what freedom means.

U.S. Marine Corps Pvt. Martin Kaylor's term of military service in the Korean War had come to an end—or so he fondly believed, until he found himself trapped deep behind enemy lines, a captive of the Chinese Communists.

The Long Way Home

By John G. Hubbell

KAYLOR," said the lieutenant, "tomorrow morning at 0600, when the regiment moves up, you are to report to S-1. Your dependency discharge has come through, and you're going back to Casual Company at Hamhung."

Bud Kaylor, marine machine gunner, was stunned, then elated. This was no foxhole rumor, this was for real. He was getting out of this frozen hell and going home. He'd be there in time for Christmas with his wife, Dorothy, and their family.

Early the next morning Kaylor said quick good-byes to his buddies. The 1st Marine Division and the army's 7th Infantry Division were moving north for an assault on the Chosin Reservoir. But for Bud Kaylor the war was over, or so he thought. This, however, was the morning of November 28, 1950, and no one knew that the stage was set for the attack by the Chinese Reds.

At S-1 the personnel officer told Kaylor he'd have to get back to Hamhung on his own. So he and Art Foley, a mail clerk, hitched a ride in the lead truck of a five-truck convoy. There were two other marine passengers in the back of their truck and another riding shotgun with the driver. Thus Bud Kaylor started the first leg of his journey out of Korea—and home.

The home he was headed for was near Hopkins, Minnesota, where Gladys and Charley Kaylor, Bud's parents, lived. It was there that the telegram was to arrive on January 5, 1951. It came from Marine Headquarters, with deep regrets: Pfc. Charles Martin Kaylor had been missing in action since November 28, 1950.

"The telegram said 'missing,' " Charley Kaylor related. "Bud is a little guy, but he's tough, cool, and a mighty quick thinker. He had always been an athlete. I figured he was still alive somewhere."

Neither could Bud's wife nor his mother nor his sisters give up. His daughter, Terry Jo, was only four, but she was sure her father would come back. Through the long months that followed, they all lived on the strength of interminable prayer and desperate hope.

Soon after Kaylor's convoy got under way that morning for the 70-mile trip, they came to a small village. The huts looked uninhabited, but in seconds a crowd of Koreans was streaming out. They shouted and pointed down the road.

"Poor gooks think the Commies are coming back," someone said.

The marines waved and laughed, and some threw candy and cigarettes. Soon they found out what the Koreans had been trying to tell them. Around a sharp bend they came upon a jeep in the middle of the road, with logs piled high on either side of it. The driver of the lead truck couldn't avoid hitting it. The jeep rolled off the road, and the driver bulled his way on.

Bud Kaylor looked over the edge of the truck. Chinese soldiers were six and seven deep in the ditches, and more were running down the hills on both sides of the road, shooting as they came. Kaylor grabbed his carbine and emptied it into one of the ditches. There wasn't time to aim, and the Reds were so thick it didn't make any difference anyway.

In a matter of seconds his ammunition was gone. He dropped flat on his back and saw two bullets sing past, within an inch of his nose. He *saw* them go by, because they had come right through the steel side of the truck, and it had slowed them down. Then one came through and got Art Foley, the mail clerk. Kaylor started to reach for Art's carbine, and he saw something yellow sail by. It was a grenade shaped like a potato masher. He leaped for it, but it wasn't there; so he thought it had bounced out of the truck. But when he lay down again, his head hit something hard; he reached back and grabbed the object. It was the grenade. He immediately threw it backward, clear of the truck, and heard it go off.

A minute later the driver was shot in the ear. The marine riding shotgun with him kept firing at the ditch on the driver's side of the road, trying to protect him. There were only two tires left, and the truck veered all over the road.

Kaylor grabbed Foley's carbine and sat up at the back of the truck. He was just in time to see a Chinese Red soldier lob one of those yellow grenades up from the ditch. It was a perfect throw, and Kaylor grabbed it by the handle and slammed it right back at him. It hit at

the Communist's feet and instantly exploded. The Red died with unbelieving surprise on his face.

Then the truck swerved off the road into the ditch. Kaylor went over the side and ran to some thin bushes. From there he could see the truck driver and his gunner running toward a frozen river about 500 yards away. The Reds shot at them from a hill, and Kaylor watched the bullets kick up the snow around their feet. Suddenly, the gunner dropped, but the driver kept right on going across the river, into the cover of thick woods.

A number of Reds showed up, and one threw a grenade that landed about five feet from Kaylor. It went off and knocked him down, and he was conscious of a burning sensation in his leg.

The Reds came up and stood all around him, looking at him and pointing their rifles. Then one moved in close and frisked him.

Kaylor saw the red stain come through his pant leg. The blood was running fast. His captors took him to a command post, where a Chinese officer called two orderlies over and gave them some instructions. Then he turned to Kaylor and made him take his parka off. The officer pretended that he was searching it, and he motioned to the orderlies to take Kaylor away. As Kaylor left, he saw the officer trying on his parka.

Bud was weak from loss of blood. He kept falling down, and the Reds kept pushing him along. Every step seemed colder than the last. It was -15°F, and all Kaylor wore now was his field cap, a shirt, pants, shoes, and long underwear. At a battalion aid station the Communist orderlies dressed his wounds.

Early the second morning, when they reached a Korean village, one of the Reds walked Kaylor to the door of a house and motioned him inside. Entering, Bud could see three Chinese officers at a table. A single candle illuminated the entire room. In a few seconds another officer came in. He was young and friendly, and his English was flawless. He put out his hand and smiled.

"I'm Lieutenant Fung," he said. "Won't you sit down?"

Fung asked his name, rank, and serial number. He translated swiftly to the three officers at the table. Then he asked Kaylor the names of marine officers in his outfit, how many tanks were there, and what kind of artillery. Kaylor started to say that he wasn't required to tell, when he felt a sharp kick at his leg. He looked around, and at the end of the bench he saw two Chinese overcoats piled over a body, with only the feet showing. Kaylor moved farther down the bench, away from the body, and told the lieutenant he couldn't answer him.

In a few minutes Fung left the room, and the body under the overcoats sat up and unveiled itself. It was the truck driver, 19-year-old Cpl. Fred Holcomb, from Hamden, New York, and he was more than a little indignant at having been captured, and all the Chinamen in Korea could go to hell.

"We don't tell them a thing," he said. "We don't have to."

Kaylor was sorry that Holcomb hadn't escaped, but glad he was finally in good marine company. They started talking about the ambush, and then Fung came back into the room. He talked to the two marines until dawn. He explained that the Chinese were not going to kill them, that they didn't even want them as prisoners.

"All we want to do with you guys," he said, "is get you out of Korea so you can't fight us anymore." He said they were going to take them to China, put them on a neutral ship, and send them back to the United States. Then he took their home addresses.

"I'd like to write you fellows after the war and see how things turn out for each of us," he said. He told them they would be moving out in the morning, shook hands, and said good-bye. And he left them with the memory of a warm and friendly person.

It was snowing heavily when they moved out with a Chinese column and started walking north. After four days they joined a group of 250 other prisoners, including 43 marines. They moved on north, Kaylor limping along on his wounded leg over the icy mountain trails. And finally, after they had walked for 11 days, and just when Bud thought he couldn't walk another mile, they stopped moving. They were in the village of Kanggye, near the Yalu River.

The Chinese divided them into two sections and billeted them in cold Korean houses, where most of them lay on the bare floor in a sleeping stupor for days. When they were strong enough to want to stop sleeping, the Chinese took their clothes and gave them Chinese uniforms. English-speaking Red officers began to interrogate them. It was kept mostly on a personal plane, and the officers kept it up until they got the answers they wanted. If Comrade Kaylor, for instance, said he earned $250 a month at his job in Minneapolis, he was obviously lying. This made the Chinese angry, and they would spend long hours explaining to him that he was among friends and there was no need for him to lie. Patiently, they would point out to him that his warmongering, capitalistic bosses on Wall Street had duped him into thinking he was well off.

When the prisoners realized what the Reds wanted to hear, they told them tales of wretched, hungry childhoods that had been lived in anticipation of joining the Marine Corps, where they could at least get some food and clothing. They told of aged parents who lived as best they could on the infrequent and niggardly charity of the Wall Street bosses. The Chinese seemed to like this.

The indoctrination began in a bleak, cold barn called the Big House. A Chinese "high commander" came out on a stage and made a welcoming speech. They were not, he explained, to think of themselves as prisoners. They were "newly liberated friends" and would be treated as such. The Chinese people were not angry with them for being in Korea, since they had been duped by their imperialistic bosses. They would be treated with kindness, but they must obey the rules set down for newly liberated friends. If they broke the rules, they would undergo severe punishment.

On Christmas night all the newly liberated friends were herded into the Big House. The Chinese had decorated the place with Christmas trees and candles, wreaths and red paper bells. There was a big sign saying, "Merry Christmas." Along the walls were signs reading, "If it were not for the Wall Street imperialists, you would be home with your wives and families this Christmas night." A high commander made a speech that repeated what the signs said, and he threw in a few unkind remarks about Truman, MacArthur, and Secretary of State John Foster Dulles.

By this time the POW's knew what the Chinese wanted of them, and word had spread that the "most promising" prisoners would be released before the war was over. So after the high commander finished speaking, a marine from Boston named McClean jumped up and shouted, "Down with the Wall Street bosses!" And another named Dickerson pulled his six feet seven inches from the floor and shouted in a Georgia drawl, "Down with the aggressive imperialists!" And a five-foot nine-inch marine named Kaylor limped over to a toothy interpreter named Lieutenant Pan, looked him squarely in the eye, and cried, "Down with the warmongers!" The newly liberated friends all over the Big House took up the cry, and the happy, smiling Chinese ran around the huge room, patting them on the back, shaking hands with them, and giving them presents. Each man received 10 pieces of candy, 6 cigarettes, and a Christmas card.

After Christmas each section was lectured every other day in the Big House. They listened to long orations by high commanders of varying rank. Sometimes the teachers spoke in Chinese, and this took the longest because an interpreter had to translate. Sometimes they would rattle along in a high-pitched, singsong English. First, they spoke on "Why Are We Treating You So Well?" Then, "Who Is the Aggressor in Korea?" Then, "Why Is the United States the Aggressor?" Then, "How You Can Fight for Peace."

After the lectures the section marched back to its house, where it would engage in a lengthy round-table discussion. An English-speaking Chinese officer would sit quietly by, listening and taking notes. Once in a while he would inject a comment, and the marines would all nod solemn approval.

The weeks stretched into months, and the pattern became routine.

And then dysentery hit. It hit everyone, and the ones it hit the worst died. Sometimes only one would die in a week, sometimes three, four, or five.

Worse than the dysentery was the malnutrition; they had nothing to eat but sorghum seed and millet. Malnutrition hit the legs with a screaming viciousness. When it hit Kaylor, he lay flat on his back for 28 days and cried and became delirious, while agonizing pains raced through his legs. When it would stop for a while, he would drift off to sleep and suddenly wake up screaming when the pains came back. Then, after days of this, exhaustion would claim him, and the pain would lie dormant while he slept. Finally, his legs felt better, and he was able to move around again.

IT WAS MARCH NOW, and the days got longer and warmer. And the rumors got thicker that some of the most "promising" friends were soon to be released. The combination kept the prisoners in anxious good spirits. But it was with some reluctance that every man in the camp signed the Stockholm Peace Petition. The Chinese thought it would be a good indication of their sincerity in their desire to fight for peace. The marines hoped that the names might somehow sift back and reach the United States.

And on March 21 the second telegram arrived at the house of Charley Kaylor in Hopkins, Minnesota. The message was from the army's provost marshal general, and it said that the name of Charles Martin Kaylor had been mentioned on an enemy propaganda broadcast out of Peking on March 16. That's all it said. But now the family's constant, desperate hope became a fire.

On Easter Sunday 60 prisoners were herded into the Big House. Inside, great care was taken to seat a certain 30 on one side of the room and the rest on the other side. Then a high commander delivered a lengthy singsong reiteration of all the lectures of the months before. He climaxed this oration with the news that one of these groups of 30 was to be released. It was felt, he said, that these men were "ready to carry on the fight for peace among their own people." The other 30 were being cited for "progress," but were being kept for a while to help instruct incoming newly liberated friends. Then he smiled and toyed with the 60 men.

"Which group is it?" he asked. "Who is going home? Is it the group on my right? Or is it the group on my left?" Bud Kaylor looked around at the faces in his group. Harrison, Estess, Dickerson, Holcomb, Maffioli—all were barracks bull-session artists, and all had given the Reds master snow jobs.

Finally, the high commander pointed to the group on his right. It was Kaylor's group. "This group," he said, "leaves tonight."

The 30 marines took the news with stone-faced joy, for they wanted the Reds to feel that they would just as soon stay there and be Communists as return home and be Communists. The other 30 also remained stone-faced, but they had trouble fighting back the tears.

The prisoners who were to be released moved out in trucks at dusk and rode for five nights. On the fifth night Lieutenant Pan, the interpreter in command, got them out of the trucks and told them they were in the Chunchon area.

"There has been an American offensive," he said. "It is too dangerous to let you go now. You might be killed."

The marines said they would take that chance, but Pan told them he was acting under orders. Then the trucks moved away, and the marines were marched to a prison camp.

They stayed in this camp six weeks. Then, on the night of May 15, the Chinese called out 19 of the 30 marines and marched them to a river. They gave them razors and soap and let them bathe and shave, then brought them chow. The food was pork and rice, and it was the first time in six months that any of them had seen anything but sorghum seed and millet. A lot of them ate too much too fast and got sick. Bud Kaylor was one of them. After they finished eating, Lieutenant Pan spoke to them.

"Word has come to release you men," he said.

Again they were loaded into trucks. On the third night they reached the Imjin River. Retreating Chinese troops were coming back across the river by the thousands. Pan turned his charges over to a field commander. The commander told them that another offensive had been started and they could not be released at this time. Then he left, saying he would be back about midnight and for them to be ready to move back up north.

T. Sgt. Charley Harrison, of Tulsa, Oklahoma, was fighting mad. He announced firmly that he was *not* going up north again. He was going home, and if anyone wanted to come with him they were welcome. U.N. artillery was whistling in close, and the guards were in foxholes. So all 19 marines sneaked off and waded across the shallow Imjin River. On the other side they ran for miles through the woods.

Just before dawn they stopped in a field where the wheat was high and went to sleep. They awoke to find four Chinese soldiers pointing guns at them and jabbering to each other. Then Harrison, who spoke Chinese, put on an act. He got up smiling. He explained that they were released prisoners of war and that the high command would be displeased if they were shot or taken back. The Chinese jabbered back at him, and then he talked some more. And then he started talking to the marines out of the side of his mouth.

"These birds aren't going to let us go," he said. "They're arguing whether they should shoot us now or take us in." Then he said something in Chinese. Then he spoke English again. "Estess and Dickerson, get the one on the left." More Chinese. "Kaylor and Hilburn, the one on the right; Nash and Holcomb, the one next to him." More Chinese. "Hawkins and Hayton, the other one." Then there was more Chinese, and finally Harrison gave the word: "Let's get 'em!"

The marines did their jobs as Harrison assigned them and completed them quickly when the others pitched in. This was a kill-or-be-killed situation. The marines overpowered the Reds and strangled them and smashed their heads with the gun butts. Then they ran.

In the next valley they came to a village. A bearded old Korean sent them up to a house on the top of a hill, where the mayor used to live, and promised to send them food and tobacco. They were to wait there until he could send a message to the American troops, who were only a few miles away.

Inside the house they lay and marveled that this was the only house any of them had seen in Korea with wallpaper. And then they heard the sound of an airplane. They looked outside and saw an L-5 artillery observer, an army plane, flying low. They quickly cut the wallpaper into strips and took it out to the rice paddy behind the house. They spelled out POW 19 RESCUE, and then they went back inside. Only Fred Holcomb stayed out in the rice paddy, waving his undershirt to attract the L-5's attention. Snipers fired at him from the hills occasionally, but they weren't coming close, and Holcomb was much too excited to care.

Soon Holcomb came running in. The L-5 had dropped a message: "Come out to the letters so you can be counted. We are sending tanks in to pick you up."

They went back to the letters, and in half an hour they saw the L-5 leading three tanks around a bend in the draw that stretched out beneath the rice paddies. Then Lt. Frank Cold, of Tampa, Florida, the only officer among the 19, lined them up in a column of twos.

"I know how we all feel about being rescued," he said. "But this is the army coming in to get us, and we're still marines. So let's be rescued like marines, in formation."

The tanks ground to a halt about 300 yards away to identify them. This was hard to do, since they were wearing Chinese uniforms. But finally they moved up close. The hatch of the lead tank opened and an army captain climbed out.

The 19 marines stood there, in columns of twos, in a soggy, worthless no-man's-land, somewhere in Korea, and tears as big as raindrops streamed down the face of every one of them. The army captain stood looking at them, and for a moment it seemed as though all Korea was silent. Then the captain said, "Come on, fellas, let's get the hell out of here!" So they climbed into the tanks and got the hell out of there, but they were rescued like marines.

IT WAS ON May 25 that the third telegram arrived at Charley Kaylor's house. It came from Marine Headquarters, and it said that Pfc. Charles Martin Kaylor would soon be home. The endless months of hoping and praying were over, and the miracle had happened. But the people in Charley Kaylor's house said one more prayer anyhow.

Almost suddenly, it was June 23, 1951, and Bud Kaylor was moving down the steps from the airplane while his eyes searched the faces at the end of the ramp. He saw them, right in front. He limped toward them. Then Dorothy was in his arms, the others clustered around him. Bud Kaylor had come the long way home.

This is the amazing account of how two daring
young Canadians established an escape route through Nazi-held
France during World War II. More than 300 Allied airmen
and secret agents followed it to freedom.

House of Alphonse

By John G. Hubbell

ONE NIGHT in January 1944 an announcer for the British Broad-
casting Corporation voiced a cheery greeting in French from
London: "Good evening to everyone in the House of Alphonse. I
repeat: Good evening to everyone in the House of Alphonse."

Across the Channel in German-occupied Brittany, in a small room
above a café in the village of Plouha, a young man named Raymond
LaBrosse, whose papers identified him as a salesman of electrical
medical equipment, switched off a radio and turned to the two other
people in the room.

"That's it," he said.

Stocky Lucien Dumais, known locally as a contractor, got to his
feet and nodded quickly to the third man, café owner François Le
Cornec. "Let's go!" he said.

The men slipped into the night.

A few minutes later the rear doors of half a dozen village houses
opened, and small groups of what seemed to be young French peasants edged silently out. They were not all peasants. Among them,
dressed in the same sort of clothes, were 13 American and 5 British
airmen who had been shot down in France. Silently, by twos and
threes, led by the French, the airmen moved through the woods behind the village. They carefully skirted the edges of open meadows to
avoid being seen by patrols of German troops.

After an interminable time they came to a stone farmhouse—the
"House of Alphonse," actually the home of Resistance worker Jean
Gicquel. Here, before a flickering candle, Dumais warned the airmen: "Many lives have been risked to bring you this far. There is just
a mile left, and it is the most dangerous you will ever travel. You will

maintain absolute silence and do exactly as you are told. There are enemy sentries and patrols in the area. If it becomes necessary to kill any of them, you are expected to help—use knives or your hands. Be quick, and above all be quiet; your lives and ours depend on it."

Then Dumais and the villagers led the airmen out again, through the darkness. Finally, they reached a cliff that dropped sharply 200 feet to the beach below. Clutching, sliding, tumbling, they scrambled down to a black cove.

From a hidden perch on the cliff, a French sailor had begun blinking the letter *B* in Morse code on a flashlight. The signal went out over the dark English Channel every two minutes.

For a long time there was no answer. Then, shortly before 2 A.M., four rowboats slid into the cove. The airmen hastily scrambled into the boats and were rowed out to a blacked-out British motor gunboat, No. 503, standing silently offshore.

The villagers returned to the House of Alphonse, where they waited for the clock to strike 6 A.M.—the hour the Germans lifted the curfew. Before going to bed in the house at Plouha, Lucien Dumais raised a wineglass to Le Cornec and LaBrosse.

"*Eh bien.* To our first success," he said. "It went off like clock-work. But we have a busy season ahead of us."

"Operation Bonaparte" was the key part of a larger escape network called Shelburne Escape and Evasion Line, which was to go on to become World War II's most successful escape route. For one of its two key men there was a prelude that began in London in August 1942, when Ray LaBrosse, a 22-year-old sergeant in the Canadian Army's 2nd Divisional Signals Regiment, was called in by a kilted British intelligence major to answer all sorts of seemingly nonsensical questions. Did he like sports? Adventure? As a boy, what games had he enjoyed most?

How did he feel about the war? About the Americans? The British? The French? As LaBrosse answered, the major sized him up. A native of Ottawa, LaBrosse was of French descent and spoke the language fluently. He was young but, according to his superiors, mature, enthusiastic, strong, imaginative.

Finally satisfied, the major put the proposition: He needed two good men to set up and run an escape organization for Allied airmen shot down in France. Capture, of course, would mean torture and a spy's death. Was LaBrosse interested? LaBrosse was.

He and a partner parachuted into France in 1943, and for six months they teamed up with the French Resistance in evacuating airmen. Then the apparatus was infiltrated by the Gestapo, and LaBrosse's partner was among those arrested. LaBrosse escaped via the Pyrenees to England. He was soon asked if he would return to help set up "Shelburne" to find, hide, clothe, feed, and evacuate escaping airmen. The role of "Bonaparte" was to get them out by sea from Brittany. He said he would.

The man selected to go with him this time was another bilingual Canadian, Sergeant Major Dumais, 38, of Montreal, a veteran of the August 1942 raid on Dieppe. (Captured there, he had escaped to England after living off the French countryside and making his way to Marseilles.) By the time the two men left England, both of them had had months of intensive training in jujitsu and the use of various types of weapons and explosives, as well as in the construction and operation of wireless sets. They were given fountain pens that fired a deadly gas, buttons that hid compasses, large amounts of francs, forged identity papers. For security reasons each had his own code, unknown to the other. Finally, on a night in November 1943, a light plane landed them in an isolated meadow 50 miles north of Paris.

The operation very nearly foundered before it got fairly started. Making their way to Paris, Dumais and LaBrosse succeeded in getting in touch with the Resistance. Soon afterward, LaBrosse went to keep a sidewalk rendezvous with one of its members, a woman. A flicker of her eye as he approached warned him just in time that two trench-coated figures idling nearby were Gestapo agents. Shaken, LaBrosse walked on past.

Soon thereafter, immutable rules for governing the escape organization were laid down. No one involved was to know anything except his own function. Cooperating Frenchmen were to be told only that if a "package" (airman) was found it was to be hidden and "rewrapped" (given peasant clothing), word passed secretly to a reliable friend,

124

instructions awaited. No airman was to be given more than the barest essential information.

Soon escape procedures and routes were worked out, villagers screened and recruited, hideouts arranged. Dumais and LaBrosse rented separate quarters in Paris and met only when necessary. Dumais made no pretense at working as the mortician his Paris papers said he was; he traveled extensively and let the story grow in his neighborhood that he was a successful black-market operator. LaBrosse appeared to be every inch the dutiful salesman. He moved about picking houses known to be safe for his radio operations and exchanging coded messages with London.

As they had surmised, the season was busy. The air war over the Continent was reaching its peak of violence; ever-increasing numbers of crewmen from crippled bombers were parachuting down all over France. Typical was Lt. William Spinning, a bomber pilot from Birmingham, Michigan, who dropped into north-central France. Bewildered, alone, knowing that any second he might be spotted and shot, he spent days and nights hiding and walking, scavenging cabbages from farms. Once he was given a meal by a huge woodcutter who wept as he watched him eat, then wrapped him in his own worn jacket, and pointed him toward Spain. He experienced a torrential rain and a feverish illness, but at last he saw two men beckoning to him from a field. They gave him hot food and drink, hid him in a warm farmhouse, told him to wait. Though Lieutenant Spinning didn't know it, the Shelburne Line had picked him up.

ALL THE AIRMEN found were funneled first toward its organization in Paris, headed by Paul-François Campinchi. Undertaker Dumais was everywhere—watching, noting, instructing. Thus, in a wine warehouse 70 miles south of Paris, he watched while Resistance men taught four Allied airmen to act like ill-humored French laborers. They were not to look angry, just sullen, like the many French who refused to speak to the enemy. If stopped for questioning, they were to show their fake identity papers, say nothing, play dumb.

"The slightest mistake can betray you," they were told. "The way you smoke, for example. You people inhale great, greedy drags and often remove a cigarette from your mouth. The Frenchman savors a cigarette; he keeps it in the corner of his mouth and lets it build an ash. He rarely removes it, and he *never* offers cigarettes to others—cigarettes are too scarce in France these days."

Next day Dumais was outside a church near Compiègne, reading a newspaper, when a farmer drove up, presented a gift of eggs to the priest, explained he was Paris-bound with a truckload of hay, and wondered if Father had "packages" he wanted delivered. The priest nodded and told the man to drive his truck around back to the church cellar entrance. There the driver picked up two airmen who had been hiding in a stack of hay.

The Canadians were nearby one night in Paris waiting to hear if Resistance interrogators thought Lt. Manuel Rogoff, an American bombardier, was a Nazi agent. Rogoff was not to be trapped. He knew that the Pittsburgh Pirates of the National League had lost no games in 1942 to the Chicago Bears of the National League, because the Bears were a football team. He knew that Dizzy Dean had never pitched for the Detroit White Sox (and that it was the Detroit Tigers, not White Sox), but for the St. Louis Cardinals. He knew what movies had been playing in the theaters on his base in England prior to his last raid. He was well acquainted with the adventures of Tom Sawyer and Huckleberry Finn.

Every airman was interrogated, because German agents were always probing. One night a Free Norwegian airman was brought in. Dumais himself questioned him. The man had been flying with the RAF, he said, and was desperately anxious to return to England and rejoin the fight.

He had all the right answers about his squadron, base, even personnel. But he became oddly vague and impatient when quizzed on things Norwegian; he said he had not spent much time in Norway in recent years. Dumais' interrogation turned savage. The "Norwegian" panicked, confessed he was a Nazi agent, and pleaded for mercy. He offered to join the organization and promised invaluable help, but no chance could be taken. Shifted to a country house near Versailles, he was pumped for all the information he would give. Then he was shot.

There was the young man who identified himself as Robert K. Fruth, a U.S. airman from Defiance, Ohio, but could not answer the most routine questions. His squadron? His bomb group? The pilot of his plane? The names of others in his crew? The target his plane had last attacked? On all these questions he drew a blank. While the Resistance was considering whether to execute him, LaBrosse tapped out a short, coded message to London.

Two days later a BBC broadcast cleverly keyed to the coded query established that Fruth was genuine. Newly arrived in England from the States, he had been roused from bed in predawn darkness his very first night to replace a gunner fallen suddenly ill. That explained why he had had no time to acquire the most rudimentary information before he was shot down.

The transfer of airmen from Paris to the Brittany coast was tricky. Too many "packages" delivered to Plouha, the principal jumping-off point for Bonaparte escapes, might attract attention. Hence, the disguised airmen were first sent to a number of other small towns nearby. One of these was Guingamp, 15 miles from Plouha.

Before an airman boarded the train in Paris, he was well briefed. In his hand or stuffed in his left coat pocket he must carry a newspaper. As he crossed the Guingamp platform, a nondescript man would jostle him and give him a swift, discreet dig in the ribs. That was the sign of recognition.

Guingamp's Resistance leader was Mathurin Branchoux, a thrice-wounded World War I veteran Among his retinue was one François Kerambrun, who drove a small enclosed delivery truck for the Germans. To airmen he was carrying to a hideout near Plouha, Kerambrun would explain that the Germans allowed him to attend to his own private business in his off-hours. And this, he would grin, was his private business—doing what he could for France.

By the middle of March 1944 LaBrosse reported in his radio code to British intelligence that dozens of fliers and secret Allied agents were hidden around the Brittany countryside. Thus, on three March nights, there came again over the BBC the welcome message, "Good evening to everyone in the House of Alphonse. . . ." and, in separate groups, they were taken out.

Cautious and vigilant, the two Canadians nevertheless knew how to take risks. Soon after the Normandy invasion in June, they had to reach Brittany for an evacuation. Rail lines had been knocked out or commandeered entirely by German forces; so they started out on bicycles. In Rennes a German military policeman took Dumais' bicycle from him. Dumais signaled LaBrosse to keep moving and meant to flee himself on foot; then he thought better of it—boldness might arouse less suspicion than humility. He stormed into German military-police headquarters, shouting that he had been robbed.

"It is imperative that I be in St. Brieuc this evening," he roared at the commandant, "and you must get me there."

The commandant, fearing that he had a wealthy, influential French collaborator on his hands, provided a staff car. When LaBrosse pedaled wearily into St. Brieuc the next day, a grinning Dumais was waiting for him.

German records later indicated that the Gestapo never came really close to untangling and destroying the undercover operation. But apart from that early near-disaster in Paris, there were many very close shaves. Once in Guingamp, with the town full of Germans, two Nazi officers hammered at the door of a house and said that it was being requisitioned for their troops. The housewife pleaded that she already was rooming several weary railroad men and had no more beds. She was given an hour to clear the rooms. The hour gave her just enough time to get rid of several Allied airmen. In François Kerambrun's truck, they were rushed somewhere else.

On another occasion German shore batteries spotted the British motor gunboat No. 503 as she approached for a pickup, and opened fire. She escaped but returned hours later in darkness and completed the rendezvous. Just as dawn lit the area, the 503 slipped over the horizon with more "packages" for London. (Eventually, the 503 came to a tragic end, though not on a Bonaparte asssignment. Four days after Germany's surrender, she struck a mine in the North Sea and sank with all hands.)

Finally, the Germans themselves paid a hair-raising visit to the House of Alphonse. One night immediately after Dumais and café

owner Le Cornec had briefed a group of airmen and left the premises, a German patrol knocked on the door and instructed its inhabitants—Jean Gicquel and his family—to come out.

Instead of obeying, Gicquel slammed the door in their faces and hustled his ailing wife, his six-week-old daughter, and five airmen up to the attic. The Germans opened fire and in the confusion wounded one of their own men. They brought the injured man into the house to patch him up. Hiding in the attic, everyone lay motionless, ready for the fight to the death they were certain was coming. But the Germans, nervous and excited, unaccountably departed without searching upstairs. Gicquel and the pilots then slipped out of the house to a nearby wheat field, where they waited out the night. Next day Dumais and Le Cornec rounded them up and later got them out.

Eight times Bonaparte's men and women led Allied airmen and agents—Britons, Americans, Canadians, Free French, Belgians, Dutchmen, Poles—through that hazardous journey to the coast. When there were no more evacuations to be made by sea, the two Canadians fought in the Maquis around Plouha.

So tightly kept was the secret of Shelburne and Bonaparte that none of the *évadés,* as the escaped airmen came to call themselves, ever was able to learn that such a network existed. Most assumed they had just fallen in with a single escape operation. But years later one of them—Ralph Patton, a Buffalo, New York, businessman—tracked down the story while vacationing in France and learned that in seven months this network had rescued a total of 307 downed Allied airmen and secret agents. Bonaparte alone accounted for nearly half of the total. There had been eight trips by the British gunboat. Of all the escape networks on the European continent, Shelburne was the most successful in that it never lost a single "package." The only casualty was the House of Alphonse itself—the Germans, suspecting it to be a Resistance hideout, returned and burned it.

As a result of Ralph Patton's discovery, 50 of the American *évadés* gathered in Buffalo from all over the country one night in May 1964 to honor those who so willingly had risked death for them. On hand were Lucien Dumais, by then a Montreal businessman, and Maj. Raymond LaBrosse, a staff officer at the Collège Militaire Royal de St. Jean—Canada's bilingual military college. From Brittany, Guingamp's Resistance leader Mathurin Branchoux brought with him photographs of houses, people, and scenes the Americans and Canadians would readily recognize.

It was the only noisy rendezvous Operation Bonaparte ever had.

His leg shattered, the East German youth lay
in the "death strip," where Western guards could
not go. Yet without help he would die.

Incident at the
Border

By Lawrence Elliott

O N THE evening of December 31, 1969, in the East German border town of Meiningen, a boy of 17 named Bernd Geis sat in a café trying to hide his loneliness behind a glass of beer. Around him strangers sang and noisily toasted the coming year, but Bernd had no one to celebrate with and nothing to celebrate. The one person he wanted to be with this New Year's Eve was his older sister, Irene, who lived across the forbidden frontier in West Germany. His mother and father had both died within the past 18 months. He had come to Meiningen to be with his married brother, but the brother had no room for Bernd in his small apartment. So every day the husky, brooding boy worked at his job as a carpenter's apprentice, and every night he came home to an empty room in a boardinghouse.

Now, at around 8:30, suddenly moved by the special melancholy that comes from being alone in the midst of great gaiety, Bernd paid up and went outside. And in the cold white night he turned, not toward his lonely little room, but down the snow-packed road that led

to the demarcation line between the two Germanys. With no fore-thought, without regard for the fact that the price of failure was prison and possibly death, Bernd had impulsively decided to flee to the West. He had no political quarrel with the regime; he had grown up under communism. He simply wanted to see his sister.

Since the Berlin Wall went up in August 1961, all sorts of people, a few even younger than Bernd, have attempted the dangerous flight to freedom. So strong is the human urge to be free that thousands upon thousands of East Germans have risked everything to cross the ugly, unnatural barrier. They have tunneled beneath it, crashed the walls with trucks, and dared the guards with false papers. But for every one who has succeeded, nine have been turned back. And on the first day of the new year, Bernd Geis, equipped with nothing but his resolve, would become the first of an estimated 10,000 who would try to reach the West before 1970 ended. Of all these, only 901 would make it.

Bernd spent that night and the daylight hours of January 1 hiding in a barn. When it was dark again, he struck out across the fields, through the deep snow, toward the place where he imagined the border to be. He knew vaguely about the border fortifications, that there were mines and high fences, yet he had no plan except that he was going to climb or burrow or run to get across.

At 8 P.M. the frightened youth came upon the barbed wire. It stood starkly revealed in the light of a cold moon, not 50 feet away. Beyond were two higher fences of wire mesh. He stood there shivering, listening, weighing his fear against his loneliness. Then he shuffled ahead through the snow and lay down on his back and in a few minutes had worked his way under the barbed wire.

It seemed so incredibly easy. Where were the guards? Was this all there was to it? He rested on his knees, brushing snow from his shoulders, measuring the next fence with his eyes. It was probably 10 feet high, but he was sure he could climb it. Suddenly he was sure of everything, that he would make it safely, that he would soon be with Irene. Up over the wire mesh he went, already gauging the last fence, and plunged toward it with joy and wild confidence.

Then Bernd's luck ran out. He was inside the 20-yard zone known as the death strip, a belt of barren land implanted with contact mines. And as he pitched through the waist-deep snow, a shattering explosion flung him forward. When he looked back, he saw that his right boot was dangling from his leg by a few shreds of flesh and that his spurting blood was staining the snow.

At that moment, about 200 yards away, on a small road that once led to Meiningen but now dead-ended at the demarcation line, a patrol of West German border guards listened intently.

"What was that?" asked recruit Wolfgang Schmitt uneasily.

"One of their mines," answered Sgt. Rudolf Romeis. "Probably set off by the weight of the snow."

But even as he spoke, an unmistakable cry for help sailed up to them and hung a moment in the cold night. Then it came again, faint, anguished. Romeis slipped his submachine gun off his shoulder and snapped at Schmitt, "You stay with the car." To the third man, Pvt. Alois Reis, he said, "Let's go!"

They struck out through a small wood that ran parallel to the demarcation line, marked on the Western side only by a series of intermittent stakes. The cries continued, drawing Romeis and Reis closer, until they came opposite the dark shape that lay crumpled in the death strip 150 feet away, just inside the wire fence.

"Hello!" Romeis called. "Who are you? What's the matter?"

And Bernd cried out, "Help! My foot is blown off. I'm bleeding very badly. I'm from Meiningen. My name's Bernd Geis. I'm trying to get away. Please help me!"

Sergeant Romeis swore aloud. At 22, he was a veteran of the federal border guards and was well aware that the pathetic souls on the far side of the fence were all too often pursued, shot at, and hauled back into East Germany. Now the life of one such human depended on him. Yet his orders were inflexible: Anyone who reached the Western side was to be protected and given every assistance; but none of his men was ever to set foot across the line of stakes that marked the actual boundary of East Germany. The Vopos—the East German guards—would need no further invitation to open fire. And as with every confrontation between East and West, this would have the potential to explode beyond a random exchange of shots.

"Listen," he called, "take your belt off and tie it around your thigh, tightly. That will stop the bleeding. Can you do that?"

"I've done that," came the reply. "But can't you help me?"

"We're going to try." He turned to Reis: "Stay here. Keep talking to him. I'm going to call headquarters."

He ran for the patrol car. It was equipped with a two-way radio, and soon, as Schmitt and a Bavarian border policeman, Paul Havlena, edged close to hear, he was detailing the situation to the duty officer at his post at Oerlenbach, 30 miles away.

"Any reaction from the Vopos?" asked the officer.

"No, sir. I think they must be celebrating New Year's. Can't we go in and get the fellow out? He won't last long in this cold."

"I can't make that decision," was the reply. "I'll contact the divisional commandant and call you back."

It would be a long time before he did. For the implications of such a confrontation were understood at every level of command, and the commandant knew that if he gave a go-ahead order, he would be held accountable. At 9 P.M. he put in an emergency call to the commanding general in Munich.

Meanwhile, Sergeant Romeis was shooting flares into the sky, turning it ghostly white. He had told Bernd that the Vopos would see them and either come to get him out or let the West Germans across the border tend to his foot. But Romeis was not as hopeful as he sounded: He had never known the Vopos to give anyone on the Western side permission to help an escapee, no matter how badly wounded. And it would take hours before the Vopos themselves could blast a safe path through the mine field. But he didn't know what else to do and kept firing flares while calling encouragement to the hurt boy. There was no response from the darkness beyond the death strip.

About 25 minutes had passed since Bernd had stepped on the mine. He lay so close to the wire fence that if he had had the strength to crawl another arm's length he could have touched it. It constituted the boundary of his world now, locking him inside with his mangled foot and the excruciating pain and the cold. He knew that without someone's help he would soon die. The pain was so bad that he began to think it would be better to close his eyes and let the cold take him.

"Please help me," he called, then put his head down on his arm.

Later, Sergeant Romeis would say: "I think that's what did it—he looked like he was giving up. Nothing we'd said to him about our orders meant a thing. All he understood was that he was dying and we were just standing there, 50 yards away."

Still there was no word from headquarters. "The hell with it!" Romeis suddenly said to Reis. "I'm going in. Are you with me?"

Without hesitation Reis replied, "Right."

Romeis ran back to the patrol car and got an ax. "We're going after him," he told Schmitt. "You cover us from here. If they start shooting, use the machine gun."

Schmitt took a deep breath: "Will they really shoot?"

"If they see us, you can count on it."

Romeis was aware that even if they got Bernd out they could all be disciplined for disobeying orders. But he didn't hesitate. Instructing Havlena, the civilian policeman, to stay where he was, Romeis stepped out beyond the line of stakes and crept across the no-man's-land to the wire fence. Reis waited at the demarcation line.

"Bernd," Romeis whispered, "we're going to get you out."

And Bernd, freezing and at the very limit of his resources, managed an exhausted, "Thank you."

Romeis tried first to pry up the wire mesh with the ax. When that didn't work, he hacked at it until, with ever more desperate swings, he broke the ax handle off. For an agonized moment he lay in the snow, breathing hard, unable to think of anything more to do. Then he bolted up and dashed back to where Reis stood: "The jack! Come on! Let's go back and get the jack!"

They ran for the patrol car, got the jack, then made their way back to where Bernd lay. They scooped snow out from under the fence and five minutes later implanted the metal extension tube of the auto jack under the mesh. Stroke by stroke, they pried the fence up. Romeis held up the mesh with his knee while Reis slithered under and began dragging Bernd through. Then they had him and hefted him up, Reis grabbing him under the armpits, Romeis by the legs. A couple of minutes later they were joined by Havlena who tried to hold the almost severed foot steady. Now, as they began slogging and staggering toward the woods, the 150 feet seemed interminable. But still there was no movement from the East, not a sound.

It was only when they reached the woods, just as they crossed over the demarcation line, that Schmitt came racing up: "It's okay, Sergeant! They just called in—the general says it's okay to get him out!"

Romeis smiled wanly. "Welcome to West Germany, Bernd," he said. "And happy New Year."

They took him directly to the hospital in Mellrichstadt, where the shattered foot was amputated at once. Two days later Irene was at his bedside. Although he was hospitalized for some time, by the summer he was settled in her house in Gelsenkirchen, learning to use an artificial foot. Later when he had a job in a chemical plant, Bernd said, "I would give the other foot, gladly, to be here."

As for the soldiers, Romeis, Reis, and Schmitt, far from being punished, they were all promoted and taken to Bonn for a special commendation by Interior Minister Hans-Dietrich Genscher for acting "as human beings in an emergency that was above the law."

But closed borders only rarely produce happy endings. Barely a year after Bernd's escape, and not far away, another young man stepped on a contact mine; although he managed to get across the border, he bled to death before help came.

This is a frank and brutal account of 15 years spent among the living dead at the penal colony in French Guiana—and of one prisoner's final escape after many failures.

Dry Guillotine

By *René Belbenoit*
Foreword by William LaVarre
Fellow, The Royal Geographical Society

IN MAY 1935 while I was on the British island of Trinidad, a slender waterlogged Indian canoe put in from the sea, carrying six starved Frenchmen—fugitives from the penal colony of French Guiana. After hearing their story, the officer of the port declared: "I am not going to turn these poor men over to the French consul. French Guiana is a plague on the face of civilization!"

Five of the six fugitives were big, powerful men—men of brute strength, brute living, and brute mentality. The sixth, in contrast, was astoundingly small, less than five feet, and weighed under 90 pounds. He had only one possession, an oilcloth-covered package containing 30 pounds of closely written manuscript—the record of 15 years of prison colony life, the most amazing document I had ever seen.

"Why don't you let me send your manuscript safely to the United States to a publisher?" I asked. "It's impossible for you to actually gain permanent freedom. You'll be lost at sea or arrested and sent back to Guiana. You must understand that."

But he refused, and I thought that I would never see him again, that his story would be lost. I was mistaken. René Belbenoit finally reached the United States, with his book, *Dry Guillotine*.

IN 1920, WHEN I WAS 21 years old, I was sentenced to eight years at hard labor in the penal colony in French Guiana, for theft.

The convict ship on which I sailed carried about 680 convicts, herded into steel cages in the hold. Each cage contained between 80 and 90 convicts, with hardly one square yard for each pair of feet.

To prevent mass rebellion, the cage ceilings had openings through which scalding live steam could be injected. Unruly convicts were sent to the hot cells, sheet-iron cubicles next to the boilers, too small for a man to straighten up in.

In the cages conversation turned naturally to Guiana and escapes.

Some prisoners had small maps of South America torn from atlases and spent their time studying these minutely, measuring distances and learning names of rivers and towns in the countries that surround Guiana, trying to pronounce words that a few months ago did not exist for them: Paramaribo, Venezuela, Orinoco, Oyapoc.

Cliques formed quickly. There was one distinct group, composed of the *forts-à-bras* ("strongarms"), the much-tattooed men who had lived many years in the military prisons in Africa and knew all the tricks. From the beginning they had tobacco and other comforts, and they quickly organized gambling games. Their lips turned suddenly into snarls, vomiting obscenities, and their bulging muscles made them the relentless bullies of the cage. During the night they stole anything they could and sold their loot to the sailors, who dropped a weighted line from the deck to the privy porthole. Each parcel of stolen goods brought five to six packages of tobacco.

One day two convicts who had long been enemies started fighting with knives made by sharpening spoon handles on the cement floor. They were out to kill each other.

We all lined ourselves up against the bars to hide the fight from the guards, and the *forts-à-bras* began singing to drown any cries of the struggling men. Suddenly, one of the fighters slipped, and the other was preparing to finish him off when the guards, becoming suspicious, entered the cage, revolvers in hand. The blood-soaked loser was taken to the infirmary, and his adversary was placed in a hot cell for the rest of the voyage.

As we reached the tropics, the heat and lack of air in the cage became terrible. Three-fourths of the men wore nothing but towels about their waists. The water became contaminated, and the sailors poured permanganate into it so it would be drinkable. Twice a day we were given a collective shower; the sailors came down into the hold with hoses and soused the steaming men with fresh salt water. It was a delicious relief.

One morning the shore appeared, and a few hours later we were being marched off the landing. A flock of blacks stood along the shore and lined our path. The black women laughed freely and gesticulated in our direction. But the many white men who were also there—*libérés* who had served their prison sentences but were still condemned to live in French Guiana—presented a miserable front. Mostly barefoot, all shabbily dressed, they seemed too wretched to be excited by our arrival.

We were taken to St.-Laurent Camp and locked into barracks in groups of 60. Presently, five men came up to the barred windows.

"Tobacco?" they whispered. "Coffee! Bananas!"

"But how are we to pay?" I asked. "I have no money!"

"With your clothes," they answered, and then quoted prices. A pair of pants was worth 40 sous; a blouse, 30 sous; a blanket, 5 francs.

One new arrival sold a pair of trousers, another a blouse. And that night everybody had his cigarettes—and a few bananas.

On the second morning after our arrival, the commandant of the penitentiary assembled everybody in the compound and warned us against trying to escape.

"Here in Guiana you enjoy great liberty," he said, "and you can try to escape whenever you like. But we have two constantly watching guardians: the jungle and the sea. I know that in less than 15 days many of you will be off into the jungle; I know also that these will return soon, and I'll see them in the cells or in the hospital, except for those who are lying as skeletons picked clean by ants."

Then came the medical inspection. Nearly all, sick or well, were pronounced capable of any kind of work. But when I showed the doctor my title to a war pension, he classed me for light work. This saved me later from many a misery.

For I discovered that all convicts who are pronounced fit—whether young or old and regardless of their former occupations—are set to the same tasks. Consequently, in that damp, hostile climate, of some 700 that arrive annually, 400 die in the first year. Hence the total number of prisoners remains fairly constant. When a convoy comes, the total rises to 3,500; the hospital overflows, some disappear in the jungle, and in the 12 months before the next shipload arrives, the count has dropped again to 2,800. The policy of the administration is to kill, not to reclaim.

Within six months after they arrive, most of the convicts are reduced to a life little better than that of primitive beasts. They must go barefoot, for the wooden shoes issued—over the protests of many governors—are unsuitable for the environment. Underclothes and socks have been sold. The men do not even wash themselves in the morning, for the water in the barracks is never plentiful.

Each convict keeps his few francs and other valuables in a hollow cylinder about three inches long, made of aluminum or other noncorrosive metal, which is concealed by inserting it into the anus.

The prisoner must be equipped with a strong constitution to resist such conditions. I was small, physically weak, unused to hardship— how long, I wondered, would I be able to last?

Eight days after our arrival, I and a dozen other men were sent to Camp Nouveau, 14 miles inland. To our utter amazement, we were shown the path and left alone to walk unescorted through the jungle!

On the trail we encountered a group of half-naked men carrying axes. Seeing we were new, they stopped for a moment. They had finished their set task of felling lumber and told us they were going back to camp for their nets. Then they would go into the forest again and catch butterflies whose wings, sold to curio dealers in Cayenne, brought in a small amount of money.

AT CAMP NOUVEAU, a thatch-covered barracks set in a clearing, the bookkeeper registered our names and numbers and then indicated our bunks—which were hard, bare boards. At dawn I was assigned to the workshop where wide straw hats are made. With a pile of *awara* palm fiber I had to plait a braid 20 yards long each day. I usually started work before daylight and had my task finished by 10 o'clock. Then I went into the jungle where I could think things out.

At Camp Nouveau many convicts had vainly tried to escape through the Dutch colony across the Maroni River. I learned from them all the details of the route and promised myself that I too would escape, though all of them tried to convince me that it was sheer folly to attempt it.

Nevertheless, when presently I made friends with a young convict who was also anxious to escape, we agreed to pool the little money he had with my information and try together. Slipping out of camp, we boarded a raft we had secreted on the creek and let it drift down the current. We had half a dozen lumps of hard bread, some tins of sardines and condensed milk, and a bottle filled with matches, collected one at a time.

When night came, we were afraid to make a fire for fear of pursuit. Mosquitoes buzzed about us by the thousands, and our faces became swollen from the maddening bites.

After many hours of struggle with the treacherous currents of the Maroni, we succeeded in reaching the Dutch bank, a few hundred yards below Albina. Then, fumbling around for a trail through the jungle, we foolishly came out into a clearing where a group of Carib Indians were at work. They immediately started toward us, brandishing shotguns and machetes.

We gave them the little money we had, hoping to buy them off, but they held their guns on us and, intent on collecting the reward for escaped prisoners, took us to the Dutch authorities. The next day a launch transported us back to French territory, where we were both locked in the blockhouse.

There are four disciplinary blockhouses at St.-Laurent, usually containing about 250 convicts. Of the 40 men in my blockhouse the majority were in for *évasion* ("escape") and had been brought back from British or Dutch Guiana. They had sold all they possessed for tobacco, and not one of them had any clothes. A few had a piece of rag wrapped around their loins. The heat was stifling, for the only air entered through six heavily barred small openings about 12 feet above the floor. At night we slept with our heads to the wall and one ankle in an iron lock. The irons clanked and rattled incessantly.

The temper of these men is terrible. Without occupation, with no money for tobacco or extra food, and crazed by the unbearable stench and heat, their misery is abject. When a newcomer comes in and they discover he has money, if he is weak, he is soon plundered. If he complains, he is apt to be murdered.

The penalty for *évasion* is usually solitary confinement for periods ranging from six months to five years. However, since it was my first attempt, I was given only 60 days. After serving my time, I was sent back to Camp Nouveau, under guard, and put to work in the jungle clearings where they were trying to grow vegetables. The first day I was terribly bitten by huge black ants, and the next morning I was so swollen and feverish that I reported sick.

The doctor refused to send me to the infirmary, and I, for my part, refused to go out to work. For this insubordination I was sentenced to 65 days in the cells—where I was most certainly better off than at work in the clearings, even though I was kept in irons and put on dry bread for two days out of three.

When I was finally released from the cells, I was transferred to the infirmary at St.-Laurent as an attendant. Here, for the first time, I had an opportunity to acquire a *débrouille*—the chance to earn some money, which is coveted by all convicts. There was a chestnut tree near the infirmary, and I began a trade in chestnuts, which I roasted on a piece of tin and sold at two sous for 20.

Every prisoner who can arrange it has his *débrouille*, his graft. One sells coffee, at four sous, made from leftovers from the kitchen. A second nightly spreads a blanket for *la marseillaise*, a form of baccarat, and takes one-tenth of the winnings. A third has a box of candy on the blanket, and the players drop two sous into it and munch a piece while they sit absorbed in the gambling. The barracks-keeper economizes on the main lamp and sells the surplus oil to the convicts for their own lamps. The hospital attendant weakens the milk diet prescribed for the dying (made by mixing water and condensed milk) and sells the extra tins of condensed milk. It is his *débrouille*.

Little by little my capital increased, and when I had got together a sufficiency of clothes, I again planned to escape. For always existence in the prison colony holds but two alternatives: escape or die. This time, I told myself, I would not fail!

The night before Christmas, when the guards were already beginning to celebrate noisily, nine of us, sworn to the last man to gain liberty or die, slunk through the silent jungle to the creek where a canoe had been hidden. We quickly pushed off downstream.

The canoe was 30 feet long, with a sail fashioned from old trousers and hammocks. It was stocked with a supply of coffee, rice, tapioca, condensed milk, dried beef, and bananas. Our water tank was a privy barrel we had submerged in the creek for several days to remove its odor—after burning it out with fire and tar.

We reached the Maroni and three hours later had traveled the 13 miles down to the Atlantic. There we set the sail and were soon out upon the open sea. Suddenly, we heard a sound like thunder. We were approaching the breakers!

Marseillais shook Basque, who had claimed to be a navigator, and shouted excitedly: "We're in danger, Basque! I don't know a thing about a boat. Take the steersman's paddle!"

Basque sat up. He began moaning and begged us to forgive him. He knew nothing about sailing, he confessed; he'd posed as a navigator just to get us to take him with us. He had hardly ended his excuses when without warning a huge roller crashed in on us from both sides. As a second roller and then a third struck us, the mast snapped and the sail fell down on us as we bailed for our lives.

When, by a miracle, we were able to steer the canoe to shore, our water supply was ruined. We had lost practically all our food. And hardly nine hours had gone by since we had left the camp.

No sooner had he set foot on the sand than Marseillais said to Basque: "Get going before it's too late," and he took his long knife out of his waistband.

I think the rest of us would have pardoned Basque and allowed him to stay with us, but we hung dejectedly in a circle and said nothing. Basque looked hard at the threatening knife and then without a word walked slowly away with hanging head into the jungle.

Without comment, we turned to our own problems. Obviously, we could not now continue by sea. Practically all our supplies had been

washed away. We agreed to rest until the next day and then set out
for Paramaribo through the jungle.

Next morning Basque returned to our camp, crying: "Everything
is flooded, I can't get through!"

In Marseillais' look I recognized Basque's death sentence. Then,
with a curse, Marseillais leaped and struck. There was a piercing
scream, and Basque sank to the ground. Marseillais dragged the body
to the water, where the tide would claim it.

After three days of tramping through miles of mud and tangles of

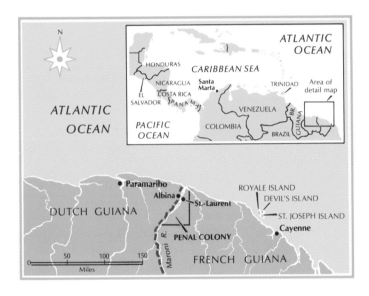

mangrove roots, we decided to get back to French Guiana as quickly
as possible. Our food was almost exhausted, but we knew that our
strength would last until we reached the Maroni River. There we
planned to spend several months catching butterflies and thus get
money for supplies for another escape. We had friends in the various
camps, on whom we thought we might depend to help us hide out.

Progress became easier now, for we emerged into higher ground.
Big Marcel and Marseillais were in the lead, slashing a trail with
machetes. I followed with three others, and a short distance behind us
were Gypsy and Robert.

Gypsy had a wooden leg, and this slowed him considerably; he fell
often on the rocks and had difficulty bending low to avoid the vines.
Robert and Gypsy had long been companions in the camp, and they

walked in the rear and helped each other when the need arose.

At the end of the second day, famished and tired, we made camp. Soon Gypsy came out of the trail and joined us. He was alone.

"Where's Robert?" Marseillais asked him.

Gypsy said that Robert had lagged behind because he was sick. He'd be along presently.

An hour went by. Robert still did not come.

So Marseillais decided to go and look for him. He traced back almost a mile. As he was about to give up and turn back, he discovered Robert's still-warm body concealed under hastily cut branches beside the trail. The back of his skull had been split by a terrific blow. Close at hand lay Robert's food bag. It was empty. Gypsy had murdered his little friend for a few mouthfuls of tapioca and milk!

Marseillais returned to camp and told us he had found no trace of Robert. But secretly he told Big Marcel what he had found. Gypsy asked innocently what Marseillais thought could have happened.

"He was my friend!" Gypsy almost cried. "My *good* friend!"

Marseillais wouldn't answer him. He busied himself getting the camp in shape, hacking palm leaves with his machete, approaching nearer and nearer to Gypsy.

Suddenly, Marseillais passed behind him, and Gypsy, suspicious, turned his head to keep an eye on him. At that instant Big Marcel leaped on him—and planted a long knife squarely in his heart!

Gypsy crumpled to the ground. I remember even now, many years later, every detail of the horrible scene that followed.

It was Dédé, the brother of Big Marcel, who proposed it. "We ought to roast his leg," he said.

Marseillais agreed. "He was but a beast—and beasts can be eaten!" The others approved. Half an hour later Gypsy's liver, skewered on a stick, was grilling over the fire—which, ironically enough, had been kindled with Gypsy's wooden leg. And Marseillais chopped off Gypsy's good leg and placed it on the coals to broil.

Then they ate—and I ate too, since I dared not incur their dislike and become an outcast from the group.

That night there was no talk—not even the most cynical, I believe, could get away from the horrible events of the day. Three bodies lay now in the trail of our escape.

Two days later we reached an Indian village on the bank of the Maroni. Here we obtained food. But as we slept, after eating, the Indians reported us to the Dutch authorities. Soon four Dutch soldiers took us by surprise, pistols in hand.

Again I served time in the blockhouse, and then, classed as an incorrigible—or "inco"—was sent to Camp Charvein, where malaria and dysentery raged and where the other incos, toiling absolutely naked under clouds of mosquitoes, were little better than maddened animals. Fortunately, however, after 80 tormented days I was restored again to the normal life of the colony by a new director of the administration to whom I had sent a petition.

During subsequent years in French Guiana I attempted twice more, unsuccessfully, to escape. As punishment I was sent to Royale, one of three islands 10 miles off the mainland. (The other two are St. Joseph and Devil's Island—the latter, made famous by Alfred Dreyfus and other political prisoners, being usually confused by the general public with the entire prison colony.)

I served time in *La Case Rouge* on Royale, the Bloodstained Barrack, where the most vicious convicts in the entire prison colony were assigned. Each morning the guards take a look in the privy to make sure that a body is not sprawled there. It has happened hundreds of times—murder for vengeance or for robbery.

No outsiders are ever allowed on these islands, and very few people have visited them for other than official reasons. I suffered there beyond the power of telling. But I kept on living while all about me blood flowed and men died.

I spent time on the island of St. Joseph in solitary confinement, entombed in a dark cell. The convicts call it *la guillotine sèche* ("the dry guillotine"). At the bottom of a sunless pit the prisoner stays 23 hours out of each 24. He has no work, nothing to read, nothing to write on—nothing to occupy himself with. The only sounds he hears are those of the sea breaking on the rocks and the screams of the demented. Here sane men are deliberately reduced to raving idiots in order to discredit their reports to the press or to high French authorities of the abuses in French Guiana.

In November 1927, after I had been in the penal colony almost six years, I was transferred to Cayenne for the first time. I had now become an established convict, familiar with the ways of the prison colony. I had also come to understand the underhanded workings of the administration. I had seen convicts buy favored positions for 25 francs; I had seen unscrupulous officials sell the government clothes and blankets, so that the convicts had to wear rags for months; I had seen guards practice systematic and incredible rackets at the expense of the prisoners. And all this revolted me even more than did the vileness of the convicts, for it was a hideous advantage to take over

145

helpless men who had no friends and no possible means of redress.

To see Cayenne is to see the depths of human degeneration. Although it is the main city of one of the oldest possessions under the French flag, it is the capital of a colony without colonists.

Back in the reign of Napoleon the Third, when the penal colony was planted, it was thought that if the convicts were made to stay on after completing their sentences, they would marry and have children, and the colony would thus become settled by hard, strong men. For this reason, the accessory penalty of *doublage* ("doubling") was resorted to. A freed convict had to serve as a *libéré* a period of exile equal to his original sentence.

But nobody wanted to have anything to do with the freed convicts. The black women would not marry them. The colony's bad name discouraged enterprising citizens in France. And so, since the days when the penal system was established, the possession has gradually dwindled into a place where lawlessness, degeneration, poverty, and misery surpass that of any other colony in the world.

French Guiana is the camping ground of futility. The only development is the penal system. And the adjacent prospering colonies of Dutch and British Guiana struggle to keep the wave of penniless convict would-be colonizers out of their boundaries.

France has long realized that the plan is a failure: Each new governor tries to develop something or other; one tries coffee, another cattle, another cocoa. But there is no element of population to sustain such efforts, and all fail completely.

The population of the capital is about 11,000, including 700 convicts and 300 *libérés.* An astonishing amount of freedom is permitted here, and convicts overrun the town by day, returning at night to be locked in the penitentiary.

WHILE I WAS ON THE ISLANDS, I had written an account of actual conditions there and secretly sent the manuscript to the new administrator of the penal colony, Governor Siadous. This interested the governor in me, and when I was transferred to Cayenne, he gave me the special task of placing the archives of the colony in order.

So for months I worked among stacks of papers, books, articles, reports on convicts, accounts of the administration, lists of food supplies, clothing materials. I took notes lavishly. Thus I got the knowledge and documentation, the facts and figures, that have enabled me since to expose irrefutably the corruptness of that hell.

I admired Governor Siadous very much. In his two years in office he tried everything to better conditions. But he had no support from the corrupt penal administration. He was all that stood between me and the administration, and when he left the colony, I was sent back to Royale and spent the last three years of my stay in Guiana in solitary confinement. The many months of long-drawn-out loneliness closed in on me as I marked each day on the wall with my fingernail. And then, on November 3, 1934, nearly 15 years after I had been sent to Guiana, a key turned in the rusty lock, and a guard handed me a document—which I could scarcely read, my eyes were so dimmed by my dark cell. I was a *libéré*—a free convict!

A *free* convict! Free to live like a homeless mongrel dog. Free to live in the jungle but condemned to the colony for the rest of my life and barred from Cayenne for 10 years.

I adopted the only trade by which a *libéré* can keep in funds. Living in a jungle hut, I caught butterflies, I made odds and ends and toys out of rubber that I collected in the forest, and these I sold to the curio dealers of the town. I managed to have a parrot to roast for Christmas—shot with a bow and arrow. I celebrated New Year's Eve over a boiled armadillo, dug out of its hole with a broken pickax salvaged from an old dump. I had no teeth left, but that did not bother me, for I rarely had anything that needed chewing.

Money! Money was what I needed—to buy an escape from this living hell. A hundred francs would buy an Indian canoe. Fifty francs would buy food for two weeks at sea.

One day as I was thus brooding in St.-Laurent, a sun-helmeted tourist beckoned to me.

"Where can I find a prisoner who speaks English?" he asked in schoolboy French.

"I speak a little English," I said.

"I want to find a prisoner named Belbenoit," he said in English. "The man about whom Blair Niles wrote her book, *Condemned to Devil's Island.*" (I had at one time sold her several manuscripts, when she had visited French Guiana, on which she had based a novel.)

I laughed for the first time in years. "I am Belbenoit!"

He explained that he was an executive of an American motion-picture company. They planned a film story about Devil's Island—one that would feature a dramatic escape. He had flown down to study the colony at first hand. Would I give him information? If a prisoner tried to escape, how would he do it?

I spent the whole night answering his questions, making rough drawings of prison cells and punishment racks, describing my three attempts to escape through the jungle, answering every question while he took a bookful of notes. By dawn he had enough. The airplane in which he had arrived soon was but a speck in the Caribbean sky. But in my hands he had left $200! The money to escape!

"This time I'll make it!" I whispered.

I searched the penal colony like a hawk—for men whose plight was most terrible and whose physical aid would be greatest. At last I selected five convicts (one a sailor).

At 6 o'clock on the night of March 2, 1935, we met stealthily and noiselessly made our way to Serpent Creek, where a Chinaman had promised to hide a boat for us. It proved to be only half the size of the craft I had bargained for—a dugout canoe barely three feet wide. The provisions contained less than half of the things agreed upon before I had passed my cash to the Chinaman. I felt as though my escape had failed before it had begun.

But something told me not to turn back. I got into the canoe, urged the others to take their places, and soon we were paddling noiselessly down the river. At the mouth we hoisted our patchwork sail. Chifflot, our navigator, took the homemade tiller. The long slender canoe began to dance over the water.

Men in their right senses would never have gone out in such a craft—but we were driven by a quite insane desire to seek freedom at any price. The night passed all too slowly. Morning found us far out at sea, unpursued.

I lighted some charcoal in a kerosene tin, and strong tea soon revived us. I would have to stretch out the Chinaman's skimpy food supply very thin. But no one, during the first day, grumbled. We all talked with nervous gaiety.

The third night found us not such good friends. The sun and glare of the open sea and the soaking of the salt spray made us miserable. Cramped for 50 long hours against each other, we had talked ourselves out of hopefulness—and then everyone began to find fault. A turbulent sea arose, and we had all we could do to keep from being swamped. We did not even attempt to keep a course. A mighty wave washed the compass from my hands, and not a star was to be seen.

When at last dawn came, we were drenched, stiff, hungry, thirsty, and sick at heart. I dipped some water out of the keg—and discovered that salt water had got in. I mixed it with condensed milk, but my companions said it tasted terrible.

"We'd better try to reach the mainland!" Dadar said. "I'd rather take a chance on the jungle—there's at least plenty of water to drink!"

"We've only been gone three days!" I said. "I told you when we started that I would not turn back. If we reach Trinidad, we are safe. If we land anywhere on the mainland, we will be turned over to a French consul." Thus we quarreled all day long, and the following days and nights were nightmares.

"Blast it!" Bébert in the bow of the canoe snarled. "Change the course! I've had enough of this. I'm going to land on the coast and take my chance!"

"Stop!" I yelled at Dadar who had begun crawling toward the sail

sheet. I reached into my shirt and drew out a small pistol I had obtained for just such a desperate crisis. I am a very little man. I should have been no match for any of my companions in physical strength. But I had made up my mind to turn neither to right nor left. The five big men glowered at me.

"Rush me if you like," I said. "Here are six bullets—and I will kill each one of you if you insist."

"Put the sail over!" Bébert shouted to Chifflot. At the same instant Dadar sprang up and tried to snatch my gun. Before I could fire, Dadar had slipped and fallen against Chifflot, and both of them tumbled against the gunwale.

"Look over there!" Casquette yelled suddenly. "It's land!"

The others stood up and looked, but, thinking it was a trick to get me off guard, I didn't budge. They couldn't fool me that easily.

"It's Trinidad! Come, Belbenoit, and see for yourself!" Cautiously, I tried to get a clear view without risking a sudden onslaught. And as we crested a whitecap, I saw that they were not trying to outwit me. There, against the horizon, were high, green mountains.

The sight wiped out all animosity. We all shouted joyously.

A few hours later, after 14 days at sea, the canoe shot up on the glistening white beach. My companions tried to leap ashore, but they were so weak that they stumbled and sprawled on the sand.

In a thatched hut nearby we found a big kettle full of rice and salt fish. We dug our hands into it and ate like wolves, then rolled over and fell into an exhausted sleep.

When we awoke we made our way to a little hamlet. The authorities listened with sympathy to our story—the British hate French Guiana as a blot on civilization. They fed us well, allowed us to rest, and presented us with a new boat. A recent Trinidad law allows all fugitives from French Guiana 24 days on the island and a means of continuing their escape.

On June 10 a British Navy launch towed our boat, amply supplied with food, out to sea. Then we were cut loose and on our way. Ahead lay the other islands of the British West Indies—stepping-stones to freedom as we headed northward for Miami.

As one day followed another, we seemed to be making good headway, but saw no land at all. Six days finally passed before we admitted we were lost.

Sixteen days after leaving Trinidad, the sea threw us up on a long barren stretch of coast, shooting us with express-train speed through the rough surf. Before we could make any effort to save ourselves, we crashed on the beach, completely wrecking our boat. We rescued only our remaining food and personal effects.

We built a fire on the beach and prepared dinner. Before we had time to eat it, a group of Indians—naked, but armed with bows and arrows and spears—came up and began inspecting our rescued supplies. When we tried to stop them, they became menacing, and at last they took everything we had, even our clothing. One of them got hold of an oilcloth package containing my Devil's Island journals, written during 15 years of imprisonment. I grabbed the package and opened it hastily to show him that it contained only papers. He gave it back to me with a humorous grimace.

The Indians disappeared behind the dunes. They were, I found out later, the Cactus Eaters, savages of the coastal desert of Colombia.

So, all of us naked and armed with only a machete that we salvaged after the Indians left, we started over the hot sand.

For four days we saw no human being as we skirted the jungle shore. We caught some fish and frogs by spearing them with sharply pointed sticks. We made a fire by rubbing dried sticks for more than an hour and carried coals in a large seashell to start new ones. We were all covered with festering insect bites. Our feet were cut and very sore. But happily we had not, as I feared, started to quarrel. Naked, we kept together out of pure fright.

At sunset of the third day we came to a long grass hut, in front of which some very old nets were drying. The fishermen were away, but we saw a large sea turtle and cooked and ate chunks of the fat meat and then climbed up into the rafters eagerly hoping to find clothes. There was not a single pair of pants or a shirt—only seven old Mother Hubbards of cheap printed calico.

"Well, a dress is better than nothing!" Bébert said as he began to twist into one.

Soon we all wore petticoats. Clothed, we found that the insects bothered us less.

Next day, however, we were discovered by a squad of Colombian soldiers. With our bearded faces, we were an astounding sight.

"We must take them to show the general," the soldiers exclaimed. "Nothing so funny has happened in years."

In an hour we reached a little town—the Colombian coast town of Santa Marta—and were taken to the barracks. The general gave us clothes, food, and medicine, but he also notified the French consul.

The next day we were behind the bars of the high-walled military prison—waiting for a French boat to take us back to Guiana. Our desperate gamble had been lost!

Under this terrible disppointment my companions began bitterly to find fault with one another, and soon a bloody fight broke out. The noise of our combat brought guards. Mysteriously, I was picked out and locked up in a solitary cell. Then, and this is hard to believe unless you know the South Americans, the prison adjutant came to my cell with some paper and pencils and said: "Belbenoit, we are going to let you escape. Your friends are a different type of fugitive; they were convicted for far more serious crimes. We've checked up on you. Spend the day writing articles for *La Prensa*. The editor will pay you for them tomorrow afternoon. At night you will find your cell door open. Bon voyage!"

All day long I wrote about different phases of the French penal administration. In the late afternoon Don Paez Reyna, the editor, came into my cell. He read what I had written and handed me a roll of bills. Some hours later I went to the door and cautiously turned the knob—the door opened. And at the end of the building I found the outside gate ajar.

Later I learned that my companions were shipped back to the dry guillotine. Of all the men who escaped with me, I alone was free!

Mind often wins over matter. I know that only one thing brought me through the terrible days that followed. It was not my muscles, for I am very weak. It was not my knowledge of the jungle or of the sea, for I had none. It was not my experience in dealing with primitive natives, for the hostile tribes I met in the coastal wilds of Colombia were as strange to me as they would have been to you. The one thing that brought me through was just this: I kept repeating over and over, "I *will* reach the United States."

When my supplies were exhausted, I obtained food from the Indians by telling them that I would pay two pesos each for butterflies—and then sneaked out of their villages at midnight to steal a canoe in which to continue up the coast. I repeated this technique a dozen times and stole as many canoes. Food hardly mattered to me anymore. My days of struggle at sea hardly mattered. Nothing mattered en route, if only I was making progress toward the United States.

In the jungles of Panama I spent several months with a friendly tribe of Indians and snared a large collection of butterflies that I later sold to a curio shop in Panama City. With this stake, and always eluding passport and identification inspection, I worked my way up through Costa Rica, Nicaragua, Honduras, and into El Salvador.

There, at the little port of La Libertad, I found a freighter loading cargo. It was northward bound, I was told. I managed to go aboard unobserved and crawled through a trapdoor into a dark room packed with coils of hawsers and wire cables. There I lay until the ship's engines started turning.

I SPENT HOUR AFTER HOUR in the black hold until I thought at least two days must have passed. The little food I had with me was finished. I was very thirsty. I decided to go on deck, if it were night, and look for food and water. I climbed the ladder and raised the trapdoor. It *was* night. Only two yards in front of me was a big dish of food—left for a dog. Beside it was a tin pan of water. The dog was playing with a ball far down the deck. I crept out, drank the water, and took the food back to my hideout.

I did not know how many days went by, for I lived in complete darkness. Twice I was hungry enough to sneak up to the deck and steal the dog's food and water. Then I heard the ship's whistle blow. We were arriving somewhere. I pushed up the trapdoor and climbed out into broad daylight. We were alongside a dock, in what I thought must be some Mexican port. At the foot of the gangplank two men in uniform were stopping each sailor who left the ship. I noticed that they only frisked the sailors. They didn't ask for identification papers.

I decided to risk everything on one lone play. An officer was going ashore; I hurried along the deck and went down the ship's gangplank behind him. The uniformed men greeted the officer cordially—in English! I opened my only possession, the bundle of manuscript, as a signal for them to search me. One of them mechanically felt my pockets and motioned me to pass on. I walked ashore.

From some laborers I learned that I was in California and that it was Tuesday. I had been in the hawser room seven days and nights.

I walked on with a springing step. I was terribly emaciated. I had no teeth. I had one pair of cotton pants. One cotton shirt. One hand-made cotton coat. A pair of ragged shoes. That was all I possessed. But I was no longer afraid. For after 22 months of almost unbelievable trials, I had escaped from the hell of French Guiana to the safety of the United States.

I entered the outskirts of Los Angeles as happy as a lark.

René Belbenoit remained in the United States on a temporary visa until 1941, when he was deported to Central America as an illegal immigrant. Determined to live in the United States, Belbenoit headed north again, swam the Rio Grande, and then reentered the country near Brownsville, Texas. He was finally, after years of legal battles, granted U.S. citizenship in 1956.

Belbenoit married and had a son. He became the owner of a clothing store in Lucerne Valley, California. He died from a heart attack on February 26, 1959, at the age of 59.

Belbenoit was born in Paris, France, and from the age of 12 he lived without parental guidance, holding such jobs as errand boy, dishwasher, valet. Convicted of stealing pearls from an employer, he was sentenced to hard labor in the prisons of French Guiana.

Belbenoit's Dry Guillotine, *published in 1938, was a best-seller and was translated into many languages. It and a subsequent book,* Hell on Trial, *are credited with playing a major role in bringing about the abolition of the French penal colony.*

The getaway was from a deserted Cuban beach under cover of night. Seven humans crowded aboard a raft made from inflated tire tubes. Their destination was the United States, many ocean miles away.

Escape From Cuba

By Joseph P. Blank

THE STORM came to an end during the darkness of early morning. Antonio Vigo Cancio was afraid to guess how far the wild north wind might have blown them back toward Cuba. It was the sixth day of their attempted escape from the Castro regime, and their raft of six patched inner tubes, roped together, was looking flimsier than ever. Then, at dawn, came the appalling sight: In the distance the seven refugees detected the faint outline of the mountaintops of Cuba, perhaps 20 miles away.

Antonio tried his best to think. Nothing was left of their rations but a half-dozen portions of water and two small cans of condensed milk. Should they go back to Cuba, land at night, try to find water, and set out again? Should they chance being caught and clapped in prison? He decided against it. Veneranda, his wife, holding their baby, read the decision in Antonio's eyes.

"You men pick up those paddles," she said. "Let's get going."

Early in the Cuban revolution, Antonio had hoped that Castro

meant democracy. By 1960 he knew that Cuba had only exchanged one dictatorship for another. He became involved in a conspiracy to overthrow the government. Caught with explosives in his possession, he was sentenced to 30 years in prison. After two attempted escapes had cost him months in solitary confinement, he decided to become a model prisoner in the hope of earning a reduced sentence. In December 1969, after serving nine years, he was paroled.

On release, Antonio was ordered to a job as a truck driver with a federal agency that employed ex-prisoners and closely observed their behavior. After working 25 days, living in a barracks with other parolees, he was permitted to spend five days with his family.

"We can't live like this, always watched," he said to Veneranda. "We have no future here. We must leave." Veneranda agreed.

As a former political prisoner, Antonio wasn't eligible for the daily refugee airlift that went to Miami. The only alternative was an illegal trip across the Straits of Florida. Antonio began to consider the problem. He decided against attempting to steal or build a seagoing craft. That way he risked arrest before he even touched water. He had to find another way.

In April 1971, after parking his truck in his agency's garage one day, Antonio found himself staring at a big inner tube from a truck tire. *That* was it—a raft composed of inner tubes tied together and enclosed in a sheath stitched from burlap bags. A special advantage: The deflated tubes could be folded and hidden in a small space.

During the next few months Antonio stole six inner tubes from the garage. Two were in fair condition; the others had to be patched. Then he found four hardwood boards and shaped them into paddles with a machete. His wife collected food and burlap bags.

On August 17 Antonio and Veneranda assembled the raft while their two sons, 11-year-old Tony and 10-month-old Carlitos, looked on. Inflating the tubes by mouth took them an hour, and they felt as if their lungs were bursting. Antonio lashed the tubes into a six-by-nine-foot raft. After slipping the raft into the sheath of burlap sacks that Veneranda had stitched together, the couple bounced on the tubes to test the patches under pressure. Everything held.

A few days later Antonio began his monthly five-day leave. Checking the weather forecasts, he learned that no storms were expected along the northern coast of Cuba during the coming week. He estimated that it would take four to five days to reach the shipping lanes off Florida, where he hoped to be picked up by a passing cargo vessel or fishing boat.

He had his crew: Luis, his wife's brother; Silvio, her cousin; Julio, a friend of the family. He had a compass: a toylike giveaway that had come with a bottle of vermouth. Everything was ready.

On the afternoon of departure, young Tony asked his mother, who had been silent for hours, *"Mima,* are you thinking of the trip?" When she nodded, he said, "Well, only three things can happen. We'll get caught, which is the worst thing. Or we'll die, but we'll die as a family. Or we'll arrive safely, which will mean happiness."

She hugged him.

Shortly before 7 that evening a friend arrived in a truck. Antonio loaded it at a casual pace to avoid attracting attention, and the family climbed aboard. After picking up Luis, Silvio, and Julio, they drove to the launching site, a narrow, uninhabited stretch of sand called Hollywood Beach, about 25 miles east of Havana.

Silently, the men carried the equipment and supplies to the water's edge, then began blowing up the tubes. When, at last, the group climbed aboard, the raft sank lower in the water than Antonio had anticipated. As the men started paddling toward Key West, 90 miles to the north, everyone on the raft soon became wet to the waist.

Antonio had no charts, no open-sea experience. By day, he intended to navigate by compass; at night, by the North Star.

The four men, sitting cross-legged or with their legs dangling in the water, paddled rhythmically for six hours. Then Silvio and young Tony got violently seasick, and Julio's arms gave out. After 24 hours Antonio remained the only consistent paddler.

The refugees were now developing painful sores on their hips, thighs, and legs. The men suffered from continual friction with the burlap as they paddled, and Veneranda from her writhing, restless 28-pound baby. Her arms felt almost dead from trying to control and provide shade for the seemingly tireless infant.

At about noon on the third day a freighter hove into sight several miles away. "We're saved!" Silvio shouted.

"Wait!" Antonio ordered. "Get under the mosquito netting."

The raft's supplies included blue-tinted netting for camouflage, and now, as they floated haphazardly, Antonio stared hard at the freighter. When it plowed a few hundred yards closer, he spotted the red and white funnels that identified it as a Soviet vessel. For a long quarter hour the group cowered silently beneath the netting while the freighter slowly disappeared in the distance.

Later that night Antonio found that food and water were being consumed faster than expected, and he began rationing for all hands except the baby, Carlitos. He also discovered, to his dismay, that salt water had killed the flashlight batteries and ruinously corroded the mirror that he'd brought for flashing signals.

On the afternoon of the fifth day the sky darkened, and a brisk north wind began stirring up whitecaps. It was the kind of wind Antonio had secretly dreaded from the outset; the raft was now being inexorably blown back toward Cuba. The waves deepened, lightning flashed, and rain slashed down, ruining the remaining bread and sugar. Hour after hour the little group merely clung to the raft. And then, with the arrival of dawn, came the disheartening sight of the Cuban mountaintops.

Shortly after the decision against returning to the island for water was made, a good south wind sprang up to push the raft away from Cuba. The men paddled, rested, and paddled again. By the end of the day the rationed water for the adults was finished, though a little remained for the baby. Luis was shaking with fever.

With the next dawn came a cloudless blue sky, and soon the sun blazed down on them. They reached into the water for seaweed and chewed on the buds. Sometimes, in a tangled mass of seaweed, they found tiny, half-inch crustaceans, which they popped into their mouths, chewed once, and swallowed.

Antonio tried to conceal his anxiety about his wife. Her bloodshot eyes were sunken, her lips deeply cracked, her blouse virtually torn off her back by the baby's frenzied clawing as he screamed from thirst. The salt water had irritated the infant's skin, and he scratched himself until the blood ran.

Then, on the ninth day, there was a fearful change. Now the baby lay mercifully quiet—too quiet. Periodically, Veneranda shook him, or Antonio reached over to play with his hand. The infant would open his eyes, gaze vacantly for a moment, then return to sleep.

Except for Antonio, the crew was apathetic—thirst and weakness were destroying them. But Antonio firmly believed they were nearing their destination. Aircraft frequently passed across the sky six or eight miles to the east, and each time he pleadingly waved his paddle with a diaper tied to it.

Early on the 11th day Antonio was alerted by a change in the air. He smelled sweet water—somewhere to the east it was raining, and the wind was blowing rain clouds in their direction.

"It's going to rain!" he shouted exultantly. "Luis, you and Julio grab a plastic bag and catch water! When the rain starts, everybody turn your face up and catch water in your mouth."

Rain drenched them for about 10 minutes. No one spoke. Each was savoring the delicious luxury of fresh water. After the clouds passed, Veneranda filled an eight-ounce bottle for the baby and let him drink half of it. He screamed for more, but his mother set aside the remainder, knowing it should be reserved for the end of the day.

Although Antonio insisted that they had to be approaching the end of their terrible passage, the other men couldn't share his optimism. They had depended on his judgment for freedom. Now, in their shattered mental state, they blamed him for their despair.

During the night a rainless storm tossed the raft. Fearful of losing a passenger overboard, Antonio shouted, "Everybody awake! Use your paddle. Sit up straight." Then, around 4 A.M., the wind died, the waves grew shallow, and stars twinkled. Not too far away Antonio saw moving lights.

"That's a boat!" he cried. More lights peeped out of the night. "Boats! We're going to be saved! Everybody paddle!" The four men screamed for help, but their pleas went unheard.

"It doesn't matter," Antonio reassured them. "There are many boats out there. As soon as day comes, they'll see us."

The men somehow found strength and, as they paddled, suddenly out of the dark-gray dawn, about 200 yards away, loomed the gigantic shape of an oil tanker, the *Key Trader,* from Wilmington, Delaware. It moved slowly toward the refugees as Antonio shouted and waved a diaper. Then, with bells suddenly clanging and red lights flashing, the tanker came to a halt.

Antonio and Silvio paddled the raft to within 20 yards of the ship. A voice from the deck shouted in English, "Who are you?"

"We are Cubans," Antonio replied. "We have escaped. We've been at sea for 12 days."

A rope dropped from the tanker's deck. Antonio grabbed it and pulled alongside. On the raft the others were chattering hoarsely, for the most part incoherently, and trying to embrace one another. In a few minutes a flexible ladder was lowered from the deck. Veneranda touched her husband and said, "The baby."

He picked up Carlitos and, incredibly, climbed the ladder with the infant clutched in one arm. At the gunwale a sailor took the baby from him. Antonio was helped to the deck, where he collapsed.

Veneranda watched her husband and baby disappear into the safety of the ship. In her numb, near-unconscious condition, she wasn't capable of feeling joy or triumph. "We've gotten through," she murmured to herself. "We are there."

*The order of execution had been given. A grave large enough
to hold 18 bodies had been dug. It seemed that only a
miracle could save the Luxembourgers from sudden death—until the
Nazi corporal took matters into his own hands.*

The Doomed Prisoners

By Edwin Muller

FOR 15 YEARS CERTAIN people in the town of Differdange, Luxembourg, had been trying to find a certain German. They had a
score to settle with him.

They knew his name, Johann Punzel. They knew his serial number
in the German Army and the fact that he had been a member of the
Nazi Party. But until June 3, 1955, they had never caught up with him.

The thing that Punzel had done, the reason they were looking for
him, had happened in the spring of 1940. The war in Poland was
over, and the vast armies of Germany and the Western Allies faced
each other along the Maginot Line; Differdange lay between them.
But Luxembourg was neutral, and the townsmen of Differdange
hoped the German invasion would never take place.

Then at dawn on May 10, they were awakened by the roar of
planes. When they looked up, the sky was full of parachutes. The
Germans had come. Soon the French came too. Columns of their
cavalry rode out from the Maginot Line and occupied the town.

By the time the first shots were fired, the roads from Differdange
were jammed with fugitives. The HADIR steelworks, which employed 4,000 of the town's 15,000 inhabitants, closed down. But one
group of employees was called together: the 40-odd steelworkers who
doubled as a fire brigade. They were free to go, the plant manager
said, but shells might hit the plant and start fires. It was to the advantage of the company and the town that the property be preserved. He
called for volunteers to stay behind.

There was a moment of silence. Then Joseph Weiler, 50, a plant
foreman and chief of the brigade, stepped forward.

"I will stay," he said.

Fourteen others volunteered, among them Nicolas Wallers, an ambulance man of the company infirmary. Wallers' wife insisted on staying too. Someone, she said, would have to prepare food for the men. Later three more men joined the group, bringing the total number to 18 men, 1 woman.

They settled down in the air-raid shelter under the main office building. Through the thick walls they could hear the terrifying rattle of machine-gun fire and the crunch of exploding shells. The battle lasted two full days. Then, on the night of May 11, the French pulled out and the German paratroopers came pouring in, followed by tanks and artillery.

At first the Germans treated the firemen in a not-unfriendly way. There was work for them to do: cleaning up debris, burying dead animals, even putting out a few fires that broke out in houses where careless soldiers were billeted.

Then, after two weeks, there was a sudden change. On May 27 and 28, Differdange was bombarded heavily by the French from the Maginot Line. The fire was extraordinarily accurate. With uncanny precision the shells found the German ammunition dumps and the areas where tanks and other heavy equipment were camouflaged. A great amount of damage was done.

Late on the night of the 29th a detail of military police went to the air-raid shelter and kicked the sleeping firemen awake. They searched everybody in the room, including Mrs. Wallers. With detection equipment they checked all wires and electrical outlets in the room, and they tested the walls with hammers. At last they went away, but guards were posted around the plant. The firemen could no longer move about freely.

At intervals the bombardment continued. Three days later the military police came again to the steelworks and ordered the firemen to assemble in the street. In a column of twos they were marched past a place where soldiers were digging a big hole. The same horrible thought occurred to more than one of the firemen: The hole was big enough to hold 18 bodies.

Farther on they were halted at a cement wall next to a small garage and lined up. A lieutenant appeared, a hard-faced man with a dueling scar on one cheek. He walked slowly down the line of men, staring each one in the face. Then he spoke:

"We have established that one or more of you have sent signals to the enemy, enabling them to direct their fire. If the guilty person or persons do not confess, all of you will be shot."

The group was then locked in a small room at the rear of a garage. It had only one barred window to admit any light. The place was cold and the concrete floor damp.

Mrs. Wallers clung to her husband, sobbing uncontrollably. Some of the men also began to weep openly; others were on their knees, saying their prayers.

Weiler spoke up in a firm voice: "Has anyone anything to say about the charge that has been made?"

Nobody did. But some began hysterically accusing others. Weiler's voice cut through the discord: "Pull yourselves together. We can get out of this only if we stick together and face the Germans like men."

The hubbub subsided. Time dragged on. At last the door opened and the lieutenant appeared. "Are the guilty ready to confess?"

Silence.

"Very well. That means that the order of execution will be carried out in precisely one hour."

The lieutenant beckoned to a corporal, a blond, blue-eyed man of some 30 years of age.

"Corporal Punzel, you will take over the custody of these men until their execution. When the hour has passed, they are to be brought out two at a time. Their grave has been dug."

The corporal saluted, and the door was closed.

JOHANN PUNZEL WAS BORN in 1910 in the Bavarian town of Pressig, where his parents had a delicatessen. In World War I his older brother was killed.

Then came the 1920's, when wild inflation nearly destroyed the middle class of Germany. The Punzel family went steadily downhill. In that decade the worst off were the youth of Germany. Their lives were frustrated and despairing—no way to earn a living, nowhere to go. The suicide rate rose.

Johann alternated between occasional jobs and helping with the dying delicatessen. In those days Hitler seemed to offer a ray of hope to youths like Johann, who joined the Nazi Party when he was 17. He saw and heard Adolf Hitler and was carried away by the glamour of that evil genius.

Presently he got a full-time clerical job at party branch headquarters in Pressig. At the time war came Johann was married to a pretty, dark-haired girl, and they had two babies. He was called into the army and did well. When his regiment, the 330th Infantry, marched into Differdange, he was a corporal.

PUNZEL STOOD outside the garage door, somewhat confused. An order was an order and must be carried out. But those people in there—and the woman he could hear sobbing. He decided to pass the buck. Leaving guards posted, he hurried off to find Lieutenant Kelch, the regimental adjutant.

Kelch was too busy to be bothered.

"The matter belongs in the judge advocate's office," he said. "Go and see them about the sentence."

Punzel returned to the prisoners, who surrounded him, clamoring their innocence. Joseph Weiler quieted them and told Punzel that the charge was without foundation, that none of them had had an opportunity to signal the French.

"You have searched the air-raid shelter," Weiler said. "Cannot further search be made?"

Punzel was impressed. And then it occurred to him that the lieutenant had spoken of carrying out the sentence against "these men." He had said nothing about the woman. He pulled Mrs. Wallers to her feet, led her outside, and found a Wehrmacht truck bound for Luxembourg City. He put her into it, and the truck drove away.

At the judge advocate's office Punzel asked the lieutenant in charge if the sentence could not be deferred until further search for evidence could be made. To his surprise, the officer said he would look into the matter and told him to come back in three quarters of an hour.

When Punzel returned, the answer was: "No. The sentence is to be carried out unless the guilty confess. But it has been decided to reprieve the prisoners for 24 hours. However, if the French bombardment is resumed, the prisoners are to be shot at once."

Punzel became more and more confused. By now he was completely convinced that the men were innocent, but he could think of no way to do anything to save them.

However, he could do some little things for their comfort. He moved the prisoners from the garage to a storeroom across the street, where the floor was dry, and he had food and hot coffee taken to them from a regimental canteen.

That night Punzel slept badly. He kept listening for the French bombardment—which would mean the immediate death of the prisoners. But they would die anyway the next afternoon.

Next morning he went again to see the prisoners. They had nothing to say except to plead for mercy. Presently, Punzel went to the judge advocate's office, not to see the lieutenant but to make sure he was away at lunch. Then the corporal went back to the storeroom, noting that there were no soldiers nearby except the guards, his own men. He had some words with them. They looked at him curiously.

Punzel went into the room and asked one of the prisoners if he could get a truck at the steelworks. The man said that he could. Punzel sent two of the guards with him.

When the truck arrived, Punzel went into the room and spoke hurriedly: "You are free, all of you. Get into the truck quickly."

At first there was only stunned silence, then a bedlam of laughing and sobbing. The men crowded around him and tried to shake his hand and give him their watches and money. He shook them off.

"Be quiet. Get into the truck and go."

Nicolas Kremer, the youngest of the firemen, asked for his name. He gave it and his serial number, 105275A. Then the truck drove off toward Luxembourg City.

Back in his quarters Punzel shook all over as if with a chill. Now the thing he had done seemed incredible. He was sure to be found out. Perhaps his own men would turn him in—though several of them had congratulated him. In any case, the firing squad would soon come and he would be done for.

But Punzel was lucky. Within an hour a general order came through: the 330th Infantry was to move up to the Maginot Line. In the commotion that followed, nobody thought to inquire about the firemen of Differdange.

Nobody ever did.

Punzel never disobeyed another order, and he ended the war as a second lieutenant. He went back to Pressig, to the dreary business of trying to make a living for himself and his family in a beaten and despairing country. He had another go at the family delicatessen. It failed. He had other jobs, but they didn't last long.

Then in 1946 he was notified that he was under investigation by a Military Government court because of his former party membership. After some thought, he wrote to the Management of Mines in Differdange, telling who he was and what he had done in the matter of the firemen. He never received an answer. But later he was notified by the court that he had been cleared.

The years went by.

THE FLEEING FIREMEN found refuge with their families or friends and went into hiding. After the Franco-German armistice of 1940 it seemed safe to return to Differdange. Some of the men went back to their old jobs in the steelworks, now under German management.

There was much speculation as to who had sent the signals to the French, but the truth was never established.

Joseph Weiler died of a heart attack. So did Mrs. Wallers. Young Nicolas Kremer rose in the world, went into politics after the war, and was elected to the Luxembourg Parliament. He was the one who concerned himself with finding Johann Punzel. But in the disorganization of beaten Germany, it proved impossible to trace a soldier through only his name and serial number.

Then Kremer heard of the letter Punzel had written to the Management of Mines. Kremer wrote to the Military Government, stating the facts of the case, but got no reply—though his letter later proved to have been helpful in getting the charge against Punzel dropped. But when he tried to locate Punzel through the Military Government, he got nowhere.

After many unsuccessful attempts over a period of years, Kremer at last tried writing to the police departments of various German cities. In the spring of 1955 the Nuremberg police sent him Punzel's address in Pressig.

Kremer wrote Punzel, inviting him to visit Differdange for a reunion with his former prisoners. Punzel, touched and incredulous at this surprising turn of events, replied that he would come.

Punzel and his wife arrived at Differdange on June 3, 1955, the 15th anniversary of the prisoners' release. The surviving firemen had contributed to an entertainment fund, as had the management of the steelworks.

For three weeks the Punzels lived in a happy daze. At a big party, the first of many, a huge meal was prepared, toasts were drunk, and a gold watch inscribed *"Als Dank Für Hilfe 3.6.1940"* ("In Thanks for Your Help") was presented to Punzel amid thunderous applause. There were automobile trips, more gifts, and invitations everywhere for lunch and dinner.

Punzel was received by the Luxembourg Minister of Justice, who, in the name of the government, thanked him for what he had done. One Sunday there was a special service in the principal church of Differdange. The pastor—who had spent three years in a concentration camp—preached a sermon of gratitude to Punzel, and the choir sang a special hymn in his honor. Punzel broke down and wept.

*Allied prisoners of war contrived many fantastic and
audacious methods of escape during World War II.
This exciting account of the infamous Nazi prison camp
Stalag Luft III is a classic escape story.*

Tunnel to Freedom

By Flight Lieutenant Paul Brickhill
Royal Australian Air Force
as told to Allan A. Michie

STALAG LUFT III, at Sagan, Germany, halfway between Berlin and
Breslau, held some 10,000 captured airmen in the spring of 1943.
Nearly all were from the British and Commonwealth air forces, al-
though Americans were beginning to arrive in numbers.

In April the camp was enlarged by the addition of the North Compound, and 700 of us were moved into it. Already, prisoners in the
working parties that helped build the compound had studied its lay-
out and paced off its distances—with tunnels in mind. Escape was the
one hope that had kept us going through the months of captivity.

A few of the officers had dug tunnels at other camps, and around
them we built "X," our escape organization. Head of "X" was Squadron Leader Roger Bushell, a tall South African who had been a lawyer in London, then a fighter pilot until shot down over Dunkirk.
Bushell had already made two remarkable escapes and once had got
almost to Switzerland before he was caught.

North Compound was a square, each side 1,000 feet long, enclosed
by two tall barbed-wire fences, parallel and five feet apart, the space
between crammed with barbed-wire coils. Ten yards inside this barrier was the warning wire; step across it and the guards shot. Numerous sentry towers, 15 feet high, each with searchlight and machine
gun, were manned 24 hours a day. Twenty-five yards outside the
wire on all four sides were dense pine woods, which cut off any view
of the outside world—but which would also cover an escape.

As soon as we moved in, notices were posted asking for volunteers
to play cricket and softball. The notices were signed "Big X." Everybody knew what that meant, and 500 signed up for the tunnel work.
It was decided to start three long tunnels, "Tom," "Dick," and

Block 104

Trapdoot to tunnel shaft concealed under heating stove

30-foot-deep shaft

Air-pump room for air-conditioning Harry

Shop for preparing timbers to shore tunnel

"Harry," in the hope that one would get by undetected. We never used the word "tunnels"; too many guards understood English.

Tom was to be dug from Block 123 to the wire, 150 feet away, and then on to the shelter of the woods. Dick was to be dug from Block 122 toward Tom, so that it could either be joined with Tom's shaft or be dug all the way to the woods. Harry was to begin from Block 104 and drive to the woods on the north.

Of course, the tunnels would have to start from within our huts. Each hut was 100 feet long, with sleeping quarters, washroom, and small kitchen. The Germans had built these huts about a foot off the ground, so that the guards could look underneath to see if we were up to any funny business. There were usually several of these "ferrets" around, easily spotted by the blue overalls they wore. With torches

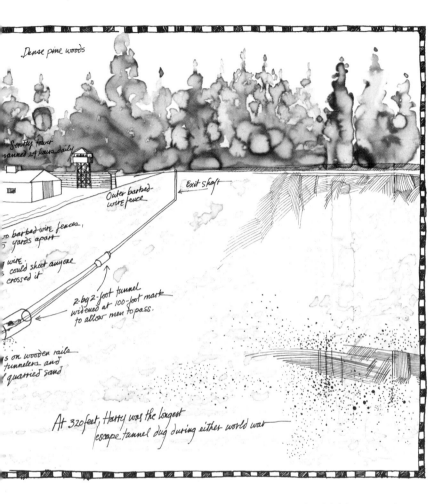

Dense pine woods

Sentry tower manned 24 hours daily

Outer barbed-wire fence

Exit shaft

Two barbed-wire fences, 5 yards apart

Guards could shoot anyone who crossed it

2-by-2-foot tunnel widened at 100-foot mark to allow men to pass.

Cars on wooden rails carried tunnelers and quarried sand

At 320 feet, Harry was the longest escape tunnel dug during either world war

and long steel probes they continually searched for hidden trapdoors and telltale sand from tunnels.

Three teams were organized, each under a veteran tunneler. Wally Floody, a Canadian mining engineer, was chief technician. Every volunteer was interviewed by the "X" chief of his block. Miners, carpenters, engineers were assigned to tunnel. Tailors were organized to turn out disguises. Artists set up a forgery shop to fake papers. Any man who spoke fluent German was assigned to make friends with a ferret, keep him always in sight, cultivate him, eventually try to bribe him to bring in items needed from the outside.

One day a new ferret, a particularly zealous one, appeared on duty and we labeled him "Keen Type." Within a month, however, a contact had so cultivated him that he lost his zest for antiescape vigilance.

He would come into the compound, walk straight to his contact's room, and say, "Keen Type here. Can I come in?" and then settle down for tea and a biscuit.

Prisoners without any special skills were assigned either as "penguins," to dispose of sand from the tunnels, or as "stooges," to keep watch on ferrets. For the next year we had 300 stooges working in shifts every day. They reported to "Big S," the head security officer, a tall, rangy American colonel.

Once the security system was working, we went ahead on the tunnels. The Germans had overlooked one detail. In each hut the washroom, the kitchen, and a small section where there was a stove had concrete floors and stood on brick and concrete foundations that had no openings through which the security guards could probe. These were the places from which we started work.

The first job was to build secret trapdoors. At any hour of the day or night the Germans would rush into a block shouting, *"Aus, Aus!"* ("Out, Out!") and then upset beds, pry into cupboards, and rip up floor and wall boards looking for tools, civilian clothing, buttons, nails, anything an escapee might use. Yet ingenuity, backed by three years of weary experience, built trapdoors they couldn't find.

By luck, we got hold of a little cement left over from building the camp. A Polish team cast a removable block to replace a slab about two feet square chipped from the floor of Block 123. When a little sand and dirt had been rubbed around the edges, nobody could spot it. This was Tom's entrance.

Dick's trapdoor in Block 122 was the most ingenious. In the washroom floor was an iron grating through which waste water ran into a concrete well three feet deep. The drainpipe that led from this sump was so placed that there was always some water in the well. While stooges kept watch outside, the Poles removed the iron grill, bailed out the well, and, with a cold chisel acquired by bribing a guard, freed the whole concrete slab that formed one side of the well so that it was removable. When the slab was in place and the cracks were sealed with soap, the waste water rapidly accumulated, making everything look most unsuspicious.

Harry's entrance was also tricky. The tall heating stove in Room 23 of Block 104 stood on tiles embedded in a concrete base about four feet square. The men moved the stove back, chipped the tiles free, and reset them in a concrete trapdoor that looked precisely like the original base. Five of the tiles cracked in the process. They were replaced by tiles stolen from a cookhouse in East Compound.

It had been risky business. Harry's floor was up for about 10 days in all, hidden from the ferrets only by a carelessly placed mattress, but we got away with it.

Now we were set for the more dangerous business of tunneling. The distances, directions, and angles of the three tunnels had been computed by rough trigonometry. We had learned that most German sound detectors could hear nothing below a depth of 25 feet, so we decided to sink shafts 30 feet straight down from the three trapdoors before heading for the woods.

The light, sandy soil was easy to dig, but it needed almost solid shoring. As a start, we made each man provide two bed slats. This first levy wasn't too bad, but by the time the fifth and sixth levies took more slats, it was hard to sleep.

Early in May 1943 the first sand was cut away. Teams worked from just after morning roll call right through to the evening roll call with only a short break for lunch.

The penguins had the troublesome job of disposing of the bright yellow sand, which showed up glaringly if dumped on the dun-colored soil above ground. Some of the sand could be stirred into the soil of our tiny gardens, but that didn't begin to solve the problem. So we took dozens of small towels and sewed them into sausage-shaped sacks. Then a penguin would hang one of these, filled with sand, in each trouser leg and wander casually out to the playing ground. There stooges would be staging boxing matches, volleyball games, or pretended brawls. Once in among the men, the penguin, with hands in pockets, would pull strings that freed pins at the bottom of the sausage sacks and let the sand trickle to the ground. There many scuffling feet would quickly discolor it and trample it into the surface. When we were

Heating stove
pushed back to
reveal
trapdoor
to shaft

going strong, we kept 150 penguins busy and disposed of tons of sand under the very noses of the ferrets.

The tunnels were scooped out with little coal shovels and iron scrapers made from our cookstoves. The bores were about two feet square and shored with box frames made of bed slats. We saved our few nails to build shaft ladders.

At the base of each shaft roomy chambers were dug for the use of carpenters and fitters and for the ventilating equipment. One day, when three diggers were thus enlarging the base of Dick's shaft, a frame began to leak sand. In a matter of seconds the leak became an avalanche. The ladder held and two diggers scrambled up. The third, Wally Floody, was almost smothered before the other two got him out. Dick's shaft filled almost to the top. It was a bitter setback, but the job was grimly done over again.

Veterans had learned that you could not tunnel far without fresh air and that holes poked up to the surface were not adequate. By luck, a copy of a modern-mechanics type of magazine came into camp, and it contained an article that described a homemade air pump. We promptly set to work to make one.

Our "tin bashers" collected Red Cross dried milk tins, cut off the ends, and fitted the cylinders together to build pipe. They wrapped the joints with German propaganda newspapers. The pipe was laid in a ditch along the tunnel floor and covered with sand. At the far end was a nozzle, which delivered fresh air. The air was forced through the pipe by shifts of pumpers who operated a bellows constructed from kit bags. This first outfit worked perfectly and we promptly built two more. Now we could close the trapdoors and work without fear of interruption from the ferrets.

Our electrical specialists rounded up odd bits of wiring left behind by the builders. Then they surreptitiously rearranged the camp wiring, gaining a few score feet in the process. They wired the three shafts and made hidden connections to the camp circuit. We stole bulbs from corridors and so had light to dig by. When the Germans neglected to switch on the power during the day, we used homemade lamps—tin cans with pajama-cord wicks burning in margarine.

The digging teams evolved a rigid system. Number one digger lay full length on his side and one elbow, hacking away at the tunnel face and pushing the sand back toward his feet. Number two lay facing the other way, his legs overlapping number one's. He collected the sand in special boxes that were placed on trolleys and hauled by homemade ropes back to the shaft.

These trolleys, strong enough to carry two sandboxes or one man, were first-class installations. They had carved flanged wooden wheels fitted with "tires" cut from tin cans. The hubs even had ball bearings, smuggled in by a tame ferret. The track rails were made from barrack moldings. When the tunnels became long, the diggers sprawled on the trolleys and pushed their way to the working face.

At times it was stifling hot in the hole. Men worked naked or in the hated long underpants issued to prisoners. Dirt stains on their outer clothes would have given the show away. Up above, we rigged rough showers where the diggers returning from the tunnel could quickly wash off all telltale sand before roll calls.

The diggers learned to take sand falls in their stride. Usually, the

One of the digging team loaded sand into boxes to be hauled back to tunnel shaft

only warning would be a slight rustling sound, and then suddenly the number one digger would be buried under a pile of the suffocating sand, which smothered lamps and air line. Then the number two man would have to work at top speed to get him out before he smothered.

By the end of May, a month after digging commenced, each of the three tunnels was about 70 feet long. It was nearly summer, the best time for escaping, for we could sleep out and live off the land.

The X leaders decided to concentrate on Tom, which had the shortest distance to go. A week later they set up the first "halfway house" at the 100-foot mark. This was a little chamber built from the end frames of our wooden bunks. In it men could turn around without having to go back to the shaft. Calculations were that Tom's halfway house was just under the warning wire. That left 100 feet to go to get inside the woods.

Other X groups were busily preparing the equipment we'd need.

173

Our forgery department consisting of 50 men turned out phony passports and identity cards. We called it "Dean & Dawson," after the English travel agency.

Some of our guards could be tempted with a gift of coffee or chocolate, and once they had smuggled in one item, they couldn't refuse more, because we might give them away to the commandant. In this way we got colored inks, pens, brushes, special types of paper, magnets to make compasses, radio parts to build the illegal receiver on which we got daily news bulletins, a camera and equipment to make photos for our fake passports, hammers, saws, nails, and maps.

A few guards, smoothly cultivated by our linguists, were even persuaded to lend us their *Zahlbuch,* combined paybook and identity card, while our forgers made copies. The faking of documents was an incredibly finicky job. Whole sheets of simulated typewriting were drawn by hand, complete with strikeovers, imperfect letters, and bad shifts. Other documents called for lines of close print or countless whorls of "engraving." Forgers ripped fine paper from Bibles and linen covers from books to make identification books. One document needed in crossing frontiers was so complicated that it would take a skilled forger five hours a day for a month to make one. Letterheads were "embossed" with toothbrush handles. German eagle and swastika stamps were cut from rubber boot heels. Altogether, the escapees were outfitted with more than 400 forged documents.

An Australian pilot made compasses—the cases from melted phonograph records, the glasses from broken windows, the needles from sewing needles rubbed on a magnet.

In the tailor shop 60 men made civilian clothes out of RAF uniforms and turned out close copies of Luftwaffe uniforms. Escapees caught wearing exact copies would be shot as spies, but by the Geneva Convention we could use imitations.

Half a dozen mapmakers traced a variety of maps and ran copies off on a makeshift duplicator. They made the gelatin from fruit jello, the ink from the crushed lead of indelible pencils.

We learned that the Americans were to be moved in six weeks to a separate compound, and they had put in a lot of work on the tunnels. So evening shifts were added to hurry things up. We had to take even greater chances with sand. More of it was dug into our vegetable gardens, and some was scattered near the freshly upturned soil around a new camp theater.

One day a probing ferret turned over some bright yellow sand in a garden. This touched off a series of frantic but futile searches. The

Germans dug a trench between Block 123 and the wire, but it was not deep enough to reveal Tom.

By the end of June we calculated that Tom had reached just under the edge of the wood, and we prepared to dig a shaft straight up to the surface. Just then a horde of Germans suddenly appeared and began to cut away the trees! It was actually mere coincidence; they had decided to build a new compound there. They chopped the trees back for 50 yards; but time for the Americans was growing short, and it was decided to break Tom out anyway and let the escapees crawl the rest of the way to cover.

We had so much sand coming up that we were desperate. Someone suggested storing it temporarily in Dick. Every evening a stream of penguins carrying cardboard Red Cross boxes would stroll across to Dick's hut and there dump sand down the shaft. Even that was not enough. The X leaders decided to take a long chance: store sand in Red Cross boxes under our beds and hope that the Germans wouldn't find it until it could be properly disposed of.

Tom was now 260 feet long, with a few yards to go to its goal. Bushell decided to lie low for a few days to allay suspicion. Then ferrets found the boxes of sand in our huts! Heavy transport wagons were brought into camp and trundled all around the area in an effort to collapse any tunnels we might have. They only wrecked our vegetable gardens.

A day or so later, in a last suspicious search of Block 123, a ferret accidentally jabbed his probe into the edge of Tom's trapdoor.

That was the end of Tom.

The ferrets couldn't find how to open the trap, so they broke it in. They dynamited Tom and incidentally blew up part of the roof of Block 123. They were so relieved at discovering Tom that they took no reprisals or even precautions.

A mass meeting decided that work would go ahead on Dick and Harry. However, it was deemed wise to do no more until winter, when we assumed vigilance would slacken because it would be a bad season for escapes.

At the end of August 1943 the Americans were moved to their new compound, and we threw a great party for them on home-brewed raisin wine as a farewell.

While we were waiting for winter, it was decided to try some aboveground escapes. For one attempt the carpenters made imitation German rifles out of wood—they got the exact measurements by sneaking up behind guards with calipers and measuring the parts.

These they leaded with pencil to resemble metal and polished them until you couldn't tell them from the real thing.

Periodically, the German guards escorted small parties of prisoners through the gates for delousing our clothes, and the idea was to stage an unofficial delousing party of our own. Three prisoners, disguised as Luftwaffe *Unteroffiziers*, took 24 other prisoners in tow, passed the inspection at the gate, and made off into the woods. A few minutes later six senior officers, including the Battle of Britain fighter ace Bob Stanford Tuck, tried to get through but were detected.

We were all forced to stand on parade for nearly seven hours while the three missing men were identified. Later, all were rounded up. One man, a fluent Spanish speaker, who posed as a foreign worker, got to Czechoslovakia and then by train almost to the Swiss border, where he got out and walked right across a narrow strip of Swiss territory without knowing it and back again into Germany, where a frontier guard nabbed him. The other two got to a Luftwaffe airdrome, sneaked into an old Junkers trainer, and were just warming up the engine when a German pilot coincidentally came along to fly it and caught them.

We were ready to start tunneling again early in 1944. Dick was almost filled in with Tom's sand, and anyway the Germans had started to build a new compound where Dick was to have broken out. That left Harry. But snow lay deep on the ground and sand disposal stumped us. One of the tunnelers suggested we put it under the theater. He had noticed the Germans never looked there.

We had built the theater ourselves and had taken care to leave no openings for the ferrets to peek through. Underneath was a deep excavation, which could take tons and tons of sand. Our engineers adjusted one seat so that it swung back on hinges, and under it they cut a trapdoor. Into this the penguins dumped kit bags packed full of sand every night.

Three teams, 10 veteran diggers in each team, pushed Harry ahead up to 12 feet per day. By the end of January, the first "halfway house" was built 100 feet out. The planners had calculated that 300 feet of tunnel in all would bring us into the shelter of the trees.

It was a long dig, and conditions were getting worse. The ground was cold and damp. Every digger suffered continuously from colds. Most of them were spitting black from breathing the fumes of our fat lamps; we had run out of electric wire. Sand falls kept occurring nearly every day.

But by mid-February another 100 feet had been dug, and the second halfway house was put in. This was just about under the far boundary wire; there were 100 feet still to go.

Then we got a small break. German workmen hooking up loudspeakers laid down two large coils of electric wire, intending to use them in a few minutes. A prisoner calmly walked off with one coil. A mock fight broke out, and in the confusion we got the second coil. The German workmen were afraid to report the loss. (At the end, when the Gestapo found the wire in Harry, three of them were shot.)

That haul gave us 600 feet of wiring, enough for stringing lights clear up to the digging face.

The chief ferret again became suspicious. Wally Floody, our chief penguin, our security chief, and half a dozen of the key diggers were suddenly transferred to a compound several miles away. That was a blow. It was bad enough losing key men, but it was worse that the Germans obviously knew we were up to something.

By March 8, 1944, the final 100-foot section was dug and a chamber excavated at the end. In four days four of the best diggers carved straight upward, fitting ladders to the side as they progressed, until they struck pine-tree roots. They estimated that they were about two feet below the surface, just inside the woods. They boarded over the top of the shaft and left the remainder to be dug on the night of the break. By March 14 the tunnel was ready. The trapdoor was closed and its sides cemented up to wait for milder weather and a night suitable for our getaway.

The very next day the chief ferret sent his men to search Block 104. One of them even ran his probe around the cement that sealed Harry's trapdoor. It held.

About 500 men had worked on the tunnels, but we estimated that only 220 would be able to pass through it during the hours of darkness. Bushell was allowed to draw up a list of 60 workers, 20 more were nominated by secret ballot because of their work on the project, and 140 names were drawn out of a hat.

The lucky ones began their preparations. We had enough money to buy train tickets for 40 men; the rest were to walk across country. Bushell and other men who'd been loose in Germany conducted lectures, giving hints and advice. A Czech pilot described the border mountains of Czechoslovakia, 60 miles away, for which most of the foot travelers intended to head.

After roll call on the morning of Friday, March 24, Roger Bushell announced that the escape would take place that night. There was six inches of snow on the ground, which was not good, but there would be no moon. Our meteorologist thought there would be a wind to drown suspicious noises.

The forgery department boys filled in their documents and stamped them with the correct date, which of course couldn't have been done until then. Some escapees were to go as foreign workers, others as neutrals, others as German officials, soldiers, and civilians—and each man's papers had to fit his story.

A digger went out to Harry's end to see how far we had to go to break through. When he jabbed a stick upward three inches, he struck daylight, much to his surprise. At least, it seemed, there wouldn't be any difficulty in getting to the surface.

We laid blankets at the bottom of the shafts to deaden sounds and nailed planks on the trolleys so the escapees could lie on them and be pulled along. When darkness came, the escapees put on their disguises. Our improvised iron rations were issued, a revolting but nourishing combination of grated chocolate, oatmeal, crushed biscuits, vitamin pills, barley, dried milk, and other concentrated foods all boiled together.

By 8:30 P.M. it was announced that all was ready. Ten minutes later the first escapee went down the ladder, turned out in a civilian suit and carrying a homemade briefcase. The second, dressed as a workman, followed. Roger Bushell, carrying an attaché case and looking like a smart businessman in his gray herringbone lounge suit, black overcoat, and dark hat, went down among the first five.

There was a bad wait when the first man was unable to pry the roof boards loose. It was almost an hour, an agonizing time for the men lying along the tunnel, before the swollen boards came loose and the earth was removed. Up above twinkled a few stars, and down the shaft came the sweet fresh air of freedom.

But when the digger cautiously stuck his head out, he got a shock. Instead of being just inside the woods, the hole was 10 feet short of the trees, its gaping opening a bare 15 yards from a sentry tower.

We were stunned when he broke the news. Would the work of 500 men for more than a year end in complete failure? But the men were in no mood to be stopped. To go out now was risky. To wait a month for the next dark of the moon and in the meantime dig another 30 feet of tunnel was equally risky. Besides, the forged papers were all dated and would have to be redone. That decided it.

The first man up crawled to a brushwood fence, paying out a rope by which he could signal when it was safe for the next man to emerge. The sentry in the tower paid no attention to the woods but played his searchlight on the barbed-wire fence and compound. Two other sentries patrolled back and forth along the wire. When both were out of sight, the rope was tugged and the second man slipped across into the relative safety of the woods.

It took more than an hour for the first 20 to make it. They were all going by train, and they headed for the Sagan railway station a quarter of a mile away. From timetables smuggled in by guards we knew exactly when the trains were due.

Back in Block 104 the initial delay had been terrible. Obviously something had gone wrong, but what? Escapees sat around, a queer collection of well-dressed civilians, workmen, and a German corporal, hoping that ferrets would not appear. Just after 9:30 the men at the trapdoor felt a blast of cold air. It could only mean that we'd broken out. A muffled cheer went around the block.

There were other interruptions. Two bad sand falls held up the show for about an hour and a half in all. Sometimes the trolleys left their rails—more delays. Men going out with suitcases or blankets wrapped around them would find themselves jammed in a narrow tunnel, afraid to pull loose for fear of causing a fall. We were running far behind schedule.

At midnight the air-raid sirens sounded, and all lights, including our illegal ones in the tunnel, were switched off. It was obvious now that not more than 100 men would get away before daylight. Lamps had to be lighted and passed along the tunnel.

We up above heard the faraway sound of falling bombs, and the huts rattled as RAF blockbusters fell crashing on Berlin, 100 miles away. At any other time we would have cheered, but that night we cursed. It was about 2 A.M. before the lights came on again. In the meantime, one by one the escapees had been crawling silently from the tunnel mouth and away into the woods.

The worst moment came at about 4:30. The sentry in the tower shouted to a guard patrolling below. The guard went up the tower ladder, and the sentry descended and walked straight toward the hole. He could hardly miss seeing it. Steam from the heat of the tunnel poured out of it, and from it to the woods led a black trail across the snow where escapees had crawled. The sentry, apparently blinded by looking at his searchlight, came on until he was a bare four feet from the hole, turned around, and squatted down. For five minutes he remained there, while the men in the shaft hardly dared breathe. At last the sentry went back to his tower. More escapees slipped through the tunnel and away.

When it was almost 5, the RAF man in charge decided it was getting too light. "Get the next three men down," he said. "Then we finish. If all of them get away without detection, the Huns won't know a thing until morning roll call, and the boys will have an extra four hours before the hunt is on."

The last three men quickly descended. Just as the third man vanished up the tunnel on the trolley, we heard the crack of a rifle.

Two escaping men had reached the rendezvous tree in the woods, another man, crawling, was halfway to it, and a fourth man had just come out of the hole when the rope signaler saw a guard approaching. If he kept on coming, he was bound to step right into the hole. The men outside froze to the ground when they felt two sharp warning tugs on the rope. The German strode on. He was seven yards away and still hadn't seen the hole.

Left, right, he strode on, probably half asleep, and one foot came down only a bare 12 inches from the tunnel mouth. When he made his next step, he almost trod on the man lying alongside the opening. He took one more pace, and then he snapped out of his daze. He didn't even notice the man lying at his feet, but he must have seen the black track across the snow. Then he saw the man lying halfway to the wood and raised his rifle to shoot. At that moment one of the escapees waiting by the tree leaped into sight and waved his arms, shouting, *"Nicht schiessen, Posten! Nicht schiessen!"* ("Don't shoot, sentry! Don't shoot!")

The sentry, startled, shot wild. The two men at the edge of the woods and the man who had crawled halfway came slowly forward, hands raised. And then, right at his feet, the last escapee, still unseen,

Of the 76 escapees, only 3 reached safety, 50 were shot, 23 were recaptured

180

rose slowly. The guard jumped back a yard and looked downward. There in front of him was Harry's gaping mouth. He whipped out a torch and flashed it down the hole into the face of the 81st escapee, hanging precariously on the ladder.

The sentry blew his whistle. In a moment guards came running from all directions.

Harry's long life had ended.

In Block 104 there was a frantic scramble to burn our lists and papers, break up equipment, and get rid of civilian clothes. The men in the tunnel were inching back along the trolleys, expecting a shot from behind. When the last man came up, the trapdoor was sealed down and the stove replaced.

In a few minutes there came a scratching sound from below. A ferret had worked his way back along the tunnel and couldn't get out. We let him stay there.

By 6 A.M. the compound was swarming with guards, machine guns covered the doors and windows, and ferrets combed Block 104 calling, *"Aus! Aus! Efferbody aus!"* As each man came out of Block 104, a ferret grabbed him and forced him to strip in the snow, boots and all, while every article of clothing was inspected.

While the search was going on, an adjutant came running to implore us to open the trapdoor. The ferret was still down there, and they were afraid he would suffocate. The other ferrets couldn't find the trapdoor. We finally decided to open it for them. The ferret down below was not a bad type—he was the only one with nerve enough to go down the tunnel.

In a matter of hours the whole countryside was roused in one of the biggest manhunts of the war. The radio warned all civilians to be on the watch for the escapees. SS and Gestapo men, Luftwaffe men, and even naval men from Stettin and Danzig were mobilized by the thousands for the search.

Back in the compound we waited for reprisals. Harry had broken the world's record for the number of escapees who got away, and we expected the Germans to take it out on us. The Gestapo arrived to investigate, but its agents, never liked by the regular army, got no help from the ferrets and found nothing. We even managed to filch two of their flashlights. But they did uncover a black market—run by the commandant and his staff! The hapless commandant was promptly whisked off for a court-martial.

Most of the 76 men who got away were nabbed within a day or so, although some got as far as Danzig and Munich. All were taken to a

Gestapo prison in Gorlitz, 40 miles away. From Gorlitz, 15 men were brought back to Stalag Luft III. We could learn nothing more.

Then, a fortnight after the break, our senior officer was called to the commandant's office. Stiffly, the German read out the official report—of the 76 escaped officers, 41 had been shot!

Our senior officer called a meeting and announced the dreadful news. Under the Geneva Convention, drastic penalties must not be inflicted upon prisoners who attempt escape. The Germans had never before done such a thing. We thought most likely the announcement was a bluff to dissuade us from further escape attempts. We held a memorial service in the compound, however, and every man defiantly wore a black diamond of mourning on his sleeve.

When the Germans posted the list of the dead, it contained not 41 but 47 names, among them the leaders—Roger Bushell; Tim Walenn, who ran the forgery factory; Al Hake, the compass maker; Charlie Hall, the photographer.

For days the compound was shaken with grief and fury. Then three more names were added to the list of dead. The Germans never gave us any reason for the shootings or why they shot only 50 of 76. A couple of weeks later they brought in urns containing the cremated ashes of the dead, which we placed in a memorial vault.

In June a letter arrived, written in Spanish and signed with a fictitious name. That was the signal that one escapee, a Dutch pilot in the RAF, had succeeded in reaching England. A postcard from Sweden, signed with two false names, revealed that two Norwegians had also made it out. With 15 men sent back to Stalag Luft III and 50 reported shot, that left 8 unaccounted for.

Not till long afterward did we learn that they had been sent to the notorious Oranienburg concentration camp. Nobody had ever escaped from a concentration camp, the Gestapo boasted. However, within a few months the eight had tunneled out. They were eventually rounded up, but by then Germany was in the chaos of collapse and they were not shot.

If the Germans shot our 50 comrades to frighten us from building more tunnels, they made a psychological blunder. X was re-formed around two veteran tunnelers, and we immediately began work on "George," which started under the theater. George was on as grand a scale as Harry, and we were almost ready to break out when we were hurriedly evacuated. The Russians were only 30 miles away. We were forced to march for weeks half across Germany. We were at Lubeck on May 2, 1945, when the British 2nd Army set us free.

After the Berlin Wall went up, thousands
managed to circumvent it in a variety of ways.
But no scheme was more audacious than the
one engineered by the Holzapfel family.

The Lion's Den

By C. Brian Kelly

A SUMMER NIGHT'S RAIN fell gently on the twin cities of Berlin, spattering the barrier that divides East from West. It soaked the four men crouched at the western base of the wall. They said nothing. They dared not even move.

High above them, on the eastern side of the wall, were the battlements of the House of Ministries, once Hermann Göring's Luftwaffe headquarters and now, in 1965, the central bureaucracy—the lion's den—of the Communist German Democratic Republic. Somewhere on the Ministries roof, beyond the brightly lit wall and the armed border guards of the National People's Army, a family of three— father, mother, young son—was crawling through the rain toward hoped-for freedom.

IT WAS HARDLY LIGHT when the alarm rang at 4:30 that morning, but Heinz and Jutta Holzapfel were already awake in their small Leipzig apartment. Their son, Günther, was still sleeping soundly.

"Günther, wake up!" his parents urged. "We have to catch the early train to Berlin."

Günther was nine years old and delighted about the trip. He would be visiting the great House of Ministries, where his father sometimes worked. He dressed quickly and stumbled after his mother and father into the cool morning air.

They took the 6:13 train to the capital. At 10:30 A.M. they stood in the vast entrance hall of the House of Ministries, surrounded by the crowd of visitors that gathered in the entrance every morning before obtaining passes and scattering in the hallways beyond. Heinz strode ahead toward the pass office, a small cubicle next to an armed

183

sentry. Jutta and Günther stayed a few paces behind. If Heinz were challenged, they could turn for home.

But no one paid attention to the slender man with the short hair and colorless features. And no one noticed that neither Heinz nor Jutta actually obtained new passes.

When Jutta stepped out of the pass office with Günther, Heinz was standing in the crowd before the sentry. Waving them through, the guard barely glanced at the outdated passes they showed (obtained on a previous visit and never returned). Inside, the three were soon lost among the throng of people.

THE HOLZAPFELS' STORY actually began in 1945, when the Russian armies captured Berlin. The son of a Leipzig cobbler, Heinz was a thin, pale boy of 14. He matured in the new schools the Communists established in the Soviet Zone and by 1953 was a member of the Free German Youth, the training ground for future comrades. He enjoyed the privilege of studying in a special economics school, where he applied himself diligently. It was there that he met a petite, brown-haired girl named Jutta, herself a Communist.

They fell in love, and in time they were married. In order to make enough money, Heinz went to work as a carpenter in a wood-veneer plant. On the side he studied Marxist economics at Leipzig University. Shortly after the Berlin Wall went up in 1961, he became an "expert planner" for 20 wood-veneer factories and a group leader for the Communist party committee in his office.

Because Heinz Holzapfel had relatives living in West Germany, he knew that he could rise only so far in the management ranks. Among his own group, however, he felt he was secure. And his wife, Jutta, was a great asset. She was first an editor of a factory newsletter and sometime later worked in the personnel department of the Leipzig trade and industrial fair. The Holzapfels were considered by most people to be "the perfect Communist couple."

Yet there were doubts, hesitant at first, then growing stronger. Neither dared mention them—until one winter evening in 1963 when it suddenly all came out in the open.

Heinz was late, held up by yet another of the interminable party meetings at the office. When he got home, he slammed the door behind him. Talk, talk, talk, he complained. Impossible production quotas. Facile exhortations to the workers. And all lies. He couldn't abide the hypocrisy any longer—the state's, the party's, his own. He wanted "to vanish from here."

Jutta was stunned. Never had she heard Heinz talk like that. What he was proposing was *escape.*

And what was she saying? Two words: "Me, too."

They stared at each other. There was nothing more to say.

In the next few weeks Heinz and Jutta discussed escape possibilities. But, as they soon learned, the borders between East and West really did form an Iron Curtain—too heavily fortified to crash openly, too heavily guarded to slip across unseen.

A year, then another six months, passed. Jutta remained at the trade fair. Heinz continued his work.

About twice a month, Heinz traveled to East Berlin on official business for his wood enterprise, which was a branch of the National Economics Council in the House of Ministries. And one day Heinz realized that the Ministries had become more than a place of business for him. At the rear of the building, only Niederkirchner Street—the "death strip"—separated it from the wall. Visiting his colleagues on the upper floors of the seven-story building, Heinz could look into West Berlin. He could see the traffic, a woman hanging wash, a boy like Günther on his way home from school.

At street level it would be easy enough to reach the border strip from the Ministries courtyard. Easy, but futile. There seemed to be no way that anyone could snip through the two barbed-wire fences, cross over the death strip, then scale the barrier itself without being stopped, or shot.

There had to be another way. Standing on the street one day, the huge structure looming above him, Heinz saw the solution in a flash. The roof! Of course. Who would expect an escape from the roof of the House of Ministries?

He also saw how it could be done. The lights that illuminated the forbidden strip of ground were the most obvious danger. But they pointed down. Anyone looking up from ground level would be blinded. The moment of real danger would come during the time of the descent. But the apparatus Heinz had in mind would reduce that exposure to only a few seconds.

That evening Heinz told Jutta his plan. It would work, he said. And Jutta agreed.

For help they turned to some of their old friends in West Germany. Routinely exercising their right to visit the Communist half of Germany, these friends met with the Holzapfels several times. They agreed to wait at the base of the wall, opposite the Ministries, on the night of the attempt.

Heinz, in the meantime, had begun a study of the Ministries roof. Fortunately, it was broken into layers, like the deck of a ship. It should be easy, Heinz figured, to drop from a seventh-story window to the sixth-floor roof, then to the fifth-floor level. From the fifth floor it was a sheer drop to the ground. How high was that level? Using floor-to-ceiling measurements made in a Ministries bathroom one day and a photograph of the building, Heinz calculated the distance at 75 feet. Next, he estimated the gap between the Ministries structure and the wall at 40 to 50 feet. All these figures were passed along to the West German helpers.

The three Holzapfels would need a hiding place—perhaps one of the sixth-floor offices Heinz visited on his official calls. But he had no key. Then, as he searched the top-floor hallways one day, Heinz passed a commonplace sign: *Herren.* Of course, the men's room!

Quickly, Heinz surveyed the building's lavatories. They were all on the wrong side, opening onto inner courts. All but one. In the most distant corridor from the wall, there was a single men's toilet overlooking the sixth floor, with only a short drop from the window to the ledge below.

Now everything fell neatly into place. At the appointed time they could retreat directly to this bathroom. It would be their hiding place *and* their escape hatch.

After they cleared pass control inside the front door that morning of July 28, 1965, the Holzapfels went their separate ways: Heinz to get a haircut; Jutta and Günther to the Ministries beauty salon. There Jutta relaxed for a bit. She had kept the briefcase containing their escape equipment. Both she and Heinz felt a woman would be less likely to be searched. As the hairdresser worked on her, Jutta had the bulging case at her feet.

When Jutta moved to the dryer and felt the hot cocoon come down over her head, her tension began to ease. Then a laugh startled her. The young woman who set Jutta's hair had the briefcase in her hand and was pretending to struggle with it. *"Mein Gott,* how heavy! What on earth is inside?"

Jutta had unaccountably left the case by the first chair.

She didn't dare answer. She felt her shaking voice would have betrayed her. So she took the case, and she and Günther left the beauty salon as quickly as possible.

Günther was too busy to wonder about anything but the fabulous building they were visiting. The gray Ministries was a small roofed city. The Holzapfels (Heinz had by this time rejoined them) visited the firefighting headquarters, the pharmacy, various shops, the huge cafeteria. After lunch, in the state bookstore, Heinz and Jutta held back a gasp as their son picked out a book on parachuting called *A Jump From the Clouds.* By late afternoon they were back in the cafeteria. Heinz and Jutta, eyes on the clock, found little to say as they lingered over a snack and a hot drink. At 4:30, with the closing hour only 30 minutes away, Heinz said softly, "It's time to get going."

He and the boy traveled the elevator to the sixth floor and locked themselves into a men's room. Jutta rode a floor higher and vanished into a women's toilet she had found earlier in the day. It was closer to the rear of the building—and the wall—than the washroom Heinz had picked weeks before. Heinz and Günther joined her there at precisely 5:05 P.M. No one observed them.

Inside, Heinz immediately opened Jutta's bulging briefcase and pulled out the sign he had prepared—"Toilet closed. Please use the one at the end of the hall." He hung it outside the door. He then secured the bathroom door with two short, heavy crossbars. It would take several men to force an entrance.

Günther watched all this in astonishment. Now they told him the plan. If he followed instructions exactly, he would be given a bicycle once they were across the wall.

Silence fell. It would be a four-hour wait for darkness. While Günther slept, Heinz examined his signal lamp, a flashlight inside a candy bag with the tip of the bag cut out. It created a pinhead of light that could be seen only from the front and not from the side. He flicked it on and off several times.

ACROSS THE WALL, the Holzapfels' four confederates, carrying a 160-yard coil of blackened wire cable, headed for an abandoned junk truck. It was standing in a deserted lot close to the wall. The truck would make a firm anchor for their end of the Holzapfel railway. Dressed in dark clothing, the confederates faded into their shadowy hiding places next to the wall.

IN THE BATHROOM a block away, Heinz and Jutta waited impatiently. Nine o'clock had passed, and although there was no moon, it was still too light. Finally, at 9:30, they awoke Günther and pulled on their harnesses and "creeping socks," old ski socks Jutta had fitted with foam-rubber soles. Heinz opened the window. They climbed through and dropped to the sixth-floor roof. There they paused to darken

187

their faces with soot. Heinz then motioned toward the rear of the building, toward the wall.

Heads down, bodies crouched, they flitted from one cover to another, shadows among the ventilation shafts and other projections that dotted the roof. They were on a ledge, framed on one side by the walls of the seventh floor and on the other by a 10-foot drop to the fifth-floor roof.

Soon they were more than halfway to the drop-off point to the fifth-floor level. But now a window threw a shaft of bright yellow light across their route. As Heinz studied it, recalling his explorations inside the Ministries months before, he realized it was the office of the *Stasi*—the State Security Service.

"Careful!" he whispered.

They nodded and followed him out to the very edge of the roof, away from the window. On hands and knees, all three Holzapfels began to pick their way carefully past the danger spot. Inside the room they saw, to their surprise, not armed police officers, but a group of men in their underwear. Seconds later the light in the room snapped off. The *Stasi* had gone to bed.

Straightening up, the Holzapfels quickly moved on.

The descent to the fifth-floor roof was easy enough, but now they were forced to crawl. There were few projections to hide behind on this final layer of roof, and a standing silhouette would be visible against the glow of West Berlin's lights.

Heinz went first, closely followed by Günther, then Jutta. Each adult had a heavy briefcase. Jutta's was full of equipment, Heinz's crammed with family papers and mementos. They both pushed their briefcases ahead, then pulled themselves forward, in a repeated push, crawl, push, crawl.

ON THE OTHER SIDE of the wall, meanwhile, a West German police patrol had stumbled on the Holzapfels' confederates and told them to leave. Early in the wall's history, West Berlin authorities had stood by to aid escape attempts. By 1965, however, the city government was anxious to avoid border incidents. And the police saw no reason to encourage this group who refused to explain their presence.

Finally, one of the confederates pointed at the gloom-shrouded House of Ministries.

"Look! There's a family up there on that roof," he told the officers. "They are planning to escape."

The police were incredulous. How could anyone escape from a

stronghold like the House of Ministries? It was quite impossible.

But the West German friends of the Holzapfels insisted, displaying the cable and explaining the operation in detail. The patrol leader heard them out, then radioed headquarters for instructions. Minutes later the conspirators returned to their posts—and 20 officers armed with submachine guns discreetly took up stations nearby.

IT WAS ALMOST 11 P.M. when the Holzapfels reached the far end of the roof of the fifth floor. Looking around for an "anchor," Heinz saw nothing close by. The only substantial thing in view was a tall flagpole at the opposite flank of the Ministries wing, at least 50 yards away. They started crawling again.

When they finally reached the flagpole, the Holzapfels were close to exhaustion. But there was no time to rest. Jutta quietly began unpacking homemade escape gear: wooden reels, a hammer, and a reel of tough nylon tennis gut. Heinz pulled out his bagged flashlight and signaled westward.

There was an answering blink.

Heinz reached for the hammer and tennis gut. He securely tied one end of the coiled gut to the flagpole, six yards from the roof's lip; the other end was attached to the hammer, which was wrapped in foam rubber to muffle the sound of its impact. Heinz stood up, swung the hammer tentatively, then hurled it with all his strength. He and Jutta heard the thin nylon feed out with a silken whisper. Then the line went taut, and they could see the brightly painted hammer on the ground, five stories down and some 50 feet away. It had landed just beyond the wall. So far, the plan was working.

After a short wait a blurred figure detached itself from the shadows near the wall and advanced toward where the hammer lay. Like a fish taking bait, it swallowed the object, then quickly retreated to merge again with the shadows.

Heinz waited—long enough, he felt sure, for his confederates to attach the cable to the gut. Yet, when he tugged at the line, it wouldn't give. Something was wrong.

On the western side of the wall, Heinz's confederates had fastened the gut to the wire cable. But the cable became snagged in under-brush, and the West Germans had to creep out to free it. Then they forgot to give Heinz any slack. His every pull continued to meet resistance. Both sides wondered what had happened. Had the others seen something they couldn't?

Finally, Heinz gave the nylon line a stiff jerk. The message was understood, for suddenly the thin line yielded. Minutes later, breathing quite heavily, Heinz and Jutta hauled the end of the wire cable over the edge of the roof. Smeared with black tar, it was barely visible. Down below, apparently unaware, the sentries remained quiet.

Moving very quickly now, Heinz looped the cable end around the flagpole, pulled the loop tight, and secured it with a snap hook. He then signaled the ground: "Ready here." They would need a few moments to draw the wire cable taut and anchor their end to the truck. Soon Heinz saw the pale green light winking.

Günther was to go off first. Even if the guards below spotted him, it seemed unlikely they could unsling their guns and aim before Günther cleared the wall. Tense and silent, the nine-year-old boy watched as his mother and father deftly attached his flimsy-looking escape vehicle to the cable. It was an eight-inch-wide wheel of hardwood with a deep groove on the cable-riding rim. Heinz had sawed hardwood pulley reels in half and installed ordinary metal bicycle hubs in the center holes. He then had glued and screwed the pulley reels

together. A pipe crossbar, inserted through the bicycle hub, was held securely in place by butterfly nuts. This provided a firm handle. Jutta, in the meantime, had made strong harness seats of extra-heavy-duty upholstery webbing, fitted to size for each family member.

Young Günther obediently crouched underneath the cable as they slipped his harness straps over the crossbar and secured them. They snapped a separate leather safety belt into place as well. Even if he lost his hold on the crossbar, Günther could not fall from the webbed seat.

But now it was quite apparent that the loop on the flagpole was too low, so low the cable pressed against the lip of the roof. If the passengers were to clear the edge, the escape track had to be lifted. Heinz quickly wedged himself under the wire cable, strained up with his shoulders—and Jutta then gave Günther a push.

The hunched figure of the nine-year-old went over the roof edge noiselessly. It was incredible how quickly he vanished into the blackness.

For young Günther, heart beating furiously, there was hardly time to realize what was happening. As the wind whipped past his face, he sensed rather than saw the lights flash past his feet. Then he struck a figure with strong, outstretched arms. In moments he was out of the harness, standing in an empty lot, the wall behind him. He had not uttered a sound during the trip.

On the roof Heinz and Jutta waited for the green blink that would tell them Günther was safe. When it came, they promptly signaled back, "Ready again."

Jutta floated down with a briefcase slung around her neck.

The police hurried Jutta and Günther to the safety of the nearest station house. The West German helpers stayed at their posts and waited for Heinz. But the cable was still. There were no warning vibrations from a third passenger.

On the Ministries roof, Heinz was desperate. He struggled to force the cable higher. It barely moved. Frantically, he tugged for more slack, but his cohorts on the ground did not understand. Finally, one of them rushed to the police station for Jutta's advice.

"He must need more slack," she said. "Loosen the cable!"

Minutes later Heinz had the added slack. Not all he wanted, but enough to raise the cable several inches. It would have to do.

Heinz hooked his harness onto the crossbar of the last reel. He eyed the cable, quivering just above the roofline. There still was no room to ride over the edge. Grabbing the cable below the reel with both hands, he jammed himself, on his back, between the cable and the lip of the roof. He forced himself to ease his legs, and finally his entire body, over the edge. Then he fell through space.

He was in his harness, however, and the wheel fell into place on the cable. Suddenly, he was rolling, faster and faster, down and away. He cleared the wall and struck the group of West Germans at the end of the cable like a cannonball.

Hours later, when dawn came, Heinz and Jutta were still up with their friends, their hotel room full of smoke and talk. Günther, soon to be the proud owner of a bicycle, was sound asleep. And back at the wall, as the cable took shape in the growing daylight, a lonely helmeted border guard was sent to haul it in.

The dramatic account of an incident in
the South Pacific during World
War II involving the escape of a future
president of the U.S.A.

Survival

By John Hersey

ONE DAY IN AUGUST 1943 an officer of a PT squadron in the Solomon Islands wrote home these distressing words: "Last night George Ross lost his life for a cause he believed in stronger than any of us, because he was an idealist of the purest sense. Jack Kennedy, ex-ambassador's son, was on the same boat and also lost his life. The man that said the cream of a nation is lost in war can never be accused of making an overstatement of a very cruel fact."

A couple of days later a mass was said in the squadron area for the souls of Kennedy, Ross, and the other 11 men of PT 109.

But sorrow at the PT base was premature. This is the account of what really happened. It shows that among all the horrible things in the Pacific war, there was one wonderful thing: the will of men to live.

SKIPPERED BY Lt. John F. Kennedy, PT 109 was out one starless night patrolling Blackett Strait in the mid-Solomons. At about 2:30 A.M. Kennedy, at the wheel, saw George "Barney" Ross, up on the bow with binoculars, turn and point into the darkness. The man in the forward machine-gun turret shouted, "Ship at 2 o'clock!"

Kennedy saw a shape and spun the wheel to turn for an attack, but the motor torpedo boat, running on only one of her three engines so as to make a minimum wake and avoid detection from the air, answered too sluggishly. The shape became a Japanese destroyer, cutting through the night at 40 knots and heading straight for the 109. All hands froze to their battle stations as the destroyer crashed into the PT and cut her in two. Kennedy thought "This is how it feels to be killed." In a moment he found himself on his back on the deck, looking up at the destroyer as it passed through his boat.

193

Only McMahon, an engineer, was below decks. He was thrown painfully against a bulkhead. A tremendous burst of flame came at him from the gas tanks. He put his hands over his face, drew his legs up, and waited to die. But he felt water hit him after the fire, and he was sucked down as his half of the PT sank. He began to struggle upward through the water. Over his head he saw a yellow glow—gasoline burning. He broke the surface and was right in the fire. He splashed hard to keep a little island of water around him.

Johnston, another engineer, had been asleep on deck. The collision dropped him overboard. The destroyer's turbulent wake took him down, turned him over and over, shook him, and drubbed on his ribs. The next day his body was black-and-blue.

The undamaged watertight compartments forward kept Kennedy's half of the PT afloat. The destroyer rushed off into the dark. There was an awful quiet: only the sound of gasoline burning.

Kennedy shouted, "Who's aboard?"

Feeble answers came from three enlisted men, McGuire, Mauer, and Albert, and one officer, Thom.

The survivors in the water answered Kennedy's hails: Ross, the third officer, and Harris, McMahon, Johnston, Zinsser, Starkey, enlisted men. Two did not answer: Kirksey and Marney, enlisted men.

Harris shouted from the darkness, "Mr. Kennedy! Mr. Kennedy! McMahon is badly hurt."

Kennedy, who had been on the Harvard swimming team five years before, dove into the water and swam to McMahon and Harris, 100 yards away, then took McMahon in tow and headed for the PT. A gentle breeze kept blowing the boat away from the swimmers. It took 45 minutes to make what had been an easy 100 yards. On the way Harris, who had hurt his leg, said, "I can't go any farther."

Kennedy, of the Boston Kennedys, said to Harris, of the same hometown, "For a guy from Boston you're certainly putting up a great exhibition out here, Harris."

Harris complained no more, and he made it to the hull. Then Kennedy swam from man to man, to see how they were doing. All were wearing life preservers. Those who couldn't swim had to be towed back to the wreck by those who could. It took nearly three hours to get everyone aboard.

The men stretched out on the tilted deck. Some collapsed into sleep. The others talked about how wonderful it was to be alive.

When it got light, the men saw, three miles to the northeast, the monumental cone of Kolombangara Island; there, they knew, 10,000

Japanese swarmed. To the west, five miles away, they saw Vella Lavella—more Japs. To the south, only a mile or so away, they actually could see a Japanese camp on Gizo. Kennedy ordered his men to keep low so that no moving silhouettes would show against the sky. The listing hulk was gurgling and gradually settling.

McMahon, horribly burned, and Johnston, who coughed continually from gasoline fumes that had gotten into his lungs, had to have room to lie down. Kennedy ordered the other men into the water and went in himself. All morning they clung to the hulk. They cursed war in general and PT's in particular. At about 10 o'clock the hulk heaved a moist sigh and turned turtle. McMahon and Johnston had to hang on as best they could.

It became clear with each passing moment that the remains of the 109 would soon sink. Kennedy said: "We will swim to that small island," pointing to one of a group three miles to the southeast. "We have less chance of making it than some of these other islands here, but there'll be less chance of Japs, too."

Those who could not swim well grouped themselves around a long timber that had been knocked loose by the collision. They tied several pairs of shoes to it, as well as the ship's lantern wrapped in a life jacket to keep it afloat.

Kennedy took one end of a long strap on McMahon's Mae West in his teeth and swam breaststroke, towing the helpless man. The salt water lapped into his mouth, and he swallowed a lot.

It took five hours to reach the island. It was only 100 yards in diameter. Kennedy lay down, exhausted. He had been in the sea, except for short intervals on the hulk, for $15\frac{1}{2}$ hours. His stomach was heavy with the salt water he had swallowed. But he kept thinking. Every night for several nights the PT's had cut through Ferguson Passage on their way to action. Ferguson Passage was just beyond the next little island. Maybe . . .

He stood up. He put a rubber life belt around his waist, and hung a .38 around his neck on a lanyard. He picked up the ship's lantern, a heavy battery affair, still wrapped in the kapok jacket. He said: "If I find a boat, I'll flash the lantern twice. The password will be 'Roger,' and the answer will be 'Wilco.' "

It took Kennedy half an hour to swim to the reef around the next island. Now it was dark. He blundered along the uneven reef in water up to his waist, making his way like a slow-motion drunk, hugging the lantern. He cut his shins and ankles on sharp coral. At about 9 o'clock he came to the end of the reef, alongside Ferguson Passage.

He took his shoes off and tied them to the life jacket, then struck out into open water. He swam about an hour, until he felt he was far enough out to intercept the PT's. Treading water, getting chilled, waiting, holding the lamp, he listened for the muffled roar of motors.

He looked west and saw flares that indicated an action beyond Gizo, 10 miles away. Kennedy realized that the PT boats had chosen, for the first night in many, to go around Gizo instead of through Ferguson Passage. There was no hope.

Kennedy started back, but this swim was different. He was very tired, and the current was carrying him off to the right. He saw that he would never reach the island; so he flashed the light on once and shouted, "Roger! Roger!"—to identify himself.

The men saw the light and heard the shouts. They thought that Kennedy had found a PT. They walked out onto the reef and waited. They waited a long time, but they saw nothing and heard nothing. They went back, very discouraged. One said despairingly, "We're going to die."

Johnston said, "Aw, shut up. *You* can't die. Don't you know that only the good die young?"

Kennedy had drifted right by the little island. He thought he had never known such deep trouble, but something he did shows that subconsciously he had not given up hope. He dropped his shoes, but he held onto the heavy lantern, his symbol of contact with his fellows. He stopped trying to swim. He seemed to stop caring. His body drifted through the wet hours, and he was very cold. Darkness and time took the place of a mind in his skull. For a long time he slept, or was crazy, or floated in a chill trance.

The tide shoves and sucks through the Solomon Islands and makes the currents curl in queer patterns. Jack Kennedy drifted in a huge circle—west past Gizo, then north and east past Kolombangara, then south. When light came at about 6, he saw that he was in Ferguson

Passage, exactly where he had been the night before when he saw the flares beyond Gizo.

For a second time he started back. He thought for a while that he had lost his mind and that he only imagined that he was repeating his attempt to reach the island. But the chill of the water was real enough, and his progress was measurable.

This time he made the island and crawled up on the beach. He was vomiting when his men came up to him. He said, "Ross, you try it tonight." Then he passed out.

In the afternoon Ross waded into the water and swam across to Island B. He took a pistol to signal with and spent the night watching Ferguson Passage. Nothing came through.

The next morning everyone felt wretched. Some prayed.

Johnston said: "You guys make me real sore. You didn't spend 10 cents in church in 10 years, then all of a sudden you're in trouble and you see the light."

When Ross came back, Kennedy decided that the group should move to a larger island to the southeast, where there seemed to be more coconut trees and where the party would be nearer Ferguson Passage. Again he towed McMahon, with the strap in his teeth, and the nine others grouped themselves around the timber as before. The swim took three hours.

The men were suffering most from thirst. When they found some coconuts lying on the ground under the trees, they broke them open and avidly drank the milk. Kennedy and McMahon, the first to drink, were sickened, and the others were careful to drink sparingly. During the night it rained, and someone suggested moving into the underbrush and licking water off the leaves. In the morning they saw that all the leaves were covered with bird droppings. Bitterly, they named the place Bird Island.

On the fourth day of their ordeal the men were low. Even Johnston was low. McGuire had a rosary and Johnston said, "McGuire, give that necklace a working over, will you?"

McGuire said quietly, "Yes, I'll take care of all you fellows."

Kennedy was still unwilling to admit that things were hopeless. He asked Ross to swim with him to an island called Nauru, to the southeast. They were both very weak, but after an hour's swim they finally made it and staggered up on the beach.

They walked painfully across Nauru to the Ferguson Passage side. There they found a box of Japanese candy and hardtack, a keg of water, and a one-man canoe. The two had a wary feast. When night

197

fell, Kennedy took the canoe and a can of water from the keg out into Ferguson Passage. But no PT's came; so he paddled to Bird Island and gave out small rations of hardtack and water.

Before dawn Kennedy started out in the canoe to rejoin Ross, but a wind arose and the canoe was swamped. Some natives appeared from nowhere in a canoe, rescued Kennedy, and took him to Nauru. They showed him where a two-man canoe was cached. Kennedy picked up a coconut with a smooth shell and scratched a message on it with a jackknife: "ELEVEN ALIVE NATIVE KNOWS POSIT AND REEFS NAURU IS-LAND KENNEDY." Then he said to the natives, "Rendova, Rendova"— the island where the PT base was located.

The natives seemed to understand just what he meant. Taking the coconut, they paddled off.

Ross and Kennedy lay in a sickly daze all day. When it got dark, conscience took hold of Kennedy, and he persuaded Ross to go out into the Ferguson Passage with him in the two-man canoe. Ross argued against it. Kennedy insisted. The two started out. As they got into the passage, the wind rose. The waves grew until they were five or six feet high, and eventually they swamped the dugout. The two men clung to it, Kennedy at the bow, Ross at the stern. The tide carried them toward the open sea; so they kicked and tugged the canoe, aiming for the island. They struggled that way for two hours.

The weather got worse; rain poured down and they couldn't see more than 10 feet. Kennedy shouted: "Sorry I got you out here, Barney!" Ross shouted back: "This would be a great time to say I told you so, but I won't!"

They saw a white line ahead and heard a frightening roar—waves crashing on a reef. It was too late to do anything except hang on for dear life and wait.

A wave broke Kennedy's hold, ripped him away from the canoe, and turned him head over heels. His ears roared and his eyes pin-wheeled, and for the third time since the collision he thought he was dying. Somehow he was not thrown against the coral but floated into a kind of eddy. Suddenly, he felt the reef under his feet. He shouted, "Barney!" There was no reply.

Kennedy thought of how he had insisted on going out in the canoe, and he again called, "Barney! Barney!" This time Ross answered. He, too, had been thrown on the reef. His right arm and shoulder had been cruelly lacerated, and his feet, already infected from earlier wounds, were cut some more.

They struggled to the beach, fell down, and slept. In the morning

they were awakened by a noise. They looked up and saw four husky natives. One said in an excellent English accent: "I have a letter for you, sir." Kennedy tore the note open. It said:

> On His Majesty's Service. To the senior officer, Nauru Island. I have just learned of your presence on Nauru Is. I am in command of a New Zealand infantry patrol operating on New Georgia. I strongly advise that you come with these natives to me. Meanwhile, I shall be in radio communication with your authorities at Rendova, and we can finalize plans to collect balance of your party. Lt. Wincote.

Everyone shook hands, and the four natives took Ross and Kennedy in their war canoe across to Bird Island to tell the others the good news. There the natives built a lean-to for McMahon, whose burns had begun to rot and stink, and for Ross, whose arm had swelled to the size of a thigh. Then they put Kennedy in the bottom of their canoe, covered him with sacking and palm fronds in case Japanese planes should buzz them, and made the long trip to New Georgia.

Lieutenant Wincote came to the water's edge and said formally, "How do you do. Lieutenant Wincote."

Kennedy said, "Hello. I'm Kennedy."

Wincote said, "Come up to my tent and have a cup of tea."

That night Kennedy sat in the war canoe waiting at a rendezvous arranged by radio with the PT base. The moon went down at 11:20. Shortly afterward, Kennedy heard the signal—four shots. He fired four answering shots.

A voice shouted, "Hey, Jack!"

Kennedy answered, "Where the hell you been?"

In a few minutes a PT came alongside. Kennedy jumped onto it and hugged the men aboard.

The PT picked up the men on Bird Island and roared back toward base. The squadron medic had sent some brandy along to revive the weakened men. Johnston felt the need of a little revival. In fact, he felt he needed quite a bit of revival. After taking care of that, he retired topside and sat with his arms around a couple of roly-poly, mission-trained natives. And in the fresh breeze on the way home, they sang together a hymn all three happened to know:

> Jesus loves me, this I know,
> For the Bible tells me so;
> Little ones to Him belong,
> They are weak, but He is strong.
> Yes, Jesus loves me; yes, Jesus loves me.

*Antis was a war dog. Born on a World War II battleground,
he became a decorated hero. Yet, to his master, Antis was
simply a friend, loyal and steadfast.*

The Dog
From No Man's Land

By Anthony Richardson

THE DEAFENING crash was followed almost at once by a long,
grinding roar. The noise was terrifying, and the German shepherd puppy, reacting frantically, struggled to get on his feet. He fell
over helplessly, uttering a tremulous cry. He was too weak from
starvation to stand up.

The farmhouse that was his home lay in no man's land between the
Maginot and Siegfried Lines. A few days earlier—it was now February 12, 1940—great thunderblasts of artillery had toppled the farmhouse walls, killed his mother and litter mates, and sent the farm
family scurrying. The puppy had lain alone in the ruined kitchen ever
since, cowering whenever the shelling recurred.

But that last blast had not been gunfire. It was the crash of a low-
flying reconnaissance plane, followed by an explosion of gasoline and
the roar of flames. A few minutes later two airmen from the French
1st Bomber-Reconnaissance Group, both lucky to be alive, spotted
the ruins of the farmhouse. The pilot, Pierre Duval, had taken a
bullet through his calf; so it was Jan Bozdech, observer-gunner, who
strode forward to investigate.

As he stepped inside past the sagging kitchen door, automatic pistol in hand, Jan heard the sound of quick, excited breathing.

"Put up your hands and come out," he ordered, covering a suspi-
cious-looking pile of rubble.

There was no reply. With pounding heart, the airman carefully
moved forward and peered over the debris.

"Well, I'll be damned," he said. Then he began to laugh.

Pierre hobbled in, trailing blood. "What is it?" he asked.

"Look! I've captured a German," Jan replied. Reaching down, he brought up the tawny German shepherd puppy. Although the animal was quivering with fright, it bared its milk teeth, snarled defiantly, and even nipped at his hand.

"Here now," Jan said, stroking the base of the dog's ears, "you've just been saved from execution. I almost shot you, you know." Under this reassuring touch, the puppy relaxed in Jan's arms.

A ground fog had thus far protected the two downed airmen from German eyes. But this might lift at any time, and it would not be safe to try for the French lines until dark. They settled down to wait.

The wounded Pierre rested in a chair and closed his eyes. Jan dug out his chocolate ration and offered a lump to the dog. It sniffed the morsel, but did not eat until Jan lit a match and melted a piece. He rubbed the softened chocolate on his fingers. Once started, the puppy happily licked the airman's fingers clean again and again. Then it snuggled into his arms and slept contentedly.

Using one hand, Jan spread out a map on the floor and studied it. It showed a wood about a mile away. If they could make this, they should be in French territory. At 6 o'clock Jan shook Pierre awake.

"It's dark," he said. "We'd better be getting on."

For a moment they studied the puppy, sleeping on the floor. They couldn't take it along, for if it whimpered it might betray them. They left some of their rations beside a pan of water. Jan pulled the sagging door off its hinges and propped it sideways across the entrance so the puppy could not follow. Then they stole away.

As they set off for the wood, an exchange of gunfire broke out. They inched forward on hands and knees. Before they had moved 30 yards, a magnesium flare sputtered almost overhead, brilliantly lighting the terrain, and the two men flattened themselves instinctively. As the flare died away, Jan heard the noise he had been dreading—the frantic yelping of a puppy who knew he was being abandoned.

The animal would have to be silenced. Jan felt for his knife and, motioning Pierre to lie still, crept back. As he neared the farmhouse, he heard the puppy hurling itself against the barrier he had braced across the entry. Two forelegs momentarily hung over the edge while the hind legs scrabbled desperately. Then the dog slipped back down.

Jan peered over the barricade, straight into the puppy's imploring eyes. He turned away. It was unthinkable to kill a dog with a knife. He searched the ground for a heavy stick with which to stun the animal, but there was none. Thinking of Pierre lying injured in the darkness, he began to panic; he must hurry. Then he heard an anguished whimper from the other side of the door.

"Oh, hell," he muttered, and the last shreds of his firm resolution snapped. Reaching down into the dark, he lifted the puppy up and slipped it inside his flying jacket.

It took the two men almost seven torturous hours to reach the fringe of the protective wood. Pierre, weakened by his wound, was at the limit of his endurance, and even Jan collapsed, utterly spent.

During all this ordeal the puppy hadn't made a sound. But now he began to whine uncontrollably.

The noise roused Jan from near-sleep. "Be quiet," he muttered.

"Listen," Pierre said. "He hears something that we can't."

Then, like a pistol shot in the dark silence, a twig snapped and half a dozen figures emerged from the trees. Jan sprang to his feet, holding the dog with one hand and reaching for his automatic with the other one. But in the shifting moonlight he saw the uniforms of the French infantry. They'd made it to safety!

Using their rifles and a greatcoat to improvise a stretcher, two of the soldiers carried Pierre to the nearest blockhouse. Next day he was sent to the hospital. And Jan, gently clutching the puppy, was driven back to his squadron base at St. Dizier.

Here he belonged to a particularly close band of seven Czech exiles. All seven had been members of the Czech Air Force before Hitler invaded their country. They then had escaped through Poland, joined the French Foreign Legion in Africa, and later had been attached to the French Air Force. All had the same fighting spirit, the same determination to strike back against the Germans at all costs.

Perhaps it was their very homelessness that made them so susceptible to Jan's puppy. They loved him at once, immediately adopted him as a mascot, and after some discussion named him "Antis" after the A.N.T. bombers they'd flown back in Czechoslovakia. As Joshka, a slight, curly-haired youth from Moravia, commented, "The name should be unique, short, and typically personal for our dog."

"*My* dog," Jan corrected. But he assented to the name.

Every night Antis slept in the blockhouse at Jan's feet. As the weeks passed, he flourished and grew and, being intelligent and lovingly instructed, he learned to shake hands with each of his friends.

France tasted defeat that spring when Hitler's panzer divisions drove south with demoralizing speed. The squadron fled from one threatened airdrome to another until the day Paris fell. Then it was assembled for the last time.

"Gentlemen," the adjutant announced solemnly, "the unit is disbanded. Now it is every man for himself. May God be with you!"

The seven Czechs held a council. "We came here to fight, not to run away," said Vlasta, the senior member of the group. "I suggest we stick together, try to get to England, and carry on from there."

There was no dissent. Within 15 minutes the seven had piled all their possessions on an ancient cart and, perching Antis atop the load, joined the stream of refugees fleeing southward. And, because they were both determined and lucky, some two weeks later they found themselves in the small Mediterranean seaport of Sète. From there they made their way to the British naval base at Gibraltar.

Once the British had satisfied themselves about the Czech fliers' credentials, they assigned all seven to the Royal Air Force and ordered them to proceed on the trawler *Northman*, bound for Liverpool. They were finally going to England!

There was, however, one small problem: No dogs were allowed on board. British regulations absolutely forbade it. A flying wedge of Czechs smuggled Antis up the gangplank in a raincoat and spirited him into the stokehold. Jan loyally remained with the dog, spreading a blanket on the grimy coal.

On the second day out the *Northman's* engines broke down, and all passengers were ordered to transfer to another vessel. Hurriedly the Czechs divided Jan's baggage among themselves so that there would be room to conceal Antis in his duffel bag. All went well until they reached the deck of the new ship, where Jan paused momentarily to shift the weight of the bag.

"Move along, please," the ship's interpreter remarked curtly, and at the sound of the strange voice the duffel bag wriggled perceptibly. As it did, Jan lost his grip on the cord enclosing its neck. Immediately Antis thrust his head through the opening and looked out—directly into the astonished eyes of the British officer of the watch. The seven Czechs all stood as if paralyzed.

"Hullo," said the officer with a grin, "a stowaway! Well, let the poor beggar out before he suffocates." He released the cord and Antis dropped to the deck, shaking a cloud of coal dust around him.

"Now get him below and give him a bath before the captain sees what a mess you've made of his deck," the officer said, turning away to check off another group of transferees. Jan was pushed along in a daze, with Antis trotting at his heels.

The rest of the trip was made in luxury—real bunks, clean laundry, washbowls in the cabins. Antis, given his freedom, regained his vitality and glossy coat.

But as they approached Liverpool, the fliers received devastating news. All animals had to be quarantined in port for six months; animals whose owners could not pay the kennel fees would be destroyed. All the money the fliers had among them would not ransom Antis for more than three weeks.

But resourceful men have coped with greater problems. And by then the Czechs were seasoned conspirators.

When the ship docked at Liverpool the next evening, Jan and Vlasta wangled the assignment of overseeing the unloading of the detachment's baggage. After the last of it had been stacked in the cargo net, they then carefully placed a large, oddly shaped duffel bag stenciled "Jan Bozdech" on top of the pile.

Within the hour the bags were stacked neatly on the platform at Liverpool Central Station, Jan's still on top of the heap. Three minutes before their train steamed in, a platoon of soldiers marched up, halted, and ordered arms. A rifle butt struck the bag labeled Bozdech, and a loud yelp of protest arose.

Immediately the military police converged on the pile. The Czech detachment, always eager to help, joined in the search, heaving the baggage about and passing Jan's bag from hand to hand under cover of the general confusion until it was well clear of the suspected area. Surreptitious yelps with an imperceptible Czechoslovakian accent also misled the pursuers.

When the airmen's train arrived, the police gave up in disgust.

A quarter of an hour later the eight comrades were on their way to their first camp in the United Kingdom. It was July 12, 1940.

For men who had been on active combat duty, going back to flying school was irksome. At Cosford, and then at the Duxford RAF station, the Czechs also spent many exasperating hours poring over a book called *Fundamentals of English.* They almost welcomed the sporadic German air attacks that disrupted their study routine.

Jan devoted his spare time to training Antis. He was no expert handler and treated the animal simply as though he were a fellow human being. Antis responded with the most devoted and intelligent obedience. He quickly mastered all the standard commands, learned to close doors when ordered, and unfailingly fetched Jan's gloves when his companion dressed to go out.

While Jan was in class, Antis stayed with the armorers. He developed an unusual ability to detect enemy aircraft and was always minutes ahead of the base's high-frequency direction finders. The warning system worked only when the planes were flying high. When the Germans came in at treetop level, it was of little use. But Antis, the armorers claimed, invariably alerted them in time to take cover.

JAN WAS SKEPTICAL, for he had always been in class at the start of the raids. But one night, when he was studying in his bunk, Antis suddenly woke up and trotted to the window, ears cocked. There was no sound except the hiss of rain, but the dog began to growl.

"Go and lie down," Jan said. "There's nothing out in this weather."

Antis whined persistently. Then, seeing that Jan had no intention of moving from the bunk, Antis flattened his ears reproachfully and lay down. Half an hour later Joshka looked in as he came off duty from the Operations Room.

"Thick out," he said. "I wouldn't have been up there tonight for anything. I'll bet the German who came over was lost."

"Tonight?" Jan asked. "I didn't hear a thing."

"About half an hour ago," Joshka said. "Very high. We were plotting him just over 15 miles away when he turned back."

"Well, I'll be damned," Jan said, and by way of apology reached down and rubbed Antis' ears. The canny dog had been right.

That fall, when the Czechs were transferred to Speke airfield, five miles from Liverpool, Antis' peculiar ability became very important. Liverpool was a major target, subject to heavy bombardment. The dog's warnings were uncannily accurate, and the men came to depend on him to alert them whenever the immediate area was threatened.

One night when Jan and Vlasta were returning from liberty in town, the dog began to whine just as they neared a massive archway beneath the Speke viaduct. Over Liverpool the air was ribbed with searchlights and the horizon blinked with exploding bombs, but as yet there had been no warning siren.

"They *must* be headed this way," Jan said as the animal's whine grew more insistent. "Come on, let's hole up under the archway."

Almost immediately they heard the approaching engines. The first bomb burst just as they flung themselves under the viaduct.

Now explosion followed explosion; a girder fell, splitting the granite pavement; masonry toppled at either end of the arch. Where there had been a neat row of houses beside the viaduct there was only rubble. A long silence ensued, then someone began to scream.

"Come on," Vlasta yelled. "We've got to get them out."

They ran into the street. A man with blood spurting from a mangled arm blundered into them.

"Save her!" he shouted. "She's under there. We were having a cup of tea . . ." His voice trailed off.

A rescue worker thrust a pick into Jan's hands. Antis, standing by the shattered remains of a kitchen cupboard, his forepaws deep in broken china, began to bark. Jan looked closely and saw five fingers moving in the rubble. Digging quickly, he uncovered a dazed and blood-streaked woman.

"Good dog," the rescue worker said. "Bring him over here, will you? There's bound to be others. Lord, what a shambles!"

Jan followed the man to a pile of smoking plaster and shattered furniture. "Seek!" he ordered.

Halfway up the heap Antis stopped short, sniffing. An RAF officer started to dig where Antis stood, and within a few minutes he had a man out who had been totally buried and was still unconscious.

They continued working until 2 in the morning. When the rescue-squad leader passed the word that the job was done, the dog's coat was matted, his paws cut and bleeding from scrambling over the wreckage.

"There's no more we can do here," Vlasta said. "Let's go back and have Antis tended to."

But Antis was straining at his leash again, dragging Jan toward a sagging brick wall.

"No more, boy," Jan said. "We've had enough—"

A crash cut him short as the wall collapsed. Horrified, he felt the leash jerk out of his hand.

"Antis!" he shouted in the din. "Antis!" Vlasta flashed his light to where the wall had been. There was now only a head-high pile of brick and timbers. Instantly Jan was on his knees, pulling up chunks of plaster and flinging them in every direction. Again he shouted almost hysterically, "Antis!"

From somewhere behind the rubble came an answering bark. The men quickly broke through to a little room knee-deep in debris. A woman, sprawled on her back under a mass of plaster, was dead. But in the far corner Antis stood by a crib; the child in it was still alive.

The rescue-squad director was visibly moved. "You know, boy," he told Antis, "we just couldn't have done the job without you."

By early January 1941 Jan, Stetka, and Josef had completed their flying-school and flight training and, with Squadron No. 311 (Czech Squadron of Bomber Command), were posted to East Wretham for combat duty. The move reunited them with the other Czechs who had been training elsewhere and gave them at long last a chance to get at the hated enemy. But it meant that Antis, for the first time, had to accustom himself to separations from Jan. For the night bombing missions, which the squadron was soon flying, ofter lasted from late evening until dawn.

For weeks Antis was moody and dispirited. Then he established rapport with the maintenance crew assigned to *Cecilia*, his master's plane, and seemed to adjust himself to the absences. The dog would accompany Jan to dispersal, see him get aboard the big Wellington bomber, then retire to the maintenance tent, which stood at the edge of the field. Once there, he would settle down for the night and not budge as long as the planes were out.

But sometimes before dawn he would suddenly rise and cock his ears, and the maintenance crew knew then that the squadron was returning. As soon as Antis discerned the particular pitch of *Cecilia*'s propellers, he commenced to bound and prance excitedly—his "war dance," the mechanics called it—and then he would trot out to watch the planes come in and to greet Jan. The ritual never varied.

But one night in June, after Jan had flown more than 10 missions, the mechanics noted a sharp departure from routine. Shortly after midnight Antis became unusually restive. "What's the matter with him?" one asked. "Are we expecting visitors?"

"No," replied Adamek, the crew chief, "no Jerries about tonight." He spoke directly to the dog. "Antis, calm down."

But the dog ignored him and went to the tent flap. Suddenly he lifted his muzzle and let out a long howl. Then he lay down outside,

not resting, but with his head up as if preparing for a long vigil.

At half past one the first returning Wellington blinked her identification lights and rumbled down the runway. She was followed at regular intervals by other planes until all but *Cecilia* were accounted for. Two hours passed; there was still no sign of Jan's aircraft.

"No point hanging on here," one of the mechanics finally said. "She'd have run out of gas by now."

"We'll give it 15 minutes more," Adamek said. When the time was up and the plane had not appeared, the crew reluctantly decided to disperse for breakfast.

"Come along, Antis," said Adamek. The dog would not move.

Just then the squadron's popular wing commander, Josef Ocelka, drove up to the tent. A longtime admirer of Antis, he had promised he would look after the dog if Jan ever failed to return from a mission.

"Any news of *Cecilia*, sir?" one of the mechanics asked, while Adamek struggled with Antis.

"Not yet. Give him a shove, Corporal," Ocelka suggested.

"It's no good, sir." Adamek replied. "He won't move until Jan shows up. I know him."

"So do I, dammit," Ocelka said. "Let's go. Perhaps he'll change his mind when he gets hungry."

After breakfast Adamek went back to the tent with a plate of liver. Antis ignored it, as he ignored the driving rain that had begun to fall. When Adamek saw that no amount of coaxing would move the dog, he spread a tarpaulin over him and left.

Late that afternoon Operations Room was informed that *Cecilia* had been hit by flak over the Dutch coast but had managed to limp back to Coltishall airfield with only one casualty. Air gunner Jan Bozdech was in Norwich Hospital undergoing treatment for a superficial head wound. The Czechs were elated at the good news. But no one could convey it to the dog.

All that night Antis stayed at his post. Next morning, at the time when the squadron customarily returned from raids, he stood up and paced about. An hour after dawn, when no plane had appeared, he began to howl disconsolately.

"He'll starve," Ocelka said, "and drive us crazy while he does. We've got to think of something."

It was the station chaplain, Padre Poucnly, who provided the solution. He went straight to the heart of the matter by telephoning the medical authorities at Norwich. Sergeant Bozdech was not seriously hurt. Would it be possible to run him out for a short trip in an ambulance and then board the dog at the hospital for a few days? (A medical consultation followed.) Yes? It would? Thank you so much.

And that was that. The ambulance arrived that afternoon, and the two inseparables rode back together to Norwich Hospital. There both of them were outrageously spoiled by the nurses until Jan recovered.

By the time Antis had waited out 30 of *Cecilia's* missions, all the crew felt that they knew his habits thoroughly. But one night shortly after the aircrew roll call the dog disappeared. Although there was no trace of him anywhere, and it was unlike him to alter a long-established routine, no one was particularly concerned. Antis had long ago proved that he could take care of himself.

When the plane leveled off at 8,000 feet, Jan gave a last worried look at the Wretham airfield, now indistinguishable in the darkened English countryside. Then he put the dog out of his mind and concentrated on checking his guns.

"Navigator to wireless operator," the intercom crackled suddenly. "Can you hear me?"

Engrossed in his own duties, Jan only half listened to the reply. But the navigator's next words jarred him to full attention.

"Am I going round the bend, or do you see what I see?" he asked.

There was a flurry of incredulous profanity. Then, "He must have got into the emergency bed by the flare-chute. Someone forgot to check it. Jan, open your turret door—we have a stowaway."

Jan knew at once what had happened. He opened the hatch and, as nonchalantly as if it were an everyday occurrence, Antis crawled into the turret and settled down between his feet.

"You villain!" Jan exclaimed. "We ought to drop you out with the bombs." But nothing could be done about it. The Wellington droned on, and Antis drifted off to sleep.

As they went over the target, a dense curtain of flak rocked the aircraft, but the dog stayed calm as long as Jan appeared unmoved. In response Jan found himself forcing signs of encouragement despite the intensity of the barrage, and thus each drew strength from the other. Then in a few moments the danger had passed, and they were on their way home unscathed.

They had just disembarked when Ocelka drove up. Since it was against Air Ministry regulations to take an animal on missions, the men braced themselves for a tongue-lashing. Like many easygoing officers, Ocelka could be vitriolic when the occasion demanded.

"How did you all make out?" he asked coolly, casting a sidelong glance at Antis. The pilot, Jo Capka, briefly described the run and the heavy fire they had encountered. The crew shuffled nervously as the recital came to a conclusion.

"Heavy fire, eh? What do you think of that?" Ocelka asked, looking Antis squarely in the eye. "Don't you think these poor boys need someone to hold their hands?"

Jan could stand it no longer. "I can explain, sir," he began, but Ocelka cut him off.

"What the eye doesn't see the heart doesn't grieve," he said curtly. "I've enough trouble on my hands with two-legged beasts without looking for any from four-legged ones. Now let's get back to Operations and make out the reports."

From then on Antis was accepted as a regular member of *Cecilia's* complement. His unruffled behavior under fire was all the more welcome because the men were nearing the end of their standard tour of combat duty. This was always a time of increased tension for any aircrew, for they all knew that more than one plane had gone down on its last trip. Unaware of their anxieties, Antis raced for the plane as if each mission were a pleasure trip, and inevitably something of his élan communicated itself to the crew.

He began to amass quite a respectable combat record and eventually sustained two wounds in the line of duty. The first occurred over Kiel, when a fragment of shrapnel lacerated his left ear, which acquired a permanent droop. The second ended his flying career.

DURING AN ATTACK on Hanover, as *Cecilia* was turning homeward after releasing her bombs, a shell exploded directly beneath the plane. The engines were not damaged, and no one reported being wounded; but when they reached East Wretham, the undercarriage jammed and they had to belly in for a landing. Only then did Jan discover that Antis had a three-inch shrapnel wound in his chest.

Jan rushed the dog to Station Sick Quarters, where he was stitched up. Thereafter Antis was grounded and barred from the field. Much as the dog resented the restrictions, they were somewhat easier to bear because he did not know Jan was still flying. While *Cecilia* was being repaired, the crew was assigned another plane, and since its propeller pitch was unfamiliar, Antis simply ignored it.

A short time later Jan completed his tour of 41 missions (of which Antis had shared 7) and was relieved of further combat duty. He spent the remaining two years of the war first as an instructor, then in flying antisubmarine patrol.

The first years of peace were blissfully happy ones for Jan. When he returned to his triumphantly liberated country, he was given a captaincy in the Czech Air Force and eventually was assigned to the Ministry of National Defense in Prague. Both he and Antis became well known to the public, for Jan wrote three books about service in the RAF. Almost every newspaper in Czechoslovakia carried tales of his war experiences with the dog.

When Jan married a golden-haired girl named Tatiana, Antis distinguished himself at the wedding by becoming entangled in the bridal veil. (He later made up for it by his steady devotion to Tatiana.) And when a son, Robert, was born to his idols in 1947, the baby became the dog's personal charge. At night he slept near the crib, instantly alert if the child awoke or cried. The dog would then rise, steal to the side of the big bed, and thrust his cold nose against the mother's bare shoulder. And if this failed to waken her, he would drag the covers away.

It was a wonderful time for all of them, but it was not to last.

On March 7, 1948, Jan Masaryk, Minister of Foreign Affairs and godfather to little Robert, telephoned from the Cernicky Palace.

"Please come round and see me, Jan," Masaryk said. "I have a present for your little boy."

As he put down the telephone, Jan knew that this summons might bring his life crashing about his ears. He had seen Masaryk only the previous day, so why should this good friend ask to see him again at this moment? There could be but one reason, and Jan approached the Cernicky Palace with dread.

"You are high on the Communist blacklist, Jan," Masaryk told him. "The blow can fall any time now. You must keep this completely to yourself. Even Tatiana must not know. You've got to get out of Czechoslovakia as soon as possible."

This then was the "present" for little Robert. But even that ruse had been necessary, since every telephone was tapped.

Acting through the Czech Communist Party, Soviet Russia was implacably taking over all the country. As the cold war intensified, everyone who had had associations in the West became suspect, and for months Jan had been aware that his apartment had been under surveillance. His friends knew it and no longer dared visit him. The Defense Ministry was now being packed with Communist informers, many of whom spoke Russian. Recently, two strange officers had been installed in his own department—ostensibly learners, but unquestionably spies.

Three days after Masaryk's warning was issued, it was grimly underscored by the fact that Masaryk himself was dead. According to the Communists, he had jumped from a Foreign Office window.

Jan faced an agonizing dilemma. He could not leave his wife and son while there was any possibility of a life for them together. But if he were imprisoned, they would be in a far worse position than if he fled. It was hard to know what to do, and for weeks he vacillated. Then one morning General Prachoska of the Czech intelligence service summoned him, and the decision was taken out of his hands.

"Sit down, Bozdech," the general greeted him. "Major Marek, my aide, would like to ask you a few questions."

"You are the author of these?" Marek began curtly, handing Jan three books and a folder of press clippings.

Jan nodded.

"And there have been broadcasts, radio plays, all glorifying the British?" Marek continued.

"I served in the RAF," Jan explained. "My writing is only a record of my experiences, without political significance—"

"On the contrary," Marek interrupted. "This work is treasonable. If you continue writing, your attention will be directed to the Red Air Force only. That is an order." He paused. "And there is one other matter. You are a member of the Air Force Club?"

"Yes, sir," said Jan. The fliers' organization was often referred to as the "English Club" because of the high percentage of members who were ex-RAF officers.

"We know that all sorts of opinions are expressed in this establishment, and we are interested in them. To put it bluntly, Captain, we want you to listen to, and if necessary encourage, criticism of the present regime. You will then report to this department the names of members whose remarks indicate that they are enemies of the state."

Jan was aghast. But as he began to protest, Marek brandished a blue document that had been lying on his desk. "I have here a police warrant for your arrest, dated Friday. You have three days to make up your mind. Is that clear?"

Jan did not return home until late that night. Long after dark he walked the streets alone, desperately seeking some way out of the trap set for him. He would never spy on his friends; that much was sure. If he remained in his post and defied the Communists, imprisonment and death were almost certain. His course was plain. No option remained but to flee the country.

To his great surprise, he woke the following morning with his mind refreshed and his nerves calm. Now that the long-dreaded blow had fallen and his intentions were resolved, his problems seemed almost preternaturally clarified.

He set off for his office at the usual time.

Some 50 yards from the Ministry of National Defense, a passerby awkwardly blundered into him.

"Excuse me, Brazda," Jan said in embarrassment, recognizing the man as a casual acquaintance, one of the instructors at the sokol physical-training college.

"If you are in trouble," Brazda said in rapid undertones, "listen to me. Tonight at 8. The Café Pavlova Kavarna at Strahove. The password is, 'May I offer you a vodka?' "

Then begging Jan's pardon for his clumsiness, Brazda left. The machinery of the underground movement had begun to turn.

AT 8 THAT NIGHT, when Jan appeared at the Café Pavlova Kavarna, the machinery caught him up smoothly. A dapper little man led him to a small upstairs room where he was confronted by two other members of the underground, a student and an elderly man who had obviously once been a soldier. The former military man, who was the leader of the group, wasted no time on formalities.

"Captain Bozdech," he said, "the deadline for your arrest is Friday. That gives us only one day to get you out of the country. It is not much time. You must make your decision quickly.

"You understand the risks, of course. If you are caught attempting to cross the frontier, they shoot first and ask questions later. So you must go alone, and perhaps we can arrange for your family to follow later by a less dangerous route. Agreed?"

Jan's heart sank, but he nodded.

"Very well," the spokesman said. "Now here are your instructions. Listen carefully." And for the next five minutes the three anonymous agents outlined down to the smallest detail what Jan would have to do the following day. Then with a warm bon voyage they dismissed him.

Tatiana was asleep when Jan returned home that night. Looking at her face, sweet in repose, he recalled Masaryk's warning, "Even Tatiana must not know." Of course Masaryk was right, Jan mused as he turned out the light. Both for her safety and little Robert's, it was best that he slip off this way. But next morning when he said good-bye to her, he found it almost impossible to keep his voice steady, and the closing of the door behind him was like a blow above the heart.

When he reached the office, he summoned his civilian clerk, Vesely. He had decided during the night that, risky as it might be, he would have to make one change in the underground's careful plans. Antis would have to come with him. Otherwise, as Jan knew from long experience, the dog would stubbornly refuse to eat; and Jan simply could not condemn him to certain starvation.

"Vesely," Jan said, "I've an appointment for Antis at the vet's at 11 o'clock. Would you go round to my flat later and collect him? I'll give you my gloves so he'll follow you."

"Very good, sir," Vesely replied.

Two hours later, when his unwitting accomplice returned with the dog, Jan knew that the time had come. The escape was now to begin. As he went out the door, he stopped for a moment casually. "I'll be back after lunch if anyone wants me," he said.

One of the Stalinist spies looked up from his paperwork. "We'll hold the fort," he said sarcastically. "Take your time."

"Thanks," said Jan. "I will."

Following the underground's instructions, he took a tram to the Vaclavska Namesti and went into the busy public lavatory there. When he asked a prearranged question, the attendant at once handed him a parcel containing a change of clothing. He was to travel as a peasant with a knapsack full of butter to sell.

The attendant kept Antis while Jan changed in one of the booths. Everything was complete, the sizes right—from the rough felt hat to the heavy boots. There were also a dozen packages of butter.

"You look a treat," the attendant muttered as Jan emerged from the booth and handed him a 500-crown note along with the parcel (which now contained Jan's smart air force uniform). "I hope you get a good price for your butter."

It was 150 yards to the Wilsonova Station. But no one took the least notice of him as he clumped through the tumult of traffic in his strange new boots, entered the station, and bought a ticket. The train came in, and he and Antis climbed aboard. Six minutes later, still following instructions, he alighted at Smichov.

This was but the beginning of a long and circuitous course that eventually brought Jan to a certain farmstead where he spent the night. Next morning a taciturn driver concealed him, along with Antis, in the back of a two-ton van. After a long ride they stopped at a remote cottage in a heavily wooded area.

"This is Anton's," the driver said. "I leave you here."

"Who is Anton?"

"A forester. He will guide you over the border."

As the van drove away, a tall, tanned man stepped from the cottage.

"What can I do for you?" he asked evenly, his eyes on the dog.

As he had been told to do, Jan offered him a package of a certain brand of cigarettes. The man turned it over in his hand ruminatively. Finally he said, "Why have you brought the dog?"

"Wherever I go, he goes too," Jan said.

Anton's face darkened. "Wherever you go, he goes," he repeated. "My God! Do you think this is a picnic outing? One bark from him and we're dead. You'll have to leave him behind."

"Then I'd better start back," Jan said.

"You'll have a warm welcome. The alarm will be out by now."

Jan realized this was true, for it was now Friday. But about Antis his mind remained stubbornly set.

"So you really want to risk your neck for the dog, eh?" Anton said. "Well, we'll see what Stefan says. He'll be coming with us."

He called into the cottage and in a moment a bearded, erect man emerged. Anton explained the situation to him, but the man said nothing, staring at Jan and Antis as if trying to recall something.

"Antis is trained," Jan said quickly. "He won't make a sound, and he may be able to help us."

"Antis," Stefan said. "That's it. I've read about you two and seen your picture in the papers. He can come, as far as I'm concerned."

Anton shrugged, then smiled at Jan. "You'd have found it a long walk back to Prague," he said. "But I like your spirit. You'll do. Now wait here, both of you."

He went into the house and returned immediately with two revolvers. "I hope we don't have to use them," Anton said, "but the positions of the observation posts are always changing. You never know."

Squatting, he began to trace a map on the ground with a stick. "Here," he said, pointing, "is our first obstacle, a forest about two miles deep. It's infested with patrols. We come out of the forest here," he indicated the spot, "then cross a small valley, which is also constantly patrolled. Then here is the West German frontier, and half a mile past it the village of Kesselholst. Once we're there, we're safe.

"We'll leave immediately. I want to reach the far side of the forest in daylight. Then we'll hole up and make the last dash across the valley after dark."

A car carried Jan, Anton, Stefan, and Antis 15 miles to the edge of the forest, and early that afternoon they plunged into the matted underbrush. Unavoidably they made a lot of noise, and as a precaution against being surprised by roving border patrols, Jan sent Antis ahead with instructions to "seek." Twice the dog stopped, growling a low warning when no other sound was audible, and seconds later the three men heard the faint, far-off sound of snapping twigs and hailing voices. They lay in the underbrush without stirring until the patrols passed, then moved cautiously on. It was almost sunset when they finally reached the far side of the wood.

From its border they carefully scanned the open valley that lay between them and Kesselholst. To their left was a narrow road and, paralleling it, a turbulent river. No patrols or strongholds were visible. As the evening light waned and the lights in the village began to go on, Anton murmured, "All right, let's go."

They had covered only a short distance when they heard Antis growl. Jan dropped to the ground, as did his companions. A moment later four dim figures stole past them down the slope.

Without warning, two searchlights suddenly split the night, sweeping across the valley. Rocks, bushes, and boulders seemed to leap out of the darkness as the light beams passed, converging, separating, then pouncing simultaneously on their prey. Four men, scarcely 50 yards from Jan, were caught scrambling frantically for the trees. They were obviously other escapees. Before they could reach the cover of the trees, machine guns opened fire, and all four fell.

As Jan, Anton, and Stefan watched, two trucks then sped up the road. Men alighted, picked up the bodies, and drove off.

"We're lucky to be alive," Anton whispered. "The way I intended to take is blocked by a new post, and if those four hadn't passed us, we'd have walked right into it. We'll have to double back and take another route across the river."

They crept silently back to the wood and then spent a hellish hour struggling blindly through the close-set firs to the riverbank. As soon as Jan stepped into the water, holding Antis by the collar, the current began to undermine his footing.

"Link hands," Anton said.

Jan clamped Antis' jaws onto the tail of his coat, and the four of them, clinging tightly to one another, edged their way toward the center of the swift-flowing river. As the current swirled about their waists, Jan slipped on a loose stone, staggered, and lost his grip on his companions' wrists. Immediately he was swept downstream, dragging Antis with him, until he struck a boulder and managed to grasp it. Recovering his balance, he saw that he had been carried into shallower water and he waded the few yards to the far shore.

Antis was with him, but there was no sign of Anton and Stefan. He dared not shout. Kneeling beside the dog, he ordered, "Seek!"

For several minutes after Antis had gone, there was no sound but the roar of the river. Jan wondered if he had been a fool to send the dog on such a hopeless errand—the current could carry a man 50 yards in a few moments. Then suddenly he felt a blow on the shoulder, and as he reached for his gun, a voice beside him began to curse. It was Anton and behind him was Antis.

"Sorry," Anton said. "I was crawling and bumped you with my head. Thank God for the dog. We'd never have got back together without him. Do you think he can find Stefan?"

At an order from Jan, the dog again disappeared. It was some time before he returned, leading his bedraggled and exhausted quarry.

"I was swept a long way downstream into a pool," Stefan explained. "But Antis found me. I think he saved my life."

After a moment's rest they pressed on, climbing toward a ridge that lay within a few hundred yards of the frontier. A dense fog shrouded the forest near its crest, and it became impossible to see a foot ahead. Antis ran from man to man, as a sheep dog handles his flock, guiding them. But at the top of the rise Anton decided that it was useless to continue the journey while the mist obscured all landmarks, and the four settled down to await the dawn.

AT FIRST LIGHT they moved behind a giant boulder to plan their final dash across the border. Jan posted Antis atop the rock as lookout.

Since Anton had no idea what new posts they might encounter, they decided to cross the valley one at a time, and Anton broke a twig in lengths for lots to see who would go first. As he extended his hand, Antis growled and leaped from the top of the boulder. There was a clatter of stones, a stifled cry, and savage snarling.

Gun in hand, Jan ran around the rock. Antis was straddling a soldier who lay sprawled on his back, his rifle useless beneath him. Anton sprang at the guard, his knife upraised.

"No!" Jan cried. Anton hesitated.

"Jan is right," Stefan said. "It would be murder."

"The swine deserves to die," Anton said, but he grudgingly got off the man's chest. Quickly they gagged him and lashed him to a tree, then ran down toward the valley.

At the edge of the wood they stopped abruptly. In the meadow ahead a single guard post, with telephone wires running from its roof, blocked their way. Helpless, they crouched in the brush for almost an hour, watching the hut. There was no sign of movement.

"Try the dog," Anton whispered, and Jan sent Antis to seek.

Antis trotted out and stood sniffing beside the closed door. Then he barked. There was no response.

"I think there was only one guard in there," Stefan said, "and now he's tied to a tree."

Jan was on his feet, shaking with excitement. "Let's go," he cried, and they sprang into the open field. Far off down the valley someone shouted, but the three men and the dog raced on, down the slope and across the stream at its base. From far behind them they heard a telephone jangling in the hut in the meadow, and the sound of a distant whistle reached them.

"On! On!" Anton cried.

Another open field lay before them and, beyond, a wood. They ran for the sanctuary of the trees, and at last they knew that their feet were on German soil.

As soon as he had delivered his charges safely to the West German authorities, Anton bade Jan and Stefan farewell. He would return to Czechoslovakia and risk his life again to keep the escape route open for other proscribed men.

"Pray God we meet again in happier times," he said in parting. "I certainly was wrong about the dog. He was our salvation."

Within a week after his arrival in West Germany Jan received some heartening news from his homeland. A Czech refugee who had known him in Prague brought word that Tatiana and Robert had suffered no reprisals and were living quietly with her parents. After he received this report, he was convinced that his decision to flee Czechoslovakia had been the right one. He applied for reenlistment in the RAF and was accepted.

On this trip to England, however, there was no squad of loyal Czechs to smuggle Antis past the inspectors, and Jan had no choice but to surrender him for the legal six-month quarantine. Now a familiar difficulty arose. Upon reenlistment Jan had reverted to the lowest rank in the service, and his entire salary would not cover the cost of the kennel fees. Thus in desperation he applied for help to the People's Dispensary for Sick Animals in London, submitting a full report on the dog's history.

The clinic's response went far beyond Jan's expectations. Not only were the fees paid, but Antis' story was widely publicized. As a result, in March 1949 he was awarded an unprecedented tribute. He became the first non-British dog to receive the Dickin Medal, the Victoria Cross of the animal world. In a moving presentation speech Field Marshal Archibald Wavell, one of England's greatest soldiers, cited

Antis' "outstanding courage, devotion to duty and lifesaving on several occasions while serving with the Royal Air Force."

"I am sure," the field marshal concluded, "that everyone will join with me in congratulating you on your award, Antis, and we wish you many years in which to wear it."

Actually there were to be few more years for Antis, but during that time he and Jan were closer than ever. Jan heard no more from his wife, son, or parents, so Antis became his only family. As Antis' sight dimmed and his muzzle whitened with age, he could not bear even the slighest separation from his beloved master.

Each year, wherever they were posted, Jan performed an unvarying ritual on Christmas Eve. Beside a miniature Christmas tree, glittering with tinsel and artificial frost, he propped up photographs of Tatiana, Robert, and his parents, thus preserving at least one tangible link with home. On Christmas Eve of 1952 Jan finished his small arrangement and went to bed early. Sometime that night he awoke, conscious of a strange weight on his chest. Reaching out, he found that it was Antis, resting his head there.

This was most unusual. Once the dog had retired for the night, he could be depended upon to stay on his blanket until morning.

"What's wrong, Antis?" Jan asked. "Go back to bed, old-timer."

Jan heard a tremulous sigh, followed by the scrabbling sound of the dog's paws on the floor, then the sound of a falling body.

Instantly Jan switched on the light. Antis was lying on his side, unable to rise. Jan carried him to his bed and began to massage his legs, continuing the treatment at intervals all that night. By noon of the next day Antis managed to stand, but he was too weak to follow his master outside, and Jan stayed with him during the base's Christmas festivities. From his window he could see the lights in his mess and hear the sound of laughter and singing, and twice friends looked in to suggest that Antis might be left for a while. Jan thanked them, but he stuck to his vigil.

He sat by the table with the Christmas tree on it and took up Tatiana's photograph. She looked radiant in her wedding dress, and he remembered how Antis had become entangled in her veil when they left the church. Now across at the mess they were playing "Silent Night," and Jan remembered Christmases at other posts. The room was full of ghosts: Adamek and Joshka, Ocelka and Vlasta; scores of them trooped in. And soon Antis would be with them.

It seemed to Jan that 100 years had passed since the day—12 years before—when he had found that small puppy in no man's land.

*Determined to escape from a Soviet
slave-labor camp near the Arctic Circle, a small band
of desperate men set out on foot on an
incredible journey of more than 4,000 miles. Only the
hardiest of the band survived the awesome
trek to reach their final goal—India.*

The Long Walk

*By Slavomir Rawicz
as told to Ronald Downing*

SLAVOMIR RAWICZ was a 24-year-old lieutenant in the Polish Army when he was arrested in 1939 by the Soviet secret police and charged with spying. Vigorously maintaining his innocence, he was subjected to a year of physical and psychological torture before he was declared guilty of espionage and plotting against the people of the U.S.S.R.

Rawicz was sentenced to 25 years of forced labor and sent to Siberia. The journey from Moscow to the prison camp was a brutal one, first by cattle car, then on foot through subzero temperatures. Rawicz has recounted the story of his ordeal and ultimate escape in a book, *The Long Walk*. Parts of that extraordinary document are reproduced here, beginning with Slavomir Rawicz's arrival in northern Siberia at Camp 303 close to the Arctic Circle.

LIFE IN CAMP 303

A FAINT EARLY-MORNING HAZE dissipated, and in the cold, clear light of day I looked around at the place to which I had been consigned to spend 25 years of my life. Camp 303, lying between 300 and 400 miles south of the Arctic Circle, was a rectangular enclosure about a half-mile long and about 400 yards broad, at each corner of which stood a guard tower raised high on solid timber stilts, manned by machine-gun crews. The main gate, around which were built the troops' quarters, the kitchens, storehouses, and administrative huts, faced west in one of the shorter sides of the oblong. Roughly in the center of the enclosure was an open stretch of ground that served as the security no man's land between the soldiers and the prisoners.

Between us and the surrounding forest were the typical defenses of a prison camp. Looking from the inside, the first barrier to freedom was an unbroken ring of coiled barbed wire, behind which was a dry moat six feet deep, its inner side cut downward at an angle of about 30 degrees and its outer wall rising sheer and perpendicular to the foot of the first of two 12-foot-high log palisades presenting a smooth surface inward but strongly buttressed on the far side. Both outer sides of the two wooden walls were protected by rolled barbed wire. The space between the two provided a well-beaten track giving access from the main gate guardroom to all four control towers. It was patrolled by armed sentries accompanied at night by police dogs, who shared kennels near the west gate with a pack of sled dogs.

Mingling diffidently with us that first morning were about a thousand men, a large proportion of them Finns, who were already installed when our bedraggled crowd of some 4,500 arrived. They came from four big huts at the eastern end of the compound.

These log-built prisoner barracks were about 80 yards long by 10 yards wide, conforming in situation with the general plan of the camp itself. The doors faced west in the narrow end and were protected from the direct blast of wind and snow by a small covered porch with a southerly opening. It was obvious that there were no accommodations for us newcomers.

Speculation was cut short by orders from the troops to line ourselves up for food. We shuffled along in line to the open window of the kitchen, one of the buildings to the left of the main gate. There was the usual issue of ersatz coffee and bread. Each man drank up as quickly as he could and returned his tin mug through another window. There was plenty of hot liquid but a shortage of utensils.

Soldiers carried a portable wooden platform out into the middle of the parade ground. Around it, under orders from junior officers and NCO's, they formed a ring. We prisoners were then hustled to form ourselves into a big circle around the troops, facing inward toward the platform. Accompanied by a small armed guard, two Russian colonels walked through the ranks to the foot of the platform. One of them stepped up.

From my place in the front row I eyed him closely. He was tall, slim, and distinguished looking, his hair graying at the temples, a typical example of a professional soldier in any army. His small gray mustache was carefully trimmed, and his lean face showed two deep lines etched from a firm mouth into a strong chin. He was facing a hostile audience, a mob of ill-treated humans whose bitter hate of all things Russian was almost a tangible thing, but he gave no sign. He stood perfectly relaxed with no movement of hands, feet, or body.

He spoke clearly and crisply in Russian. "I am Colonel Ushakov," he said. "I am commandant of this camp. You have come here to work, and I expect from all of you hard work and discipline. I will not talk to you of punishment since you all probably know what to expect if you do not behave.

"Our first job is to provide shelter for you. Your first task, therefore, will be to build barracks for yourselves. How quickly you get inside out of the weather depends on your own efforts.

"If you have any complaints, I will always listen to them, and I will do what is in my power to help you. There are no doctors here, but there are trained soldiers who can administer first aid. Those of you who are now too sick after your journey to work will be housed in the existing barracks while the rest of you get on with the new buildings. That is all I have to say."

He stepped down. Immediately the other colonel took his place. He did not step up so much as leap forward in eagerness. There was nothing relaxed about this man. If there was a sense of restrained authority about Ushakov, this fellow wore his power like a flaunting banner. He was better dressed than the commandant. He wore a sheepskin jacket, and his well-made high boots were of soft leather, brightly polished. He was young enough to have been Ushakov's son.

If I ever knew his name, I do not remember it. He was the political officer, and we never called him anything but the Politruk, the short title by which all such officials were known.

He stood for fully a minute just looking at us, smiling faintly, eminently sure of himself, a picture of well-being and arrogance. The men stirred uneasily and stayed quiet.

He spoke strongly, harshly, and insultingly. "Look at you," he said, hunching his shoulders and placing his gloved hands on his hips. "You look like a bunch of animals. You are supposed to be the highly civilized people who fancy they can run the world. Can't you now appreciate what stupid nonsense you have been taught?"

Fortified by his anonymity in the restless crowd, one brave man had the temerity to answer back. His voice shocked the silence of the pause that the Politruk had allowed himself for dramatic emphasis after his opening onslaught. "How can we look any different? You won't let us shave; there's no soap and no clean clothes."

The Politruk turned in the direction of the voice. "I'll get your food ration stopped if I am interrupted again."

He was not interrupted again.

"After a time here," he went on, "and under the guidance of Comrade Stalin, we shall make useful citizens of you. Those who don't work don't eat. It is my job to help you to improve yourselves. You can attend classes to correct your way of thinking. We have an excellent library, which you can use after working hours."

There was some more in the same vein. Then, briskly, "Any questions?" A prisoner asked, "When does spring come here?" Replied the Politruk, "Don't ask stupid questions." The meeting ended.

The first few days of building the new prisoners' barracks were chaotic. All were willing enough to work, but it was most difficult to direct the men with the best qualifications to the work for which they were suited. The positions sorted themselves out smoothly enough after about three days. There were teams of architects and surveyors to plan out the ground and mark with stakes the plots for each hut. There were teams of young laborers hacking away at the frozen earth to make deep postholes for the main structural timbers. There were builders, men skilled in the use of axes to rough-shape the virgin wood from the forest. The main labor force issued forth from the camp gate every morning at 8, in the charge of armed soldiers.

I joined the forest workers. The camp was awakened by a bugle at 5 A.M., and there was an early morning procession of half-asleep men to the latrine trenches inside the wire behind the building site. The lineup for breakfast would follow. Tools were issued from the store on the left side of the gate, carefully checked out, and as scrupulously checked in again at the end of the day. As we marched out of the gate, a tallyman ticked off our names against his lists.

The forest was mainly of pine, but there was also an abundance of birch and larch. I worked in a felling team, handling one end of a heavy, crosscut, two-man saw. Occasionally I was able to get some variation by lopping with an ax the branches of the trees. Since the days of my boyhood at Pinsk I had always been handy with an ax, and I enjoyed the work. I found my strength coming back daily. I became absorbed in the bustle and activity. There was a glow of pride and satisfaction in being able to use my hands again. At 1 P.M. we went back to the camp, manhandling for delivery to the builders the timber we had cut. We received a midday issue of soup and returned to the forest to work until the light faded. Each day the line of huts increased in length.

Two weeks after our arrival the huts were finished. They lay in two lines with a wide "street" between each line of 10 huts. I was allocated a bunk in one of the last half dozen to be completed, and I well remember the wonderful feeling of shelter and warmth, protection and comfort I felt the first time I came in out of the chilling night into my new home. The air smelt deliciously of fresh-cut pine. Down each long side wall of heavy timbers were 50 three-tier bunks, simply made of planks laid out within a strong, four-post framework. Three square, sheet-iron stoves equally spaced out down the length of the room blazed red into the gloom, fueled by short pieces of sawn log, of which a supply was brought in daily by the forest working parties. Following the example of those already installed in their huts, we had brought in as much moss as we could carry in our kapok-padded jackets, called *fufaikas,* to spread on the hard boards of our beds. There were no chimneys for the stoves; the smoke issued from a short stovepipe and curled away through vents in the roof.

We had to spend many hours in our huts. After 6 P.M. all prisoners had to be back in their own quarters. A certain amount of movement in and around the huts was allowed as long as there was no standing about in large groups. Both lines of barracks were under close supervision from the towers at the eastern end of the compound, but as long as prisoners obeyed the strict order to keep away from the wire, the guards took no action. There was nothing much to do in the huts. There was nothing to read and no light to read by. The only activity permitted after the 6 P.M. deadline was a visit either to the Wednesday night lecture by the Politruk or to the library, the other Politruk-controlled enterprise.

It was a lively, cynical, and entertaining Czech occupying a bunk near me who persuaded me to go with him to one of the Politruk's Wednesday night talks, compulsory for all off-duty troops. The Politruk made no secret of his pleasure at seeing us and addressed a few special remarks to us before proceeding to deal with his military class. He spoke of the might of Russia, of her dominating place in the world (with asides to us on the decadence of the evil capitalist system). Soldiers asked questions, and the Politruk answered with the dogma of Marx and quotations from the speeches and writings of Lenin and Stalin. He was smiling as we left. He would not have been smiling a few minutes later had he watched the Czech put on a magnificent show for the benefit of the prisoners in our hut of the Politruk's education of the Red Army. I joined in the uproarious laughter. The Czech was a born actor and mimic.

BY THE END OF the first month the camp had settled into a disciplined rhythm of life, and there was a general feeling that, harsh though existence was in this remote, winter-bound spot, conditions could have been much worse. All working prisoners were given 400 grams (some 14 ounces) of bread a day. The bread was issued with the early morning coffee; part was eaten then, another portion went down with the midday soup, and the rest was taken with the hot drink handed out at the end of the day's work.

There was an occasional treat on Sunday when we were given dried fish, but bread remained our staple diet and the most important single factor in our lives. Tobacco, too, was important. There was a fairly generous issue once a week of the coarse *korizhki*, with a sheet of very old newspaper to act as cigarette paper. Bread and tobacco were the only commodities of value in the camp. They were the currency of the camp, the only means of payment for services.

The mortality rate continued high in that first month. Many of the men who survived the death march wrecked in body and mind never did any work. They were given bunks in the existing huts when we arrived and, worn-out beyond endurance, just lay there day after day until they lost their feeble grip on life. Volunteer burial parties from among their friends carried their bodies under armed escort to a clearing about a quarter of a mile from the camp, labored to hack graves out of the frozen earth, and committed them at last to rest.

Twice I went out with burial parties and in so doing discovered that the commandant was provided with an airplane. Our way took us past what seemed to me to be an inadequate runway cut out of the forest at its highest point. The plane, protected by tarpaulins, stood under the shelter of some trees. It was a small Tiger Moth trainer type. One of the guards said Ushakov piloted it himself to attend conferences at area army headquarters at Yakutsk.

The Russians interfered very little with our lives outside working hours. Inspection of our quarters was infrequent and perfunctory. Prisoners working in felling teams in the forest found new friends and at first sought permission to change from one hut to another to bunk near their teammates. The authorities offered no objection and let it be known that such moves could be made as a mutual arrangement between prisoners. Most men could be persuaded to switch places from one hut to another by a bribe of tobacco, and there was therefore a constant movement in those early weeks as men sorted out themselves and their friends.

I knew none of my companions particularly well, although I still occasionally saw Grechinen, who had been my companion on the march to Siberia. Apart from him there was only the Czech, whose wit and gaiety I admired but who was never a close friend.

I used to lie on my bunk in the long evenings looking up to the smoke vent 20 feet above me and think about it all. The insistent, hammering thought always was, "25 years in this place." Many of the men I now knew would die as the years passed. There would be fresh entries. And I would get older and older. Twenty-five years. As long to go as I had already lived. But how to get out? And having beaten the wire, the moat, and the formidable wooden fences, where would one escape to? Did anyone ever get out of Siberia? No man could hope to fight his way out alone against the crushing hazards of this country with its immense distances. Where, having planned an escape, could one find resolute men to make the attempt? These and other questions I put to myself. And I had no answers.

I fell in with Grechinen on the way to the latrines one evening. "Grechinen," I said, "if I could one day think up a plan of escape, would you come with me?" A frown creased his forehead. "Are you serious?" I nodded. Grechinen ran his fingers slowly through his beard. "Rawicz," he answered finally, "I will think about it tonight and tell you tomorrow."

Cautious Grechinen. I saw him the next day in the wide space between the two rows of huts.

"No," he said. "I would come with you if there was a chance, but the snow and the cold would kill us before we could get anywhere, even if the Russians didn't catch us." I shrugged my shoulders. "I still don't want to die young," added Grechinen.

I put the same question to the Czech. He thought at first that I was joking. Then he sat down on the edge of his bunk and motioned me down beside him. He put his hand on my shoulder. Quietly, in a voice just above a whisper, he said, "Yes, I would come with you, but you want strong and healthy men. My stomach plagues me, and I think it will eventually kill me. If I came with you I would die that much sooner out there, and you would suffer for having me with you." We sat there in silence for a few minutes after that. Then the Czech spoke again. "If you get the chance, clear out, my boy. Keep your eyes peeled, pick your men. I shall wish you luck, anyway."

We worked hard for six days and had an easy day on the seventh. Sunday was the day when the commandant addressed the prisoners. He would talk of the work target for the following week, draw attention to any infringements of camp rules, and make any necessary announcements affecting the life of prisoners.

We had been there a month when the commandant called for volunteers for a new job. He wanted men who had experience in making skis. There was no response at first. Said the commandant, "Volunteers will receive an immediate increase of their daily bread ration, and there will be more if the skis turned out are of good quality."

Sixty men volunteered, and I was one of them. I had once made a pair of skis. I could not claim to be an expert, but for an extra three or four ounces of bread a day I was willing to try my hand.

The ski shop was the other half of the building occupied by the library. Half a dozen of the volunteers were real experts at the job, and by common consent they divided the rest of us into a team of handymen for the actual process of manufacture and an outdoor crew for felling the birch trees, sawing the wood into the right lengths, and keeping up a steady supply of the right timber to the shop. My achievement in having once made a pair of skis earned me a job inside the hut on the last stage of steaming and shaping.

Working in the warmth of the ski shop, with the big stove roaring all day for the steaming of the wood, I felt I was getting back toward my full strength again. It should have made me resigned to my sentence, but instead it turned my thoughts more and more to escape. I began to wonder how I could preserve and hide some of my extra bread. I still had no workable plan, and I could not know then that I was soon to get help from a most unexpected quarter.

THE WIFE OF THE COMMANDANT

I HAD VOLUNTEERED ONCE and struck it lucky. I volunteered again one cold blustery Sunday morning in mid-March as flurries of snow swept about the hunched-up prisoners at the weekly parade.

"In my quarters," said Ushakov, "I have a radio set. It is called a Telefunken. Is there any one of you who knows this make of set well enough to do a repair job?"

I knew the Telefunken, because we had one at home—a German make. Men turned their heads to see who might step forward. There was a full minute of silence, and nobody made a move. I knew the set, but could I repair it? If I could, there was the exciting prospect of hearing some news from the outside world. I had a sudden panic that somebody else would get the job. I stuck up my hand and called out. An NCO stepped up and took my name and my place of work. "I will send for you when I want you," said the commandant.

It was to be a fateful decision, launching me into the last and most extraordinary phase of my stay at Camp 303. In this isolated community of between 5,000 and 6,000 men under sentence and a battalion strength of officers and men, there was but one woman. The defective Telefunken was to be the means of my meeting her, and, so far as I knew, I was the only prisoner who ever talked to her.

The following afternoon, as I worked in the ski shop, the commandant's messenger, a moon-faced private named Igor, called for me. "The commandant wants you," he said. "Come with me." As we left, the other men in the shop called out, "Find out how the war's going," and "Get us some news from Poland," and so on. I waved my hand. I confess I felt nervous as I walked away from the ski shop, across in front of the big gate, past the officers' mess to the commandant's house standing on the other side of the camp at the northwest corner of the parade ground. It was, like all the other buildings, built of logs with the typical porch opening south to keep the wind and snow away from the front door. As I stepped inside, I saw it only differed from the style of the prisoners' barracks in that it had an inner skin of smooth plank walls, a wooden ceiling and floor, and a stovepipe that went all the way up through the roof.

Igor ushered me in. Ushakov stepped forward toward the door, dismissed Igor, and motioned me in. "I have come to look at the set, *Gospodin Polkovnik,*" I said in Russian, using the old Russian style of respectful address to a colonel.

"Yes, of course. I will show it to you." He stepped past me.

The woman sat in front of the stove, which had been placed so that it protruded through the partition that divided the house into two rooms, thus heating both halves. The colonel murmured a conventional introduction to his wife. I bowed and said something formal, and she smiled with a small inclination of her head. I found myself staring at her. She was the first woman I had met since I left my mother in Pinsk. I felt awkward and ill at ease, painfully aware of my ugly clothes, my beard, and my long hair that curled over the neck of my jacket. I could not take my eyes off her.

She stood up, and I saw she was tall for a woman. She wore a long thick skirt and a dark woolen cardigan over a white, flower-embroidered cotton blouse. Her brown hair, tightly plaited and wound in the Russian style like a halo around the head, had a live, well-brushed sheen, and I was struck by the clearness of her skin. I was never much good at guessing women's ages, but I think she would have been nearing 40. She was not beautiful, but she had that quality of essential womanliness, a way of holding herself, an ease of moving, a way of looking at one, that would command attention anywhere. I came out of my fleeting trance to find her blue eyes regarding me with frank pity and sympathy. I turned my head away and saw Ushakov standing in the doorway between the two rooms looking at me in that preoccupied and detached manner of his.

"Let me show you the radio," he said.

The inner room was their bedroom and his office combined. Along one wall nearest to the stove was a heavy wooden bunk, at the head of which was a cupboard in which I could see his uniforms hanging. Near it, against the wall farthest from the door, was a solid wooden chest. The bed was to my left as I walked in through the partition door, the chest immediately in front of me. The part of the room to my right was Ushakov's office. Hanging on the wall was a big contour map of eastern Siberia. There was also a plan of the camp and a colored portrait of Joseph Stalin. On a bench under the all-seeing eye of Stalin was the radio, a brand-new, battery-operated Telefunken.

Ushakov gave me a Pushki cigarette, fetched over a kerosene lamp, and set it down on a bench near me. I took the back off the set and began running my fingers along the leads, suspecting a loose connection somewhere. Ushakov asked me questions about the set—where it was made, what it cost, how it worked.

Hesitantly, I inquired where he had got it.

"I happened unfortunately," Ushakov answered, "to be in charge of troops in Poland in 1939, and I acquired it there."

My mind seized on the use of the word "unfortunately." It tied in with the theory that the prisoners expressed that even to be commandant of a camp in Siberia was in the nature of a punishment. I had the impression then—and it was later to be strengthened—that Colonel Ushakov owed his appointment to Siberia to some indiscretion on his part during the Polish campaign.

He went back to the fire and sat down on the polished bench with his wife. I worked on, unhurriedly checking the circuit. After about half an hour I was aware that she was busying herself in the next room, and then he called me to the fire, while she poured out two mugs of tea, saccharine sweetened. The colonel drank first and then gave his mug to me. I went back to the radio, and as I worked, I surprised myself with the thought that I was not going to rush this job, that this was my most pleasant experience since my arrest, and that I must make it last. When Igor came to take me back, I explained that checking all the leads and valves was a slow business.

"Very well," said Ushakov, "you must come again. I will send for you." He gave me another cigarette, and I went off with my escort.

"What's the news?" the men called out to me when I got back.

"I haven't got the set going yet," I said, "but I'll tell you what's happening as soon as I do."

Igor fetched me again the next day. As I fiddled with the set, the colonel and his wife both talked to me. She was impressed by the fluency of my Russian. I told her my mother was Russian.

"What did you do to get sent here?" the colonel asked.

"Nothing," I said.

"You have 25 years, haven't you?"

"Yes."

There was a short pause, and then she spoke again. "Twenty-five

233

years is a long time. How old are you?" I told her that I was 25.

The three-way conversation was interspersed with some odd silences. They sat close together on the bench; I was on my haunches looking over the top of the Telefunken. Surprisingly, Ushakov asked me if I thought Russia would be involved in another war. The last war for Russia, as far as he was concerned, was that of 1914. I mentioned Finland and Poland. "Ah," he replied, "that wasn't war; it was liberation." I wondered if he really believed it. I popped my head over the top of the radio and looked at him. He was gazing up at the ceiling, and his face was expressionless. He returned to the question of Russia being involved in war.

"In Poland," I said, "it was common knowledge that Goering came to us to get us to give the Germans a corridor through which they could attack Russia. Germany is ready, and the attack is inevitable." I gabbled it out fast. I expected to be told I was talking too much. But neither Ushakov nor his wife made any comment.

It occurred to me that they did not seem anxious to hurry the repair of the radio. I had found what I believed to be the fault, a loose battery lead. But I just did not want to put the back on the set,

Slavomir
Rawicz

connect the radio, and switch it on. I thought my visits must then end.

She asked me about prewar Poland. What were the women's fashions? They were often elegant, I said, straight from Paris. And high-heeled shoes? Yes, I said. They, too, were very attractive.

Two days went by before I was summoned again.

On this third visit I started straightaway to get the Telefunken working. Ushakov was busy at his desk, and the woman did all the talking. She asked me about the films I used to see and was surprised to hear that Russian films were banned in Poland. As she talked, I switched the radio on. It hummed into life, and I began to turn the dials. Ushakov left his work and came over beside me. We heard a concert from Moscow. I went from station to station, picking up fragments of news, and finally we heard the voice of Hitler, ranting in his own unmistakable fashion, at a youth rally in the Ruhr.

Ushakov gave me a whole packet of korizhki tobacco and a sheet of old newspaper. As Igor stood in the doorway waiting to escort me away, Ushakov said, "If the set needs any attention, I will send for you again. I am afraid we do not understand how it works." I went back and told the men all I had learned from the wireless. Their greatest interest was in Germany and the speech by Adolf Hitler.

It was now nearing the end of March. I worked uninterruptedly for several days in the ski shop and began regretfully to think that the Telefunken episode was over. Just about that time I came to know a remarkable man named Anastazi Kolemenos. I had seen him come in occasionally to warm himself at the big fire. He was one of the finest physical specimens I have ever seen, over six feet tall, blond-haired and blond-bearded, with curious gray-green eyes. In spite of the privations he had endured, he must have weighed close to 200 pounds. He was a kind and helpful giant of a man, whose job it was to carry the birch logs and split them for use in the ski shop.

I was standing outside the ski shop door watching him one day. I walked across to where he had piled some logs and went to lift one to take it over to him. The end came up easily enough. I tried to get a grip around the middle to hoist it up. It defied my efforts. Then, suddenly, Kolemenos was beside me.

"That's all right, friend," he said, "I'll do it."

He bent down and swung the log onto his shoulder in one powerful movement. I did not regard myself as a weakling, but this man's strength was phenomenal. I spoke to him, spontaneously telling him who I was. Kolemenos told me his name and volunteered the information that he had been a landowner in Latvia and was now 27 years of age. The old escape idea came surging into my mind, but this was no place to talk of it. "We will have to talk some time," I said.

"I shall be glad to," answered the giant.

Over the clatter of workshop activity they called out to me, "Your friend has called for you again."

Igor stood stolidly inside the door and beckoned. I put down a ski I was testing, dusted myself off, and walked out with him.

Ushakov was there and so was she. He told me that the set was not working too well. I tested it, and it seemed to function, although the signal strength was down a little. I told him he would be advised to get spare batteries, and he said he would arrange that. He put on his greatcoat, murmured something to her about having to attend an officers' meeting, and went out. There was great understanding between these two, and they were completely devoted to each other.

"I will make some tea for you," she smiled. "You can find me a station with some good music."

235

She talked on for a while about the music she liked, praised Chopin, but declared that her favorite composer was Tchaikovsky. She told me that she played the piano and that having to leave her piano behind was one of her greatest hardships here in Siberia.

I found her the kind of music she wanted, and, with a symphony orchestra as the background, she talked about herself. She talked to draw me out, to get me to tell her about myself. It was as though she were saying, "This is me; this is my life. You can trust me."

I didn't quite know why this was happening to me. I said to myself that in spite of his exalted position here, these are really exiles and outcasts. She, especially, is almost as much a prisoner as I am. She is here only because he is here, and probably the real ruler of Camp 303 is the Politruk.

We sipped hot tea, and she kept her voice low. This was the story she told me. Her family had been army officers for generations before the revolution. Her father had been a colonel in the czar's personal guard and had been shot by the Bolsheviks. Her young cadet brother died of wounds received in the defense of the Smolny Institute. Her mother had fled with her from their home near Nijni Novgorod, and when, later, the mother died, she had adapted herself to the new order of life, got herself a work card, and found a job. She did well and earned herself a state holiday with other favored workers at Yalta. And there she met Ushakov. I gathered that from then on he was the only man in her life.

She was very loyal to Ushakov. She did not tell me why he had suddenly been posted from Poland. He went first to Vladivostock, and she had no word from him for six months. She knew some party people with the right influence. They told her that he was going to be put in charge of a camp in Siberia, and she strove unceasingly until her friends got her a travel permit to join him.

All the time I was telling myself: She talks to me because I am a prisoner and she is sorry for me and because she cannot talk about these things to her own people. Yet, amid lingering doubts, there was the conviction that this was an intelligent, sensitive, and most compassionate woman, and this camp, which surrounded her with the evidence of cruelly wasted lives, had shocked her. It was no place for a woman. She was a Russian, and she believed passionately in the great destiny of Russia. But she was also a woman, and I don't think she liked what she now had to see, day after day, month after month.

Those clear blue eyes held mine. "Do you ever think of escape?" The question panicked me. There was awful danger in it. I had my mouth open but could not speak. I put the cup down with a clumsy thump. And her eyes, wide open and blue and candid, still held me and watched my flutterings of fear.

The quiet voice was going on. "You do not answer, Rawicz. You do not trust me. I thought you might want to talk about it. There is no danger in talking to me about it. . . ."

Escape. It was as though she had looked into my mind and plucked out that one word of danger and longing and hope. Yes, I wanted to tell her about my perilous dreams. But she had shocked me into silence. The words would not come.

Then came Igor, and I turned to go, disconcerted and miserable, like a man who has turned his head from the extended hand of a friend. She spoke coolly and formally. "You will come again if the set needs adjusting?" My words came in a rush. "Yes, yes, of course I will. I shall be glad to."

I felt a slow burn of excitement as I waited through the next few days to see if I would get another call. I met a man named Sigmund Makowski, a 37-year-old captain in the Polish frontier forces. A precise, clear-thinking fellow, he was fit, active, and bore the stamp of the regular army officer. I marked him down, as I had marked Kolemenos, but I said nothing of my plans at this stage. I do not know what I expected of the colonel's wife, but at least I thought she would be in a position to advise.

Call for me she did. She was alone, and when I had tuned in the radio, dallying round the dial to pick up some news items for my friends, she started to talk of the approaching short Siberian summer.

I took the plunge. "I am sorry about the last time," I said. "Of course, I do think of those things, but the distances are so great, the country so difficult, and I have no equipment to face such a journey."

"You are only 25," she answered. "You need not have been afraid to admit that you do not look forward to the next 25 years in these surroundings. I am quite well looked after here. We have comfortable quarters, better food than yours, and as many cigarettes as we need. But I couldn't spend 25 years here. So escape must be an idea close to your heart, and it may do you good to tell me what you think."

So we talked of it as an abstract thing, as though it were being contemplated by some third person. We posed the question: Supposing a man could get out of the camp, where could he head for? The only possibility for such a man, in my opinion, would be to make a dash due east the short 600 miles to Kamchatka and from there find his way ultimately to Japan.

The attempt would be a failure, in her opinion. The Kamchatka coast was a number one security commitment and would be heavily guarded. Could he smuggle himself onto a westbound train, maybe find himself a job in the Ural mines, and possibly make his way out of Russia later? There would be difficulties of travel and work permits and other vital papers, she said.

That was all the exploring we did that day, and it was not until I lay on my bunk that night thinking things over that I realized the one escape route she appeared deliberately to have ignored—south, past Lake Baikal. Whence from there? Afghanistan was the name that popped into my mind. It sounded sufficiently neutral and obscure.

It was the colonel himself who next sent for me. He genuinely could not work that simple radio set, a fact that greatly surprised me, for he was an intelligent man. He seemed to be a little in awe of it and liked to have me find the stations for him. He wanted news, and as I got it for him in various speeches and bulletins, he said he now felt certain that Russia would soon be involved in war. I don't think he wanted war, but in war obviously lay his chance to get out of Siberia and back to the real job of soldiering for which he was trained.

There was no fanciful talk of escape when the commandant was there. I imagine he would have been horrified to know that his wife had ever broached such a topic with a prisoner.

When the time came for me to go, he stayed near the radio and she walked behind me to the door.

"Don't worry," she said. "You will be all right."

That night I spoke to Makowski. I walked him over to the latrines. "What would you think of an escape?"

"Don't be crazy, man. We have nothing to escape with, even if we got outside the camp."

"I might get a little help."

"If you can, I'm with you. To hell with this place."

The colonel's wife appeared to be actively enjoying her role as conspirator in chief. I have been unable to decide whether she ever believed I would really attempt an escape. It might be that all this was an intriguing exercise for the sharp wits of a woman bored by depressing camp life.

The business had emerged from the abstract. She was planning away as the radio gave us one of her favorite Tchaikovsky symphonies. "You will want a small number of the fittest and most enterprising men. You, from your extra rations, will save a quarter of a kilo of bread each day, dry it at the back of your ski shop stove, and then you will hide it. I will find some sacking to make into bags. Skins you will need for extra clothing and footwear. The soldiers trap sables, and the officers shoot them. They hang them on the outer wire. The men working outside must grab one a day. No one will miss them. Plan your own way out and then head south. Wait for a night when it is snowing heavily, so that your tracks are covered."

And then, almost as an afterthought, "Colonel Ushakov will be leaving for a senior officers' course at Yakutsk shortly. I would not want anything to happen while he was in command."

A very loyal wife, this one.

I sought out Makowski immediately. "We are getting out," I said. "There will be a little help for us."

"How many men will you want?"

"About half a dozen," I said.

"Good. We'll find them. I know one I can recommend."

I thought of Kolemenos. "I know one, too. We'll start rounding them up tomorrow."

PLANS FOR ESCAPE

"THERE HE IS NOW." Makowski, standing beside me at the midday break the next day, indicated a prisoner standing a little apart from the rest. "Let us wait here a couple of minutes so that you can look him over." The man's shoulders were squared, and the shapeless clothes could not disguise that ramrod back.

"You are a cavalry man," said Makowski at length. "You should recognize the type."

"Who is he?"

"He's a Pole. Sergeant of Cavalry Anton Paluchowicz. He's 41, but strong and fit, well-trained, experienced. I'd go anywhere with him. Shall we talk to him?"

We went over and talked. I liked the look of Paluchowicz. He accepted the proposition like a good soldier undertaking a mission of war. He was glad to know I was a lieutenant of the Polish cavalry.

"We shall do it," he said. "It won't be easy, but we shall do it."

That evening I came up behind Kolemenos. I tapped him on the shoulder, and he turned. He smiled. "Oh, it's you again."

"Kolemenos, I am getting out of here with some others. Would you like to join us?"

He put one big hand on my shoulder. "You mean it? Seriously?" I nodded. "Yes, seriously. Perhaps very soon."

The big man smiled happily through his blond beard. "I shall come." He laughed and brought the weight of his hand down twice on my shoulder. "I could carry you on my shoulders if necessary."

Now there were four of us. We began to plan with a sense of urgency. It was the end of March, and I felt we had not a great deal of time. We began to watch things closely. We noted, for instance, that the starting of the dog patrol around the perimeter at night was always signaled by the yelping and whining of the sled dogs showing their annoyance at being left behind. That signal came only once every two hours. We discovered the patrol always went around counterclockwise, covering the long south side first. We decided the escape must be through the southerly defenses and that therefore we must get ourselves established in the end hut on that side. We began to bribe and cajole ourselves bunks in that hut.

Paluchowicz brought Zaro into the scheme. Eugene Zaro came from the Balkans, a Yugoslav I think. He was 30 and, before the Russians had caught up with him, had been a clerk. "If you want some fun on the way," said our sergeant, "Zaro is the man."

Like an inspection committee, Makowski and Paluchowicz and I watched him in the food queue. He was a well-built man, below average in height, and his almost black eyes had a constant gleam of laughter and mischief. The men around him roared in joyous gusts, and Zaro stood there, his eyes twinkling in a mock-serious face.

"All right," I pronounced, "we'll have him."

"I've always wanted to travel, and this sounds good," was Zaro's answer to my approach.

"It's going to be the worst trip you ever had," I told him.

"I know," he replied, "but I'm coming with you anyway." There was a pause. "The Russians have no sense of humor. It will do me good to get away from them."

So Eugene Zaro came in, and we were five.

I went on with my daily chore of drying a quarter of a kilo of my bread behind the big stove to add to the growing store hidden beneath the pile of rejected skis in the far corner of the shop.

Escapee number six was brought in by big Kolememos. He was a 28-year-old Lithuanian architect named Zacharius Marchinkovas, tall and spare-framed, with alert brown eyes. I was impressed by the manner in which he had already weighed the odds against us and decided that the slightest hope of success was worth the attempt.

When Sergeant Paluchowicz brought into our hushed deliberations the name Schmidt, I thought this must be one of the Russo-German colony who had joined our prison train at Ufa in the Urals. These Russians with German names were descendants of German craftsmen imported by Peter the Great.

"Is he German?" I asked the sergeant.

"His name is Schmidt, but I do not know," was the answer. "He speaks Russian very well and easily. He stands apart from the others. He does a great deal of thinking by himself, and he gives me excellent advice on everything. I recommend him to you."

Makowski and I announced our intention of meeting Mr. Schmidt the next day. "I will point him out to you, then," said the sergeant with a smile.

Schmidt was coming up to the window of the kitchen for his coffee when Paluchowicz indicated him with a jerk of the head. Makowski and I strolled over.

My first impression was that he might be too old for the rigors of the adventure we were planning. I judged him to be about 50. He was well built, wide-shouldered, and slim-waisted. His thick hair and beard were tinged with gray. He had seen us coming and, probably because the sergeant had warned him of the meeting, showed no surprise when I spoke. "We would like to talk to you."

I spoke in Russian. He answered in Russian, "Walk toward the huts, and I will join you." He moved on and we walked away.

Holding his mug of coffee, he fell in with us and, clear of the crowd, we stopped. He faced us and smiled. "Gentlemen, my name is Smith. I understand you have a proposition."

Makowski and I stood there, mouths agape. *"Smith?"* We repeated the name together.

"I am Smith, Mr. Smith. I am an American." He grinned happily at our astonishment. "You are surprised, gentlemen."

We just could not believe our ears. His Russian was impeccable. I could detect no trace of an accent.

"It is hard to believe," I said. "How did you get here?"

He had an easy, patient, almost professorial manner of speech. "Let me repeat, I am an American. By profession I am an engineer and was one of a number cordially invited by the Soviet government to help build the Moscow Metro. There were about 50 of us. That was 9 or 10 years ago. They arrested me in 1936, convinced themselves I was a professional foreign spy, and gave me 20 years." He drank his coffee. We were still looking at him like a pair of fools.

"Now I'll take my mug back and we shall walk together to the huts."

The three of us walked slowly to the huts. By now, the beginning of April, Makowski and I had got ourselves bunks near the door of the end hut. Kolemenos had also managed the switch, and the others hoped to join us within a few days.

We invited Mr. Smith into our hut. Sitting on Makowski's bottom bunk, I cautiously outlined our plans. I told him I had sound reasons for believing that only the long road south held any chance of success, although some of the others were still reluctant to drop the idea of the short route east to Kamchatka.

He did not rush to answer. He asked a few shrewd questions. We sat silent as he thought things over. And then, "Gentlemen, it will be a privilege to join you. I agree that the south route is the best. You can count on me."

We sat long with Smith. All our histories, our Russian dossiers, followed a similar pattern. Smith was different. He was the odd man out, and he intrigued us. He told us much, but neither then nor ever did he tell us his Christian name. Later, when we six Europeans addressed one another by our first names, the American was always, as he first introduced himself, Mr. Smith, the "Mister" somehow being accepted as a substitute for the name we were never told.

He had a ridged scar curving lividly from right to left from the crown of his head to the nape of his neck, some eight or nine inches long. He received it, he explained, when some scaffolding fell on him during the Metro building.

"Apart from the accident that give me this scar," he told us, "I had a good time in Moscow for a few years. The work was interesting, I was highly paid, and I found the Russians easy to work with. They had skilled engineers themselves, but key positions went to foreigners like myself. The reason, I think, was that this Metro scheme was a great prestige prospect, and if anything went wrong, national pride would be saved by having a foreigner as a scapegoat. I was quite happy. I had wanted to see Russia, and I was being financially well rewarded for the experience."

In a Moscow obsessed between the wars with its five-year plans, Smith and his friends, installed in well-appointed apartments and with money to spare to buy luxuries in shops where the entry permit was either a party membership card or a foreign passport, must have been conspicuous. Smith had a car and traveled around freely—a circumstance that must have earned him an underlined report in secret police records. He had a Russian girl friend; the police would not have liked that. But they let him go on, working hard and playing hard.

"I never saw the blow coming," he went on. "After a year's work, the Russians, without any move from me, doubled my salary, which had been fixed by contract, to show their appreciation of the steady progress that was being made with the work. From then on I thought I was well in with them."

Smith was in his flat with the girl after midnight one evening in 1936 when the NKVD called in force. They were quiet, determined, and most efficient. Smith and the girl were both arrested. He never saw her again. Other occupants of the flats probably never saw or heard a thing. When dawn came, Smith was occupying a cell in the Lubyanka—it was to be his home for the next six months. They refused his demands to see someone from the United States Embassy.

"What a transition," mused Mr. Smith. "One day a successful engineer, the next a professional foreign spy. It seems that apart from keeping a general watchful eye on my activities they had been opening my mail home. The main charge was that I had been sending out information about Russia in my letters to my folks in America.

"The trial was secret and farcical. I got 20 years, as I told you. They confiscated my car and all my possessions, so perhaps they got back most of the extra salary they had so generously awarded me."

He questioned us closely about our plans. He wanted as clear and detailed a picture as we could give at this stage. He asked us very shrewdly about the distances involved. Had we realized it would be 1,000 miles of foot slogging to the borders of Mongolia alone? We talked, almost in whispers, for a long time, as other occupants of Hut Number One came in past us, stamping snow off their boots, calling out to friends, standing in groups around the three red-hot stoves. I told him we would help him make the move from his hut in the middle of the line to this one. I urged that time was short.

He stood up, nodded thoughtfully. "Good-bye for now," I said. "Good-bye, gentlemen," he answered and walked out. The others readily accepted the seventh and last recruit to the party.

BY THE END OF the first week in April we were all in the same hut—a triumph of preliminary organization. We were gathering an impressive store of skins, most of them pulled off the wires by Kolemenos on his frequent trips to pick up the birch logs for the ski shop. On the grindstone in the ski shop I flattened and sharpened a six-inch nail into an instrument that could be used to cut and pierce holes in the tough pelts. Our final collection included sable, ermine, Siberian fox, and, a real prize, the skin of a deer that one of the officers had shot for the pot. We cut long thongs of hide for lacing up the simple moccasins we fashioned in the nightly gloom of the hut. We plaited thongs together and used them as belts. Each man made and wore under his fufaika a warm vest with the fur turned inward toward the body. To protect the legs, we made fur gaiters.

Our acute fear at this time was that we might be betrayed. Our feverish efforts were bound to attract some attention. Had a word been dropped to the Russians, the informant would have been well paid in extra bread and tobacco. But there was no Judas.

I told the colonel's wife that I had found six friends. She did not ask me who they were, and I do not think she wanted to know. She gave me a gift that was to be of inestimable value—an ax head.

"That will be on my conscience all my life," she said. "It is the first thing I have ever stolen."

I made a handle for it, and Kolemenos wore it for safekeeping inside the back waistband of his trousers.

One other priceless article I made in the ski shop was a fine three-inch-wide and foot-long knife. It was originally a section of broken saw blade, which I heated in the workshop stove, hammered into shape, and ground on the grindstone. The handle was two pieces of wood tightly thonged together by long strips of deerskin. As Kolemenos became the keeper of the ax, so I took over the custody of the knife. These were perilous possessions inside the camp. The discovery of either would have wrecked the whole scheme.

The problem of making fire was one we already had the answer to. Here, where matches were counted a luxury, there existed an effective, if primitive, method that made use of a thick fungoid forest growth that the Russians called *gubka* (literally "sponge"). It could be tugged off the trees in sheets. It was then boiled and dried. The fire-making equipment was completed with a bent nail and a piece of flintstone. The dry gubka, a supply of which we all carried stuffed into our jacket pockets, readily took the spark from the flint and could be blown into a red smolder.

The word reached us that in a week's time it would be Easter Sunday. It fell in 1941 on April 13, as I have discovered since then. The Sunday before, April 6, marked the end of our preparations. Our escape wardrobe was then complete with the making of seven balaclava caps of fur with extension flaps down the back that could be tucked into the necks of our jackets. We were all tense and ready to go, worried about our valuable new possessions—the skins, the ax, the knife, the store of dehydrated bread—and fearful that at this point some of them might be stolen.

And on that day the colonel's wife sent for me and said, "My husband has gone to Yakutsk. That is why he did not attend the parade today. I have made seven bags out of provision sacks. You will have to take them out one at a time." She was perfectly calm. My heart was hammering with anxiety. When she handed me the first of these bags, I saw that she had provisioned it, too, and I wondered how we could possibly hide it. I tucked the bag under my arm inside my jacket, stuck my hands in the deep pockets, and walked back to the prisoners' lines hunched up and bending over like a man in deep thought. Six times more in the next few days I made that hazardous trip, knowing each time that if any Russian guard discovered what I was carrying, disaster would be sudden and complete. We made pillows of the bags, covering them with bits of animal skin and moss. Every hour we were away from the hut we sweated in apprehension.

We acquired in those last few days a discarded and well-worn soldier's sheepskin jacket. I told the others of an old poacher's trick in which a sheepskin was dragged along behind to put the gamekeeper's dogs off the human scent. We could try the trick ourselves, I suggested. The others agreed.

We watched the weather, so essential a part of our escape plan. We wanted snow, big-flaked, heavy-falling snow, to obscure our movements. Monday was cold and very clear. On Tuesday there was wind-driven, icy sleet. Midmorning on Wednesday a lead-gray and lowering sky gave us the boon we sought. The snow thickened as the day went on. It began to pile up in the untrodden no man's land between us and the wire. At the midday break the seven of us met briefly. The word went around: "This is the day."

At 4 P.M. I left the ski shop for the last time with my fufaika bulging with my hoard of bread and the knife blade cold against my leg in my right boot. We drank our evening mug of coffee, ate some of the day's bread issue, and walked to the hut in ones and twos.

There were frequent walks to the latrines as we tensely talked over the final plans. It was Smith who advised that we must not start our break too early. The camp must be allowed to settle down for the night before we moved. Midnight, he thought, would be a reasonable time to run for it. Meanwhile, we must try to keep calm. And the blessed snow kept falling in big, obliterating cottonlike flakes, covering everything.

It was Zaro who had the preposterous idea of attending the Politruk's Wednesday evening indoctrination. We laughed at first, and then Makowski said, "Why not?" So we went, all seven of us, leaving our precious, moss-camouflaged bags on our bunks and telling ourselves that now, on this last night, nothing could go wrong. We sat ourselves at the back, and the Politruk beamed a faintly surprised welcome at us. We smiled right back at him and tried not to fidget.

It was the most exciting political meeting I have ever attended, although the element of excitement owed little to the speaker. The Politruk, now the camp's senior officer in the absence of Ushakov, was in good form. We heard again about the miracle of the Soviet state, about the value of toil, of self-discipline within the framework of state discipline, of the glorious international ideal of communism.

There was about an hour and a half of it before we stood up to go.

"Good night, colonel," we chorused.

"Good night," he answered.

Back in Hut Number One the men were beginning to settle for the night. Smith and Zaro, in the bunks nearest the door, were to give us the starting signal. We all broke up and climbed onto our bunks and lay there. Six of us lay wide awake and waiting, but big Kolemenos in the bunk below me was gently snoring.

I lay thinking and listening to the thumping of my heart. I remembered I had not said good-bye to the colonel's wife. I decided she would not have wanted me to.

The hours dragged by. Gradually the hut grew quiet. There was a loud snoring from someone. A man babbled in his sleep.

Smith tapped my shoulder. "Now," he whispered.

Gently I shook Kolemenos. "Now," I repeated.

THE GETAWAY

WE SWUNG OUR BAGS off the bunks by the rawhide straps that we had fitted for slinging them across our backs. We piled the moss coverings back in pillow form at the heads of our beds. "Everybody ready?" I whispered. From all around me came the hissed answer, "Yes." "Anybody changed his mind?" There was no reply.

"Let's go," said Makowski.

I dropped my bag near the door and stepped outside. The camp was silent. It was snowing as heavily as ever. I could not see the nearest wire. In the southeast guard tower, our nearest danger, they

246

could not have had 20 yards visibility. We could be thankful that in this place of no piped water supply and no electricity, there were no searchlights to menace us.

The inner wire was 100 yards from the hut door. The success of the first part of the operation depended on the observation that the frost-stiffened wire coils did not faithfully follow the contours of the ground. There was a dip in the ground straight ahead of us, which we reckoned would provide a couple of feet of clearance if we burrowed through the snow and under the wire.

We went out one by one with about a minute's interval between each. Zaro went first, and I prayed he found the right spot at the first attempt. Then the Lithuanian. Then Mr. Smith. Then Makowski and Paluchowicz. Kolemenos turned and whispered to me, "I only hope they've made a great big hole for me to get through."

I watched him run off into the night like the others, carrying his bag in front of him, ready, according to plan, to shove it through the gap ahead of him. Then it was my turn, and the palms of my hands were moist with sweat. I took a last swift look around. The men in the hut were sleeping on. I turned and bolted.

When I reached the wire, Smith was under it and slowly wriggling forward. Two were through. The rest of us crouched down and waited. Agonizing minutes passed by as first the sergeant and then Makowski squirmed and grunted, bellies pressed flat against the earth, under the wire. The big bulk of Kolemenos went head first into the gap, and I held my breath. He was halfway through when the barbs took hold on the back of his jacket between the shoulder blades. He shook himself gently, and little pieces of ice tinkled musically down the coils of the wire.

"Lie still, Anastazi," I whispered. "Don't move at all."

Someone on the other side had pulled his bag through and was reaching through over his neck to try to release him. The minutes ticked by. I was aware that my jaws were clamped tight, and I was trying to count the passing seconds on my fingers. Kolemenos lay very still as the hand worked between his shoulders. Someone spoke on the other side, and the big man went forward again. I let out my breath in a long sigh and followed through. The first obstacle was behind us. It had taken a full 20 minutes.

We knelt down along the edge of the dry moat and looked across to the first tall wooden fence as Kolemenos slithered in and braced himself against the steep-sloping near side. We used him as a human stepping-stone, and as we clambered over him, he took our feet in his

linked and cupped hands and heaved us one by one onto the ledge at the base of the 12-foot palisade. More vital minutes were lost in pulling Kolemenos out of the ditch. By standing on his shoulders and reaching out at full stretch, we hauled ourselves over the top. Then perched on the lateral securing timber on the other side, we were able to lean over and help up the later arrivals.

Anchorman Kolemenos again posed us a problem. Straddling the top of the fence, our legs held firm, Makowski and I leaned heads downward and arms outstretched to haul at him, one arm each. Three times we got his fingers to within inches of the top, and three times we had to lower him down again. We paused, trembling with exertion and near despair, and tried again. His fingers scrabbled for a hold on the top, gripped. To our straining he began to add his own tremendous strength. He came up, up, and over.

To clear the coiled wire at the foot of the fence, we threw ourselves outward, landing in a heap in the deep snow. One or two failed to leap quite clear enough and were scratched as they pulled themselves away. We were in the patrol alley between the two fences. Time was running out. If I had heard the sound of the sled dogs announcing the start of a patrol, I think I might have been physically sick.

We ran the few yards to the outer fence and this time shoved Kolemenos up first. We were probably making little noise, but it seemed to me the commotion was deafening. This time I was last up, and it was Kolemenos who swung me up and over. In a final mad scramble we leapt and tumbled over the last lot of barbed wire at the foot of the outer fence, picked ourselves up, breathlessly inquired if everyone was all right, and, with one accord, started to run. Round my waist was tied the old sheepskin jacket. I tugged it free, dropped it, and heard it slithering along behind me attached to the thong looped on my wrist.

We gasped and choked and wheezed, but we ran and kept running into the great forest among the looming, white-clothed trees. We ran south, with the camp at our backs. One and then another stumbled, fell, and were helped to their feet. The first headlong rush slowed to a steady, racking lope. We jogged along for hours, into the dawn and beyond it to another snow-filled day, our packs bumping and pounding our backs as we went. When we stopped to draw air into laboring lungs, I made them start again. And I made them struggle on until about 11 A.M., when hardly one of us could have moved another step. I picked up the old sheepskin and held it under my arm. We looked around at one another. Paluchowicz was bent over double with his hands on his knees, his shoulders heaving, fighting to get his breath. Two of the others were squatting on their haunches in the snow. All of us were open-mouthed, panting like spent animals.

This place was a shallow, bowl-like depression where the trees grew more widely spaced. We had stumbled down into it and could not, without a rest, have attempted the slight climb out of it. We stood there for about 10 minutes, too breathless to speak and in a lather of sweat in spite of the subzero temperature.

The snow still came down, thinning a little now, and there was a moaning wind through the trees that made the gaunt branches shake and creak miserably. Like hunted animals, we were all straining our ears for sounds of the chase from behind us. In all our minds was the thought of the dogs. But there was only the wind, the falling snow, and the stirring trees.

Up the slope to our left the trees grew more closely together. "We will get up there," I said, finally. "There is more shelter, and we shall be better hidden." There were groans of protest. Smith joined in, "Rawicz is right."

So we labored our way out of the hollow and picked the broad base of a great tree as the location for our shelter. We scooped the snow away down to the tree roots and cleared a space a couple of yards square. Then we built up the snow around into a solid low wall. Kolemenos cut branches with his ax, and we laid them on top in a close mesh, piling on more snow to complete the roof. It was a lesson we had learned the hard way in Siberia: Get out of the wind, because the wind is the killer. Just wrap snow around you, and you'll sleep warm as though you were in a feather bed.

Here it was that we had our first real look at the contents of our packs. Each man had a flat baked loaf, a little flour, about five pounds of pearl barley, some salt, four or five ounces of korizhki tobacco, and some old newspaper. All this in addition to the dried ration bread I had managed to save. On the top of each pack were the spare moccasins we had made and the leftover pieces of skin. We crawled into the little snow house, all jammed closely together, and talked in low voices. There was a discussion as to whether we should smoke. We decided the additional risk was quite slight and the benefit to jangling nerves great. So we smoked and lay close together in the warm blue haze of burning tobacco.

There was, this relatively short distance from the camp, no question of lighting a fire, so we wolfed some of our bread. And in so doing we made a discovery about Sergeant of Cavalry Paluchowicz.

251

He had not a tooth in his head. Eating this hard bread was agony for him. The only way he could cope with it was by soaking it—in this case, where there was no water, by kneading it with snow.

"I had a nice set of dentures when they took me prisoner," he explained. " Then those bastard NKVD fellows knocked them out of my mouth, and they smashed on the floor. They laughed at that trick, but it was no joke to me, trying to get my gums around that prison bread, I can tell you. First thing I do when we get to where we are going will be to treat myself to another set of teeth."

"And have them gold-plated. You'll deserve them." This from Zaro. We laughed, and Paluchowicz joined in, too.

We slept through the remaining few hours of daylight, only one man remaining awake at a time to keep a listening guard near the small opening. Kolemenos went off to sleep like a tired child and snored gently and musically. No one had the heart to stir him for guard duty. Marchinkovas roused us as the light outside began to fade. We ate some more bread, smoked one cigarette each, and then crawled out. The snowfall had diminished to light flurries, and the wind was getting up. It was very cold, and we were stiff and sore.

All seven of us knew it was imperative that we should get clear of the camp area as soon as possible. All through that second night we alternately ran and walked. It never seemed to be completely dark, but the going was nevertheless difficult through two and three feet of crisp snow, the undulations of the ground masked by close-growing trees. Near morning we crossed a frozen stream, steeply banked on the other side, and when we scrambled up and got away from it into the continuing forest, we made our camp.

For the first four or five days we stuck to this night movement and daylight holing up. There was no sign of pursuit. Hopefully, we decided that, our tracks having been well covered by the first night's snow, the hunt had probably been organized eastward as being the shortest and most feasible escape route. Cautiously we congratulated ourselves on the choice of the flight to the south. We started to travel by day, advancing roughly abreast in a spread-out formation and making up to 30 miles a day. Watching the occasional watery sun, reading the sign of the moss growing on the sheltered side of the trees, we held to an approximate course south. Several more ice-bound streams were negotiated, and I judged they were all flowing southward to drain into the great Lena River. It was a time of hardship, of a constant battle against cold and fatigue, but our spirits were high. Most of all at this time we wanted to be able to light a fire, and we spurred ourselves on with the promise that we should have one as soon as we sighted the Lena.

After about a week of travel we began to sort ourselves out. The two regular soldiers, Makowski and Paluchowicz, kept close together. Marchinkovas, reserved and serious but with an occasional unexpected dry wit, was befriended by Kolemenos. Smith, now completely accepted as a kind of elder counselor of the party, was my own particular companion. The buoyant, fun-loving Zaro was impartially friendly with everyone and moved happily from group to group. A rare fellow, this Zaro. I saw him, at the end of a grueling day when we had to flog our aching muscles for the energy to build the night's hideout, mocking at his own and our weariness by squatting down in the snow, hands on hips, and giving us a lively version of a Russian dance until Kolemenos was bellowing with laughter, tears running down into his beard. Nothing could ever daunt Zaro. Of all the gallant jokers I had met, Zaro was undoubtedly the greatest. He taught us all that the grimmest twists of life were not entirely humorless.

ON THE EIGHTH or ninth day the going was unmistakably easier. The ground was falling away in a long, gradual slope southward. The bare earth between the trees began to show tufts of the typical tough, rustling Siberian grass; there was more moss on the tree trunks. In the early afternoon the forest suddenly thinned out, and we saw the Lena River, ice-sheathed and well over half a mile wide, at this point already a mighty waterway with still some 1,500 miles to run to its many-mouthed outlet into the Arctic Ocean. We stood, partially under cover in an extended line, listening and watching. The day was clear, and sounds would have carried well, but all was silent.

The American walked quietly over to me. "We'd better stay on this side tonight," he suggested, "and cross over at first light tomorrow."

I agreed. We built a shelter, and as darkness came on, we lit our first fire, setting it off with gubka moss and dry twigs that we had carried for days inside our jackets against our fur vests.

Quietly, as the wood smoke curled up into the upper branches of the trees and disappeared into the night, we celebrated with a hot dinner—a steaming *kasha*, or gruel, made of water, pearl barley, and flour, flavored with salt. Our only cooking pot was an aluminum mug of about one-pint capacity. We had a couple of crudely made wooden spoons, and the mug was passed around the circle, each man taking a couple of spoonfuls at a time. When the first lot disappeared—and it went very quickly—we melted some more snow and made a fresh mugful. The sergeant was allowed to soak his bread in the gruel, and we all congratulated ourselves on a fine meal. All night long we kept the fire going, the man on watch acting as stoker.

In the faint light of the day's beginning we silently crossed the Lena, mightiest river in this country of many great rivers, and came to the steep bank on the far side. There for some minutes we stood, looking back across the ice. Some of the tension of the past weeks was already falling away from us. In all our minds had been the idea we might never reach the Lena, but here we were, safe and unmolested. We could face the next stage with fresh confidence.

Inconsequentially, someone started to talk about fish. It set me on a train of thought and memory. I told the others that in winter back home in Poland it was possible to catch fish by hammering a hole through the ice.

"And having made the hole," interjected Zaro, "what do we do next—whistle them up?"

No, I explained, the fish, stunned by the hammering, will be forced out through the change of the air pressure when the ice is broken through. The others laughed and bantered, congratulating me on my ability as a teller of tall tales.

"All right then," I said, "let's try it."

Kolemenos went off and returned with a solid piece of timber, and we walked out about 20 yards onto the river ice. Kolemenos wrapped his arms around the timber, Zaro and I took hold near the bottom to direct the business end, and we started thumping away with pile-driver blows. Eventually we broke through. The water gushed up like a geyser, swirling icily around our feet. And yes! There were fish— four of them, about the size of herrings. We swooped on them and picked them up. We were all as excited as schoolboys. The others crowded around me, slapping me on the back, and Zaro made a little speech of apology for having doubted my word. Then Smith, looking anxiously around, said we had better not play our luck too hard and should get moving under cover again. We had a drink of the cold, clean Lena water and moved off.

We turned south again, climbed the riverbank to the higher ground beyond, and headed on the next leg of our journey with Lake Baikal as the immediate objective.

That first night across the river we spent in a copse of trees on a low hillock and lightly grilled our fish spitted through the gills on a skewer-pointed twig, ate sumptuously of our first fresh food, and finished up with more gruel.

By now the issue of rubber boots had been discarded as worn out. Our feet were still wrapped in the long strips of thick linen that had been handed out in the camp. All of us were now wearing moccasins with skin gaiters wound round with straps of hide. Movement south was at the steady rate of about 30 miles a day, and we kept going for a full 10 hours daily.

A FUGITIVE GIRL

OUR WAY LAY THROUGH TREES for some days. On about the third day we were enveloped in an early-morning ground mist as we started out. We abandoned for once our practice of advance in extended line and pushed on through the mist in a bunch. Somebody hissed urgently for silence. We stopped dead and listened.

Ahead of us and quite near came a violent thumping on the ground and a succession of crashing noises as though some heavy body were hurling itself toward us through the undergrowth. We stood as still as a collection of statues. Then I reached down for the knife, and Kolemenos heaved his ax up to his shoulder.

The furious commotion stopped. We waited a full minute, straining our ears. Faintly came the sound of choked, labored breathing. Another minute went by. The uproar exploded again, and we felt the vibrations as the earth was pounded. Kolemenos came up beside me.

"What is it?" he whispered.

"Must be an animal," I said.

"Well, it's not coming any nearer," said the big man. "Let's go and look." We spread out and went forward.

Through the mist a few yards away I saw an animal thrashing convulsively from side to side, its head down and hidden from me. I made the remaining short distance at a crouched run. The others came up fast behind me. There, kicking, snorting, and struggling, its muzzle flecked with spume and its breath pumping out steamily to join the morning's white mist, was a full-grown male deer. It was trapped and could not run. The fine spread of antlers was locked fast in the tangled roots of a fallen tree.

From the chaos around, from the beaten ground and the fact that the animal was almost spent with its efforts to break free, it seemed that it must have ensnared itself hours earlier. We looked at Kolemenos, and Kolemenos looked at the stricken beast.

He stepped up onto the trunk of the fallen tree and swung the shining ax blade down with a vicious swish. The edge struck home where the back joined the neck and the deer slumped, quite dead. We all ran forward and unitedly tried to get the head of the animal free. Kolemenos got his shoulders under the roots and heaved upward, but even he could not release the antlers, and eventually he brought his ax out again and hacked the head from the body. We hauled the carcass into a clear space, and I cut it open and carefully skinned it.

The thing had happened very quickly, and in the flurry of killing and cutting up the animal, we had not spoken much, until Makowski, speaking to us in a general way, but with his eyes on Mr. Smith, said, "What are we going to do with this lot?"

"We had better have a conference," said the American.

Mr. Smith opened the meeting with the statement that we could not carry all this meat, and we could not afford to leave any behind.

Marchinkovas propounded the obvious solution: "We must stay here for 24 hours and eat as much meat as we can hold. What's left we ought to be able to carry."

Zaro, licking his lips, said he was quite sure he could help to greatly lighten the load.

"All agreed, gentlemen?" asked Mr. Smith. There was an instant chorus of approval.

Paluchowicz busied himself gathering wood, laying and lighting a fire, while the rest of us built a shelter and completed the butchering. Within an hour we had choice cuts of venison grilling on a wooden spit over the flame, and the melted ice and barley gruel was steaming fragrantly with the addition of tidbits of liver and tender meat. We could not wait for the joints to cook through; I kept hacking slices off and handing them around. It took a bit of chewing, but it was excellent meat. Paluchowicz borrowed my knife and cut his share into small pieces because of his lack of teeth, and we let him later have the first go at the mug of gruel. We ate and ate, the fat of the meat running down into our beards, and we belched loudly and laughed, congratulating ourselves on our miraculous good fortune. All of us smoked and dozed in the shelter for an hour or two afterward and then decided we must get to work on the skin.

The preparation of the skin took some time. We armed ourselves with some pieces of wood and painstakingly scraped off the adhering lumps of fat. We made moccasins, 14 pairs of them. We each put one pair on over those we were wearing and packed the spare pair in our sacks. And there was still a piece of skin left for each of us. I carried mine rolled on the top of my sack. We broke off from our shoemaking to cook and eat another great meal, and again at night we fed off venison until our bellies were blown out with food. Not quite so heartily, but still willingly, we ate meat again just before dawn and distributed the best of what was left among our packs.

We continued on our southern course for Lake Baikal. And as the weeks slipped by into the middle of May, we noted gratefully the first signs of the short Siberian spring. The wind was milder, and there were a few buds on the trees. The streams we crossed were still frozen hard, and the carpet of snow lay undisturbed, but conditions generally were much easier.

The last thing we wanted was to meet other men, and in this our luck held. We crossed occasional roads only after thorough reconnaissance. There were nights when we saw afar the lights of a village. There were days when we saw the faraway outlines of buildings and tall chimneys plumed with white smoke. In these areas we proceeded with extra caution.

Then we began to meet real roads, probably of secondary importance but far better than anything we had encountered since we broke from camp. Borne on the wind from the direction of the lake came the sound of a distant factory hooter.

We came to a high point from which we could look down at the beginning of Lake Baikal. Miles away to the west groups of factory buildings caught the eye. Far below, between us and the water, there wound a road alongside which were telephone poles with their big white insulators carrying a weight of wires that indicated the presence of a fairly important highway. Our difficulty was to discover at what point we had struck the lake. We talked it over and finally made up our minds that we had swung too far west and were now somewhere near the northeast corner. This meant that we should have to follow the north shore westward until it turned down to point our route through southern Siberia.

For upward of an hour the seven of us squatted there, absorbed in the widespread scene below. We were in good humor at the thought of having attained another objective on our long trek south, but we faced the fact that our food supplies were down to a few scraps, including some small pieces of high-smelling venison.

Smith finally broke up the session. "Let's go down and take a look around," he suggested.

It took longer than we expected to reach the road. A weather-beaten signboard showed the direction and distance of a town, or village, named Chichevka, which must have been the place with the factories we had seen from the heights. We bolted across the road and into the undergrowth on the other side. Between us and the lakeside was a mile of flattish country in which junipers grew in profusion amid oak, ash, birch, lime, and willow. We broke through a fringe of small trees to find ourselves on the edge of a river.

We had to decide whether or not to cross. It was only about 150 yards wide, but the ice had broken up in the middle channel, and the brown water swirled on a swift current. Here we found that all of us could swim. The general opinion was that as we should have to negotiate many rivers from now on, there was no point in delaying our first test. I volunteered to go first.

We unwound our yards of rawhide strap from about our waists to make a safety line. Each man had up to seven turns of the stuff around him; the joined line was impressively long. The others kept watch as I trod carefully out on to the ice edge. It gave way suddenly with a crack, and I was in the water and gasping to get my breath. I struck out the short distance to the ice across the channel, reached it, and tried to climb up. The ice broke away and I tried again. It seemed a long time before I was able to haul myself out. Chilled and wet, I signaled the others to follow.

It was not so difficult for the rest but no less uncomfortable. They came across with the line to guide them, one by one, and Smith, the last to cross, was hauled over with the other end of the line around his waist. The next time I went over one of these half-frozen rivers, I took the ax with me and chopped away at the ice until the blade bit in, using it to help me out of the water.

We ran under cover as quickly as we could and then took off our three garments—the padded trousers and jackets and the fur vests— one by one and wrung out as much water as we could. We put them on again to dry on our bodies and went off briskly toward the lake to bring back circulation to our limbs.

LATE IN THE afternoon we huddled together to make plans for the next immediate stage of the journey. Common sense dictated that to hug the lakeshore too closely was to invite discovery by inhabitants of fishing villages that were well spaced here in the north but clustered thicker together on the southern side toward the sizable cities within reach of the Trans-Siberian Railway. The proposal we all approved, therefore, was to bear away north and make our way clear of roads and towns on a course parallel with but safely distant from the lake.

We accordingly set off obliquely northeast, aiming to cross the road again farther along. Our clothes were still damp, and we moved at a fast pace to dry ourselves off. We had covered about five miles when we saw ahead of us a line of trees marking the bank of another river.

Over to my right Zaro gave the halt and alert signal with upraised arm. I repeated the signal, and the advancing line straggled to a stop. Zaro pointed urgently in the direction of the river. I saw something moving between the trees. It could have been an animal, or it could have been a man—at this distance of several hundred yards in the fading light it was impossible to tell—but we had to investigate. I went over to Zaro and asked him what he thought he had seen.

Zaro said, "It might be a man. Whatever it is, it acts as though it has seen us and is trying to hide."

The others crept up to us. "If it's a man," said Makowski, "we shall have to hit him on the head and throw him in the river. We can't risk anyone giving us away."

We spread out again, Smith and Zaro on my left, Paluchowicz, Makowski, Marchinkovas, and Kolemenos on my right. Crouching low we moved forward from bush to bush until we were able to see that the line of trees was about 50 yards from the river, its waters now clearly visible. About 10 yards from the first of the belt of trees I stopped and listened. The others pulled up, too, and everyone peered ahead. Suddenly, a figure that had been motionless behind a tree trunk threw itself forward and downward into a clump of bushes. In that flash of movement I saw trousers and heavy boots. I broke cover and ran forward, the others at my heels.

The boots were rubber soled, felt topped, and knee length. They stuck ludicrously out from the bush as I threw myself on them and hauled outward to bring the owner into view. The next instant I was asprawl with the boots held in my hands. Kolemenos was breathing heavily down my neck, peering down at a ridiculously small pair of linen-swathed feet and slim ankles. And from beneath the bush came terrified, heartbroken sobbing. We looked at one another, still panting from our run, in sudden embarrassment. Someone whispered in awed tones, "It must be a woman."

Kolemenos bent down, shouldered aside the bush, and gently lifted. We all crowded around. It was a girl—a slip of a girl, round-eyed with fright, her tears making clean rivulets through the grime of her face. Moments ago we had been a bunch of desperate men who could have contemplated killing to prevent discovery. Now we stood around, clumsily contrite, like a crowd of romping boys caught in mischief and seeking the words to repair some act of over-rough horseplay. Through her tears she stole a look at my face and cowered back.

"Don't be afraid of us," I said in Russian.

She looked at me again, and her eyes went from me to the other six solemn and anxious bearded faces. She went on crying, and I cannot blame her; we must have looked like the worst gang of desperadoes she had ever had the ill luck to meet.

"Please don't cry, little girl," said Sergeant Paluchowicz.

She was still very frightened. She was fighting hard to stop her sobbing. "We won't hurt you," I tried to console her. "We all have sisters and sweethearts of our own."

Everything she wore seemed too big and bulky for her. Her thin shoulders were hunched in a long, wide, padded winter jacket, and her slim ankles emerged incongruously from a pair of heavy padded trousers. Like our own, both garments were of some somber black heavy material. Beneath the jacket showed the upper half of a well-worn and dirty purple velvet dress, the skirt of which was tucked into the trousers. From two sleeves of a green woolen sweater she had made herself a scarf, which was wrapped about her neck. Her tear-brimming eyes were very blue. Wisps of chestnut hair strayed out from under a moth-eaten fur hood. She looked like a schoolgirl masquerading in the clothes of a grown man.

She lifted her hands to draw the jacket sleeves across her face, and I saw she was holding a little crucifix. She dropped her hands, looked down at her feet, and turned her eyes on me. She was standing all but barefoot in the snow—and I was still holding her boots. I bent down and helped her slip her feet back into them.

She spoke then, in a quaint mixture of Polish and halting Russian. "I have lost my way to the kolkhoz where I work. I am Polish, and I was deported here to work." The look she gave us was apprehensive.

Paluchowicz and Makowski both pushed forward. I talked and they talked in a rush at the same time. In the gabble of explanation she finally understood we were telling her that we were Poles, too, that we were escaping prisoners, and that she had nothing to fear. Impulsively, she flung herself into my arms and cried her relief and sudden happiness. Over and over again she repeated, "God is good to me." The other two Poles awkwardly patted her head and shoulders.

Smith had moved apart and had been keeping an anxious watch. In Russian he called out: "Break it up. Are you forgetting where we are? For God's sake, let's get under cover."

The group quickly broke up. We moved off to find a hiding place.

HER NAME WAS KRISTINA POLANSKA. She was just 17. She had not eaten for two days, and she was very, very hungry. We rummaged in our bags and handed her our scraps of food. She ate like a half-starved wild animal, with absorbed concentration, every now and again sniffling and rubbing her padded sleeve across her nose. She fascinated us. We squatted on our haunches and never took our eyes off her. Only Mr. Smith sat back a little, watching her, too, but with a more detached air of appraisal.

"I am not lost from the kolkhoz," she volunteered. "I ran away. I have been running for many days." She paused. "And you are the first gentlemen I have met since I left my home." She put a lot of emphasis into the word gentlemen.

"Where was your home, Kristina?" I asked.

"My father had a farm near Luck, in the Polish Ukraine," she said. "I last saw it in 1939. I have no home now."

Quietly, the American interposed with a question about our immediate plans. It was getting dark, he pointed out, and he thought we should make some distance along the riverbank northward to a point that looked favorable for a crossing early the next day. He suggested that it would be senseless to give ourselves another soaking that night. At least we could sleep dry.

There was no argument. We walked for four or five miles along the tree-fringed river. I saw the girl several times looking at Smith. She did not speak to him. I think she sensed that in this calm and thoughtful man was the only likely opposition to her presence among us. We Poles talked to her, but Smith said nothing.

It was quite dark when we found a place to rest. We built a shelter against a fallen log. We laid down our food sacks for her, and she curled up among us, completely trustful, and slept. Ours was a more fitful rest. Throughout the dark hours we took sentry duty in turns, according to our practice. She slept on like a tired child, oblivious of the chill of the night. She still had not awakened when, in the first hint of day, Mr. Smith touched me on the shoulder and beckoned me away from the group.

He came to the point at once. "What are we going to do with this young woman, Slav?"

I had known it was coming, and I did not know what to say. It might be a good thing, I said, to find out from her what her plans were. It was evading the question, and I was well aware of it. Out of the corner of my eye I saw Makowski talking to Paluchowicz. They strolled over to us. On their heels came Kolemenos. A minute later the other two joined us.

"Very well," said the American, "we'll make it a full conference."

We talked, but we did not come to the point. Were we going to take the girl with us? That was the only question. We decided that we would talk to Kristina first, then reach some decision afterward.

Kristina
Polanska

We woke her gently. She yawned and stretched. She sat up and looked at us all. She smiled in real happiness to see us. We grinned back through our beards and basked in that rare smile. Busily we fussed around to scare up some food, and we all quietly breakfasted together as day began to break. Paluchowicz, clearing his throat embarrassedly, asked Kristina how she came to be where we found her and where she was heading.

"I was trying to get to Irkutsk," she said, "because a man who gave me a lift on a farm truck and was sorry for me told me that if I got to the big railway junction there I might steal a ride on a train going west. He dropped me on the road a few miles away, and I was trying to find a way around the town."

Her glance rested on the American. He returned the look gravely. Her fingers fluttered to the strands of hair straying outside her cap and tucked them away in a gesture pathetically and engagingly feminine. "I think I should tell you about myself," she said. We nodded.

It was a variation of a story we all knew. After the First World War Kristina Polanska's father had been rewarded for his war services by a grant of land in the Ukraine under the reorganization of central European territory. He had fought against the Bolsheviks, and General Pilsudski was thus able to give a practical expression of Polish gratitude. The girl was an only child. They were a hardworking couple, her parents, and they intended that Kristina should have every advantage their industry could provide. In 1939 she was attending high school in Luck, and the Polanskas were pleased with her progress.

Then came September 1939. The Russians started moving in. The news of their coming reached the Ukrainian farm workers ahead of the Red Army "liberators." The well-organized Communist underground was ready. It needed only a few inflammatory speeches on the theme of the overthrow of foreign landowners and restoration of the land to the workers, and the Ukrainian peasants were transformed into killer mobs. The Polanskas knew their position was desperate. They knew the mob would come for them. They hid Kristina in a loft and waited. "Whatever happens, stay there until we come back for you," said her mother.

She heard the arrival of the mob, the shouts of men, the sounds of destruction as hammers and axes were swung. Kristina thought she recognized the voices of men from the nearest village. Outside in the yard her father called by name to some of the men he knew. The appeal came through clearly to the terrified child in the loft. "Take away what you want, but don't destroy our home and land." Silence for a minute or two after this. A growling murmur followed, then someone began to harangue the men loudly. The phrases were violent and venomous. Kristina heard her father's voice raised once more; however, it was immediately drowned out by a sudden uproar. Her mother screamed again, piercingly, and then Kristina pressed her hands over her ears to shut out the sound.

Kristina stayed in the loft for what seemed like hours, but she thought perhaps it was not really very long. The men had gone. The house was very still. All the personal servants had fled the day before. Kristina crept down through the silent house and into the yard. Her father and mother lay dead in the yard, near the side of the house. She crept to them and looked upon them for the last time. They had been beaten and then strangled with pieces of barbed wire.

I watched Kristina's white face closely as she told of the horror of that bright September morning. She spoke flatly, with little or no change of expression, as a person does who is still under the influence of profound shock.

"I went back into the house then," she said, "and I picked up some food and wrapped it in a cloth. I ran very hard for a long time."

She did not remember the next few days in detail. Some compassionate people in villages she passed through gave her a night's shelter and some food. She was obsessed with the idea of having to keep ahead of the Russians and out of their hands. Ironically, they caught her in the act of crossing the border when she did not even know she was near it. The Red Army handed her over to a civilian court, which swiftly sentenced her to be deported to Russia as a kolkhoz worker in the Yenisei River area of western Siberia.

Vividly she described her life on the Soviet farm. Most of the workers were strapping, big-bosomed, tough Russian women, and Kristina was the only Pole among them. On the second day after her arrival she was set to threshing and moving huge sacks of corn. The other women taunted her for her refinement and her weakness. They laughed at her failure to do the heavy work they managed themselves with ease. Aching from head to foot, she would cry herself to sleep at night. Food was poor, and the main item was one kilo of bread a day—for her as for the other workers.

But it was not the women who eventually caused Kristina to run. The farm was controlled by a foreman, whose attentions the other women were always inviting. Kristina was frightened of him and tried to keep out of his way. He was a big fellow, she said, swarthy and powerful. He would occasionally seek out the girl and try out some heavy pleasantries, telling her how different she was from the Russian women and that she needed someone to look after her.

There came the day when she was told she would not accompany the other workers in the horse-drawn farm cart but would report to the foreman's house "for interrogation." His intentions were obvious from the start. He promised there would be no more heavy work for her if she were kind to him.

Kristina panicked and appealed to him to let her go after the others and join them. What followed was a plain attempt at rape. Kristina screamed, clawed at his face, and frenziedly kicked out with her heavy boots. Surprised at the fury of her resistance, he relaxed his hold just long enough for her to break away and bolt blindly out and back to the women's quarters. He called vile names after her and threatened that he had means to make her change her mind.

She waited until the light began to fade in the afternoon, expecting all the time that he would come for her, but he did not show up. When she felt that the return of the other women must be imminent, she slipped out, keeping the kolkhoz buildings between her and the foreman's house, and ran. She slept that night in reeds by a river, and after following the river along for many miles the next day, finally reached a road and was given the first of two long lifts eastward by drivers of big farm trucks.

"All Russians are not bad," said Kristina. "These two were sorry for me and gave me some of their bread to eat. The second one told me to try to get to Irkutsk, but he could not take me any farther."

She looked around at us all, and her eyes finally rested on Mr. Smith. "So that is how I came to be here," she added.

The American dug his hands into his fufaika pockets. He spoke levelly. "We are not going near Irkutsk; we are heading south around the other side of the lake. What are you going to do now?"

Kristina looked surprised and taken aback. She turned an appealing gaze on the other six of us. We said nothing. We knew what we wanted but were content to let Mr. Smith handle this his own way. Her lips trembled slightly. Then she jutted out her little chin. "I am coming with you. You can't leave me on my own."

The American looked over her head for some moments at the river beyond. "Can you swim?"

"I swim very well," she said, and there was no mistaking the note of pride. "In school I was a very good swimmer."

Through Mr. Smith's gray-streaked beard came the glimpse of a smile. We relaxed as we heard him tell her: "Forgive me, child, if my questions have seemed to be abrupt. We just thought you might have plans of your own. All we can offer you is a lot of hardship. Our food has run very low, and we have a great distance to travel. You must consider, too, that if you are caught with us you will not get off as lightly as you would if you remained on your own. If you want to join us, however, we accept you completely."

"Thank you," replied Kristina simply. "The only thing I wanted was to be with you."

THE GIRL WENT AWAY from us then into a screen of bushes, and in her absence I called for a check on food. All seven sacks were opened up, the rolled-up skins set on one side, and the food brought out. We were, as we feared, badly off. There remained perhaps a couple of pounds of barley among the lot of us, a little flour, some salt, and a few pounds of almost black deer meat. We decided on strict rationing to one small meal a day until we could replenish our stocks. The only item still in plentiful supply was the gubka moss for fire lighting.

Probably each one of us had, in addition to the communal food openly displayed, at least one piece of hard, dried bread, stuffed deep down in his long jacket pocket. I know I had one, and there was evidence later that the others also had this tiny personal cache. There was nothing dishonest or antisocial about it. To hide away bread was a prisoner reflex, a symptom of captivity. A prisoner holding one crust of bread felt that he still had a hold on life, as a man in civilized surroundings will carry around with him a lucky coin to insure that he will never be penniless. It was a measure of the great affection we developed for this waif Polish girl that later on one and another of us would dig out this last piece of bread to allay her hunger.

We ate hurriedly there that morning and decided to make an immediate river crossing. This first hour of daylight gave promise of a fine spring day, and we had a common desire to make distance fast and to return as soon as possible to a straight course to the south.

For the girl this first river was a new ordeal. We persuaded her to take off her warm jacket, trousers, and boots. I had a moment of great pity for her as she stood with us in the shelter of the trees in her faded purple dress. I went carefully out to the edge of the ice with the line paying out behind me, the ax stuck firmly in the back waistband of my trousers, and I made it fairly quickly across the open channel to the other side. Kolemenos crossed, holding her rolled-up clothes, with some difficulty, above water. Paluchowicz and Makowski came over together, the girl behind them with the bight of a length of spare line about her, the ends held by the two Poles. The other three followed, one of them bringing the girl's boots. We ran for cover, winding in the line as we went.

Kristina was blue with cold, and she could not stop her teeth from chattering. Kolemenos handed her her clothes.

"Don't stand still, child," the American told her. "Run off from us now and take that dress off. Wring it out quickly, wipe off as much water as you can, and jump into your dry trousers and jacket."

She nodded and ran.

We stripped, danced around, wringing out our garments as we did so. The operation did not take long, and in our wet rags we waited a few minutes for the girl to rejoin us. She came running, with her dress and underwear under her arm in a soggy bundle.

"Did you see? I *can* swim, can't I?"

Mr. Smith grinned. "Yes. I saw." And, aside to me, "The little lady is not going to be much trouble, after all."

We walked hard all through the day, halting for only the briefest rests, and Kristina kept up with us uncomplainingly. The midday May sun was pleasantly warm, helping, with the heat of our exertions, to dry out our clothes. We must have covered 30 miles northeast away from Lake Baikal by nightfall, and we all slept easier for being back among tall timber.

On the third day after leaving the lakeside, I judged we were in a position for turning south on a route that would take us down to the border, with Baikal lying some 50 miles to our right. It was guess-

work, but I don't think the estimate was far off, although it would have been impossible to maintain a truly parallel course. The country was hilly and well wooded, and our progress was a series of stiffish climbs, with scrambles down into steep-sided valleys carrying small rivers and streams. These valleys ran almost uniformly southwest. Many of the streams were fordable, although the current, swollen by the breakup of the ice, was strong. Kolemenos led the way across these, prodding ahead of him with a long sounding pole.

I marveled at the way the girl stood it all. I fear we all still had misgivings about her frailty, and I am sure she was aware of them. In these early days she never once held us up. She was even lively and happy when we were soured and foot-weary after a particularly trying march. She treated us like a crowd of big brothers—all except Mr. Smith. Between those two there grew almost a father-daughter relationship. Often in the night shelter she would get him to tell her about America, and on more than one occasion I heard him suggest that when this was all over, she should come to the states with him. He would gently tease her about her big Russian boots and then say, "Never mind, Kristina, in America I will buy you some beautiful dresses and elegant high-heeled shoes." And Kristina would laugh with the wonder and promise of it.

She grew on us until there was not one of the bunch who would not cheerfully have died to protect her. She would wake in the morning, look at the unhandsome collection around her, and say, "It is wonderful to see you all. You make me feel so safe." On the march she loved to get Zaro up to his funny business. Even Zaro sometimes was glum, but Kristina never failed to chaff him back to his normal sparkling humor. Zaro, spurred on by her interest, would effervesce with fun. Sometimes as I watched them together, I found it hard to realize we were on a desperate mission, half starved and with the worst of the journey yet to come. Most reserved of the party was Marchinkovas, the Lithuanian. He talked little and generally only gave his advice when he was asked for it. Kristina would walk alongside him for miles, talking softly and seriously, and then there would be the phenomenon of Marchinkovas smiling, even laughing out loud.

Now, too, the party had a nurse. Kolemenos began limping with sore toes. Kristina bathed his feet for him, tore strips off her petticoat, and bound up the raw places between his toes. When my leg wound opened up, she dressed that. A cut or an abrasion was her immediate concern.

When the bandages were finished with, Kristina washed them in stream water, dried them, and then put them away for further use.

Approaching what was probably the Bargusin River, about half-way down the lake, Kristina was herself a casualty. She began to drop behind, and I saw she was hobbling. I stopped the others and went back to her. "My boots are hurting me a little," she said.

I took them off. The soles and backs of the heels were raw where blisters had formed and burst. She must have had hours of agony. The boots had been much too heavy and too big for her. All seven men fussed about Kristina while she insisted that she was quite well enough to continue. I bandaged her feet with some of her own linen and then finally persuaded her to let us throw the boots away and make her some moccasins.

So I made Kristina a pair of moccasins. I lavished on them all the care and artistry of which I was capable with the materials at hand. The others watched every cut of the knife and every stitch of the leather thonging. I doubled the soles so that they would be stiff and long-wearing, and I lined them with sable. Everybody congratulated me on my handiwork, and Kristina planted an impulsive kiss right in the center of my forehead.

We began to feel that the girl was good luck for us. We suffered no real slowdown until, only five days after turning south at the lake tip, we reached, at night, the Bargusin River.

THE TRANS-SIBERIAN RAILWAY

THE BARGUSIN CROSSING took place at the end of May and was the last of the major water hazards. On the south bank the Siberian summer seemed to be waiting for us. The sun beat down, all was green, there were flowers, and the birds were back from their distant migrations. In six weeks we had walked out of the bitter tail end of central Siberian winter into the warm embrace of the southern summer, where village orchards in the distance were gay and beautiful with blossoming cherry and apricot trees. Sleeping out became less of an ordeal, even when it was considered prudent not to risk lighting a fire. During the day we were forced to discard our fur vests, but we put them on again after sunset to protect us against the night's chill.

For a full two days after crossing the Bargusin we ate nothing, and the thought of food obsessed all minds. Then it was that we saw the horse through the trees betraying its presence with restless movement in the shafts of a crude sledge. It had scented our approach and obviously did not like what it smelt. Zaro and I went forward for a close look. The horse turned the whites of its eyes over its shoulder toward us. It had every reason to suspect our intentions. We were all quite ready to eat horsemeat.

Zaro and I saw it at the same time—an old single-barreled 12-bore shotgun, stock and barrel held together by windings of copper wire. It lay across the sledge alongside a little leather pouch, which we guessed to be for the ammunition. The thought struck me hard: We must get that gun before the owner can reach it. I ran forward with Zaro and whipped it quickly under my arm, barrel pointing down. I waved the others forward. Kristina, with Mr. Smith's arm protectively about her shoulder, stood well back as the rest of the party came up to Zaro and me. Kolemenos went toward the horse to talk to it and to try to quiet its restiveness, but the animal shied from him.

The man must have been quite near, near enough to hear the nervous movements of his horse. We faced him in a tense bunch. He was about 60, a solid, broad-shouldered woodcutter, his big ax held on his right shoulder. He was heavily bearded, but both his beard and long hair were neatly trimmed. His approach impressed me. He saw us, but his slow, deliberate walk did not falter. His eyes looked steadily ahead and took in the fact that I held his gun under my arm. He gave no sign of fear or alarm. He went to the horse's head, ran his hand through the mane, turned aside, and swung the blade of his ax into the bole of a tree, where he left it.

He looked at me and beyond me to where the girl stood with the American. "Who are you?"

Smith answered, moving forward as he did so. "We are prisoners escaping. We shall not harm you. We only want food."

"Times have changed," said the man. "At one time you would have found food waiting for you and no questions asked."

There was a simple dignity about the man. He looked us all over with easy frankness. He turned his head toward Kristina again, and I thought he was going to ask us about her. But he said nothing. Instead, he walked around the horse's head and reached down to the sledge for a long, slim sack, which he picked up. His fingers busied themselves with the leather thong around the neck.

"You don't have to worry about me," he said. "I live alone, and I am the only man for miles around here."

From the sack came treasure. A loaf of dark brown bread. Four smallish dried fish. A thick, mouth-watering hunk of salted fat pork.

From his belt he took a long hunter's knife. These were the provisions of a man who was intending to be away from his home for a whole day, and it was evident he had not yet eaten. We watched his performance with concentrated attention. Carefully, he cut off one slice of bread and one slice of salt pork, which he replaced in the sack. He motioned to Kolemenos, positioned nearest to him. Kolemenos took a couple of paces forward, and the woodcutter put into his big hands the loaf of bread, the lump of pork, and the dried fish.

Kolemenos stood for so long looking down at the food in his hands that eventually I said to him, "Put it in your bag, Anastazi, and we'll portion it out later."

The sound of my voice caused the Russian to turn toward me—and to the gun I was holding. There was an unspoken question in his eyes. I walked over to Smith, and we talked about the gun. We agreed the thing would be useless to us. We could not hunt with it because the noise of it would attract attention to us, especially in the well-populated southern areas we were now approaching. Nevertheless, security demanded we should not leave it with the woodcutter. Paluchowicz and Makowski added their opinions, and the final decision was that we could not afford to take the slightest risk of the gun being used against us or as a signal to summon assistance.

I faced the Russian. "We are sorry, old man, but we have to take your gun with us."

For the first time he appeared perturbed. He lifted his hands as though to appeal to us, dropped them again. "It will not be safe for you to use it," he said. "I understand the way you feel. Hang the gun on a tree somewhere, and perhaps one day I shall find it."

We turned to go. Once more he looked at Kristina. "Good luck to you all," he called after us. "May you find what you seek."

We moved on for about an hour without much talk, all of us feeling a nagging sense of guilt at having taken that shotgun, a thing of inestimable value to a man like the woodcutter.

About five miles from the scene of the encounter I hung the gun on the low branch of a tree overhanging a faint track, having first bound a piece of deerskin around the breech. It was the best I could do.

The food remained untouched until that day's march ended at nightfall. Kolemenos divided it into eight portions. So small was each lot that I could have bolted down mine in a couple of minutes and still remained hungry. But the well-developed instinct of hoarding food against the possibility of even worse trouble prevailed with all of us. We decided to use what we had as an iron ration spread over three days—a little for this night and the two following nights. Kristina listened to our talk and ate as we did, one-third of her small store. She looked very white and tired that night, I remember.

In spite of the natural preoccupation with food, our progress remained good as we pressed south over a succession of low ranges. The farther we went, the more the signs of human settlement increased. Our method was to approach the top of each hill warily and scout from there the country ahead. Frequently we saw people moving about in the distance. We swung off course to avoid roads along which went telephone poles—always the mark of an important route—and which carried a fair amount of truck traffic. On other occasions we heard men calling to one another and the clatter of tractors. There was often the sound of a not-far-distant factory hooter.

DAYLIGHT TRAVELING WAS getting hazardous. One day after the last of the woodcutter's food was gone, we sat down to review our situation. This was a day, I recall, when Kristina had been unable to keep up. Several times she had slipped away and held us up. There had been good-natured grousing. She was away from us now as we discussed plans for covering the dangerous terrain between us and the border.

"What is the matter with the little girl?" asked Paluchowicz.

I turned rather sharply on him. "There is nothing the matter with her that a day's rest won't cure. Don't forget she is a woman. All women become unwell. Have you forgotten?"

Paluchowicz' face was a study of consternation. "I hadn't thought of that," he said slowly. Nor had the others, apparently. "The poor child," murmured Makowski.

Mr. Smith spoke up. "We shall have to revert to night marches very soon. We might as well start the new scheme now, and Kristina can have her rest. Slav, you are the youngest of us. You have a quiet word with her and tell her we won't start until she feels fit to go."

I met her as she came out from among the trees. "Kristina, we are all going to rest for a day and then start traveling at night."

"Is it because of me?" There was a bright pink spot in each cheek.

"No, no. It will be safer at night."

"I have been holding you back today. I am very sorry. But I could not help it, Slav. I am very tired today."

"I understand. Please don't worry."

She turned away. "You are very kind, Slav. You are all very kind. Thank you." And I led her back to the others. And everybody was immediately talkative in an elaborately casual way. Then Kristina sat down beside Mr. Smith and said, "Tell me some more about what the women wear in America." He smiled and talked. She listened without saying a word, her chin on her knees.

The new arrangement was a pleasant one. We slept during the heat of the day and had the light of the moon to guide us through the pleasant cool of the night.

It was in bright moonlight that hunger forced us for the first and only time to raid a village. The scattered lights of houses about a mile and a half away stopped us on the crest of a rise. A single, thin squeal of a pig came to us clearly.

Zaro made a sucking noise through his lips. "My mother used to make beautiful pea soup with a pig's tail in it."

Kolemenos touched my shoulder. "Let's go and find that pig."

We weighed the risks. We had to eat. Smith offered the strongest opposition, then gave in. The pig-hunting party was selected—Kolemenos, with the ax, I with the knife, and the Lithuanian Marchinkovas as a third member.

The big Latvian and I set off, Marchinkovas following us a few yards behind. We made a beeline in the direction from which we thought the squeal had come and came to an orchard of young trees on the fringe of the village. Grass grew thickly among the trees.

At the edge of the orchard we left Marchinkovas on sentry duty and started a hands-and-knees crawl toward a small, barnlike wooden building at the other end. We looked up to the roof of the building to make sure it was not after all a human dwelling place. We were reassured. There was no chimney.

I crept forward and flattened myself against the side of the building with my ear pressed against the wood. I could hear the pig moving around in rustling straw. He had scented me, too, and was snuffling at me inches away on the other side. Kolemenos joined me. We felt along for a door. There was none. "It must be around the other side," I whispered to him. The other side faced the village and its few lighted windows.

I found the door on the far side. It opened by a simple latch and creaked and groaned for lack of oil as I sweated to inch it open. Kolemenos squeezed in after me into the blackness. I moved over to the far side where from outside I had heard the pig moving about. By feel I discovered a small gate that lead to a penned-off corner. I jumped as the pig grunted a foot away from me and brought its snout against my leg. Kolemenos came from behind me, slipped his powerful arms gently around the animal, and gave a tentative heave to test the weight. "It's surely much too heavy for us to carry," he said.

There was only one alternative. We had to persuade the pig to come with us. "Make friends with it," I whispered. "Tickle its belly. Then get behind it and be ready to give it an occasional push." Kolemenos and I got to work. The pig grunted with pleasure. I took it by the ear and started toward the door. Kolemenos encouraged it from behind. There were a few breathtaking seconds of indecision before it moved. We went out, shutting the door after us, got into and through the orchard, crouching low and murmuring endearments to keep the animal in the right frame of mind to stay willingly with us.

A white-faced Marchinkovas met us at the top of the orchard and fell in behind us to cover our retreat.

With the luck of desperate men we made it. About a hundred yards from the rendezvous with the others, Kolemenos dispatched the pig with one swift ax blow. It died soundlessly. I felt a sharp pang of regret. It had been a very trustful pig. We worked fast, gutting the carcass in the moonlight and crudely cutting it up into pieces that could be carried by the seven men.

The killing had taken place only about three-quarters of a mile from the village, and the signs could easily be found in the morning. There was an extreme urgency about putting as much distance as possible behind us before daylight. We were jogging along most of the hours before the sun began vaguely to show in the east. We climbed a rock-strewn hill and, when we had almost despaired of finding a hideout, stumbled finally on a dank cave with a narrow opening well screened by dwarf trees.

As the sun came up, we had a clear view across a plain to a long ridge a couple of miles away in the direction from which we had come. There were no signs of life, but we took great care not to expose ourselves. The meat-heavy sacks were dropped well inside the cave. Anxiously we deliberated what to do with the pork. In this June warmth it would not long remain edible, and we knew it must be cooked quickly. The solution again must be to gorge as much meat as we could while it was fresh-cooked. There was no alternative to the risk of lighting a fire.

The fire was set going with the driest wood we could find well back inside the cave. Kristina turned the stake on which the joints of pork were spitted. The fire spluttered and hissed as the sizzling fat dropped on the burning wood. A delicious smell of roast pork and wood smoke filled the cave.

Throughout that day we cooked and ate and slept, maintaining one man on sentry duty in approximately two-hour shifts. By midafternoon I was in the throes of the most racking stomachache. Smith, Paluchowicz, and Makowski were also rocking in sheer agony, holding their clasped hands across their stomachs. All of us suffered from the effects of loading our digestions, idle for days, on the rich fattiness of half-cooked pig meat. Toward evening the cramping pains eased, and we drove ourselves to eat more.

Someone made the suggestion that we should try to smoke the meat we were to carry with us so as to preserve it. Dusk was falling as we piled green juniper boughs on the flames. The smoke billowed up, causing an epidemic of coughing and streaming eyes. For a couple of hours we smoked the lumps of meat until they were dark brown. Then we packed them in our sacks and set off on the night march.

At this stage of the journey I knew we must be within a week's travel of the border. The knowledge made us edgy, silent, and exaggeratedly watchful. I had the feeling that we were moving among hostile people and that the odds were that we must at some time run into some of them. I feared the imminent crossing of the Trans-Siberian Railway even more than I did the frontier. Already we were near enough to have heard in the far distance the passing of trains. Mr. Smith shared my fears.

"The railway will be heavily patrolled," he said anxiously.

"We will cross at night," I replied.

It was difficult to sleep during the day. There was no need to post sentries. Everybody was alert. Only Kristina seemed to enjoy peace of mind. Her trust in us was absolute.

From high ground we saw through the clear air of a June morning the Trans-Siberian Railway five miles distant from us. Near the track and separated by four or five miles were two small villages; on the outskirts of each, hard against the side of the tracks, was a signalman's or maintenance man's stone house. On our side of the railway, the northern side, was a protective belt of trees, beyond which could be seen some kind of fence, both having the purpose of preventing snow from drifting and piling up on the line. All day we watched. Several long trains passed in both directions.

The advance toward the railway was made immediately after dark. The fence offered no difficulties. At the foot of the embankment there was a ditch. We climbed into and out of it. We crawled slowly up onto the tracks and lay there listening. I put my ear to the nearest metal rail. There was no sound.

"Come on," I jerked my arm, jumped to my feet, and leapt for-

Mr. Smith

Anastazi Kolemenos

Sigmund
Makowski

ward, taking Kristina with me by the elbow. There was an agitated scramble down the embankment on the far side, and then we were all running like crazy fools. We had covered about a hundred yards when someone shouted, his voice sharp with panic, "Down! Down! Get down!"

I glanced over my shoulder and saw the lights of an oncoming passenger train. I dropped, pulling the girl with me. The train rushed past, in a whirlwind of sound.

It had been a near thing. If anyone on the train had seen us, we would have been ruthlessly hunted down. And there was still the chance that someone had caught a glimpse of us. We had to move on quickly.

The morning found us, after hours of hard travel, basking in sunshine on the secluded bank of a clear-water river. Smith said he thought it would be better if we got over to the other side as soon as possible. Unlike the rivers of the Baikal Range, these waters moved slowly and were warm. The swim across was pleasantly refreshing. The country on the south side of the river was fairly flat and gave us good cover. We made good time.

We were very near the border when we ran into two Buryat Mongols. There was no avoiding the meeting. We saw one another at the same moment at a distance of not more than 50 yards, and there was nothing to do but continue toward the pair.

One was middle-aged, as best as I was able to determine, and the other one was definitely a young man. They could have well been father and son. They stopped and waited for us to come up to them and grinned widely and nodded their heads. They bowed together as we came to a halt.

The conversation was embroidered and

276

ornamented with politenesses, and I took the pattern from them. They spoke slowly in Russian. They inquired solicitously whether our feet carried us well in our travels. I assured them that our feet had carried us well and returned the inquiry. The older man was naively curious to know about us.

"Where do you come from?"

"From the north—Yakutsk."

"And where are you going?"

"We are traveling very far south."

The old man looked shrewdly at me from beneath his wrinkled lids. "You go perhaps to Lhasa to pray."

I thought that was an excellent idea. "Yes," I replied.

But the old man hadn't finished. He looked us over carefully. "Why do you have the woman with you?"

A bit of quick thinking was required.

"She has relatives who live on the way," I said. "We promised to deliver her there."

The two Mongols exchanged smiling glances as though approving of our protecting the girl on her journey. Then they both dug their hands deep in their pockets and withdrew them clutching fistfuls of peanuts, which they cheerfully handed around.

Each in turn wished us that our feet would carry us well and safely to our destination. They turned away together and walked from us. We waited to see them out of sight. They had gone only a few yards when the old man turned back alone.

He walked straight up to Kristina, bowed, and gave her a big handful of peanuts for herself. He repeated his good wishes to her and to us all and left us beaming goodwill.

We set off at a fast pace. We were too near the frontier to take chances now.

Eugene Zaro

Zacharius Marchinkovas

Anton Paluchowicz

277

PHASE ONE OF THE ESCAPE ended with the crossing of the Russo-Mongolian border at the end of the second week in June. It was notable for two circumstances: the ease of the crossing and the fact that we stepped out of the Buryat-Mongol Autonomous Soviet Socialist Republic with about 100 pounds of small early potatoes pulled out of a field only a few hours from the frontier. The timing of the potato-field raid—at dawn on the day in which later we were to make our exit from Siberia—was particularly gratifying to me. I felt that, having gone into captivity with nothing, we were leaving with a valuable parting gift, even though the donors were not conscious of their generosity.

We reached the crossing point in late afternoon. There was nothing to challenge our progress. The dividing line was marked by a nine-foot-tall red post surmounted by a round metal sign carrying the Soviet wheatsheaf, star, hammer, and sickle emblems over a strip of Cyrillic initials. To east and west one more post was clearly visible in each direction. They were so spaced in accordance with the contours of the country that an observer standing at any one post could always see two others.

I stepped around the post to see what might be inscribed on the other side of the plaque, but the reverse was blank.

There was the sound of sudden laughter as Zaro called out, "What's it like in Mongolia, Slav?"

Zaro cavorted across to me with a hop, skip, and a jump. The others followed with a rush. We pranced and danced, slapped one another on the back, pulled beards, and shook hands. Kristina ran around, kissed each one of us in turn, and cried with happiness and excitement. Mr. Smith put a stop to the noisy rejoicings by pointedly swinging his potato-filled food sack onto his back and moving off. We ran after him, still laughing.

"Let's get away from this place," Mr. Smith said, "as fast as we can go. We can't be sure how far below this border Russian influence extends. We don't know where we are or where we are going."

We walked fast after that, our sacks bumping against our backs. Behind us the frontier markers were swallowed into the distance and the darkness. The American had started a train of serious thought. I

278

estimated that we had covered about 1,200 miles in not much more than 60 days. It was a feat of speed as well as endurance.

Paluchowicz broke in on my thoughts. "How far do we have to travel now?"

I thought about it. "About twice as far as we've traveled already," I guessed. Paluchowicz grunted his dismay.

Here it was that we first discussed seriously where we were going. Up to now we had thought ahead no farther than the escape from Siberia. Back in the camp I had talked, without any great conviction, of making for Afghanistan. It sounded like a safe, out-of-the-way small country where we might be received without too many questions asked. Now we turned our thoughts toward India. And the key to this, I think, lay in the talk we had had a day earlier with the two Mongols. Lhasa. It was a word we could use in a country where few knew our language, a sound that could be understood and that would always evoke the response of a flung-out hand to indicate direction. We talked mainly of Tibet in that first hour. India then seemed too far to contemplate.

The American spoke truly when he said we did not know where we were. We had no maps, and there was no one to tell us.

We were climbing steadily into the mountains two hours after leaving the border. Sweat oozed from us. The thunder spoke out nearer and nearer, and a warm, sighing wind blew up from nowhere, rapidly increasing in strength as we plodded on.

Around midnight the gathering storm exploded. The first overhead thunderclap boomed like a near-at-hand battery of long-range artillery firing a simultaneous salvo. It was an assault on the ears. Lightning streaked and blazed across the black heavens while the thunder rolled, crashed, and reverberated about us. A few large raindrops urged us to look for cover, but the lightning revealed only a wilderness of rocky slopes. The torrent was upon us as we groped in the tumult. The rain dropped down by sheer weight, its vertical fall unaffected by the whining wind.

My clothes were soaked in a matter of minutes. Streams of water trickled down the back of my neck inside my jacket. It was the worst electrical storm I have ever experienced.

We lasted that night out, the eight of us, in a shallow crevice between two smooth rocks. Only the innermost couple enjoyed any degree of comfort. The girl, in the most favored position, huddled shivering in her wet clothes throughout the unending dark hours, bewildered at the unabating fury of the storm.

It was a relief to get moving at first light. The rain sheeted down all through the day as though it would never stop. It went on teeming throughout the next night and until evening of the second day. Then the downpour ceased as spectacularly as though someone had turned a tap off in the heavens. In the morning a hot sun transformed our dreary world, and steam rose in clouds from the rocks. We dried our clothes and again began to take an interest in our position.

The continuing ascent was tiring but not difficult. The 15 to 20 pounds of potatoes each of us carried did not make the effort any easier, but no one grumbled on that account. From the heights on the fourth day there was a clear view of the range running roughly east and west and splaying out to the south like a series of great probing fingers. Our accidentally chosen route crossed the middle of three ill-defined peaks, its summit a broad, uneven-surfaced plateau.

The negotiation of the mountains took about eight days. The last stages of the descent were notable because we were able to find wood to light a fire and cooked the last of our stinking pig meat. We laid a flat stone across one corner of the fire and roasted potatoes, which made a memorable meal.

COMING DOWN ONTO THE PLAIN from the cool heights was like stepping into an oven. Off came the bulky fufaikas, and we sweltered bare-armed in our camp-made fur vests. Kolemenos carried Kristina's padded jacket, and she walked along with her faded purple dress opened at the neck. The ground was hard as cement and coated with a powdery reddish dust. The mountains outcropped in an odd succession of low, oval mounds. Our exposed arms turned bright red, blistered, peeled, and finally took on a deep tan. The 20 to 30 miles a day we imposed on ourselves were infinitely tiring, and the nights brought with them a severe chill.

The treatment of sore feet became a preoccupation. Deep cracks developed between the toes, and there were raw patches where the fine dust chafed inside our moccasins. We had occasion to bless the foresight of Paluchowicz, a chronic foot-sufferer, who had collected the fat drippings from the cooking pork back in the cave in Siberia and carried it in a roughly hollowed wooden cup shaped like half a coconut shell. This fat we applied to the cracks and sore patches.

The country, we discovered, was crisscrossed with rivers, but we marched a couple of days before we struck the first one. At noon on a sun-scorched day through a shimmering heat haze, the promise of its cool waters sent our dragging feet lifting over the dry ground. It was a beautiful sight, about 100 yards wide, its banks green-clothed with grass, its verges supporting flourishing growths of the long-stemmed, bamboo-jointed water plants we had met all through Siberia. We lay on our bellies and drank, then we sat in bliss soaking our aching feet. We washed ourselves, using fine sand as a scourer, and soaked the dust out of our clothes. We baked and ate some of our potatoes and lay down in the grass with a sense of relaxed well-being.

Along the river an hour after our arrival came a small sampan-type boat, high-built at bow and stern, broad-bottomed, and with a flimsy canopy amidships. Athwartships, just forward of the canopy, ran a long stout pole extending beyond the boat a few feet on each side to the ends of which were lashed two thick bundles of sticks riding an inch or two above water. At first I thought they were fenders, but afterward I concluded they were stabilizers, which, dipping into the water as the craft slewed, would keep it on an even keel. The boatman was Chinese. He was barefoot and wore a coolie sun hat, linen trousers ending below the knees, and a loose flapping shirt with ragged sleeves torn off at the elbows.

The sampan was poled along with a length of strong bamboo. The spectacle was new to all of us, and we waved as the sampan glided by. The boatman grinned and waved back. Three or four more craft moved past while we rested there. Propulsion was the same for all—a long bamboo pole—although one had a stumpy mast that could have been used for a sail.

There were many other boats on many other rivers in Outer Mongolia, but the men who plied their trade in them were always Chinese. On the roads I never once met a Chinese. Road travelers always seemed to be Mongols.

Our face-to-face meeting with the natives of the country occurred after we had crossed the river and moved a few miles to the south. We were following no track but planning our progress according to the lay of the land—avoiding small hills, seizing on a landmark ahead, and then walking steadily toward it. Our path was cut eventually by a road lying east and west.

Coming slowly from the west was a group of travelers, and it was obvious that if both they and we maintained our pace, we must meet. We were less than 50 yards from the road when the Mongols drew abreast. They stopped and waited for us. They were talking busily among themselves as we came within earshot but became silent as we halted before them. They smiled and bowed, keeping their eyes on us all the while.

There were a dozen or more men, one camel, two mules, and two donkeys. The animals were lightly laden and were also saddled for riding. Only the camel was being ridden now. Perched comfortably on it was an old man with a wispy gray beard. The men might have been a family party, of which the old man was the patriarch. All wore the typical Mongolian conical caps with their long earflaps turned back alongside the crown, in material that ranged from leather to quilted homespun cloth. All wore calf-length boots of excellent soft leather, and the old man's boots, in green leather simply embroidered on the outside of the leg in colored silk or woolen threads, were of especially fine quality.

When the bowing on both sides had been completed in silence, the graybeard got down from his camel. We bowed again, and he returned the greeting. He spoke in his own language, and we shook our heads. Mr. Smith whispered to me, "Try him in Russian, Slav." The old man heard and turned his attention to me.

"May your feet carry you well on the rest of your journey," I addressed him in Russian.

A long pause followed.

In Russian, haltingly and with an obvious searching for words in an unfamiliar tongue, came the answer: "Talk more, please. I understand you well, but I speak little Russian. Once I spoke this language, but not for many years."

I talked slowly, and he listened intently. I said we were going south, that we had crossed a river some hours before. I didn't know what else to say. There was such a long silence when I finished that I thought the parley was over. But the old gentleman wanted to satisfy his curiosity and, as it turned out, was grappling with his rusty Russian in order to phrase his questions. The conversation, in the fullness of time, proceeded thus:

You have no camels?—We are too poor to have camels.

You have no mules?—We have no mules either.

You have no donkeys?—No donkeys.

Having established us on the lowest stratum of society, he went on to question me about our journey. The word Lhasa came up. He pointed to the south.

"It is a very long way," he said. "and the sun will come around many times before you reach this place."

The question he had been itching to ask came at last. He looked at Kristina. Her hair, bleached several shades lighter by the sun, was in sharp contrast to the dark tan of her face, from which the blue eyes

frankly returned the old man's gaze. He asked how old she was, if she were related to any of us, and where we were taking her. I answered as I had done that other old man to the north.

This leisurely catechism had taken over half an hour and the patriarch had appeared to enjoy it immensely. I suspect he was proud of the opportunity of showing his younger kinsmen how he could converse in a foreign tongue.

He turned from us and spoke in his own language to the others. They smiled among themselves and bustled about the packs on the animals. From the packs they brought him food, and smilingly he distributed it among us. He handed around nuts, dried fish, some partly cooked swollen barley grains, and scone-sized oaten cakes.

We all bowed, and I, as the spokesman, thanked him in the finest phrases I could lay tongue to.

We parted with many expressions of felicitation for our respective journeys and many kind wishes for the continuing health of our feet. It was perhaps our most interesting encounter in Mongolia, but we were to find that all these people, whatever their station in life, had those typical qualities of courtesy, complete trust, generosity, and hospitality. The help we received was according to the means of the giver, but that help was always cheerfully given.

By the end of our first two weeks in Mongolia our methods of advance had been modified from those employed in Siberia. No longer was it necessary to post night sentries. The urge to keep on the move persisted; it had become a habit of our existence. But we were not now bedeviled by fears of imminent recapture; we could make contact with the people of the country. We did long day marches from the cool hour before dawn until the late evening setting of the sun, but we had adopted the hot-country custom of resting in shelter for the two hours of fiercest heat at midday.

To relate time and distance has been the greatest of my difficulties in recording the story of this bid for freedom. Particularly is this so concerning the passage through Mongolia, where we had no common speech with the inhabitants and where, even if we were given the names of rivers, villages, or other landmarks, there was no means of setting the sounds down to help the memory in later years. But I believe our progress through inhabited Outer Mongolia to the wastes of Inner Mongolia occupied us from six to eight weeks.

This much I remember: The entry into the Gobi Desert was not an abrupt transition. Twice we thought we were in it as we traversed long sandy stretches, but on each occasion a range of fairly tall hills intervened, and at the foot of the second range there was the boon of a shallow, sandy rivulet, beside which we camped for the night. That was our last drink of fresh water for a long, long time.

Toward nightfall of the next day we encountered a caravan trail at right angles to our course, alongside which were seated four Mongolians watching over a steaming iron cauldron suspended from a metal tripod over a fire. They all appeared to be aged between 30 and 40.

The usual courtesies were exchanged, but this time none of our hosts knew Russian. They motioned us to sit on one side of the fire while they faced us across the flames.

These were poorer travelers than those we had first met. I noticed that their jackets had been neatly patched in places. They had one mule among them, on which the bare necessities for their journey were carried. More water was added to the pot while we grinned and gestured futilely to show our pleasure at the unexpected meeting. In deference to Smith's gray-streaked beard, the oldest-looking Mongol directed his attention to the American, whom he obviously regarded as the senior member of our party and therefore its leader.

Eventually, Mr. Smith used the magic word Lhasa, and the Mongol, after a minute of deliberation, pointed the direction we should take. Then from inside his coat he withdrew a contraption that I can best describe as a metal cylinder on a long rod. From this cylinder he drew out a length of silk ribbon in the manner that a Westerner will produce a tape measure of the mechanically retracting kind. The silk was covered with symbols in a series of frames like the separate pictures on a movie film. He spent some time tranquilly contemplating the ribbon and finally, with a spinning motion of the hand, returned the roll within its case. This performance we took to mean a prayer for the happy completion of our pilgrimage. Mr. Smith bowed his acknowledgment.

The man in charge of the cauldron produced a brick of compressed tea, black in color, broke off a piece, and fed it into the water. For several minutes he stirred the brew with a large long-handled wooden spoon, and the fragrance from the boiling pot assailed our noses most agreeably. Next was produced a wooden jar from which the lid was removed to reveal a substance that looked to me like honey but which later turned out to be butter. Spoonfuls of the stuff were added to the brew, and the stirring and simmering went on for some time.

Two mugs were produced. The procedure for passing around the tea was rather amusing, since it involved guessing our ages in order that the more senior on both sides should be served first. About Mr.

Smith they had no difficulty. The first two cups dipped into the brew went to him and the oldest Mongol. When we turned over our own mug to the cook, he filled it and passed it without hesitation to Paluchowicz. I saw the sergeant make a face of great distaste at his first gulp, look at the American, and then smack his lips as Smith was doing to show appreciation of what he was drinking. Mr. Smith had sipped away with great composure.

Kristina and I were the last to be served. While we awaited our turns, I teased her about the custom of a country that ruled "Ladies last." She replied that placing her last might mean only that they recognized her as the youngest of us. The Mongols watched the laughing exchanges between us, and I am sure they would have loved to know what we talked about. When our turns did come, I could sense the others looking at us surreptitiously. The tea was comfortingly hot, but it tasted foul. We kept our faces straight and avoided each other's eyes.

The savor of the fragrant leaves was overborne by the sickening tang of rancid butter, which floated in glistening globules of fat on the surface. But we got through it, and I had to exercise great self-control to stop from laughing out loud as Kristina gave out a couple of decorous lip-smackings.

The Mongols' hospitality was rounded off with the gift of a little tobacco and a few nuts. We all stood and made our farewells. We walked away, and when I looked back from 50 yards away, they were squatting down again, their backs toward us. In that short distance we had passed out of their lives and they out of ours.

I was to remember later that they thought our trail to Lhasa merited a special prayer. We were striding into the burning wastes of the Gobi, waterless and with little food. None of us then knew the hell we were to meet.

HUNGER, DROUGHT, AND DEATH

TWO DAYS WITHOUT WATER in the hillocky, sand-covered, August furnace of the Gobi and I felt the first flutterings of fear. The early rays of the sun rising over the rim of the world dispersed the sharp chill of the desert night. The light hit the tops of the billowing dunes and threw sharp shadows across the deep-sanded floors of the intervening little valleys. Fear came with small fast-beating wings and was suppressed as we sucked pebbles and dragged our feet on to make maximum distance before the blinding heat of noon. From time to time one or another of us would climb one of the endless knolls and look south to see the same deadly landscape stretching to the horizon. Toward midday we stuck our long clubs in the sand and draped our jackets over them to make a shelter. Alarm about our position must have been general, but no one voiced it. My own feeling was that we must not frighten the girl, and I am sure the others kept silent for the same reason.

The heat enveloped us, sucking the moisture from our bodies, putting ankle irons of lethargy about our legs. Each one of us walked with his and her own thoughts, and none spoke, dully concentrating on placing one foot ahead of the other interminably. Most often I led the way, Kolemenos and the girl nearest to me, and the other ones bunched together a few yards behind. I was driving them now, making them get to their feet in the mornings, forcing them to cut short the noon rest.

As we still walked in the rays of the setting sun, the fear hit me again. It was, of course, the fundamental, most oppressive fear of all—that we would die here in the burning wilderness. I struggled against a panicky impulse to urge a return the way we had come, back to water and green things and life. I fought it down.

We flopped out against a tall dune, and the cold stars came out to look at us. Our bone-weariness should have ensured the sleep of exhaustion, but, tortured with thirst, one after another twisted restlessly, rose, wandered around, and came back. Sometime after midnight I suggested we start off again to take advantage of the cool conditions. Everybody seemed to be awake. We hauled ourselves upright and began again the trudge south. It was much easier going. We rested a couple of hours after dawn—and still the southerly prospect remained unaltered.

After this one trial there were no more night marches. Makowski put a stop to it.

"Can you plot your course by the stars?" he asked me. The others turned haggard faces toward me.

I paused a long moment before answering. "Not with complete certainty," I confessed.

"Can any of us?" he persisted. No one spoke.

"Then we could have been walking in circles all through the night," he said heavily.

I sensed the awful dismay his words had caused. I protested that I was sure we had not veered off course, that the rising sun had proved us still to be facing south. But in my own mind, even as I argued, I had to admit the possiblity that Makowski was right.

In any case, the seed of doubt had been sown, and we just could not afford to add anything to the already heavy burden of apprehension we were under.

So we went on through the shimmering stillness. Not even a faint zephyr of air came up to disperse the fine dust hanging almost unseen above the desert, the dust that coated our faces and beards, entered into our cracked lips, and reddened the rims of eyes already sorely tried by the stark brightness of the sun.

The severely rationed food gave out on about the fifth day, and still we faced a lifeless horizon. In all this arid world only eight struggling human specks and an occasional snake were alive. We could have ceased to move quite easily and lain there and died. The temptation to extend the noonday halt, to go on dozing through the hot afternoon until the sun dropped out of sight, invited our dry, aching bodies. Our feet were in a pitiable state as the burning sand struck through the thin soles of our worn moccasins.

I found myself croaking at the others to get up and keep going. There is nothing here, I would say. There is nothing for days behind us. Ahead there must be something. There must be *something*. Kristina would stand up and join me, and Kolemenos. Then the others in a bunch. Like automatons we would be under way again, heads bent down, silent, thinking God knows what, but moving one foot in front of the other hour after desperate hour.

On the sixth day the girl stumbled and, on her knees, looked up at me. "That was foolish of me, Slav. I tripped myself up." She did not wait for my assistance. She rose slowly from the sand and stepped out beside me. That afternoon I found to my faint surprise and irritation that I was on my knees. I had not been conscious of the act of falling. One moment I was walking, the next I had stopped. On my knees, I thought . . . like a man at prayer.

I got up. No one had slackened pace for me. They probably hardly noticed my stumble. It seemed to take me a very long time to regain my position at the head again. Others were falling, too, I noticed from time to time. The knees gave, and they knelt there a few unbelieving seconds until realization came that they had ceased to be mobile. They came on again.

There was no dropping out. These were the signs of growing, strength-sapping weakness, but it would have been fatal to have ac-

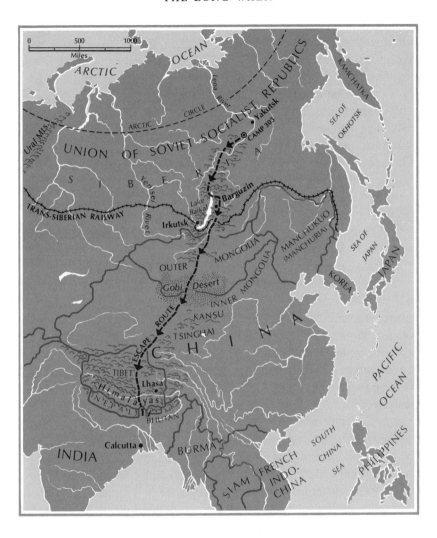

knowledged them for what they were. They were the probing fingers of death, and we were not ready to die yet.

The sun rose on the seventh day in a symphony of suffused pinks and gold. Without much hope we watched Kolemenos climb laboriously to the top of a high mound. One of us did this every morning as soon as the light was sufficient to give clear visibility southward to the horizon. He stood there for quite a minute with his hand over his eyes, and we kept walking, expecting the usual hopeless shrug of the shoulders. But Kolemenos made no move to come down. He flung out his right arm and pointed. My sight blurred over. For some

289

seconds I could not focus. I rubbed my eyes and looked again. There was *something*, a dark patch against the light sand. It might have been five miles distant from us. Through the early morning haze it was shapeless and defied recognition. Excitement grew as we looked.

"Could it be an animal?" asked Paluchowicz.

"Whatever it is, it certainly is not sand," Mr. Smith replied. "Let's go and investigate."

It took us a good two hours to cover the intervening distance. There were *trees* all right—real, live, growing, healthy trees, in a clump, outlined against the sand like a blob of ink on a fresh-laundered tablecloth.

"Where there are trees, there is water," said the American.

"An oasis," somebody shouted, and the word fluttered from mouth to mouth. "An oasis!"

Kristina whispered, "It is a miracle. God has saved us."

If we could have run, we would have done so. We toiled that last half mile as fast we could flog our legs along. I went sprawling a few times. My tongue was dry and felt swollen in my mouth. The trees loomed larger, and I saw they were palms. In their shade was a sunken hollow, roughly oval shaped, and I knew this must be water. A few hundred yard from the oasis we crossed a clearly defined east-west caravan track. On the fringe of the trees we passed an incongruous pile of what looked like rusting biscuit tins, like some fantastic mid-desert junkyard.

The trees, a dozen or more of them, were arranged in a crescent on the south side of the pool and threw their shadows over it for most of the day. The wonderful cool water lay still and inviting in an elliptical depression hemmed with big, rough-worked stones. The whole green, life-giving spot could have been contained inside half an acre.

Zaro had the mug, but we could not wait for him to fill it and hand it around. We lay over the water lapping at it and sucking it in like animals. We allowed it to caress our fevered faces. We dabbed it around our necks. We drank until someone uttered the warning about filling our empty bellies with too much liquid. Then we soaked our food sacks and, sitting on the big stones, gently washed our cracked and lacerated feet. The very feel and presence of water was an ecstasy. Our spirits zoomed. We had walked out of an abyss of fear into life and new hope. We chatted and laughed as though the liquid we had drunk was heady champagne.

The full extent of our good fortune had not yet been discovered. Some 20 yards east of the pool, on the opposite side from which we had approached, were the remains of a still-warm fire and the fresh tracks of camels and many hoofprints, telling of the recent halt of a big caravan. It had probably departed at sunrise. These men, whoever they were, had cooked and eaten meat, and the bones, as yet quite fresh and untainted, were scattered around the wood ashes. They were the bones of one large and one small animal, and the meat had been sliced from them with knives, leaving small, succulent pieces still adhering. We portioned out the bones and tore at them with our teeth, lauding our luck. Poor toothless Paluchowicz borrowed the knife from me and did as well as anybody. When there was no more meat, we cracked each bone with the ax and sucked out the marrow.

For two or three hours during the heat of the afternoon we lay stretched out near the water under the blessed shade of the palms. The sun's rays began to slant, and I came out of a sleep haunted by blazing light and never-ending desert. I picked up the mug, climbed over the stones, scooped up water, and drank again. The American stood up, stretched, and joined me. Soon we were all up and about.

"I'm going to have a look at that pile of tins," Zaro said.

THE PUZZLE OF THAT DUMP of civilized junk in the heart of the south Gobi must remain unsolved. There were about a hundred of the boxlike metal containers, and they had been there so long that, even in the dry air of that place, they had rusted beyond use. From beneath the pile, half buried in the sand, Zaro pulled out a complete coil of rust-covered quarter-inch wire held together by circlets of thinner wire that broke away at a touch. I held a handful of sand in a fold of my sack and rubbed away at the heavy wire until I cleared the rust. The coating was thin; the wire was strong and sound. No one had any clear notion what to do with it, but we just could not bring ourselves to leave treasure behind. Since we had to take it with us, the discussion finally boiled down to shaping it into an easily portable form.

That was how we came to spend hours that day cutting off about four-foot lengths, turning the ends into hooks, and making loops that could be slung around the neck. The metal was tough, and bending it required hard work with the back of the ax head while the wire ends were jammed and firmly held in interstices between the close-set stones. When each of us had been supplied with a loop, Zaro and a couple of others made a few metal spikes about two feet long, one end beaten out to a point and the other looped to hang on the belt. Plenty of wire still remained when we had finished, but we thought we had all we could carry. The operation gave us a sense of achievement.

Inevitably came the question of when to depart. Two of our problems were insoluble. The oasis had water but no food. We had nothing in which to carry water. Makowski argued that if we waited here a few days, we stood a chance of meeting a caravan and securing ourselves a stock of food for the next stage. But I wanted to go. I said that, as we had just missed one caravan, there might not be another for weeks. We would wait on for days until we were too weak from lack of food to move at all, and the next travelers might find us dead from starvation. We were in desperate straits, and we had to decide immediately one way or the other. The thing was decided late that evening. We would set out before dawn.

We were on our way when the sun came up, and for half a day we could look back and see the trees of the oasis. I was glad when I could no longer see their shapes against the skyline.

For the first three days I thought we moved surprisingly well. On the fourth day the inescapable, strength-draining heat began quite suddenly to take its toll. This was the pre-oasis journey all over again. Stumbles and falls became increasingly frequent, the pace slowed, speech dried up into short grunted phrases. I remember Makowski saying, "Hell can't be hotter than this bloody desert."

On the fifth day Kristina fell to her knees. I turned slowly around to look at her, expecting her to get to her feet as she had done before. She remained kneeling, her fair head bowed down on her chest. She was very still. I moved toward her, and Kolemenos stepped back at the same time. Before we could reach her, she swayed from the hips and slumped forward, her face in the sand. We reached her at the same time and turned her on her back. She was unconscious. I opened the neck of her dress and started talking to her, gently shaking her, while Mr. Smith set to work with a stick and fufaikas to provide some shade for her.

She came to quickly. She looked at our anxious ring of faces, sat up, smiled through split lips, and said, "I feel better now. I must have fallen over—I don't know how it happened."

"Don't worry," I consoled her. "We'll rest here awhile and then you'll be all right again."

She leaned forward and lightly patted the back of my hand. "I won't fall down again."

We sat there awhile. Kristina reached down to scratch her ankle, and my eyes idly followed her hand. I saw that the ankle was swollen so that the skin pressed outward against the narrow-fitting ends of her padded trousers.

"Has anything bitten you, Kristina?"

"No, Slav. Why?"

"Your leg looks swollen."

She pulled up the trouser leg and looked, turning her foot about as she did so. "I hadn't noticed it before," she said.

We struggled on for a few more hours. She seemed to be refreshed. Then she fell again, and this time her knees buckled and her face hit the sand in almost one movement without even the action of putting her arms out to break the fall.

We turned her over again and wiped away the sand that had been forced into her nose and mouth. We put up the shelter. She lay with eyes closed, breathing in harsh gasps through her mouth. I looked at her ankles, and they were a pitiful sight. Both were badly discolored and so swollen that it seemed they would burst the restricting bottoms of the trousers. I took out my knife and slit the cloth upward. The skin appeared to be distended by water right up to the knees. I touched the swelling, and the mark of my fingers remained plainly visible for some seconds.

Kristina was unconscious for about an hour while we tried to stifle our gnawing anxiety with banalities such as, "It must be just a touch of sunstroke." I had a feeling like lead in the pit of my stomach. I was very frightened.

She was quite cheerful when she came around. "I am becoming a nuisance," she said. "What can be the matter with me? My legs are getting quite thick."

"Do they hurt you, Kristina?"

"No, not at all," she quickly replied. "They must be swelling because I have walked so far."

The time was afternoon on the fifth day. She walked on for hours without more than an occasional small stumble and was still keeping up with Kolemenos and me when the sun had gone and we stopped for the night. Sitting there among us she stole frequent looks at her legs. She said nothing, and we pretended not to notice.

It was a disturbed night. Everyone except Kolemenos seemed too weary and worried for sleep, Kristina lay very still, but I sensed she remained wide-awake.

During the first two hours of the sixth day the air was cool, and walking was as pleasant as ever it can be in the desert. But soon the sun began to blaze at us from a sky empty of clouds.

I took Kristina's elbow. "Can you keep going in this?"

"Yes, I think so."

Five minutes later she had folded up and was out, face down in the sand. Again we ministered to her and waited for her to open her eyes. She appeared to be breathing quite normally, like a tired child.

I stood a few steps away from her, and the others came over to me. "She is very swollen," I said, my voice lowered. "Do any of you know what that means?"

Nobody knew the symptoms. We went back to her and waited. I flapped my cap over her face to make some air.

She smiled at us. "I am being a bother again." We shook our heads. "I am afraid you had better leave me this time."

We all broke into protest at once. Kolemenos dropped down on his knees beside her. "Don't say that. Don't be a silly little girl. We shall never leave you." She lay there for another half hour, and when she tried to force herself up on her elbows, she fell back again.

I spoke to Kolemenos. "We must give her a hand." We lifted her to her feet. "I can walk if you stay near me," she said.

Amazingly, she walked, Kolemenos and I lightly holding her elbows. After a quarter of a mile we felt her start to fall forward. We steadied her, and she went on again. She pulled herself erect, and there was not a sound of distress, not a whimper. The next time she slumped forward we could not hold her. She had played herself utterly out; even the gallant will in that frail body could not produce another torturing effort. We were all in a bunch around her as the sun climbed up over our heads. Kolemenos and I each put an arm about her and, half-carrying, half-dragging her, set off again. A mile or so of that and I had no reserve of strength to give her. We stopped, and I bent over double fighting for breath.

We made a shelter there and remained for perhaps three hours through the worst heat of the day. She lay still—I do not think she could move. The ugly swelling had advanced past the knees and was heavy with water.

The sun began to decline. Kolemenos bent down and swung her into his arms and trudged off. I stayed with him, and the rest were all about us. He covered fully a quarter of a mile before he put her down that first time. He picked her up again and walked, her head pillowed on his great shoulder. I can never in my life see anything so magnificent as the blond-bearded giant Kolemenos carrying Kristina, hour after hour, toward darkness of that awful sixth day. His ordeal lasted some four hours. Then she touched his cheek.

"Put me down on the ground, Anastazi. Just lay me down on the ground. Please, Anastazi."

294

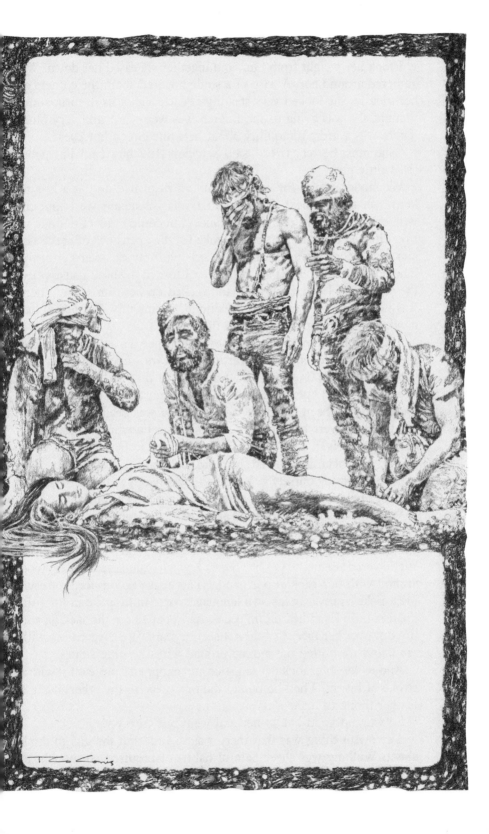

I took her weight from him, and together we eased her down. We gathered around her. A wisp of a smile hovered about the corners of her mouth. She looked very steadily at each one of us in turn, and I thought she was going to speak. Her eyes were clear and very blue. There was a great tranquility about her. She closed her eyes.

"She must be very tired," said Sergeant Paluchowicz. "The poor, tired little girl."

We stood around for several minutes, dispirited and at a loss to know what to do next. The shoulders of Kolemenos were sagging with exhaustion. We exchanged glances but could think of nothing to say. I looked down at Kristina. I looked at the open neck of her dress, and in a second I was down at her side with my ear over her heart. There was no beat. I did not believe it. I turned my head and applied the other ear. I lifted my head and picked up her thin wrist. There was no pulse. They were all looking at me intently. I dropped her hand, and it thumped softly into the sand.

The American spoke, hardly above a whisper. I tried to answer but the words would not come. Instead the tears came, the bitter salt tears. And the sobs were torn from me. In that godforsaken place seven men cried openly because the thing most precious to us in all the world had been taken from us. Kristina was dead.

I think we were half crazy there beside her body in the desert. We accused ourselves of having brought her here to her death.

The American intervened, his voice cold and flat. "Gentlemen, it is no use blaming ourselves. I think she was happy with us." The talk ceased. He went on, "Let us now give her a decent burial."

We scraped a hole in the sand at the base of a dune. Little pieces of stone that we sifted from the grains as we dug deeper we laid apart. I slit open a food sack and laid the double end gently under her chin. We lowered the body. On her breast lay her little crucifix. We stood around with our caps in our hands. There was no service, but each man spoke a prayer in his own language. Mr. Smith spoke in English, the first time I had heard him use it. As I opened out the sacking and lifted it over her face, I could not see for tears. We covered her with sand, and we dotted the mound around with the little stones.

And Kolemenos took her tall stick and chopped a piece off it with a stroke of his ax. Then he bound the one piece to the other, using a leather thong to make a cross.

So we said good-bye to her and went our empty way.

The awful thing was that there was so little but the girl to think about. Walking was sheer painful habit—it required no thought to

296

perform. The sun beating down hour after hour would addle my brains and check the orderly sequence of thinking. I found I could imagine she was still there, just behind my shoulders, and I'd scuff along for mile after mile, seeing her. But there always came a time when the idea of her presence was so strong that I must turn my head, and bitter grief would knife at me all over again. I awoke slowly from a troubled, thirst-ridden sleep that night, and I was sure once more that she remained with us. And each fresh realization of her death renewed the agony.

It took another bitter tragedy to dull the sharp edges of our memory of Kristina.

On the eighth day out from the oasis, Sigmund Makowski pitched over into the sand. His arms were still at his sides when his face thumped down, and he had made no effort to use his stick to prevent the fall. He lay there a minute or two and was barely conscious. We looked down at him and saw the telltale sign. Over the tops of his moccasins the flesh was soft and puffy. We exchanged glances and said nothing. We turned him over and flapped our sacks in his face, and he recovered quickly. He got to his feet, shook his head from side to side, grabbed his stick, and plunged off. He keeled over again and again, but he kept going. And all the time the sickening flabby swelling grew upward and weighed upon his legs.

Makowski lasted longer after the first onset than Kristina had. On the ninth day he must have slumped down half a dozen times in a couple of hours.

That night he seemed to sleep peacefully, and in the morning of the 10th day he was not only still alive but appeared to have regained some strength. He set off with the rest of us, dragging his feet but unaided. He moved for half an hour before his first fall, but thereafter he pitched over repeatedly until Kolemenos and I again went to his rescue. When the time came to make our noonday halt, he was draped about our shoulders like a sack, and his legs had all but ceased to move. Mr. Smith and Paluchowicz eased his weight away from us and gently laid him down on his back. Then we put up the shelter and squatted down around him. Makowski lay quite still—only his eyes seemed to be alive.

After a while he closed his eyes, and I thought he had gone, but he was still breathing quietly. He opened his eyes again. The lids came down, and this time he was dead. There was no spasm, no tremor, no outward sign to show that life had departed the body. Like Kristina, he had no words for us at the end.

The dossier for Sigmund Makowski, aged 37, ex-captain of the Polish Frontier Forces, was closed. Somewhere in Poland he had a wife. I would like her some day to know he was a brave man. We buried him there in the Gobi. Kolemenos made another small wooden cross; we said our prayers and left him.

I tried hard to keep count of the days. I tried, too, to remember if I had ever read how long a man can keep alive without food and water. My head ached with the heat. Often the blackest pall of despair settled on me, and I felt we were six doomed men toiling inevitably to destruction. With each hopeless dawn the thought recurred: Who will be next? We were six dried-out travesties of men shuffling, shuffling. The sand seemed to get deeper, more and more reluctant to let our ill-used feet go. When a man stumbled, he made a show of getting quickly on his legs again. Quite openly now we examined our ankles for the first sign of swelling, for the warning of death.

In the shadow of death we grew closer together than ever before. No man would admit to despair. No man spoke of fear. The only thought spoken out again and again was that there must be water soon. All our hope was in this. Over every arid ridge of hot sand I imagined a tiny stream, and after each waterless vista there was always another ridge to keep the hope alive.

The only life we saw in the desert about us were snakes. They lay still, heads showing, with the lengths of their bodies hidden in deep holes in the sand. I wondered how they lived. They showed no fear of us, and we had no desire to molest them.

THE LAST OF THE GOBI

Two days after Makowski's death, Slav Rawicz and his five companions were reaching the end of their endurance, yet they staggered on across the blistering sands of the Gobi Desert. Each man knew that if a miracle did not happen soon, they could never expect to survive. Then a chance discovery revealed an almost dried-up creek. It gave them enough muddy water to stave off immediate death. But still there was nothing to eat.

"I think snakes are our only chance," the American, Smith, said. "It's not unknown for men to eat snakes. The poison is in a sac in the head. When you cut off the head, you remove the poison."

Unquestionably, it was the snakes of the Gobi that saved them, Slav Rawicz later wrote. Two were soon caught, skinned, cooked, and eaten. They were just the first of many the men ate, as the dreadful southward trek across the flat, never-ending desert went on and on.

Then one morning they awoke to make an exciting discovery. The land far ahead was beginning to slope upward to a series of foothills, and beyond, perhaps 50 miles away, was a mountain range.

So UNINFORMED WERE WE of central Asian geography that we speculated on the possibility that the tall eastern barrier could be the Himalayas, that somehow we had bypassed them to the west, that we might now even be on the threshold of India. We were to learn that the whole considerable north-to-south expanse of Tibet, ruggedly harsh and mountainous, lay between us and the Himalayas.

We plodded on for two more exhausting, heartbreaking days before we reached firm ground, a waste of lightly sanded rocks. Lifeless and naked, the rocky ridge sloped easily into the distance above us. In my mind was the one thought that over the hump there might be water. We rested a couple of hours before we tackled the drag upward. We took off our moccasins and emptied them of sand. Then we went up and out of the Gobi.

Over the ridge there was more desolation. By nightfall we had dropped down into a stone-strewn valley. In the morning we climbed again. We did not reach the next summit for several hours. From the top there was the view again of the great range to the east, looking even more formidable than at our first sight of it. Below us the floor of the valley appeared to be covered with sand, and we decided to get down before dark to search for snakes.

It was the merest accident that we did not miss the water on our way down. We had all passed it when Zaro turned around and yelled the one wonderful word. It was no more than a trickle from a crack in a rock, but it glinted like silver. It crept down over the curve of a big round boulder and spread thinly over a flat rock below. We turned quickly and scrambled back. We found that the source of the little spring was a crack just wide enough to take the fingers of one hand. The water was sparkling, clean, and ice-cold. We channeled the tiny stream to a point where we could lead it into our battered and much traveled metal mug. The mug was passed around, and each man took a gulp. No nectar of the gods could have tasted so wonderful. Again and again we filled the mug and drank.

The time was around the middle of the day. We agreed readily that we should stay close to the spring for another 24 hours.

The next morning we were on our way again. We traveled down the long slope, across the hot valley, and up the hillside facing us—a total of at least 15 miles. From the top of the ridge we took fresh bearings. Directly ahead were some formidable heights, so we set our course over easier ground about 10 degrees east of the line due south. Toward evening we were all heartened by the discovery of the first vegetation we had seen since the oasis. It was a rough, spiky grass clinging hardily to dry rootholds in fissures between the rocks.

The wearing trek went on day after day. Our diet was still confined to an occasional snake—we lived on them altogether for upward of three weeks from the time of our first sampling back in the desert. The specter of thirst receded as we found clear-running rivulets. It was rare now that we had to go waterless for longer than a day.

There came a morning when we breasted the top of a long rise and looked down unbelievingly into a wide-spreading valley, which showed, far below, the lush green of grazing grass. Still more exciting, there was a flock of about a hundred sheep, crawling like specks five miles or more distant from and below us. We made the descent fast, slipping and sliding in our eagerness to get down. We had about a quarter of a mile to go to reach the flock when we saw the two dogs, long-coated liver-and-white collie types. They came racing around the flock to take up a station between us and their charges.

Zaro called out, "Don't worry, we won't hurt them. Where's your master?" The dogs eyed him warily.

Kolemenos growled, "I only need to get near enough to a sheep for one swing of my old ax. . . ."

"Don't get impatient, Anastazi," I told him. "It is fairly obvious the shepherd has sent his dogs over here to intercept us. Let us swing away from the flock and see if they will lead us to their master."

We turned pointedly away. The dogs watched us closely for a couple of minutes. Then, apparently satisfied that they had headed us away from the sheep, they ran off at great speed together toward the opposite slope of the valley. My eyes followed the line of their run ahead of them, and then I shouted and pointed. A mile or more away rose a thin wisp of smoke.

"A fire at midday can mean only one thing—cooking," said Marchinkovas hopefully.

The fire was burning in the lee of a rocky outcrop, against which had been built a one-man shelter of stones laid one above the other as in an old cairn. Seated there was an old man, his two dogs, tongues lolling, beside him. He spoke to his dogs as we neared him, and they got up and raced off back across the valley to the flock. Steaming over the fire was a black iron cauldron. The American went to the front and approached bowing. The old man rose smiling and returned the bow and then went on to bow to each of us in turn.

He was white-bearded. The high cheekbones in his broad, square face revealed a skin that had been weathered to the color of old rosewood. He wore a warm goatskin cap with earflaps turned up over the crown in the fashion of the Mongols we had met in the north. His felt boots were well made and had stout leather soles. His unfastened three-quarter-length sheepskin coat was held to the body by a woven wool girdle, and his trousers were bulkily padded, probably with lamb's wool. He leaned his weight on a five-foot-tall wooden staff. There was no doubt of his friendliness and his pleasure at the arrival of unexpected visitors.

He talked eagerly, and it was a minute or two before he realized we did not understand a word. I spoke in Russian, and he regarded me blankly. It was a great pity because he must have been looking forward to conversation and the exchange of news. I think he was trying to tell us that he had seen us a long way off and had prepared food for our arrival. He motioned us to sit near the fire and resumed the stirring of the pot that our coming had interrupted. I looked into the stone shelter and saw there was just room for one man to sleep. On the floor was a sleeping mat.

As he wielded his big wooden spoon, he made another attempt at conversation. He spoke slowly. It was no use. Mr. Smith cleared his throat. He gestured with his arm around the group of us. "We," he said slowly in Russian, "go to Lhasa."

The shepherd's eyes grew intelligent. "Lhasa, Lhasa," Smith repeated, and pointed south. From inside his jacket the old shepherd pulled out a prayer wheel that appeared as if it had been with him for many years. The religious signs were painted on parchment, the edges of which were worn with use. He pointed to the sun and made circles, many of them, with his outstretched arm.

"He is trying to tell us how many days it will take us to reach Lhasa," I said.

"His arm's going around like a windmill," observed Zaro. "It must be a hell of a long way from here."

We bowed our acknowledgment of the information. From out of his pocket he produced a bag of salt and invited us to look into the cauldron as he sprinkled some in. We crowded around and saw a bubbling, grayish, thick gruel. He stirred again, brought out a spoonful, blew on it, smacked his lips, tasted, and finally thrust out his tongue and ran it slowly around his lips.

He chuckled at us like a delighted schoolboy, and his good humor was so infectious that we found ourselves laughing aloud in real enjoyment for the first time in months.

The next move by the old man had almost a ritualistic air. From his shack he produced an object wrapped in a linen bag. He looked at us, eyes twinkling, and I could not help thinking of a conjuror building up suspense for the trick that was to astound his audience. I think we all looked suitably impressed as he opened the bag and reached into it. Into the sunlight emerged a wooden bowl about five inches in diameter and three inches deep, beautifully turned, shining with care and use, of a rich walnut brown color.

Into the bowl he ladled a quantity of gruel and laid it on the skin rug. He disappeared into the shack and came out holding an unglazed earthenware jar, dark brown and long necked. It held about a gallon of ewe's milk, a little of which he added to the gruel in the bowl. He handed the bowl and spoon to Zaro, who was seated nearest to him.

Zaro ate a spoonful, smacked his lips, and made to pass the bowl around, but the shepherd indicated he was to finish the portion.

Zaro made short but evidently highly enjoyable work of it. "By God, that tastes wonderful," he exclaimed.

IT WAS MY TURN NEXT. The main ingredient seemed to be barley, but some kind of fat had been added. The sweet, fresh milk had cooled the mixture a little, and I fairly wolfed it down. I belched loudly, smacked my lips, and handed back the bowl.

The shepherd saw to the needs of each of us in turn before he ate himself. To what was left in the cauldron he added several pints of milk and started stirring again, making enough extra to give us each another bowlful.

He took the cauldron off the fire to cool off, moving it with some difficulty because it had no handle, although I noticed there were the usual two holes in the rim. To our unspeakable joy he then produced tobacco from a skin pouch and handed us each enough for two or three cigarettes. Out came the pieces of hoarded newspaper. We lit up with glowing brands from the fire.

We were happy in that moment and brimming over with gratitude toward a supremely generous host. And he, bless him, sat there cross-legged and basked in our smiles.

Away he went after about half an hour, refusing offers of help, to wash the cauldron and the precious bowl at a nearby spring. He came back, stoked the fire, and made us tea, Tibetan style, and this time we even faintly approved the taste of the rancid butter floating in globules on the surface.

I felt I wanted to do something for the old man. I said to Kolemenos, "Let's make him a handle for his cauldron out of one of the spare wire loops." Everybody thought it an excellent idea. It took us only about 30 minutes to break off a suitable length, shape it, and fasten it. Our host was delighted.

We tried to think of some other service we could render. Someone suggested we forage for wood for the fire. We were away about an hour and came back with a pile of stuff, including a complete small tree which Kolemenos had hacked down with his ax.

The shepherd had been waiting for our return. As we came in, he was finishing sharpening his knife on a smooth piece of stone. He had his two dogs with him again. He made us sit down and, with his dogs at his heels, strode off.

He returned shortly, dragging by the wool between its horns a young ram, the dogs circling him in quiet excitement as he came. In something like five minutes the ram was dead, butchered with practiced skill. He wanted no help from us on this job. He skinned and gutted the carcass with a speed that made my own abilities in this direction seem clumsy. The carcass finally was quartered. Salt was rubbed in one fore and one hind quarter, which were hung inside the stone hut. He threw the head and some other oddments to the dogs.

Half the sheep was roasted on wooden spits over the blazing fire that night, and we ate again to repletion. We made signs that we would like to stay overnight, and he seemed altogether willing that we should. The six of us slept warm around the fire, while the shepherd lay the night inside his hut.

From somewhere he produced the next morning a batch of rough barley cakes—three each was our share. There was more tea and, to our astonishment, because we thought the limit of hospitality must already have been reached, the rest of the ram was roasted and portioned out, and a little more tobacco distributed.

We left him in the early afternoon, after restocking his fuel store. We did not know how to thank him for his inestimable kindness. Gently we patted his back and smiled at him. I think we managed to convey to him that he had made six most grateful friends.

At last we stood off a few feet from him and bowed low, keeping our eyes, according to custom, on his face. Gravely he returned the salute. We turned and walked away. When I looked back, he was sitting with his back to us, his dogs beside him.

I THINK IT PROBABLE that at the time we encountered the old man and his sheep we had not even entered Tibet but had come out from the desert into the highlands in the narrow neck of the Chinese province of Kansu lying along the northeastern border of Tibet. The time then was about the beginning of October 1941, and it was to take us over three months to cover about 1,500 miles of difficult country to the Himalayas. We tried always to do at least 20 miles a day. Often we did more. There were occasional days, too, when we did no traveling, glad of the rest and refreshment provided by friendly Tibetan villagers. The tradition of hospitality to travelers was an innate and wonderful part of the life of these people; their generosity was openhanded and without thought of reward. Without their help we could not have kept going.

We came across our first village some five days after leaving the shepherd. We had been on the move for about an hour after dawn when I saw, over to the left of our course and about 10 miles distant, a smear of smoke. We were hungry, stiff, and not very warm. We decided to investigate. We came down a hill that was scrub-covered on its upper reaches, giving way to grass of good sheep-grazing quality. As we got nearer, we saw the smoke came from several fires and knew we were approaching some kind of settlement, hidden from us by the rounded shoulder of the opposite hill.

It was well past noon when we reached the village. The hill threw out a green-clothed buttress like a long arm, and 10 boxlike houses nestled there like a child in the crook of its mother's arm. Each house was about 20 feet by 12 feet, flat-roofed with overlapping wide boards weighted down with stones. The roofs sloped slightly forward in the direction of the overlap. A few of the dwellings were backed by a fenced-in enclosure containing a small outhouse a couple of yards square. The slopes around were dotted with dozens of long-haired sheep. We came in slowly on an almost due west-east track, frequently pausing to look around so that the villagers would have ample warning of our visit. We did not know then what reception to expect.

A closer view of the village revealed the presence of a number of children, some chickens, goats, and the first yaks any of us had ever seen outside a zoo. At a leisurely shuffle, strung out in couples, we came near to the first house and stopped, interested in the novel spectacle of a man harnessing a yak to a high two-wheeled cart. He had seen us but had his hands too full with the task in hand to do anything about it. Half a dozen shy but frankly inquisitive children, the eldest about 10 years old, positioned themselves about the cart and eyed us. The yak, its long silken hair riffling in the breeze blowing through the valley, was being difficult and was doing its best not be attached to the cart. Possibly it had got wind of us and did not care for the evidence of its nose. (I couldn't have blamed it for any adverse opinion based on the smell of us!)

The villager decided suddenly to give up the struggle. He dropped the harness and let the beast go free. We stood our distance as he turned toward us. We bowed, our eyes on his young, flat, glistening face. Meticulously he returned the salutation. The children watched silently. Kolemenos and I stepped forward a few paces, smiling. The children broke out into a chatter at the impressive stature of Kolemenos, surprised by his long blond beard and hair. We stood in front of the man and bowed again. He talked, and I talked, but all the pair of us learned was that we could not understand each other. The small children grouped themselves behind the man and listened to the exchange. All the time they kept darting glances at the blond giant. The villager turned around and motioned us to follow. The children ran ahead through the village to spread the news of our coming.

At about the middle of the uneven row of buildings the guide stopped. This dwelling followed the same unassuming pattern as the others, but it was distinguished from them by being slightly larger and having a porch formed of two sturdy timbers at its door.

"This looks interesting," Mr. Smith whispered to me as the man disappeared through the door.

"I think he's gone inside to fetch the mayor," said Zaro.

There was not much time for further speculation for, almost as though he had been waiting behind the door, a new figure emerged through the porch. I judged him to be about 50; he wore the normal dress of the country topped with a loose sheepskin jacket. We exchanged the usual greetings before he spoke in the language of the country. I shook my head and replied in slow, precise Russian. His face lit up, and he beamed at me.

"Welcome," he said in Russian. "Now we shall be able to talk."

We were rather taken aback. He spoke Russian easily and without hesitation. I had to remind myself that there could be no danger in a chance encounter with a Russian so far south of the Soviet Union.

He waited a moment for me to reply, and when I did not, he went on eagerly, "I am a Circassian, and it is a long time since I met anyone who could speak Russian."

"A Circassian?" I repeated. "That is most interesting." I could not think of anything less banal to say. I knew little of the region in the Caucasus where he was from.

His questions tumbled over themselves. "Are you pilgrims?" he asked. "There are not many Russians who are Buddhists. You came through the Gobi on foot?"

"Yes, on foot."

"It must have been a terrible experience for you. Once I myself nearly died on that journey."

He was going to ask more questions but suddenly stopped, remembering his duty as a host. He apologized and invited us into his home. We trooped inside. A stone partition divided the one big room. I caught a glimpse of a woman I took to be his wife hustling three or four children out of the front half of the room, presumably to the kitchen at the rear.

Within half an hour of our arrival we were being regaled with tea and oaten cakes. Nobody spoke much until the food was gone. We were too busy filling our empty stomachs. Then our host produced a pipe and bowl of tobacco and handed the bowl around. Soon the place was a haze of blue smoke, which drifted out through the open door.

"So you are going to Lhasa," he said between puffs of his pipe. He said it politely, more as a conversational gambit. I do not think he necessarily believed it.

"Don't forget," he warned us, "that the nights are fiercely cold, especially on the heights. You must never be tempted to seek sleep without adequate shelter. You must never be too tired to build yourselves a fire. If you go to sleep unprotected on the mountains, you will be dead in the morning.

"You are going in the right direction for Lhasa. There is a track from here for the next stage of your journey that you will find easy to follow. Tonight you must all stay here, and in the morning I will show you how to go.

"If you come across any village toward nightfall, stay there until the morning. You will always have a roof over your heads and be given a meal. No one will ask you for payment."

"Our trouble," Mr. Smith broke in, "is that not one of us knows the language."

Our host smiled. "That is not such a handicap. If you bow to a

306

Tibetan and he bows back, no other introduction is needed. You are accepted as a friend."

In the early evening we were treated to a meal of roasted mutton, which one of the Circassian's elder sons had killed soon after our arrival. While we ate, the father cut off strips of meat for the younger children, and they ran out through the door with the meat in their hands. Salt was produced in a bowl to help our eating, and I fear I ate a lot more of it than a thoughtful guest should have. It was a delight to savor its sharp piquancy again.

After the evening meal half a dozen men neighbors joined our party. The hardworking Tibetan wife produced more tea. Each of the neighbors proudly produced a fine wooden bowl of the kind that the lone shepherd had shown us five days before. Here again it was quite evident that these were very precious possessions.

The men drank tea from their bowls, and when they had finished, the bowls were taken away and washed. Although they all looked alike to me, each man knew his own bowl, and they were affectionately stowed away in linen bags before the pipes were brought out and the tobacco handed around. Smoke was puffed out in great clouds. The Circassian was kept busy translating the busy talk between us and his neighbors. In this community he was obviously of great eminence, much respected for his gift of tongues and knowledge of matters of the big world outside the valley. He was human enough to enjoy his role, but he carried it off with dignity and modesty.

THE NEIGHBORS BADE US good night and went their way. They went like men who have had a rare and enjoyable evening. I could imagine that we had provided them with material for many a reminiscent talk to brighten their uneventful lives.

We slept in bunks—our first night under a roof since our escape. I felt able to relax. I had a glorious feeling of complete safety. I slept a deep, refreshing sleep and only half woke at the urging of the rising sun. They let us lie on until the day was a few hours old. The household had long been astir, and two of the younger children were peering in at us as we sat up in our beds. They ran out, and I heard them chattering to their father.

Our benefactor came in with some squares of thick homespun linen over his arm. "Perhaps you gentlemen would like to wash?" he inquired with a smile.

"This is real hotel service," Zaro joked. He bowed to the Circassian. "Just lead us to the bathroom."

The Circassian joined in the laugh. "It is at the end of the village—nice, clean, flowing water."

The six of us went down to the stream. The morning air was sharp, but we stripped to the waist, immersed our heads in the cold water, gasped, splashed, and rubbed vigorously. We were tempted to wash our jackets and fur vests but decided that we should have to wait too long for them to dry.

We were given more meat, more oaten cakes, more tea. Then it was time to go.

"When you come back this way," said the Circassian earnestly, "do not forget this house. It will always be a home to you."

The American answered, "Thank you. You have been very kind and generous to us."

I said, "Will you please thank your wife for all she has done for us. We are grateful."

He turned to me. "I won't do that." he said quietly. "She would not understand your thanks. But I will think of something to say to her that will please her."

He spoke to her, and her face broke into a great smile. She went away and returned with a wooden platter piled with flat oaten cakes, handed them to her husband, and said something to him.

"She wants you to take them with you," he told us. We portioned them out gratefully.

There was one other parting present—a fine fleece from the man, handed over with the wish that it might be used to make new footwear or repair our worn moccasins. We never did use it for that purpose, but later it made us half a dozen pairs of excellent mittens to shield our hands from the mountain cold.

He walked with us out of the village and pointed out our way. For the only time in our travels we received specific and detailed instructions of our route.

"Some of the tracks you will follow will not be easy to find," he warned. "Don't look for them at your feet; look ahead into the distance—they show up quite clearly then."

He described landmarks we were to seek. The first was to be a crown-shaped mountain about four days distant, and we were to take a path that would lead us over the saddle between the two north-facing points of the "crown." From the heights we were to set course for a peak shaped like a sugarloaf, which we would find to be deceptively far way. It might take us two weeks to reach it, he thought.

More than that he could not from here tell us accurately, but eventually we should reach a road that at some point forked east to the city of Lhasa and southwest to the villages of the Himalayan foothills. We left him there, a little knot of children at his heels. When we turned around, he made a most un-Mongolian gesture—he waved his arm in farewell to us.

Marchinkovas spoke for us all when he said, "These people make me feel very humble. They do a lot to wipe out bitter memories of other people who have lost their respect for humanity."

We disciplined ourselves not to touch our oatcakes until the third day—we had three each—and then we spread out the eating of them as an iron ration. Our track was clearly marked, and the way was not too hard. At the end of the fourth day we camped at the foot of the crown-shaped mountain our host had described and started our climb at first light the next day. The ascent was long but not difficult, and the crossing took us two days.

It had been fully a week since our last real meal when we came across a mixed herd of sheep and goats and found the two houses of the Tibetans who owned them. The day was warm and brightly sunny after the freezing temperatures of the heights. There were scattered bushes of a species of wild rose, attracting the eye with gay blooms of yellow and red and white.

The house into which we were taken by the Tibetan herdsman was in the same style as that of the Circassian but smaller and not so well equipped. But the courtesy and the hospitality were of the same impeccable standard. We were given milk to drink on arrival and later two massive meals of goat meat. By signs we were urged to spend the night and willingly accepted the offer. The whole family turned out to bow their farewells in the morning.

The explicit directions of the Circassian led us to the looming bulk of the sugarloaf mountain and over it. On the other side we found a stretch of country that presented comparatively easy traveling.

ON TO THE HIMALAYAS

THE WEEKS DRAGGED ON, October made way for November, the days were cool, and the nights were freezing. Over long stretches of country too barren to support even sheep and goats, we sometimes went for four and five days without food. There were bleak, mist-enveloped mornings when I felt leadenly dispirited, drained of energy, and reluctant to flog my weary body into movement. The meals we were so generously given from time to time in the villages we came to were massive, but we lacked fresh greenstuff. The result was that we continued to be ravaged by scurvy. But we counted ourselves fortunate that no member of the party suffered a major breakdown in health, and the march went on. We swam turbulent rivers when we had to. We negotiated formidable-looking peaks that turned out on closer acquaintance to offer surprisingly little difficulty; we struggled over innocent-looking hills that perversely offered precipitous resistance to our advance.

It was about this time that we discovered a use for the strong wire loops we had brought with us out of the desert. One day we found our way blocked where the track over a hill had been broken away by a fall of rock. To get around it we had to face the climber's hazard of an overhang surmounted by a sharp spur. We made a 10-foot length of plaited thongs, tied it firmly to Kolemenos' loop, and had him from his superior height try to lasso the tip of the rock spur. It took a dozen throws before the wire settled over. Then, gradually, Kolemenos put the strain of his still considerable weight on the rope. It held firm. Zaro, as one of the lighter members, volunteered to go up first. He climbed with great care, not trusting absolutely to the rope but making use of what slight handholds and footholds there were. With Zaro tending the anchored end, we all made it quite easily, Kolemenos climbing last.

There was a well-spaced-out succession of unremarkable villages and hamlets, alike in their simple architecture and in the full measure of hospitality they accorded us. They presented no feature by which I can remember them individually.

In the fullness of time we came to a fork in the rough trail that we confidently accepted as that mentioned to us by the Circassian—the eastward branch leading to Lhasa and the other southwest to India. A few hours later we saw far off in the distance a big caravan of possibly 50 men and animals creeping slowly away from us in the direction we imagined to be Lhasa. It was the only large traveling group we ever saw in the country.

We found this to be a country not only of rugged ranges but also of great lakes. Near the end of November our way led us to a vast sheet of water like an inland sea. We bathed in the fresh cold water and camped the night around a fire that did not throw out quite enough heat to keep out the damp night air from the lake.

Then followed a period of comparatively easy progress. The lakeshore was our guide for many miles. A couple of days later we were in broken country again. There was a cluster of a few houses where we stayed for only one meal, and upon our refusal to stay overnight, we were given food to carry with us. We were moving well and our morale was excellent.

Three or four days after leaving the great lake, we camped in a valley strewn with stark rocks. We settled down in a shallow cave to eat what still remained of our flat cakes made from coarse-milled flour. We sat together for warmth. There was nothing then to warn us that this was a setting for tragedy.

As ALWAYS WE SLEPT, with the exception of Kolemenos, fitfully. One and another would awake mumbling from half-remembered dreams to get up and tend the fire. It was Zaro who rose and went out as another day began palely to light the still desolation of the valley. I lay propped on one elbow as he came back.

"There's some mist about, and it's cold," he said to me, "Let's get moving." He stepped over the others, rousing them one by one. Paluchowicz lay next to me, and Marchinkovas was huddled between Smith and Kolemenos. I stood up and stretched, rubbed my stiff legs, flapped my arms about. There was a general stirring. Kolemenos pushed me with elephantine playfulness as I limbered up.

Zaro's voice cut in on us. "Come on, Zacharius. Get up!" He was bending over Marchinkovas, gently shaking his shoulder. I heard the note of panic as he shouted again, "Wake up, wake up!"

Zaro looked up at us, his face tight with alarm. "I think he must be ill. I can't wake him."

I dropped on my knees beside Marchinkovas. He lay in an attitude of complete relaxation, one arm thrown up above his head. I took the outstretched arm and shook it. He lay unmoving, eyes closed. I felt for the pulse, laid my ear to his chest, and lifted the eyelids. I went through all the tests again, fearful of believing their shocking message. The body was still warm.

I straightened up. I was surprised at how small and calm my voice was. "Marchinkovas is dead," I said. The statement sounded odd and flat to me, so I said it again. "Marchinkovas is dead."

Somebody burst out, "But he can't be. There was nothing wrong with him. Nothing! I talked to him only a few hours ago. He was well. He had no complaint. . . ."

"He is dead," I said.

Mr. Smith got down beside the body. He was there only a minute

311

or two. Then he crossed the hands of Marchinkovas on his chest, stood up, and said, "Yes, gentlemen, Slav is right."

Paluchowicz took off his old fur cap and crossed himself.

Zacharius Marchinkovas, aged 28 or 29, who might have been a successful architect in his native Lithuania if the Russians had not come and taken him away, had given up the stuggle. We were all stunned; we could not understand it, and we did not know how death had come to him. Perhaps he was more exhausted than we knew and his willing heart could take the strain no more. I don't know. None of us knew. Marchinkovas, the silent one with the occasional shaft of cynical wit, Marchinkovas, who lived much with his own thoughts, the man with a load of bitterness whom Kristina had befriended and made to laugh—Marchinkovas was gone.

In the rocky ground we could find no place to dig a grave for him. His resting place was a deep cleft between rocks, and we filled up the space above him with pebbles and small stones. Kolemenos carried out his duty of making a small cross, which he wedged into the rubble. We said our farewells, each in his own fashion. Silently, I commended his soul to God. The five of us went heavy-footed on our way.

The country changed again, challenging our spirit and endurance with the uncompromising steepness of craggy hills. We learned to use our wire loops as climbing aids on difficult patches. We tried always to find a village to spend the night under cover, but all too often the end of the day overtook us with no human settlement in sight.

Once from the heights we saw, many miles off, the flashing reflection of the sun from the shining roofs of a distant, high-sited city, and it pleased us to believe that at least we had seen the holy city of Lhasa.

The days were cold now, the nights colder. Snow-charged clouds hung menacingly over the distant, gaunt foothills of the Himalayas. We stayed one night in a poor hamlet of four stone-built shacks and the next morning spent several hours making warm mittens from the Circassian's gift fleece.

There came one clear day when we saw the snowcapped, cloud-topped soaring hump of the Himalayas, deceptively near. We were, in fact, a long way off and were to find the intervening distance fraught with trial and hazard.

Winter had overtaken us, and the night temperatures fell well below zero. There were occasional heavy snowfalls, sleety rain, winds that whipped down off the hilltops with the chill of the heights in them. Bitter though the conditions were, they had not the severity of the Siberian winter. But they were grim enough for us, underfed and weakened as we were by nine long months of continuous foot travel.

In February we encountered our last village, just eight or nine houses snuggled in a hollow a couple of hundred feet above a narrow valley. Behind the village reared the forbidding rampart of tall hills over which we had struggled for two days. Across the valley, hazy in the light of a wintry afternoon sun, another range heaved itself up toward the clouds. The houses had, for Tibet, a rare distinction. They were the only two-story buildings we had seen in the whole country, or, indeed, since we had left Siberia. We had descended to a point west of and below the little settlement and had to climb up to it along a rough track. We were profoundly tired, miserable, and very hungry. Paluchowicz was limping on his right foot, the arch of which had been bruised when he had stepped on a sharp stone.

The Tibetans, when they understood by our signs whence we had come and where we intended to go, showed amazement at our hardihood, or our foolhardiness. We were gently ushered into one of the houses, made to sit down on low benches polished with years of use, fussed over, given steaming hot tea, and fed with mutton and the usual filling oaten cakes..Paluchowicz was given some grease to rub into his sore foot. From all the houses men and children came to look at us. There was much smiling and bowing and slow nodding of heads. Undoubtedly, our arrival was an extraordinary event and it would long be a topic for wondering talk.

When we left the little mountain hamlet, we were loaded down with food, which included a complete side of a roasted sheep. Up to now we had kept whatever food we had been given in one sack, which was carried in turns. We decided at this stage to share the meat and flat cakes equally among us because of the danger of losing the lot if the precious single sack disappeared with its owner on one of the increasingly difficult climbs we were now encountering.

That night, around a small fire, we sat talking for hours trying to assess our position and how much farther we had to go. When the conversation flagged, the extraordinary stillness and silence of the brooding mountains engulfed us. I had a feeling of great pity for myself and for us all. I wrestled with a desperate fear that now, with thousands of heartbreaking miles behind us, the odds might be too much for us. Often at night I had these bouts of despair and doubt. The others, too, I am sure, fought the same battles, but we never voiced our waverings. With the coming of morning the outlook was always more hopeful. Fear remained, a lurking thing, but movement and action and the exercise of the mind on the daily problems of existence pushed it into the background. We were now, more strongly than ever, in the grip of the compulsive urge to keep moving. It had become an obsession, a form of mania. Like automatons we set out each morning, triggered off by a quiet "Let's go" from one or another of us. No one ever pleaded for half an hour's respite. We just went, walking the stiffness out of our joints and the chill of the dark hours from our bodies.

We rationed the food out thinly, and it lasted, one meal a day, for over two weeks. It was insufficient for the heavy climbing and the perilous descents in which we were now involved, but at least we had the comfort of knowing we could not starve while it lasted. Several times we were caught out on the heights and had to resort to the lessons of our Siberian experience in making a snow dugout and holing up sleepless until the dawn of another day.

Of the art of mountaineering we learned much as the weeks crept by. I had done some climbing in Poland before the war, but it bore little resemblance to this grim Himalayan business. Then I had stout spiked boots and all the civilized paraphernalia, plus the services of an expert guide. And we had climbed in summer, for sport.

Here we would claw our way upward for hours, sacks lashed on our backs, only to find our way blocked by a sheer, smooth, outward-thrusting rock face. We would cling to our holds and rest our toes, cramped and sore with their prehensile curling inside the soft moccasins for footholds. Then we would turn about and go down and down until we found a place from which to attempt a different approach to the summit.

Under these circumstances the going was very slow. Our total mountaineering equipment consisted of one strong rawhide rope limited in use by its short length, the ax—by far the greatest single asset—the broad-bladed knife, and the loops and spikes we had made back in the heat of the Gobi.

We climbed as individuals, but in set order. Zaro, the lightest man, led the way upward, testing the holds with the ax, breaking through the ice crust on the snow, blazing a trail for the rest of us. I came next, sometimes changing over leadership with Zaro to give him a rest, then Kolemenos, Mr. Smith, and Paluchowicz. We tried to make things as easy as possible for the two older men, but they always insisted on taking the lead on the descents.

We still carried our trusty sticks, and on gentler slopes we used them for probing through the snow to detect hidden crevices. At other times we carried them stuck through our belts at our backs.

Zaro would have made a skilled and intrepid climber in any company. A clumsy device we thought up and made for getting us past bulging overhangs of rock was a weighty piece of smooth, hard, black stone, waisted in the middle like a figure 8, to which we tied our rope. This we would throw up and over, again and again and again, until eventually, unseen somewhere above, it would jam itself and take hold. Kolemenos would haul gently at first at the rope until it took his full weight. Then Zaro heroically would start to climb while we watched from below with our hearts in our throats, knowing that the penalty for a slip was death. When on a few occasions I saw by what flimsy chance the stone had taken hold on the original throw, my stomach turned over.

Occasional bright days brought the additional trial of sun glare off the white snow. We were distressed, too, by a new experience of intense physical discomfort: The cold struck at our foreheads until they seemed to be held in frigid bands of ice. This trouble we overcame by making sheepskin masks with slits for the eyes, the upper parts held under the rims of our caps and the lower parts hanging loosely at nose level.

The masks were effective for the purpose for which they were designed. They also seemed to help with the trouble of snow glare, but we found that moisture gathered beneath them, trickled, and froze around the nose and mouth. There were times when I had to stop and thaw out the gathering ice by holding the lower part of my face in my mittened hands. We kept our hands covered as much as possible, but when climbing demanded the use of the fingers, our mittens hung from our wrists by thongs.

With the masks around our heads and tied at the back of the head, and the earflaps of our Russian-style caps in position, we found it difficult to hear one another. Irritation piled on irritation. We were deadly tired, morose, always hungry. My nerves were strung as tight as piano wires.

THE ABOMINABLE SNOWMEN

TOWARD THE END OF MARCH 1942 we were convinced that at last we were very near the sanctuary of India. Barring our way ahead reared the tallest and most forbidding peaks we had yet seen. We told one another that one final effort must bring us to the country where we were sure ultimate freedom, civilization, rest, and ease of mind awaited us. Individually we needed all the assurances and encouragement we could get. I was tortured with the fear that the exertion of one more great climb would finish me. I feared the onset of the insidious sleep on the heights from which there was no awakening. All my fears were sharpened by that shared conviction that after 4,000 miles we were near success. I could not now banish the specter of bitter failure.

We sat around a fire made from the last of our hoarded scraps of fuel and ate the last crumbs of our rations. We got out the rawhide rope, the ax, the knife, the wire loops, the slim spikes, and examined them and tested them. We gave ourselves a couple of hours before dark for repairing footwear. When we had finished, we were as well prepared for the last assault as we could be. The fire burned down and became ashes before midnight, and we spent a restless night until the first glimmer of dawn. Zaro wound the rope about him, took the ax from Kolemenos, and started off. I was relieved to be on the move.

We were blessed with fair weather. The wind was cold, but the sun shone strongly enough to attack the top layer of snow so that it melted sufficiently to re-form in the freezing night temperatures into a skin of crisp, treacherous ice. We climbed more surely, more cautiously, than ever before. Zaro double tested every foothold and each handhold as he led the way upward, chipping away with the ax, steam issuing in little clouds from his nose and mouth beneath the mask.

At the beginning of the third day we were over the top, only to find ourselves confronted with another peak. It was the stuff of which nightmares are made. Always it seemed there was another mountain to block our way. Two days were spent scrambling down the south face from our exposed high perch, and I found it more wearing on the nerves than the ascent. Down in the valley we made ourselves a snow shelter out of the whip of the wind and managed to get ourselves an uncomfortable few hours sleep in preparation for the next ordeal.

This next mountain was the worst in all our experience. From valley to valley its crossing took us six days and taxed our endurance to such a degree that for the first time we talked openly of the prospect that we might all perish. I am certain that one blizzard of a few hours duration would have wiped us out.

Two days up, the top still hidden by swirling white clouds, I dug my knife into a crevice to give myself extra purchase in hauling myself up from a narrow ledge. With my body pressed close against the rock, I loosened each hand and foot in turn so that I could flex my cramped fingers and wriggle my stiff toes. Then I reached for the knife handle above me and began to haul on it with my right arm. Suddenly the knife sprang like a live thing, leaped from my hand, and flew over my head with the steel singing. I took fresh hold and, digging in with fingers and toes, dragged myself to safety. The knife was gone. There was no sign of it. I felt as though I had lost a personal friend.

Near the summit on the third day the climbing became easier, but we began to doubt seriously whether we could make it. The cold was terrible, eddying mist dropped down about us and lifted, dropped and lifted again. The effects of high altitude were draining from us what slight reserves of stamina we still had. Every step was a fight against torturing lassitude, making one want to sit down and cry with weakness and frustration. I could not get enough air into my bursting lungs, and my heart thumped audibly, hammering against my chest. Willpower became a flaccid thing. Any one of us, alone, could have given up thankfully, lay down happily, closed his eyes, and drifted into death. But somebody was always crawling on, so we all kept moving. A final refinement of misery was nosebleed. I tried to stop mine by plugging the nostrils with bits of sacking, but the discomfort of breathing only through the mouth was too much and I removed the plug. The blood poured down into my beard, freezing and congealing there.

We knew we would have to spend the night in this rarefied atmosphere, and the knowledge did our spirits no good.

"We must keep going while there's light," Zaro said. "We must try to get over the top before dark."

So we went on and on, painfully. We made long traverses to right and left to avoid the impossible extra exertion of a frontal assault. I do not remember going over the summit. I remember only the point at which I noticed with vague surprise that Zaro, leading, was slightly below me. We climbed again a little, and then we knew with certainty that the descent had begun.

That night was the crisis of the whole enterprise. On a broad, flat ledge where the snow had drifted and piled, we axed through the hard crust of the surface and dug laboriously through a few feet of snow to make ourselves a barely adequate refuge against the rigors of the night. We had no fire. We were all so bone-weary we literally could have slept standing up, but we knew it would be courting death even to attempt to doze.

It was the longest night of my life. We huddled there standing, with our arms about one another. Sleep lay on our lids like a solid weight, and I found myself holding my eyes open with fingertips pressed against the eyeballs under my mask. Three times Kolemenos, the arch-sleeper, let his chin sag on his chest and began to snore, and each time we punched and shook him back to consciousness. Each man was his brother's keeper, watching for drooping eyelids and the nodding head. At intervals we would stamp slowly around in a close ring. Even during this grotesque dance I began to swim down into beautiful, velvet sleep, but the American dragged me back by gently cuffing me, pulling my beard, and shaking me hard. There came that awful predawn period when fatigue and cold together combined to set me shivering in an uncontrollable ague from head to foot.

"Let's get going," said someone. "Let's get down to someplace where we can breath again."

Paluchowicz spoke: "I could not last another night like that."

It was barely daylight, but we broke out and started on our way, Paluchowicz leading and Zaro and I in the rear. Even now I could not convince myself we would make it. Once, around noon, we were marooned for fully an hour when the track of our descent ended abruptly on a foot-wide shelf over a terrible drop. We inched our way back, climbed upward in our old tracks, and tried again in another direction. This time we succeeded, but not without great danger and frequent use of the rope and ax.

In about 10 hours of grueling toil we must have come down about 5,000 feet before nightfall. Breathing became easier, morale improved, hopes rose a little again. We dragged on through another depressing, wakeful night and continued the descent the next day until we were able to see the valley below quite clearly.

IN THE AFTERNOON we found a cave. It was untenanted, but there was a stack of brushwood near the entrance. If we had needed a sign that Providence was still on our side, this was it.

Hanging from a peg in the roof was something wrapped in soft lambskin. Someone lifted it down and unwrapped it. Inside was a leg of goat meat, partly smoked and nearly black. We were too hungry to be fastidious. We decided to get the fire going and cook it.

What a fire that was. We stoked it until the dancing flames lit up the far corners of the cave. Watching the meat cooking, we thawed out for the first time in weeks. Without the knife we had to do some crude carving with the ax, leaving half the joint to be eaten in the morning and tearing up the rest in strips. Toothless Paluchowicz took longer than the rest of us to eat his portion, but we all managed to take the edge off our hunger.

We slept the night through. When we awoke, the day was already a couple of hours old, and the fire had long since died out. Hurriedly we ate the rest of the goat meat cold and left.

It was profitless to speculate any further on how near we might be to our journey's end. Not even now were we out of the mountains. The lesser peak we set ourselves to surmount two days after the cave episode was, had we known it, the last outpost of the Himalayas, beyond which the foothills led down into northern India. I do not remember any of the details of this last climb, but I know we pulled ourselves up the northern face for two days without attaining the height that brought on altitude sickness. When we started down the other side, the sun was shining brightly and the air was startlingly clear. Southward the country fell away dramatically. I knew I was looking, at last, at India.

In all our wanderings through the Himalayan region we had encountered no other creatures than men, dogs, sheep, goats, and yaks. It was with quickening interest, therefore, that in the early stages of our descent of this last mountain Kolemenos drew our attention to two moving black specks against the snow about a quarter of a mile below us. We thought of animals and immediately of food, but as we set off down to investigate, we had no great hopes that they would await our arrival. The contours of the mountain temporarily hid them from view as we approached nearer, but when we halted on the edge of a bluff, we found they were still there, 12 feet or so below us and about 100 yards away.

Two points struck me immediately. They were enormous, and they walked on their hind legs. The picture is clear in my mind, fixed there indelibly by a solid two hours of observation. We just could not believe what we saw at first, so we stayed to watch. Somebody talked about dropping down to their level to get a close-up view.

Zaro said, "They look strong enough to eat us." We stayed where we were. We weren't too sure of unknown creatures that refused to run away at the approach of men.

I set myself to estimating their height on the basis of my military training for artillery observation. They could not have been much less than eight feet tall. One was a few inches taller than the other, in the relation of the average man to the average woman. They were shuffling quietly around on a flattish shelf that formed part of the obvious route for us to continue our descent. We thought that if we waited long enough, they would go away and leave the way clear for us. It was obvious they had seen us, and it was equally apparent that they had no fear of us.

The American said that eventually he was sure we would see them drop on all fours like bears. But they never did.

Their faces I could not see in detail, but the heads were squarish, and the ears must have lain close to the skull because there were no projections from the silhouettes against the snow. Their shoulders sloped sharply down to powerful chests. The arms were long, and the wrists reached the level of the knees. Seen in profile, the back of the head was a straight line from the crown into the shoulders—"like a damned Prussian," as Paluchowicz put it.

We decided unanimously that we were examining a type of creature of which we had no previous experience in the wild, in zoos, or in literature. It would have been easy, had we merely seen them waddle off at a distance, to dismiss them as either bears or big apes of the orangutan species. From close range they defied facile description. There was something of both the bear and the ape about their general shape, but they could not be mistaken for either. The color was a rusty kind of brown. They appeared to be covered by two distinct kinds of hair—the reddish hair that gave them their characteristic color forming a tight, close fur against the body. This mingled with long, loose, straight hairs, hanging downward, which had a slight grayish tinge as the light caught them.

Dangling our feet over the edge of the rock, we kept them closely under observation for about an hour. They were doing nothing but moving around slowly together, occasionally stopping to look around them like people admiring a view. Their heads turned toward us now and again, but their interest in us seemed to be of the slightest.

Then Zaro stood up. "We can't wait all day for them to make up their minds to move. I am going to shift them."

He went off into a pantomime of arm waving, Indian war dancing, bawling, and shrieking. The things did not even turn. Zaro scratched around and came up with half a dozen pieces of ice about a quarter-inch thick. One after another he pitched them down toward the pair, but they skimmed erratically and lost direction. One missile kicked up a little powder of snow about 20 yards from them, but if they saw it, they gave no sign. Zaro sat down again, panting.

We gave them another hour, but they seemed content to stay where they were. I got the uncomfortable feeling that they were challenging us to continue our descent across their ground.

"I think they are laughing at us," said Zaro.

Mr. Smith stood up. "It occurs to me they might take it into their heads to come up and investigate *us*. It is obvious they are not afraid of us. I think we had better go while we are safe."

We pushed off around the rock and directly away from them. I looked back and the pair were standing still, arms swinging slightly, as though listening intently. What were they? For years they remained a mystery to me, but since then I have read of scientific expeditions to discover the Abominable Snowman of the Himalayas and have studied descriptions of the creature given by native hillmen. I believe that the five of us that day may have met two of the animals. If so, I think recent estimates of their height as about five feet are wrong. The creatures we saw must have been at least seven feet.

I think that, in causing a deviation of route, they brought our final disaster upon us.

It was about midday when we set off to continue our descent. Everything went well, and we made good time. Our spirits were up in spite of our empty bellies. We found an almost ideal cavity among the rocks to spend the night and were greeted by another clear, fine April morning breaking through a thin, quickly dissipated mist.

Two hours later it happened. Zaro and I had the rope's end belayed around our two stout sticks at the crest of a slope. I was laughing at something Zaro had said about the two strange creatures of the day before. The slope was short and hardly steep enough to warrant the use of the rope, which lay loosely thrown out as a safety line in case Paluchowicz, crawling down backward on all fours, should slip into an unseen crevice. Behind him were Smith and Kolemenos, well spaced out. All three were astride the limp rope without holding it.

I saw Paluchowicz reach the end of the slope. I turned to Zaro and in that instant saw the rope jerk about the sticks and become slack again. Simultaneously there was a brief, sharp cry, such as a man will make when he is suddenly surprised. Zaro and I swung together. It was a second or two before the awful truth struck me. Smith was there. Kolemenos was there. But Paluchowicz had vanished.

Like fools, the two of us stood there calling out his name. No one answered. The other two, with their backs to Paluchowicz, did not know what had happened. They had stopped at our first shout and were looking up at us.

"Come back!" I called out to them. "Come back! Something has happened to Anton."

They clambered back. I hauled in the rope and tied the loose end

about my waist. "I am going down to see if I can find him," I said.

I reached the point where, from above, the slope appeared to fall gently away. Zaro took in the slack of the rope and I turned around as I had seen Paluchowicz do. The sight made me catch my breath. The mountain yawned open as though it had been split clean apart with a giant ax blow. I was looking across a 20-yard gap, the narrowest part of the chasm that dropped sickeningly below me. I could not see the bottom. I felt the cold sweat beading out on my forehead. Futilely I yelled, "Anton, Anton!"

I turned and went back to join the others, so shaken that I held tightly to the rope all the way.

They all talked at once. Had I seen him? Why was I shouting? Where was he?

I told them what it was like down there, that there was no sign of Paluchowicz.

"We will have to find him," said Kolemenos.

"We will never find him," I told them. "He is gone."

Nobody wanted to believe it. I did not want to believe it myself. With difficulty we broke a way to a new point from which we could look down into the abyss. Then they understood. We heaved a stone down and listened for it to strike. We heard nothing. We tried a bigger stone and dropped that down. We listened, straining our ears, but there was still no echo of the strike.

We hung around there a long time, not knowing what to do. The disaster was so sudden, so complete. One minute Paluchowicz was with us, then he was gone, plucked away from us. I never thought he would have to die. He seemed indestructible. Tough, toothless, devout old Sergeant Paluchowicz.

"All this way," said the American. "All this way, to die so stupidly at the last." I think he felt it more than any of us. As the two older men, they had been close together.

Kolemenos took his sack from his back and very deliberately tore it down the seams. We all stood silent. He put a stone in the corner and threw it out into space. The stone fell out and the sack floated away, a symbolic shroud for Paluchowicz. He took his stick and with the blunted ax chopped an end off and made a cross and stuck it there, on the edge of the abyss.

We climbed on down, trying to keep in sight the spot from which Paluchowicz had disappeared, vaguely hoping we might discover his body. But we never found the bottom of the great cleft, and we never found Paluchowicz.

There were some quite warm days after this. We could look back and see the majesty of the mountains we had crossed. We were in terrible need of food, and now that the supreme effort was over, we could barely keep ourselves moving. One day we saw a couple of long-haired wild goats, which bounded off like the wind. They need not have been afraid. We hardly had the strength to kill anything bigger than a beetle. The country was still hilly, but there were rivers and streams and birds in trees.

We had been about eight days without food when we saw far off to the east on a sunny morning a flock of sheep with men and dogs in charge. They were too far off to be of any help to us and were moving away from us, but our hopes rose at the sight of them. Soon we must certainly be picked up.

Exhausted walking skeletons of men that we were, we knew now for the first time peace of mind. It was now that we lost, at last, the fear of recapture.

They came from the west, a little knot of marching men, and as they came closer, I saw there were six native soldiers with an NCO in charge. I wanted to wave my hands and shout, but I just stood there with the other three watching them come. They were very smart, very clean, very fit, very military. My eyes began to fill, and the tears brimmed over.

Smith stepped forward and stuck out his hand.

"We are very glad to see you," he said.

INDIA

IT WAS HARD TO COMPREHEND that this was the end of it all. I leaned my weight on my stick and tried to blink my eyes clear. I felt weak and lightheaded like a man in a fever. My knees trembled with weakness, and it required real effort to prevent myself from slumping down to the ground. Zaro, too, was hunched over his stick, and one of Kolemenos' great arms was drooped lightly about his shoulders. The rough, scrubby country danced in the haze of a warm noon sun. The soldiers, halted but five yards from us, were a compact knot of men in tropical shorts and shirts swimming in and out of my vision.

I dropped my head forward on my chest and heard the voice of Mr. Smith. He talked in English, which I did not understand, but there was no mistaking the urgency in the tone. His speech went on for several minutes. I had to flex my knees to stop their trembling.

The American came over to us, his face smiling. "Gentlemen, we are safe." And because we remained unmoving and silent, he said again in Russian, very slowly, "Gentlemen, we are safe."

Zaro shouted, and the sound startled me. He threw down his stick and yelled, his arms above his head and the fingers of his hands extended. He threw his arms about the American, and Smith had to hold him tight to prevent his running over to the patrol and kissing each man individually.

"Come away, Eugene," he shouted. "Come away from them. I have told them we are filthy with lice."

Zaro started to laugh and jig inside the restraining arms. Then he had the American going around with him in a crazy, hopping polka, and they were both laughing and crying at the same time. I do not remember starting to dance; but there we were, the four of us, stamping, kicking up the dust, hugging one another, laughing hysterically, until all of us collapsed one by one on the ground.

Kolemenos lay sprawled out repeating softly to himself the American's words: "We are safe . . . we are safe. . . ."

The American said, "We shall be able to live again."

I thought a little about that. It sounded a wonderful thing to say. All that misery, all that sorrow, the hardship of a whole year afoot, so that we might live again.

We learned from Mr. Smith that this was a British patrol on exercise. They would take us, if we were not too weak to march, a few miles to the nearest rough road where they had a rendezvous with a military truck from their main unit. He had told them that we had come so far a few more miles would not kill us. With the main unit there would be real food.

The patrol produced groundsheets from their packs and rigged up a shelter to protect us from the sun. We lay beneath it resting for about an hour. My head throbbed, and I felt a little sick. We were handed a packet of cigarettes and some matches. Even more than food just then I wanted to smoke. To handle so ordinary a civilized commodity as a box of matches gave me a warm thrill. The smoke itself was bliss. From somewhere came a big can of peaches, ready opened, and we dug our fingers in, stuffed the peaches in our mouths, and crushed the exquisite juice and pulp from them. We drank water from army water bottles and were ready to go.

It seemed to me that none of us could have recalled details of that cross-country trek. The patrol adjusted its pace to our weary shamble, and it must have taken about five hours to cover 10 miles. Zaro marched with me, and we buoyed ourselves up with the pretense that we were getting along at a swinging military pace.

"The heroes' return," Zaro said with a grin. "All we need now is a band to lead us."

The altogether delightful quality of everything that happened to us at the end of the march was that it required no resolution or decision from us. There was a bumping ride by truck at that breakneck speed that is the hallmark of army driving anywhere in the world. We were as thrilled as schoolboys with the trip. We were in the process of being gathered up, looked after, told what to do, tended, and later even pampered. The British took over completely.

I never found out exactly where we were. At that time I did not care. Any guess I might make from perusal of maps could be hundreds of miles off. Smith must have found out, but if he ever told me, the information did not register. I hugged to myself only the great revelation that this was India.

The young British lieutenant who watched us ease ourselves down over the truck tailgate was amazingly clean, spruce, and well shaven. I observed him as the American told him our story. His expression as he stood listening in the shade of the trees at the small roadside encampment was incredulous. His eyes kept wandering from Smith to us. He was trying to understand. He asked several questions, nodding his head slowly at each answer. I thought how young he looked. Yet he was about my own age.

The American told us, "He believes me now. He says he will make arrangements for us to be deloused and cleaned up here because he can't take us back to their base in this condition. He says he will have to isolate us from his troops until this is done but that we will be well fed and cared for. He says we need not worry."

That night we were given a hot meal that ended with stewed fruit and steamed pudding. I had my first experience of hot, very strong canned-milk army tea, lavishly sweetened. We were given cigarettes and first-aid treatment for our torn and bruised feet. And that night we slept secure, wrapped in army blankets, in a tent.

The novelty, the bustle, and the excitement of it all kept me going. There was no time for me to stand still and discover how near to collapse I was. Breakfast the next day absorbed my attention—more tea, corned beef, Australian cheese, butter from cans, and, unbelievably, white bread, canned bacon rashers, and marmalade.

The delousing was a very thorough affair. We stripped off all our clothes—the sheepskin surcoats, fufaikas, fur vests, caps, masks, padded trousers, sacks, and skin gaiters—and piled them in the open. The blankets we had slept in were thrown on top of the heap. Head and body hair was shorn off, bundled, and thrust among the clothes. Over the lot they poured gasoline, and suddenly it erupted into a roaring bonfire, billowing black smoke into the sunny, clear air. Everything went, consumed in flame.

Kolemenos said, "I hope those bloody lice die hard. They have had a good time at my expense."

I turned to him and he to me. Then we were all exchanging looks, and the laughter was bubbling out of us. We had realized we were seeing one another for the first time—really seeing for the very first time the lines, the set of the mouth, the angle of the chin, and the character of the faces of men who for 12 months and 4,000 miles had shared the wretched struggle for survival.

It seemed the most comical thing that had ever happened to us. I had never thought of what might lie beneath the matted hair, and neither, I suppose, had they. It was like the midnight revelation from some fantastically prolonged masked ball.

"Why, Zaro," I said, "you are a good-looking man."

"You look all right yourself," Zaro answered.

And Mr. Smith was not as old as I had thought him to be, now that he was shorn of his graying hair. And Kolemenos, in spite of the ravages that marked us all, was as handsome as a big, fine-bodied man could be. The four of us sat there laughing and joking in our nakedness while the fire roared.

Scrubbed clean, our cuts, sores, and scratchings anointed, we were made ready for our reentry into a civilized community. We received white, crisp new underwear, bush shirts, stockings, canvas shoes, and, to top the lot, dashing Australian-type light felt hats. Smith dressed in a leisurely, careful way, but the other three of us hurried through the operation in an enthusiastic race to be ready first. We looked one another over and liked what we saw. We joked about the stark whiteness of our knees.

They drove us away westward. I had a curiously detached feeling about it, like an exhausted swimmer allowing himself to be carried along in a tide race. We came to a military garrison, but I had no chance to look at it. We were immediately lodged in sick quarters.

The army doctor had been waiting for us. He examined us gravely, eyes narrowed behind thin tortoiseshell spectacles. He nodded his head, thinning on top, in acknowledgment of Smith's answers to terse questions. He was aged about 40, quick-moving, sympathetic behind his professional facade of impersonal efficiency. We needed a lot of care, he told Smith. We needed to take things easy. Recovery might take quite a long time.

For a few days they kept us there. The doctor dosed us with medicines and pills. We lounged and lay about, chatting and dozing. We ate most magnificently and were plied with fresh fruit. Kolemenos amused the small staff with his huge appetite. We were allowed to smoke as often as we pleased.

Here it was that we temporarily parted from Smith. He said he was being taken away to see the American authorities. "You three will be taken to Calcutta. Whatever happens I shall see you there."

We shook him by the hand. There didn't seem to be anything any of us could say.

"Just keep your spirits up," Mr. Smith said. "The doctor tells me that we are all going to be very sick before we recover from our trip. But he says that with the proper attention we shall get in a big hospital, we should pull through all right."

I thought we were not as ill as that and said so. I did not appreciate then that I was feeling a quite spurious sense of well-being, that I was a little drunk with the excitement of these wonderful last few days, that the reckoning was yet to come.

He went away from us like a figure slipping out of a dream. Zaro said, "We shall be seeing him in Calcutta," as though India were a small place and Calcutta were just around the corner. It was the way we felt. Everything was taken care of. We were spent forces, content to be carried along. All the hammering urgency and the iron-hard resolution of the last bitter year had drained from us. We were more sick than we knew.

I HAVE SMALL RECOLLECTION of the journey to Calcutta, except that it was long and tiresome and I was shrouded in black depression. We smoked incessantly.

It was a symptom of our condition, I suppose, that when we were driven in a bus through the teeming Calcutta streets, we were all bright as crickets, pointing out the sights one to the other, almost hysterically good-humored. I could have persuaded myself then that recovery had already begun. I was being fooled again by the fever of a new excitement.

The bus drove between the tall main gates of a hospital, and an orderly took Zaro, Kolemenos, and me away for a preliminary medical examination. At first we were bogged down in language difficulties. After some time it was understood that between us we spoke Russian, Polish, French, and German—but no English. Eventually we were interviewed by an orderly who spoke French. They wanted medical histories from childhood, so Zaro told the orderly about our measles and our whooping cough and our operations. It all went down on a set of stiff cards. We were examined by doctors, weighed, measured, given a bath, decked out in pajamas, and tucked in bed in a long ward, Zaro and Kolemenos in adjoining positions on one side with me directly opposite.

I remember my awakening the next morning quite clearly, a spotless vision of a nursing sister standing beside my bed laying her strong brown arm against my white one and joking with me until I smiled up at her. Then came the breakfast of fresh eggs with wafer-thin white bread and butter.

I went back to sleep that morning and dropped into a bottomless pit that stole all mind and recollection from me for nearly a month. I learned all about it later, and it was Mr. Smith who gathered the story and told it to me.

They gave me sedatives and kept a day and night watch over me. Meanwhile, Zaro and then Kolemenos went under. At night I screamed and raved in madness. I ran from the Russians all over again; I crossed my deserts and my mountains. And each day I ate half my bread and slyly tucked the remainder under the mattress or in the pillowcase. Each day they gently took away my precious little hoard. They talked to me and brought in great white loaves from the kitchens and told me that I would never have to worry again. There would always be bread. The assurances meant nothing. I kept collecting bread for the next stage of my escape.

The climax came after about 10 days, I was told. After that I was quieter, very weak, exhausted, and on the danger list. Kolemenos and Zaro, too, were in a bad way.

But, said the hospital staff, neither of the others matched the performance I put on during the second night of my stay in the ward. I got out my saved-up bread from where I'd hidden it; rolled up my mattress, bedclothes, and pillows; and, to their astonishment because they had not believed I had that much strength left, set off staggering under the load for the door. By the time I had rolled up my bedding, the night sister had the doctor there.

He had said, "Leave him; let us see what he does."

At the door the doctor, the sister, and two male orderlies blocked my way. The doctor talked quietly as he would have done to a sleep-walker. I went on. The orderlies held me, and I dropped my burden and fought with savage fury. It took all four of them to get me back to bed. I have no memory of the incident.

Four weeks after my admission to the hospital, I awoke one morning feeling refreshed, as though I had slept the night through dreamlessly and restfully. I could not believe it when I was told that my night had been a month long.

Mr. Smith came to see us. He looked lean and spruce in a light-weight civilian suit. For a week, he said, he had been close to death. He had been to see me a couple of days earlier, but I had shown no signs of recognizing him. He had talked to the doctors about us, told them in detail what we had been through.

"You are going to be all right now, Slav," he said. He gestured over to where Zaro and Kolemenos were sitting up in bed and beaming across at us. "And so are they."

One of the soldier patients in the ward wanted to know our names. The American told him, but the soldier had difficulty in getting his tongue around the unfamiliar syllables. A compromise was reached. We became Zaro, Slav, and "Big Boy."

Our story got around. From other parts of the hospital, staff members came along to take a peep at us. The British soldiers in our ward showered us with kindnesses. One of them went around with his hat collecting cigarettes, money, chocolate, and little personal gifts and shared the offerings among us.

The American came to see us again later. He gave me a silver cigarette case and some money.

"What are you intending to do when you are better, Slav?"

I told him there was only one course open to me. As a Polish officer I must rejoin the Polish Army.

"Are you sure that is what you want to do?"

"It is the only thing I can do."

"We shall meet again after the war, of course," the American said. "Where shall it be, Slav?"

"In Warsaw," I replied. And I wrote down for him the address of my family's house in Warsaw.

"I should like that," he said. "We will meet in Warsaw."

A British officer and a Polish interpreter came to see me. It was a long talk, but the characteristics of security interrogation were not overstressed. A long catechism about Poland, its people, and its politics tested my bona fides. Then I was called upon to repeat once again the stories about the Russians, the prison camp, and the journey.

The interpreter returned alone the next day, bringing me a gift of half a dozen white handkerchiefs and an Indian ivory cigarette holder. He told me that transport was being arranged through the British for me to join up with Polish forces fighting with the Allies in the Middle East.

The night before I left, Kolemenos, Zaro, and I had a farewell celebration in the hospital canteen.

Mr. Smith came to the hospital to see me off on that last day, bringing me a small fiber case in which to pack my few belongings. I had resolved to make the parting from Zaro and Kolemenos as painless as possible. We said good-bye in the ward, and the soldiers called out "Good luck" and "All the best, Slav," and things like that.

I walked toward the door, Smith ahead of me. Zaro and Kolemenos followed behind. I wanted them to stay where they were, but they kept on walking. I turned at the door, and big Kolemenos ran forward and hugged me, and then came Zaro. And the tears came so that I had to drag myself away. The American walked with me, blowing his nose in his handkerchief.

He rode on the bus with me into Calcutta, where they dropped him off. "Look after yourself, Slav," he said. "And God bless you."

The bus pulled away toward the transit camp where I was to await a troopship that would take me to the Middle East. I looked back at him once, and he waved.

I felt suddenly bereft of friends, bereft of everything, as desolate and lonely as a man could be.

Slavomir Rawicz served with the Polish armed forces in the Middle East during World War II, then was sent to England. He was in training with the Royal Air Force when the war ended. Rawicz remained in England, married an English girl and settled in the Midlands. His escape story came to the notice of a newspaperman, Ronald Downing, and together they produced this chronicle. No contacts were ever established with the other three survivors of The Long Walk.

The only chance of escape for the shell-torn
frigate and her crew was to make a suicidal dash
down the Yangtze River to the sea.

The Epic
of the *Amethyst*

By George Kent

THE THIRD OF AUGUST is no holiday in Hong Kong, but on that day in 1949 the city was a riot of flags; firecrackers exploded, bands played, and on the decks of British and American men-of-war crews in dress uniform stood at attention. The object of all this celebration was a low-slung, battered frigate with shell holes in her hull and haggard men at the rails. The 1,430-ton *Amethyst* had come into port after a heroic exploit—the latest in the long exploit-starred history of the British Navy.

The story begins on April 20, 1949. The *Amethyst,* one of several warships assigned to furnish sanctuary and protection to British citizens caught in the war between Nationalist and Communist Chinese, was making her way up the Yangtze River. Large Union Jacks were painted on her sides, proof of her neutrality.

As she approached Rose Island, Communist guns, hidden behind tall reeds, let go without warning at point-blank range. Shells blasted the *Amethyst*'s bridge and wheelhouse and entered her hull above and below the waterline, killing 17 men, wounding 30 others. The skipper fell by the binnacle. The doctor dropped in the shattered sick bay. The second and third officers were both badly wounded. The helmsman slumped lifeless over the wheel, slewing the vessel aground in the Yangtze mud.

The destroyer *Consort* dashed up, guns blazing. She in turn was fired on, losing 10 dead, 21 wounded. The following day the cruiser *London* and the frigate *Black Swan* attempted a rescue and together lost 13 dead, 22 wounded. All three vessels finally retired under the relentless fire.

Below decks on the *Amethyst* a petty officer with a piece of shrapnel in his neck emptied fuel and ballast tanks to lighten the ship and get her off the mudbank. Another with a crippled shoulder unraveled the tangled electrical system. And communication with the outside world was maintained by Jack French, the frigate's only radio operator, who stayed on duty for five days and nights, taking only occasional catnaps.

Finally the *Amethyst* shuddered free of the mud and moved into a creek, which seemed safe. A volley from the Red batteries reminded her that such was not the case. Here most of her wounded were taken ashore and put aboard a Sunderland aircraft that landed with a doctor. Both plane and wounded were fired on.

The next day the ship moved to a position off Ta Sha Island, where she remained, under the muzzles of Communist guns, until the dramatic night of July 30.

On April 22 Lt. Comdr. John Simon Kerans, Royal Navy, entered the scene. A tall, thin man of 33 with a brilliant war record, he was ordered from his post as assistant naval attaché in Nanking to take command of the *Amethyst*. A comfortless situation confronted him. Seventeen dead men, roughly sewed in canvas, awaited disposition. Below were the wounded who had been unwilling or unable to move. The deck was a litter of blood and torn metal. Hundreds of rats had come aboard through shell holes.

Kerans found that most of the crew were youngsters fresh out of England with no battle experience.

"I gave them plenty to do," he later reported, "because I wanted them tired, too tired to think." He also ordered the best meals the ship's stores could provide.

He had the remaining wounded ferried over to the Nationalist side of the river, whence they were helped overland to Shanghai. Then he read the prayer over the dead and consigned them to the yellow waters of the Yangtze.

He used up his slim store of disinfectant to remove the gore from the decks. He had the shell holes stuffed with tightly rolled hammocks and kit bags and destroyed the damaged radar lest it fall into the hands of the enemy.

The Communist artillery was now emplaced on a commanding high knoll nearby, and trigger-happy sentries patrolled the shoreline. Ships were halted for inspection of papers by bursts of machine-gun fire aimed across their bows, with bullets frequently spattering the *Amethyst*'s deck.

Early in May, Kerans had the first of 11 talks with the Communists concerning a safe-conduct. Col. Kang Mao-chao, the officer in charge, made it clear that the slightest move downriver would mean the annihilation of the *Amethyst*. Kerans soon realized that nothing would come of these talks. Methodically he began to plan a getaway.

To escape, he needed an adequate supply of oil; and to conserve it, he began shutting off power for 24-hour, then 59-hour, periods.

"Living in a ship with nothing running," said Kerans later, "was a

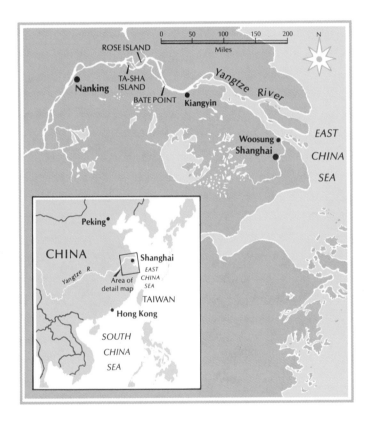

most unpleasant experience. It was like living in a grave."

Fans, too, had to be turned off, and the temperature below decks rose to 110° F, but sleeping on deck was frequently impossible because of the rains. Rats were everywhere. They ate the books—valuable morale-builders—raided the stores, and ran over the sleeping men. Mosquitoes were also bad, but a daily dose of paludrine kept all hands free of malaria. Prickly heat was the universal curse.

By the beginning of July, Kerans suspected that the enemy was

TRUE STORIES OF GREAT ESCAPES

going to try to starve him into submission. He cut rations in half. Meanwhile, he pored for hours each day over the shrapnel-shredded, blood-stiffened chart, learning it by heart. The piece showing the river immediately ahead was gone.

The Yangtze is a twisting stream, with mudbanks, hairpin curves, and a narrow, constantly shifting channel. It is one of the rivers on which the Admiralty permits its vessels to use pilots. In daylight pilots will not travel faster than five knots; at night they are reluctant to travel at all.

Part of Kerans's scheme was to mislead the Reds. In letters to his commanding officer, Adm. Sir Patrick Brind at Hong Kong—letters he knew the Communists read—he complained bitterly of his lack of fuel and kept asking for charts and a pilot. He also made it a point to give the vessel's top speed as 16 knots. Actually, helped by the current, the ship could do $22\frac{1}{2}$ knots. Moreover, Kerans knew he had fuel enough to cover the 140 miles from his anchorage to the sea with a little left over.

On July 24 Kerans had his 11th futile talk with Colonel Kang. The next day he made up his mind. He could not consult in code with Admiral Brind, because the code books had been burned in the shelling. So he communicated in double-talk, demanding instructions on how to behave should a typhoon arise. It was a question no British officer would ask; he is supposed to know.

Sir Patrick got the point. His reply was: "The golden rule of making an offing and taking plenty of sea room still applies." It was clearly permission to go.

On Friday, July 29, Kerans ordered the crew to pack the anchor chain with burlap and to place canvas, covered heavily with oil, beneath it, so that the chain could be slipped into the water noiselessly. By thus leaving chain and anchor behind, they could get under way in a matter of minutes. This was the only hint to the men that something was brewing.

At 8 o'clock the next night he explained to the crew that the breakout was to start in two hours. "If we don't get away now, we may never have another chance," he said.

On instructions from Kerans, the crew placed crates and boxes on the superstructure; over them and over the guns went yards of black canvas, altering the ship's silhouette to resemble an LST's, many of which, converted to commercial use, plied the river regularly. Buckets of black paint were splashed over the gleaming bridge and forward sections.

The *Amethyst* was beginning to get up steam, but the smoke would mean nothing to the Communists. Smoke had been pouring through the funnel all day from the stoves in the galley.

At 10 o'clock a brightly lighted steamer flying the Communist flag came chugging slowly downriver. Here was a break. The moment it was past, Kerans ordered his men to let go the anchor. The chain slipped silently into the water.

In a matter of seconds the ship was under way, and Kerans murmured the old Admiralty prayer: "Lord, Thou knowest how busy I shall be this day. If I forget Thee, do not Thou forget me."

The *Amethyst* trailed the steamer—the *Kiang Ling Liberation*—by about 200 yards. Kerans hoped that the glare from its lighted portholes would blind the Communists ashore and that in the flurry of inspection his ship might slip through unnoticed. Just as the *Kiang* came abreast of the shore batteries, flares illuminated the water brilliantly. A moment later the *Amethyst* inched past. Flares challenged her. Kerans's only reply was to increase speed.

With that, all hell broke loose. Machine-gun bullets ricocheted from the *Amethyst's* bridge, even from Kerans's tin hat, which fell off. As he stooped to pick it up, another burst cut the aerial wires close behind him. Then came the roar of the heavy stuff. Meanwhile, through the voice pipe, he could hear the man at the echo sounder chanting his minute-by-minute report of the river's depth: "Seven fathom, seven fathom, six fathom . . ."

A Communist gunboat anchored below the batteries began firing hysterically, mostly at the Red batteries ashore. The *Amethyst,* capable of using only one four-incher because of her shortage of men, let fly a single shell, then blazed away with her antiaircraft batteries. From her funnel poured a black smoke screen.

A 75-millimeter shell slammed into the *Amethyst* forward of the bridge, above the waterline. "Full speed ahead," the bridge telegraph clanged. But the vessel had acquired a sharp list to starboard and did not pick up speed. "Under heavy fire and am hit," said its radio. The helmsman was having trouble with the wheel; where ordinarily a touch did the trick, now he had to spin it hard over. Kerans swore. Here was disaster before he had gotten well under way. But he was able to note with satisfaction that his shots had started a great blaze ashore. In the water were two other fires: the *Kiang Ling Liberation* and the gunboat, both burning briskly after having been hit by the Red batteries.

The *Amethyst* continued to move like a man with a pain in his side,

and Kerans scanned the shore, looking for a place where he could beach her. He had planned for this emergency also. Twenty-four detonators were cached in the stern. Should it become necessary, he would blow her up.

Suddenly—Kerans still doesn't know how it happened—the ship returned to an even keel. At 10:15 she passed Rose Island, where the original shelling had taken place. At 12:24 Sunday morning, July 31, she went by Bate Point at a fast clip. At both places there were guns, but the speed of the *Amethyst* caught them unprepared. In the engine room, with sea doors shut and fans off, the stifling heat passed 150° F.

One-third of the run having been completed, the chart was now usable. To appreciate Kerans's feat, it must be remembered that the always unstable Yangtze was in flood; markers and landmarks had been covered or washed away. The flood helped the ship over the shallow places, but there was always danger that she would miss the course and run aground. It was a tar-black night, and the *Amethyst* was doing better than 22 knots.

Shortly after midnight a junk loomed suddenly under the bow. Before the *Amethyst* could swerve, she had sliced the craft in two. But there was no time to pause.

At 12:57 the *Amethyst* reached the forts at Kiangyin. Her speed again caught the Reds napping, and she was abeam before the guns began to fire. Once more the funnel vomited black smoke and the shells buried themselves in vapor. "Under heavy fire at Kiangyin," said the radio.

Twelve minutes later the radio spoke again: "Still under heavy fire, nearing boom."

The boom, a river block, consisted of a row of sunken merchant vessels, with only a narrow passage marked in normal times by two lights. On this night there were no lights. Kerans inched up to the boom, finally spotted the narrow lane, and drove through.

Machine guns on the boom let go a rattle of bullets, but Kerans rushed on. There was no heavy artillery to overtake him.

Now only 40 miles remained, and there was only one major obstacle, perhaps the most serious one yet encountered—Shanghai's heavily gunned forts at Woosung, which guarded the confluence of the Whangpoo and the Yangtze. But Kerans knew that the cruiser *Concord* was awaiting him at the mouth of the river, prepared to open fire on Woosung should it become necessary.

At 5:03 A.M., with the sky graying, Kerans saw Woosung's powerful searchlights sweeping the river. Somehow they missed the *Ame-*

thyst. Perhaps the tricky light of early dawn explains their failure to focus on the ship.

A half hour later Kerans was in the open sea alongside the *Concord* and radioing: "Have rejoined the fleet. No damages or casualties. God save the King."

Then in return Admiral Brind promptly sent a radio message: "Welcome back to the fleet. Your passage today will be epic in the history of the Navy."

King George sent this message: "The courage, skill, and determination shown by all have my highest commendation. Splice the main brace." In the British Navy the main brace is spliced by a formal gathering of all hands around a barrel of rum to drink His Majesty's health. This was done immediately.

Another message announced the award to Kerans of the Distinguished Service Order, one of Britain's highest decorations. From his old schoolteacher Kerans received this telegram: "Well played. Your mathematics must have improved."

One award that caught the public's fancy was the Dickin Medal given to the ship's cat, Simon, for valiant service in keeping down the rat population. The crew's version of the citation read: "Though recovering from wounds, Simon did single-handedly and unarmed stalk and destroy Mao Tse-tung, a rat guilty of raiding food supplies."

At Hong Kong, Malta, Gibraltar—wherever the ship paused on her trip home—there were festive celebrations. Finally, on November 1, the *Amethyst* docked at Plymouth. Shortly thereafter the ship's company paraded for the people of London and was received personally by King George.

What Kerans and his crew had done was summed up admirably in *The Illustrated London News:* "The affair of the *Amethyst,* measured by worldly reckoning, is a very small affair—a remote river incident. But measured in terms of the human spirit it matters a great deal, more perhaps than the brave men who manned her at the time realized."

*Slipping elusively from the role of theologian to that
of secret agent, the Irish-born monsignor engineered
the escape of thousands of Allied servicemen in wartime Italy
from under the very noses of the Nazis.*

Vatican Pimpernel

By Lt. Col. Sam Derry
with David MacDonald

IN ROME, LONG AFTER the end of the Second World War, my wife
and I crossed the vast expanse of St. Peter's Square to the top
steps of the basilica.

"Right here," I said, "he used to wait for us."

So often, during the German occupation of 1943-44, I saw Msgr.
Hugh O'Flaherty standing there large as life. Over six feet in height,
with a rugged Irish face bent over a breviary, glasses glinting on his
big nose, he'd look over the square for a familiar figure—one of our
agents—while murmuring Latin in a Kerry brogue. To sightseeing
Wehrmacht soldiers, he was just another priest at prayer. Nothing
about him suggested that this was the "Vatican Pimpernel," up to his
clerical collar in wartime intrigue.

As a theologian for the Holy See, Monsignor O'Flaherty officially
dealt in Catholic dogma. *Ex officio*, he led the underground British
Organization in Rome, which saved almost 4,000 runaway Allied
prisoners of war from the Germans. The key to its amazing success
lay in Monsignor O'Flaherty's makeup. Besides awesome courage,
sharp wits, and the impish ways of an oversized leprechaun, he had
more compassion than anyone I've ever known.

We met when I was 29. A British Army major, captured by Rommel's Afrika Korps and held in Italy for 15 months, I jumped off a
POW train in October 1943 and landed with a partisan farmer less
than 15 miles from Rome. Since several Allied envoys were still
inside the neutral Vatican, a village priest agreed to take a note there
for "anybody English." Back came money—and a summons to Rome
from someone he called "my superior."

Dressed as a laborer and smuggled into Rome under a cartload of cabbages, I was eventually led to the Vatican by a courier named Aldo. A burly man in black gazed down from the basilica's left-hand steps. Muttering "Follow me," he bustled through the Bernini colonnades, up an alley, into a building marked Collegio Teutonico—the German College—outside the Vatican but still on neutral ground. Escorting me into a small bedroom-study, he said with a twinkle: "Make yourself at home! Me name's O'Flaherty and I live here."

But why was I here? The 45-year-old priest grinned mischievously. "Ye'll soon find out," he said. "Meanwhile, how would you like a nice warm bath?" I must say I wasted no time in accepting.

At dusk, both clad in cassocks, we bluffed our way past the Swiss Guards and jackbooted Germans to the Vatican's nearby Ospizio di Santa Maria, the home of the refugee British legation. Our minister there, Sir D'Arcy Osborne, told me about Hugh O'Flaherty.

As a young seminarian from Ireland, he'd been posted to Rome in 1922, the year Mussolini's dictatorship began. A Vatican monsignor by 1934, he was deeply devoted to golf and assorted good works. In the early war years he used to tour Italian POW camps, seeking out new prisoners still "missing in action" and reassuring their families whenever possible via Vatican Radio as to their physical condition.

After the Allied forces' landings and Italy's capitulation in September 1943, thousands of POW's—mostly Britons—were let loose, and many reached Rome, just as German troops seized it. Recalling O'Flaherty, the ex-prisoners turned to him for help and advice. He hid hundreds with Roman friends or with rural partisans, meanwhile scrounging money to support them. But now, Sir D'Arcy related, an officer was needed to lend a hand.

"*That* is why we sent for you," Sir D'Arcy told me. "Are you prepared to take the command?"

Fascinated by O'Flaherty, I readily agreed. He decided we'd share his room at the Collegio. To the monsignor's mind—now devious, now direct, always unpredictable—a British conspirator should be safest in a place filled with German clergy. So he let me sleep on his sofa, obtained a civilian suit for me, and produced identity cards converting me from Sam to "Patrick" Derry and from an Anglican to a Dublin-born Catholic employed by Holy Mother Church.

Tramping around Rome with him, I marveled at how his organization had so far concealed more than 1,000 ex-POW's—in convents, in crowded apartments, on outlying farms. His favorite such billet was an apartment directly behind SS headquarters.

"Faith," he chortled, "they'll not look under their noses."

Given the tacit blessing of Pope Pius XII, the monsignor secured aid from an odd collection of monks, nuns, Communists, nobles, a Swiss count, two Free French secret agents, and a cockney butler, John May, at our U.K. legation. As John put it: "Our Irish friend knows everyone, and they all adore him."

A notable exception was SS Col. Herbert Kappler. Chief of SS forces in Rome, he'd learned of an escape line run by a mysterious priest and, unknown to us, had Gestapo men scheming to catch him.

The colonel almost succeeded. Once when the monsignor called on Prince Filippo Doria Pamphili, a prominent anti-Fascist who backed the network with money, Kappler raided the Palazzo Doria. As rifle butts banged on the front door, O'Flaherty fled to the cellar, where sacks of coal were just then tumbling through a trapdoor. He quickly stripped to trousers and T-shirt, stuffing his cassock and clerical hat into one bag. Smeared with soot, he crept out behind the delivery truck, shuffled past a score of SS officers, and vanished before they could realize that the "coalman" carried a full sack *away*.

As chief of staff to this artful dodger, I ordered all our escapees to stay under cover lest they compromise the Italian *padroni* ("patrons") who courted death by harboring them. Yet the gravest security problems were posed by the monsignor himself. He delighted in deliberately flirting with danger.

After we'd long kept a British general cooped up in a secret room, O'Flaherty took that star boarder, garbed in Donegal tweeds, to a papal reception and introduced him as an Irish doctor—to the German ambassador! I was furious.

"Ah, now," he said, winking, " 'twas a nice break for him."

As POW's turned up, the monsignor usually guided them to their secret billets or "cells"—often in clerical robes—because he couldn't bear asking anyone else to run the risk. But early in 1944, with the Allied armies pinned down below Monte Cassino about 100 miles away, O'Flaherty himself was compelled to take cover.

First, an escapee in one of our rural billets was recaptured. Threatened with torture, he turned in 12 other POW's and their *padroni*. O'Flaherty's reaction was typical, a gentle "God forgive him."

I couldn't. A further betrayal led the SS to 16 more POW's in two Rome hideouts where the monsignor and I were known. Some were shot. The German ambassador then informed O'Flaherty that he'd been denounced to Colonel Kappler as the escape line's leader. "If you ever step outside the Vatican, you will be arrested." he warned.

Under pressure from German authorities, his church superiors also ordered him to stay put and to get his "guest" out of his rooms. So I covertly moved into the British legation, carrying on our clandestine business as before. Undeterred, the monsignor met our agents openly on St. Peter's steps.

One day a former helper named Grossi brought word of an injured POW in a village 30 miles from Rome. Without telling me, the monsignor promised to go there the next Sunday. A last-minute message from another agent saved his life: Grossi has sold out to Colonel Kappler, who'd baited a diabolical trap for O'Flaherty by playing on his known Samaritan sympathies.

The Allies finally broke through at Monte Cassino on May 18 and swept toward Rome. When the city awoke on June 4, the gray hordes were gone, retreating north as Allied troops rolled into the Eternal City to a tumultuous welcome.

While some 250,000 people massed in St. Peter's Square for the pope's benediction, I went looking for Monsignor O'Flaherty. He was in the German College, giving thanks to God.

In nine months Monsignor O'Flaherty's makeshift organization had taken care of 3,925 escapees, including 1,695 Britons. (In all, 122 men were recaptured and half a dozen shot.)

Yet O'Flaherty *couldn't* stop there. Overnight, his boundless compassion embraced our foes as well. When U.S. Gen. Mark Clark came to pay his respects, O'Flaherty quizzed him sharply to make sure that German prisoners were well treated. In a plane lent by the Allied commander in chief, Gen. Sir Harold Alexander, the monsignor flew to see thousands of Italian POW's in South Africa and then visited Jewish refugees in Jerusalem.

He was awarded a CBE (Commander of the British Empire), the U.S. Medal of Freedom with silver palm, and other decorations from Canada and Australia. But when Italy's first postwar government awarded him a lifetime pension, he never accepted one lira of it. He wanted nothing for himself.

While I stayed in Rome, arranging repayments to all those who supported O'Flaherty's network or otherwise aided the Allies, many Fascist collaborators came to trial. Among them were two double agents, a doctor who'd rented one of our hideouts and the courier Aldo who'd first taken me to the Vatican. Incapable of spite, the monsignor testified on their behalf.

"They did wrong," he admitted. "But there's good in every man."

He sincerely believed it. After SS Colonel Kappler was jailed for life as a war criminal, O'Flaherty often went to visit him. "To me," Kappler once wrote, "he became a fatherly friend." And when Colonel Kappler later entered the Catholic Church, he was baptized by Monsignor O'Flaherty.

Although seldom together following the war, the monsignor and I kept in close touch. Made Notary of the Holy Office, he remained at the Vatican until 1960, when he suffered a stroke and retired to his sister's home in County Kerry.

Three years later I was maneuvered into a London television studio, the unwitting subject of *This Is Your Life*. Before an audience of former POW's, colleagues from the British Organization in Rome came forth to share old memories. A white-haired Monsignor O'Flaherty appeared on film, sending greetings from Ireland in a halting, quavery voice, because, it was explained, his doctors had warned him not to travel. But suddenly the monsignor appeared and walked slowly out on stage. Blinking in the limelight, he grinned and threw his arms around me. We both wept for joy.

That was our last time together. Within months, he died peacefully at 65, after a good life that another priest summed up in these few, true words: "Hugh O'Flaherty was above all a generous honest-to-God Irishman. His big heart was open to any and every distress."

*All that was needed to bring about the escape
of the Irish patriot Eamon de Valera from the
English prison was a sense of humor.*

This Way Out

By Frank Kelly

IN MAY 1918 Eamon de Valera, who subsequently became president of the Irish Free State, was arrested for his nationalist activities in Ireland and was imprisoned in Lincoln Jail in England.

The following year, in February, De Valera managed to engineer an escape that was an ingenious affair of keys. Keys drawn on a postcard; keys conveyed by cake. No disguises were used, no tunnels dug. Even the rope ladder, kept handy for emergency, never dangled from the prison walls. Nor did the initiative come from outside as so often happens in jailbreaks. It was De Valera's own inspiration, planned by himself. Later on many others came into it.

Lincoln town is old and steep, full of odd and twisty byways. Outside the town stood the jail. Here, in this medieval city on the east coast of England, Eamon de Valera and other leaders of Sinn Fein had been locked up.

It was a stirring time. History was being made outside. World War I had ended in November 1918. A general election followed. In Ireland it resulted in an almost complete swingover to Sinn Fein. It was a republican landslide. The first Dail Eireann met in Dublin in the following January and adopted the Declaration of Independence. But there were only 26 members present at that first meeting of the elected representatives of the people. Thirty-six more were held in various British jails. Others were deported or "on the run."

The world was in a ferment. The countries of Europe, rising from the ruins of the war, were planning a peace conference. Every small nation in the world was getting its case ready—every small nation but Ireland, whose leader was behind prison bars.

No wonder De Valera chafed in jail. Were he free, he could bring

347

Ireland's case for the first time into international politics. He could go to the United States and there raise a national loan. At home, with the people now behind him, he could do so many things.

Of all those things he was thinking day after day in Lincoln Jail. Thinking of the future and of the immediate present with its constant urge to escape.

One Sunday morning he saw the prison chaplain's passkey lying in the sacristy beside the chapel. Perhaps that key would fit the gate to freedom? But how to get an impression, and how to get a key made from it afterwards? In a drawer in the sacristy were some wax candle ends thrown aside from the candlesticks. He collected them in an empty tin tobacco box. Then he waited his opportunity.

De Valera usually served Mass, but on the following Sunday he asked another prisoner to take his place. When the sacristy was empty, he slipped quietly in. There was the chaplain's key lying in its usual place. De Valera produced the wax, which he had kept warm with the heat of his body. In a few moments he had taken an impression; not only an impression of the surface of the key but of its thickness and length as well. The next problem was to get the impression out and a copy of the key in. The prisoners could not make a key there. It had to come from Dublin.

A snatch of an old music hall song came into De Valera's head. It went something like this: "He couldn't get the latchkey in, he couldn't." The tag ran through his mind. It haunted him. Somewhere in that comic song lay the solution. But where? What did it suggest? He examined the matter in his mind. A drunken reveller coming home late at night, too unsteady in the hand to fit the latchkey of his home into the keyhole. That was it! He got the idea.

Sean Milroy, one of the prisoners, was a great hand at drawing comic sketches with pen and ink. So De Valera got him to draw two sketches on a postcard; they were of a fellow prisoner, Sean McGarry. In the first sketch McGarry was depicted with a key in his hand, trying to open the door of his house. Underneath was written: *"Christmas 1917—he can't get in."* In the second sketch McGarry was sitting disconsolate in a prison cell. He was staring at a large keyhole, and the caption was: *"Christmas 1918—he can't get out."*

The idea behind the sketches was clever. The key and the keyhole were full size. Everything else in the sketches was diminished. There was the plan.

The postcard was brought out by a warder who was quite unconscious of its importance. After many vicissitudes it was posted to Sean

McGarry's wife in Dublin. While this comic postcard, showing the good spirits of the Lincoln prisoners, was going the rounds of their friends in Dublin, let us go back a little while in time.

Two men who had escaped the May roundup were Michael Collins and Harry Boland. Since that month they had been on the run, but working like mad as the brunt of leadership and organisation had fallen upon them. It was a vital time at home. Suppression alternated with organisation, a tense and exciting time.

Collins and Boland had hourly expected the release of the prisoners following the end of the war. They thought, however, that the British would grudge them a glorious jail delivery, a mass return home with bands and banners and all the enthusiasm of a national welcome. More likely the British technique would be to release the men one by one from this or that jail, without notice.

This is where I came in. I was working at the old Sinn Fein Headquarters at 6 Harcourt Street, Dublin, at the time. Collins and Boland decided to have someone stationed in Lincoln to watch the jail closely and send word of De Valera's sudden release. I was chosen for the mission, and my advance message would give them time to organise a mass welcome.

So I went to Lincoln City, took up my quarters at a hotel, and haunted the jail gates from dawn till dark.

But the jail gates did not open. Two weeks passed and nothing happened. I got in touch with Collins for further instructions. The answer was the sudden appearance of Collins and Boland themselves.

There had been a change of plans. It now looked as if the British had no intention of releasing the prisoners until after the peace conference. This was alarming news. De Valera was urgently needed. The only thing was to get him out.

Back in Dublin Sean Milroy's comic postcard had found its mark at last. It had been going the rounds for weeks before somebody saw the point. I think it was Collins who spotted it first.

It was now clear to those outside that a jail escape was being planned by the prisoners themselves. But more must be known about it. We must try and get in touch with them. My orders were to stay in Lincoln and do this while Collins and Boland returned to Dublin to get their end ready.

Instead of watching the jail, now I followed the prison warders around the town. I picked them up, talked to them in pubs, drank with them. I had to be careful, deadly careful, for a false move, a word, might ruin everything.

349

At last I decided on a more direct approach. I called on the prison chaplain and asked him to take a message in to John O'Mahony, who was a great friend of mine. The message was innocently worded, but I hoped that John would bite. John replied, but he did not bite.

Then a significant letter arrived in Dublin from Lincoln Jail. It had been smuggled out by a friendly official who used to carry small but harmless messages. This time he carried dynamite, though he did not know it. The letter was from John O'Mahony to a friend in Leeds. It was written in three languages, Irish, English, and Latin. The Latin part asked that the enclosure be sent to Mrs. Sean McGarry. In English, it demanded a bottle of wine for John. The kernel was in the Irish. It explained the postcard and asked for a key. Details of the proposed escape were given.

The key was made in Dublin. Mrs. McGarry put it into a cake she had baked. And over to Lincoln travelled Fintan Murphy, a HQ staff man, with the key in the cake.

Fintan had a bad moment at the jail gate, for he had to sit in the waiting room while a warder prodded the cake with a long knife. Somehow the warder missed the key. Had he spotted it, then the whole game would have been up.

This first key was tried out by Sean McGarry on a cell door, but it broke in the lock. They dared not leave it there. So they prised it out hurriedly with wire before a warder came along. Again a key was made; another cake was baked. I brought it to the jail gate.

At this point Collins and Boland arrived in Lincoln again. Another letter went in by the prison chaplain. It bore a code in Irish interspersed with English words. Back comes a letter from the prisoners asking for files and keys, blank keys this time.

So a third cake was baked. It was Mrs. O'Sullivan, housekeeper to Liam MacMahon of Manchester, who made it, and an Irish girl working in England who took it to the gate.

This cake held more hardware than raisins. Its weight was terrific. Instead of almond icing there was a thin coating of plaster of paris to keep the cake from breaking. Why they didn't spot the fictitious nature of the cake was a miracle.

It was third time lucky. With the files and blank it contained Peadar de Loughrey, another prisoner, cut a perfect master key. He actually took the lock off a disused cell door with no other instrument than a little typewriter screwdriver belonging to De Valera.

And so, many anxious weeks after the despatch of the postcard, a night was fixed for the escape. Now we were to be up against the worst of it. Although the war was over, wartime conditions still prevailed in England. Lincoln was an armed camp. It was an RAF base. Opposite the back wall of the prison, near the gate marked as the escape gate, was a large emergency hospital for troops. Military traffic on the road near it was unceasing. Every night the wounded Tommies would drift back to hospital. They'd linger outside for hours with their girls before they went in.

Now that the plan was ready, the whole of Dublin Headquarters staff came on the job. Collins's genius for brilliant organisation came into full play. Every man was allotted his post and job. Every possible contingency was provided for. The whole lie of the land was mapped, roads drawn, distances and vital points marked.

The night of February 3, just before lockup was the time chosen. All along the route of escape the Irishmen were at their posts. It was after dark when Collins and Boland arrived at the jail. Down in the town standing by with a taxi was Paddy O'Donoghue.

Collins and Boland had guns. My weapon was a combined dagger and knuckle-duster, a nasty-looking thing. The final getaway might end in a fight. Among our equipment was a coiled rope ladder that made an enormous parcel, heavier than any of the Lincoln cakes. This was to be the last resort.

The back of the jail faced the Wraggly Road with fields in between. This was the road I mentioned that was crowded with military traffic.

Collins and Boland took the ladder and went towards the jail wall while I scouted the Wraggly Road.

On the stroke of the appointed hour Collins and Boland flashed their torch upwards from the dark fields outside. From a high jail window a sudden light flashed in answer. This light, by the way, was made by a number of matches lit together, which De Valera, who was watching from the window, himself ignited.

Down the long dim prison corridors De Valera hurried with the two men he had asked to escape with him, Sean Milroy and Sean McGarry. Like shadows across the grass sped Collins and Boland to meet them. Now Collins reached their first objective, the lock in the postern gate of the back wall. He thrust his duplicate key into it and turned it. But the key would not turn. It stuck. He tried again and to his horror the slight pressure snapped it. Both men stood in dismay, Collins with the handle of the broken key in his hand.

Inside, the escaping prisoners were having better luck. De Valera's master key had already brought them safely through three inner doors, each of which was opened and locked again with great precision. They had escaped from their own wing and passed through its door; they had crossed a courtyard and then had to enter a second building. Out of this building they made their way and across the last yard, which led to the jail wall. Here there was an inner door. Once more the master key did its work, and this door too swung open. But not to freedom, for there, between the prisoners and their rescuers, stood the last door of all, an iron-covered gate. And it was in this gate that Collins's key had broken and stuck.

In whispers they conferred through the iron gate. "I've broken the key in the lock, Dev," said Collins, with a sob in his voice.

It was a terrible moment. Breathing a prayer, De Valera inserted his master key into the last lock. Very carefully he put it in. It met the stub of Collins's broken key and pushed the broken key before it. The lock turned. The outer gate swung open. They were free.

Five shadows now crossed the fields and bore towards the five-barred gate that separated them from the Wraggly Road. The Tommies were drifting back to hospital, lingering with their girls at the gate. There was no way out but through the groups of courting couples. As the five conspirators passed, the cheery Harry Boland called out, "Good-night, chums."

Then they walked down the steep streets of Lincoln to Paddy O'Donoghue and the first waiting taxi. Here they scattered, the escapees taking the taxi while Collins and Boland went for a train.

The rest of the De Valera escape was timing and organisation. The rest of the story belongs to Mr. O'Donoghue, who took them on the first stage to Worksop; and to Mr. Fintan Murphy, who put them on the road to Sheffield, and to Mr. Liam MacMahon, who did the rest. It was much more difficult than it seems. There were heavy wartime restrictions on petrol and on the use of taxis.

In Liverpool Collins's underground transport organisation was running to perfection. From Liverpool smuggling was easy. So three weeks after the jailbreak De Valera came home by that port. But not to public acclamation. His new position of escaped prisoner prevented that. But public welcomes were no longer necessary. His amazing prison coup had already set all Ireland aflame.

Following his escape, De Valera went to the United States to raise more than $5 million to help win Irish independence from Britain. At various times he served as prime minister and as president of the Irish Republic until his retirement from public office in 1973. Eamon de Valera died in Dublin, Ireland, August 29, 1975.